NATION AND STATE IN LATE IMPERIAL RUSSIA

NATION
and
State
— *in* —
LATE IMPERIAL RUSSIA

Nationalism and Russification

on the Western Frontier,

1863–1914

T H E O D O R E   R . W E E K S

NORTHERN

ILLINOIS

UNIVERSITY PRESS

DeKalb 1996

© 1996 by Northern Illinois University Press
Published by the Northern Illinois University
Press, DeKalb, Illinois 60115
Manufactured in the United States
using acid-free paper
All Rights Reserved
Design by Julia Fauci

Library of Congress
Cataloging-in-Publication Data
Weeks, Theodore R.
Nation and state in late Imperial Russia :
nationalism and Russification on the
western frontier, 1863–1914 /
Theodore R. Weeks.
p.   cm.
Includes bibliographical references and index.
ISBN 0-87580-216-8 (alk. paper)
1. Russia—History—1801–1917.
2. Russia—Ethnic relations.
3. Nationalism—Russia. 4. Russification.
5. Minorities—Russia.
I. Title.
DK221.W28   1996
96-7364
947.08—dc20
CIP

To my mother

and to the memory

of my father

Contents

List of Maps

List of Tables

Acknowledgments

In the long process of research, writing, more research, and rewriting to produce this book, I have incurred numerous debts, intellectual, moral, and financial. I owe my greatest intellectual debt to my teachers at the University of California at Berkeley and most particularly to my dissertation committee, Professors Nicholas V. Riasanovsky, Reginald Zelnik, and Simon Karlinsky. They taught me by example what it means to be a scholar, and I can only hope that my own puny efforts in that direction may meet their exacting standards. Many scholars in the United States, Europe, and Israel encouraged my work; and my thanks go out to all of them. I would particularly like to thank those who took their valuable time to read the entire manuscript and offer helpful suggestions: Professors Hans Rogger, Edward C. Thaden, and John Klier. I must thank the Slavonic Library of Helsinki University and its wonderful staff for providing me with a warm, comfortable intellectual home on many occasions. Serafima Igorevna Varekova at the Russian State Historical Archives in St. Petersburg greatly facilitated my research there. Finally, I wish to express my gratitude to the History Department at Southern Illinois University for believing in me enough to give me that rarest and most valuable of all prizes: a job.

The research for this work was carried out over a period of years, on three continents. Among the funding organizations that made my research and writing possible were the University of California Education Abroad Program, the Fulbright-Hays DDRA program, Fulbright/IIE, the American Council of Learned Societies, the Social Science Research Council, the American Philosophical Society, and the Golda Meir postdoctoral fellowship fund at the Hebrew University in Jerusalem. Research was also funded in part by a grant from the International Research and Exchanges Board (IREX) with funds provided by the National Endowment for the Humanities, the U.S. Information Agency, and the U.S. Department of State, which administers the Title VIII Program. It goes without saying that I am solely responsible for the views and errors expressed here.

I would also like to express my gratitude to the marvellous staff at NIU Press for their prompt, careful, and always cheerful attention to this manuscript. The book's maps were designed by my colleague at Southern Illinois University, Kay Carr. One map is slightly revised from Edward Chmielewski's *The Polish Question in the Russian State Duma*, for which I thank Professor Chmielewski.

Part of chapter 8 appeared in slightly different form in *Russian History/Histoire Russe* 21, no. 1 (spring 1994), pp. 23–47. My thanks go to Dr. Charles Schlacks, publisher, for allowing me to publish that material here.

NATION AND STATE IN LATE IMPERIAL RUSSIA

One

Nation, State, and Nationalism
and the Romanov Empire

Ich, der Staat, bin das Volk
(I, the state, am the nation).

—*Friedrich Nietzsche*

The existence of nations cannot be justified rationally; at
the present stage, however, one must
deal with it as a fact.

—*Czeslaw Milosz*

❖ We live in a world permeated with nationality and nationalism, a world in which identity is defined to a great extent by membership in a national, linguistic, and cultural group. But the world was not always so. Our world in which "nationality" and "the state" loom large in everyday life is barely a century—or in some cases, two centuries—old. Our unconscious and pervasive identification of one state with one nationality and, usually, with one language and culture is a new (and, one might argue, pernicious) phenomenon on the historical stage. The present study looks at the Russian Empire in the final half century of its existence, and specifically at the concepts of "state" and "nation" that prevailed during those years of rapid economic and social change.

During that period the issue of "nationality" in the Russian Empire took on a fresh urgency, which forced Russia's rulers to come to terms with nationality and to transform hitherto subconscious assumptions and expectations into explicit legal form. And yet the Russian Empire was not, and could not be, a nation-state. Any effort to make the Russian Empire into a national Russian state was doomed to failure. More important, the ruling class of the Romanov Empire did not conceive of "their" state in those terms. The complicated interaction between "Russian" as a national category and the Russian Empire as a multinational state will form the fundament for this study.

Before we go on, we must pause for a moment and define certain terms. "State" and "nation" will be discussed in greater detail below, but I cannot overemphasize the need to hold apart these two concepts in any understanding of East-Central and Eastern Europe (not to mention the rest of the world). Thus when I speak of "nation" here, I will never use the term as a synonym for "state." Nor will "nationality" here be coterminous with "citizenship." Rather, for our purposes the terms "nation," "nationality," and "ethnicity"—even, in certain contexts, "tribe"—will function as synonyms. Similarly, "national" will never designate state policies but will always be used as an adjectival form of "nation," that is, ethnic or cultural group. These terminological considerations should indicate already that we are entering a new conceptional world or, rather, that our own world's preconceptions and tacit assumptions about nationality will not fit the case described here. Keeping these key terms and concepts in mind, we may now proceed to the matter at hand: nation, state, and nationality in the Russian Empire.

In the final decades of its existence, the Russian Empire underwent startling, even revolutionary, changes. Between the defeat in the Crimean War and the outbreak of World War I, imperial Russia was transformed in the economic, literary, intellectual, and even political spheres—a process that amounted in many respects to the crumbling of the old order. And yet, when faced by the onslaught of the Central Powers in 1914, the Romanov Empire still proved strong enough to defend itself for three long years against the combined forces of Turkish, Austrian, and German armies. For all its weaknesses (and these were many and obvious to Russian society and government figures), the Russian Empire retained its fundamental political structure to the end; that is to say, it remained an "old regime" state: popular participation in government remained severely curtailed, and both government and bureaucracy continued to harbor a deep suspicion of mass movements of any kind, including those espousing Russian nationalism. Despite the presence of such "new men" as Sergei Witte and Peter Stolypin in the upper echelons of government, the tsarist bureaucracy remained for the most part dominated by cautious and conservative supporters of the "old regime."[1]

The Great Reforms of the 1860s had aimed to lay the foundations for a modern, industrial Russia. Serfdom was abolished; elective organs of local self-government were introduced; press censorship was somewhat eased; a modern judicial system was inaugurated; the army was reformed. Despite these changes, Russia remained an autocracy, and Alexander II's plans to inaugurate a mitigated form of popular participation in government were cut short by his assassination in March 1881. His son, Alexander III, crushed the incipient revolutionary movement in Russia and worked throughout his reign to limit the level of public participation in government. This reactionary trend was continued by his son, Nicholas II (or, as he was called even during his reign, "Nicholas the Last"). To simplify matters more than somewhat, the two and a half generations between the Crimean defeat and Gavrilo Princip's fateful shot in Sarajevo witnessed in Russia a period of cautious reforms followed by attempts to limit the damage—both real and potential—that any extension of the public sphere might entail for autocratic power. This period was characterized by an acute tension between the admitted inadequacy of existing conditions in the empire—economic, social, administrative—and the profound fear of the political consequences any meaningful reform could have.

The "nationality policy" of the Russian Empire during these decades followed a similarly tortuous path. Indeed, the word "policy" seems far too definite a term for the confused, disparate, and uncoordinated actions of the Russian administration vis-à-vis its non-Russian subjects. There is no doubt that the empire pursued a far from enlightened "nationality policy"—as the well-known restrictions on Jews, Poles, Armenians, Moslems, and others illustrate. A balanced historical understanding of the complex interplay between nation and state in the late Romanov Empire requires more, however, than an enumeration of repressions. In this study I shall attempt to describe this relationship mainly from the point of view of the Russian public and imperial bureaucracy. I argue that the Russian imperial government, far from pursuing a consistently nationalist course, reacted rather than acted and was plagued by the fundamentally non-national (or even anti-national) nature of the empire.

One may well consider A. Avrekh's term *lavirovanie* appropriate as a description for imperial "nationality policy."[2] Avrekh had in mind Stolypin's "tacking" back and forth between right and left during the Duma period, but this zigzag metaphor precisely captures the reality of tsarist Russia's policy toward non-Russians as well. Imperial Russia was not, and could not be, a nation-state, and yet the desire to equate Russia with the Great Russian nationality and the Orthodox church was at times irresistible. This study, I hope, will make clearer the contours and the logic of this zigzag course.

Nation and State

All too often we take the meaning of the basic terms "nation" and "state" for granted, ignoring the complexity of their use and their changing meanings through historical time. In English (particularly American English), for example, one speaks of "the nation's capital," or "a nation divided within itself," or "the nation of Islam." Clearly the word takes on a different meaning in each case. Even in scholarly works, we find a degree of confusion and overlap between the two terms. One indication of this terminological jumble is the sociological term "nation building," which actually refers to the building not of a nation but of a state—and most particularly, of a Western

European nation-state.[3] In English and French the blurring of "nation" and "state" both linguistically and historically can be traced back to the rough equivalency of the two concepts based on a long tradition of relatively strong and stable states, which were able over time to establish a hegemonic unity in political, linguistic, and even religious spheres. To be sure, this unity was never absolute even in France or England, but, speaking in relative terms, the nation/state nexus was far stronger there than in Central and Eastern Europe.[4]

In Central and Eastern Europe, the distinction between nation and state is more clear-cut, even linguistically. In German one speaks of *Volk* or *Staat;* in Polish *naród* as opposed to *państwo;* in Russian *narod* or *gosudarstvo.* When dealing with the world outside Western Europe, however, we must take pains not to muddle these two terms, not to assume that a nation "naturally" has its state. Even at the end of the twentieth century, the much-vaunted nation-state of liberal West European pride remains an ideal somewhat tarnished by events since 1914, and one that has been taken up by few of the nearly two hundred "states" now represented in the United "Nations." Let us attempt, then, to establish, however tentatively, a working definition of these two words.

"State" is probably the easier of the two to tack down. The most straightforward, if rather abstract, definition of the term is Max Weber's: as that entity which holds the monopoly over legitimate violence.[5] On a more concrete level, the state is that agency which organizes armies, levies taxes, builds schools, imprisons or executes socially deviant elements, and generally serves (in principle, at least) to keep a given society in order. There are many diverse and contradictory theories of state, ranging from the liberal Jeffersonian night watchman to the twentieth-century total state of Hitler and Stalin. For the nationalist, a nation needs its state. The state will protect the nation against foreign intrusions and help foster the national language, culture, and perhaps religion. From a nationalist point of view, a nation without a state is a forlorn thing indeed, in the long run doomed to extinction. For this reason, "nation" and "state" inevitably come together as complementary concepts—at least for nationalist thinkers. And who, at the end of the twentieth century, remains untouched by nationalism?[6]

"Nation," on the other hand, proves almost impossible to tack down precisely. Certain factors are vital in different cases. A few contemporary instances demonstrate the complexity of the situation. Serbs and Croats speak essentially the same language, and yet the perceived national difference between them can be a matter of life and death. Belgians speak Flemish or French but form one nation.[7] Catholics and Protestants in Northern Ireland speak the same tongue (and even with the same accent), share a broad range of cultural affinities, and yet do not consider themselves one people. Language is certainly one important factor: it is probably the single most important determining factor for modern nationalism.

Depending on the specific cases, however, religion may take on crucial importance (as between the Croats, Serbs, and "Moslems" in the former

Yugoslavia). And we cannot ignore the role of the state in fostering the "nation"—witness present-day Austria, which linguistically, religiously, and culturally differs little from neighboring Bavaria. Indeed, in 1918 the Austrian parliament petitioned to be allowed to join the German Empire. Three generations later, Austrians are proud of their own nation and rather strictly differentiate themselves from the neighboring Germans. To complicate matters further, and specifically in the western borderlands of the Russian Empire, there is the issue of the "Jewish nation," a concept alternately strongly defended and bitterly opposed both within the Jewish community and among Russians. All these intricacies and ambiguities must signal to us the impossibility of finding only one answer to the question, What is a nation? Rather, we must observe carefully the situation that existed at a given point in history and, in the final decision, allow individuals to determine their own national affiliation. At the same time, we need to recognize that this "liberal solution" was for the most part not recognized by most states, including the Russian Empire, and runs directly counter to the ideology held dear by most nationalists.[8]

Nations are not a given in history but rather arise as a by-product of a nationalist movement. Ernest Gellner speaks of "two especially promising candidates for the construction of a theory of nationality: will and culture," before dismissing both as not "remotely adequate." In the end he does not provide a specific definition of "nation" but acknowledges, "It is nationalism which engenders nations, and not the other way around."[9] This rather commonsensical conclusion runs counter to the rhetoric not only of nationalists but of much scholarly writing. The reification of "nation" and its abstraction from historical circumstances lead to such absurdities as the lamentable attempts to claim St. Vladimir (St. Volodymyr) for either the Russian or the Ukrainian nation. We now "naturally" think in national categories, but this mind-set has not necessarily been in existence throughout history. Furthermore, our categories and criteria for belonging to a certain nation may not coincide with those that existed in the past.

Gellner's definition is not the only one. Benedict Anderson defines the nation as an "imagined political community." In a similar vein Peter Alter, another specialist, wrote, "The nation is the politically mobilized people."[10] For the Russian Empire at the turn of the last century, neither of these definitions can be accepted without qualification. In 1900 and even in 1914 the Ukrainian nation (just to name one) could hardly be described as politically mobilized. Indeed, the Russian *narod* (nation, *Volk*) itself was hardly a political community in 1914. Although a variety of competing nationalisms were gaining strength in the Russian Empire in the late nineteenth and early twentieth centuries, the traditional "pre-national" mentality of the peasant masses seems to have remained predominant, despite the impressive gains of nationalist movements before 1914.

Thus, faute de mieux, we find ourselves obliged to accept Gellner's concept—that nationalism creates nations—as most appropriate for the condition in the Russian Empire before 1914. This definition may well seem unacceptable to nationalists and, admittedly, suffers from an overly "macro-" perspective. But it avoids such problems as whether, for example, Jews are "really" a nation: if they believe so then we must accept it, or (to quote a Russian proverb), "If they say they're mushrooms, put them in the mushroom box." Still, we are left with the phenomenon one might call "Tuzenbach's dilemma." Consider the heartfelt outburst of this character in Chekhov's *Three Sisters*: "You might think, that German [Tuzenbach himself] is getting over-excited. But on my word of honor, I'm Russian. I can't even speak German. My father is Orthodox." Clearly, by the end of the nineteenth century, "Russians" with "foreign" names (such as Tuzenbach, or Gessen, or even Krzyżanowski) felt the need to emphasize their "Russianness" more than previous generations.

On a more concrete level, it is necessary to give some characteristics that often (but not always) indicated nationality in the Russian Empire. We must constantly keep in mind that no strict legal definition of any nationality—whether "Russian" or "non-Russian"—existed during the imperial period. Generally speaking, these terms were defined anew in specific laws or for specific privileges (or restrictions, as in the case of the Poles). One possible definition of a Russian (*litso russkogo proiskhozhdeniia*) is found in a government document from 1904: "Persons of Russian descent will be considered exclusively those of the Orthodox faith, including *edinovertsy* and Old Believers."[11] Thus, Russian and Orthodox (*pravoslavnyi*) go hand in hand. On a practical level, to the end of the imperial period, religion remained possibly the single most important determining factor for the imperial government's definition of the Russian nation.[12] This may be explained in part because the religious affiliation of all Russian subjects (unlike their nationality) was a matter of official record and could be changed only with difficulty. By itself, however, religion was not enough to determine nationality: there arose the never-resolved difficulty of Catholic Ukrainians (especially in the Kholm area) and Belorussians. The situation was further complicated by the shadow presence of the Uniates in the region, despite the official conversion to Orthodoxy of all Uniates in the Russian Empire by 1875.

The search for a precise and definitive decision on what constituted a nation in late imperial Russia is doomed to failure. Certain factors and characteristics may, however, be set down. In the late Russian Empire, the two decisive factors were religion and language.[13] These distinctions became complicated, however, by the issue of the disputed existence of the Ukrainian and Belorussian languages (neither was officially recognized by the imperial bureaucracy) and by contradictory attitudes on whether Jews (either as a nation or as a religious group) could be considered as belonging to the Polish or Russian nation.[14] While it is impossible to offer a precise theoretical definition of "nation" or even of "Russian" during this period, it is more important to bear in mind the ambiguities present in this historical situation than to offer a deceptively clear-cut abstract definition. In any case, as Russian administrators nearly always argued, on the ground level the decision was almost always considerably less difficult than theory might suggest.

Many conjectures have been advanced to explain the complex phenomenon of modern nationalism, which blossomed—or rather, exploded—
onto the political scene in the mid- and late nineteenth century. Ernest Gellner has presented an elegant theoretical model that I shall try to apply to
the Russian case. It must be pointed out, however, that Gellner, like most
theoreticians of nationalism, concerns himself primarily with the problem of
nationalism as a political movement, that is, the nationalism of Garibaldi,
Kossuth, or Yassir Arafat.[15] The present study examines "official" governmental nationalism, which is rather a different thing. Indeed, as we shall
see, the Russian Empire's "nationality policy" was far from modern nationalism: its primary goal was to preserve the unwieldy, utterly non-national
empire, and only in second place to strengthen Russian culture. Furthermore, the nationalist's desire to see the state as the embodiment of the nation—or the national spirit—was quite alien to the conservative Romanov
state. However, "official nationalism" and modern, populist national movements reflect each other in a certain complicated and distorted manner, and
Gellner's theoretical model can help us understand the social and political
processes at work in the Russian Empire in the decades before 1914.

Gellner's thesis (to compress a delightfully intelligent and witty book
into a rather crude nutshell) is that "modernization" begets nationalism.
Modern industrial society is characterized by bureaucracy, "rationality,"
and the need for a flexible, ever-changing, and highly trained workforce.
Industrial societies take for granted change, growth, and improvement
("progress"). For states, economic growth is vital in order to maintain or
even expand existing power bases; the would-be modern state that cannot
deal with this necessary social flexibility will be hard-pressed to retain its
power and prestige in the international arena. Gellner refers to the modern
world as "the society of perpetual growth," where previously hallowed
roles, traditions, and social relationships make way for universal education
and social mobility. "Roles become optional and instrumental. The old stability of the social role structure is simply incompatible with growth and
innovation."[16]

As estate privileges and status conferred by birth decrease in importance, education takes on an ever greater role in preparing the individual
for life as a social actor. People live out their lives not as members of a sub-
group (peasant, noble, cleric) but as "fully socialized individuals," differing
little in education, speech, and social customs from any other member of
society. In effect, people are "made" by the educational system: "At the
base of the modern social order stands not the executioner but the professor."[17] And, in this educational system the role of exact and standardized
language is of utmost importance because of a new imperative characteristic of modern industrial states (but not, for example, their agrarian predecessors) for communication over much greater distances and in much
greater detail. Thus, centralization and "homogenization" in modern industrial society would seem to demand a state that defends one culture
and one language.

To be sure, Russian society in 1914 (much less in 1894) can hardly be described in terms of the kind of mass society with universal education that Gellner's paradigm describes, and no modern state resembles this model exactly. Still, these modernizing tendencies (increasing literacy, burgeoning urbanization, a growing professional class, social mobility increasingly predicated on higher education) were present and came to the fore after 1906, during discussions in the State Duma regarding the proposed use of Ukrainian as a language of instruction in elementary schools (to name just one example).[18] For whatever reason, throughout our period and especially after 1905, the Russian Empire did indeed feel the unwelcome pressure of nationalistic activity. Nationalist movements among Armenians, Tatars, Jews, Poles, Lithuanians, and even Russians became part of the empire's political landscape only from the final decade of the nineteenth century. And St. Petersburg could hardly remain immune from these tendencies. For example, Stolypin's "nationalist" stance was to a great extent a reaction to the nationalist strains (both of "true-Russians" and of "minority nationalities") felt by the Russian government in the Duma period.

Gellner sees industrialism (based on a universal education system), with its need for rapid change and mobility of personnel, as the key stimulus of nationalism. After all, communication must take place in a certain language, and in the modern industrialized world, unlike traditional agricultural society, a high degree of linguistic precision is required. To quote Gellner, "In an age of universalized clerisy and Mamluk-dom [that is, the modern age], the relationship of culture and polity changes radically. A high culture pervades the whole of society, defines it, and needs to be sustained by the polity. *That* is the secret of nationalism."[19] And this "universalized clerisy" provides employment and a means of social advancement. This side of nationalism should not be neglected: in championing the cause of "the nation," nationalist intellectuals frequently further their own careers.[20]

Another scholar, Benedict Anderson, locates the origins of nationalism in the decline of religious feeling and most especially in the rise of "print-capitalism."[21] Defining a nation as "an imagined political community" and "a sociological organism moving calendrically through homogeneous, empty time," Anderson emphasizes the socioeconomic aspects of nationalism and national consciousness. Most pertinent for this study are Anderson's comments on "Official Nationalism and Imperialism." He specifically considers the example of the Russian Empire, extensively, and at points inaccurately, describing a putative policy of russification. Most interesting are his general comments on the antithetical nature of dynastic rule (that is, the "old regime" state) and nationalism:

> The "naturalizations" of Europe's dynasties—maneuvers that required in many cases some diverting acrobatics—eventually led to what Seton-Watson bitingly calls "official nationalisms," of which Czarist Russification is only the best-known example. These "official nationalisms" can best be understood as a means for combining naturalization with retention of dynastic power, . . . or, to put it another way, for stretching the short, tight skin of the nation over the gigantic body of the empire.

Leaving aside the issue of russification and of the origin of the phrase "official nationalism," Anderson's point here—of the fundamentally antagonistic nature of old regime ("dynastic") and national politics—is well taken: the above quotation continues, "'Russification' of the heterogeneous population of the Czar's subjects thus represented a violent, conscious welding of two opposing political orders, one ancient, one quite new."[22]

Indeed, Anderson underestimates just how incompatible nationalism and the old regime state really were. Hans Rogger describes the "dilemma of nineteenth-century Russian nationalism" in the following terms: "it could only with difficulty, if at all, view the tsarist state as the embodiment of the national purpose, as the necessary instrument and expression of national goals and values, while the state, for its part, looked upon every autonomous expression of nationalism with fear and suspicion." In fact, the Romanov tsars saw their legitimacy as a matter of history and divine plan; such a belief precluded any stooping to nurture "national feeling" among their subjects.[23]

Considering the Russian case in particular, a recent work by Liah Greenfeld argues that Russian nationalism (both governmental and "popular") grew mainly out of a single factor: *ressentiment* of the West. That is to say, Russians compared their own political, intellectual, and "spiritual" situation with that existing in Western Europe (most particularly in France and England) and were deeply unhappy with the uncomplimentary light such a comparison shed on Russia. To quote that work, "The cognitive construct born out of the anguish and humiliation of the eighteenth-century [Russian] elite became the identity of its nineteenth-century descendants."[24] This stark conclusion is buttressed with the rather flimsy support of literary sources. And yet it cannot be said that Greenfeld is entirely wrong, though she does overstate her point. Russian government and society did look to the West for models of "civilization," and even when rejecting these models Russians were influenced by them. For example, Russian centralism grew out of the very real need for the Muscovite Grand Duchy and later Russian Empire to maintain its grasp on its far-flung territories. By the late nineteenth century, however, the model of French centralization and efficiency in administration could not be ignored, however much tsarist officials might insist that Russia could only be governed according to her own historically determined institutions.

The nation/state nexus in the Russian Empire differed profoundly from relations existing in any other European state, and this difference was reflected in the ambiguous policies adopted toward non-Russian peoples. On one hand, we should never lose sight of the close link between Russian ethnicity, Russian language, and (possibly most important of all) Orthodox faith with the Russian Empire. On the other hand, "loyal" nationalities such as the Baltic Germans made excellent careers in the Russian Empire and on the whole retained their culture and privileged position in the Baltic region.[25] Even the Poles, a national group openly distrusted by Russian officialdom, were present in relatively large numbers in the imperial civil and military services, despite the restrictions placed upon them. In many respects the Russian Empire cared far less about "nationality" than we do. It mattered not at all that the tsars took foreign princesses as wives. (Of course, these princesses had to accept Orthodoxy and in this sense became "russified.") The fact that Nicholas II's family spoke English at home caused no murmurings among the populace. But on a practical level the empire had to be kept together, and the Russian Empire was unabashed in its belief that, as loyal subjects of the tsar, non-Russians could—and should—learn the "governing language," respect the Orthodox church (but not necessarily convert), and conform to certain "European" cultural expectations.[26]

Past historiography has at times posited or presupposed the existence of a master plan on the part of the imperial government vis-à-vis the non-Russians. To use the term "master plan" is to put the matter rather baldly. However, there still persists a tendency to speak of russification as if the Russian state was guided by a coherent nationality policy that aimed at the total elimination of cultural and linguistic differences and at the conversion of Russia into a nation-state on the German or French model.[27] Only recently have scholarly studies begun to tackle the vexing complexity of the national problem that faced the Russian government and the contradictory realities that hitherto had been masked by the term "russification." Edward Thaden, for example, differentiates between administrative and cultural russification in the Baltic region and in Finland during the late imperial period. From the point of view of St. Petersburg, however, "administrative russification" may have been seen as nothing more than a "rational" and natural process of centralization and the elimination of local privilege.[28]

Without question, the Russian Empire in the late nineteenth and early twentieth centuries attempted to expand the use of Russian and conversely restricted the prerogatives of local non-Russian languages and cultures. This overall policy has been generally described using the term "russification." That the Russian government wanted to encourage assimilation of non-Russians into the Russian nation seems on the whole undeniable, though not entirely unproblematic (consider the Jewish example). Thus some kind of russification was indeed fostered by the Russian state. But more than a few observers, both then and now, saw in it a more sinister design. The most extreme theory held that the imperial government consistently pursued a policy aimed at transforming all subjects of the empire into Russians. Clearly this conception is unacceptable as it stands: the imperial government lacked even the resources to educate its "rooted Russian" population, much less to mount a cultural offensive against minority nations. This fact is frequently repeated by individuals sympathetic to (or a part of) the imperial government in nearly every account of the treatment of minority nations. S. Witte points out in his memoirs, for example, that Nicholas II's *gofmarshal* was Benckendorff, a Catholic, while the minister of the imperial court was Baron Freedericksz, a Lutheran. Witte does, however, point out the contradiction between the presence of these non-Orthodox men at court and "the superficial ultra-Orthodox tendencies that have crept into high places since the unrest of 1905." Figures of the Russian nationalist right loudly bewailed the government's failure to secure the rights of the Russian nation, but even such Russian nationalists seemed to consider the "russifying" of Poles, for example, to be quite impossible and not even particularly desirable. For example, Vladimirov complains bitterly of the lack of interest in defending the Russian nation among imperial bureaucrats in the Northwest and bewails their friendliness to the local Poles.[29]

One cannot, to be sure, simply dismiss accusations of russification as mere moanings of disgruntled anti-Russian nationalists. How else to explain, for example, the dismantling of Polish universities in Vilna (Wilno in Polish) and Warsaw or the total suppression of Ukrainian language and culture in the Russian Empire from 1847 to 1905? To take the government view just for a moment, both can be explained without resorting to the thesis of russification. In the former case, the Polish universities were seen as hotbeds of Polish nationalism and anti-Russian, anti-imperial conspiracies that came to the fore in 1830 and 1863. For sound raison d'état, these subversive centers had to be shut down or (in the case of the Szkoła Główna in Warsaw) replaced by an institution that would instill loyalty to the tsarist regime and, not quite incidentally, Russian culture.[30] As for the suppression of Ukrainian culture, from the point of view of St. Petersburg, this could hardly be a case of "russification" since the inhabitants of Ukraine were indisputably Russians already. The measures that were taken aimed at preventing seditious regional separatists from driving a wedge between the "Little Russian" peasantry and the tsar's government.[31] In both the Ukrainian and the Polish cases, as in the Jewish one, the tsarist government became entrapped in its own rhetoric and thus unable to perceive the significant changes that had occurred within these national groups during the nineteenth century.

Considering the government's own explanations of its policy does not mean accepting or defending them. It does, however, offer another means of approaching that policy and of answering the question of why such a policy was followed. If Polish students or Ukrainian intellectuals were conspiring to undermine the integrity of the Russian Empire, then from the view of St. Petersburg it would seem obvious that steps must be taken to neutralize these threats. Once we grant the Russian Empire, just as a thesis, the right to exist in its present (that is, 1863–1914) boundaries, and we attempt to fathom its own peculiar logic, nationality policy begins to look considerably less sinister, although perhaps no less wrong-headed and ultimately destructive.

If russification is dethroned as the guiding factor of tsarist nationality policy, what takes its place? First and foremost, the government aimed to defend the unity and integrity of the Russian state. After all (to quote the very first article of the fundamental law of 1906), "The Russian state is one and indivisible." It was the task of the imperial government and bureaucracy to defend this indivisibility. A recent study by Andreas Kappeler on the historical preconditions of Russia's nationality problem stresses the generally conservative nature of Russian "nationality policy": "First priority [of the nationality policy] was always the preservation of the Empire's power and security, both domestically (loyalty of all subjects, the most conflict-free rule over an ethnically heterogenous population) and on the international stage (great-power politics, strategic considerations)."[32]

Although Kappeler is here referring to an earlier period of Russia's history, he admits that the guiding principles of Russian "nationality policy" remained generally constant throughout the imperial period. "While a shift towards russification is not to be denied, even at the end of the nineteenth century no fundamentally new orientation of the tsarist nationality policy took place. Rather, one observes only a temporary change in methods." That is, the Russian government's policy toward national minorities, at least from St. Petersburg's own view, remained defensive and sought to preserve the unity of the Russian state and, especially in relation to the Poles, to prevent the loss of Russian ethnic identity among peasants of the western region.[33]

Any nationalist movement could be seen as a centrifugal force and hence as dangerous to the empire's integrity. Almost no effort was made, even during the Duma period, to co-opt minority nationalists on the Austrian model. Of course, the state in question here could not be detached from Russian nationality and culture or the Orthodox religion: Orthodoxy, Autocracy, and Nationality were three aspects of one trinity. In this way, russification can easily slip in through the back door, as it were. The imperial government's prime concern was not necessarily to refashion Poles, Lithuanians, and Germans into Russians, but because of the state and its bureaucracy's Russian nature, ambitious members of minority nationalities entering the imperial bureaucracy would often assume aspects of Russian nationality and culture, at least in part. This process concerned, however, a minimal proportion of the population and, moreover, was not a conscious policy but rather a natural outcome of individual desires for social advancement.[34]

So we should not overestimate the conscious, planned aspects of imperial nationality policy. Russia was a poor country with a relatively small bureaucracy considering the country's size, and these bureaucrats were not known for their ruthless efficiency.[35] Perhaps the best argument against the thesis of a conscious and consistent policy of russification can be found in the repeated complaints of Russian nationalists who denounced government inconsistency in its governing of the western borderlands. One should not forget that significant numbers of the propertied and noble classes in the western territory and in Russian Poland belonged to the Polish nationality. Thus the Russian government, unless it wished to rule exclusively on the basis of bayonets and terror, had to achieve some degree of cooperation with these local elites.

One should not mistake inefficiency and lack of administrative ability for sympathy or liberalism. A key stock in trade of Russian nationalists was a belief in the profound tolerance of both the Russian people and the Russian state. Leaving aside the issue of the "Russian soul," it is clear that the "toleration" of the Russian state—especially before 1905—remained within quite narrow limits, which expanded only slightly after the October Manifesto. Here the limitations placed on Jews were only the most egregious example. Catholics and Poles were regarded with a good deal of suspicion both by the tsar himself and within the government bureaucracy and were subject as well to specific restrictions, for example, on the purchase of land in the nine Western Provinces.[36] In general, the imperial government's policy toward non-Russians often reminds one of Witte's statement to Alexander III that, since it was impossible to drown all Jews in the Black Sea, the Russian government had to find other methods of dealing with them. Substitute "Ukrainians," "Poles," "Lithuanians," and so on for "Jews" and one obtains a simplified but on the whole fair view of imperial Russia's "nationality policy." The tsarist government preferred to ignore the national issue rather than deal with it and, when forced to acknowledge and face the problem, preferred sweeping restrictive measures (often soon circumvented or ignored) to either co-optation or cooperation.[37]

A final historiographical problem surpasses the bounds of history and reaches into epistemology: what is truth? what is objectivity? Obviously, this issue looms large in any attempt to write history, but the problem would seem even more daunting in the field of nationality studies. In constructing a historical narrative and argument from various sources, historians often use differing, sometimes contradictory, accounts to supplement and support one another. Historians of nationality do the same. But their task is complicated by a phenomenon I would like to call (if I may be forgiven the Russianism) "national daltonism": the extreme difficulty nationalists had (particularly in Europe between 1848 and 1945) in perceiving and appreciating the viewpoints or needs of members of other nationalities.[38] Like those afflicted with color-blindness (*dal'tonizm* in Russian), writers and thinkers of a nationalist persuasion seem incapable of perceiving the legitimate wants or needs of other nationalities. Speaking metaphorically, one may say that, where one nationalist sees the figure "6," a nationalist of differing ethnicity sees the figure "9." Though not completely blind to the other's views, the nationalist almost inevitably perceives an issue in a manner quite alien to that of his "national other." While not wishing to posit this phenomenon as a universal truth, the historian cannot help but be overwhelmed by the pervasiveness of national daltonism around the turn of the century and up until 1914 in Russia. One need mention only Petr Struve's campaign against Ukrainian "separatism" or the Polish-Jewish conflict that exploded in the years immediately before World War I. Nearly all the primary sources from the period, whether official or publicistic, suffer from this tendency, and the historian must constantly bear this in mind when evaluating sources.

This phenomenon is also present (in a muted form) in historical literature, which brings us back to the issue of partisanship. By concentrating research on one nationality, usually the nationality of the historian or of his or her ancestors, there has arisen a one-sidedness in the historiography. One tends to see tsarist nationality policy from the victims' point of view and to ignore the "inner logic" (however peculiar from our present point of view) of the national mentality of the imperial government. Trying to fathom and reconstruct the attitudes and prejudices that "made sense" of restricting Jewish, Polish, and Ukrainian rights, for example, does not in any way mean that these restrictions become less morally repugnant or even more politically acceptable. What this approach does entail is a willingness to accept the existence of thought patterns and a political morality different from our own and to examine the logic and utility of these policies from an alien standpoint: that of the Russian imperial bureaucracy under Nicholas II. Attempting to understand the motivations of "nationality policy" in no way undermines a critical attitude toward the suffering caused by the restrictions themselves. *Tout comprendre* definitely does not mean *tout pardonner*.

❖   The relations between state and nation in the post-reform Russian Empire were complicated by two factors in particular. First, as a state's subjects become literate and more vocal in their political demands, the government must necessarily in one way or another adapt itself to public wishes. Or, at the very least, a government must be aware of these demands and offer some sort of plausible explanation as to why they cannot be met "at this time." Hence there arises the possibility of nationalism as a political tool, either as the fulfillment of the political demands of a segment of society or as a smoke screen to distract public discontents from other, more delicate areas. The formation in 1912 of the Kholm Province, for example, could be interpreted either as the legitimate safeguarding of Russian Orthodox peasants from polonization (Bishop Evlogii's line) or as a cynical political tactic by the government to assure the loyalty of its rightist allies in the Duma (the interpretation of Russian liberals and the Polish Koło).[39]

Second, the smooth functioning of a modern bureaucracy demands a good deal of standardization. A modern state will probably find it difficult to tolerate a large amount of local privilege: "centralization," in one form or another, becomes the order of the day. Such centralizing pressures may be observed also in the Russian Empire during Nicholas II's reign—for example, efforts to limit Finland's autonomy and make the grand duchy more dependent on imperial orders; plans to draw up a unified legal code for the entire empire; projects to introduce zemstva to the borderlands of the empire—that is, to eliminate differences in administrative practice between center and periphery. These standardizing and centralizing tendencies almost inevitably contain a nationalist element or at least can be perceived as nationalist encroachment by the region that is being brought into line with the center.[40]

Thus the "modernizing" government is caught between two often contradictory demands. On one hand, it must allow greater participation in government, especially at the local level, in order to defuse popular discontent. On the other hand, the government must centralize and standardize to assure maximum administrative efficiency. These two demands will often clash in areas populated with minority nationalities: the local leaders will oppose efforts from the center to impose bureaucratic *Gleichschaltung*, which will probably entail the elimination of certain local rights and privileges. Again, it must be stressed that such difficulties do not always and inevitably arise or prove insurmountable in a multinational state. Still, such are the probable bottlenecks in the process of political reform of an old-regime state. Certainly, the Russian imperial government was exceedingly, not to say morbidly, aware of the contradiction between the desirability of more political representation (for example, the introduction of zemstva and municipal self-government) and the possibility that these organs of local administration would fall under control of untrustworthy local elements (read: Poles).

To conclude, the Russian imperial government during the reign of Nicholas II found itself confronted by the need to modernize and reform its political structure and to allow the inhabitants of the empire a greater voice in their political future. In this context, the administration of the Western Provinces and Russian Poland became doubly problematic because of the putative (and, at least to some extent, quite real) disloyalty of the local population and because of the strategic importance of these border regions in case of war. Although the imperial government's "nationality policy" never aimed to destroy ethnic groups as such, neither did the government wish to entrust these groups (particularly Jews and Poles) with political power. Thus the perception of these nationalities as problem groups helped shape the policy adopted in these regions.

This book aims to present an explanation of the Russian Empire's "national mentality" based concretely on the treatment of non-Russians in one specific region, the Western Provinces and the Kingdom of Poland, or "Vistula land." The limits of this study are defined geographically, not ethnographically, because this focus better reflects the complex reality of the national question facing the rulers of the Russian Empire. After all, St. Petersburg had to maintain and enforce its political power over entire regions and could not abstract the "Polish question" or the "Jewish question" from the real-life issues of economics, politics, and social issues in this territory.

The next five chapters will approach the national issues in this region from several distinct viewpoints. Chapters 2 and 3 present overviews of Russian society's and the Russian government's perceptions of nationality. Chapter 4 attempts a description of the administrative, socioeconomic, and national relations existing in the region. Chapter 5 details government policy in the area from the time of the Polish Insurrection of 1863 through the post-1905 Duma period. Chapter 6 recounts briefly the development of national movements among the diverse national groups in the Western and Polish provinces.

These first chapters will provide a background for the discussion of three specific government projects, or case studies, concerning this area: first, the introduction of limited local autonomy in the form of zemstva to the Western Provinces; second, the introduction of elected municipal government to the Kingdom of Poland; and third, the creation of a separate Kholm Province out of the eastern districts of Siedlce and Lublin Provinces. In all three cases, nationality issues loomed large in the discussions of local reform. It is hoped that these final chapters will serve as concrete illustrations of the realities of "nationality policy" in the late Russian Empire and will give us new insight into the rhetoric and the reality of Russian "official nationality" in the final years of the Russian Empire.

Two

Talking about Nationality

Non-Russians in Russian Public Discourse

The Russian intelligentsia has one quality that sharply
distinguishes it from all other hegemonic
nationalities in multi-national states. That is its more
or less total neutralization of
nationalistic characteristics.

—*M. Slavinskii (1910)*

❖ In any place or time, speech and communication are subject to an underlying and largely subconscious set of rules and categories. This "prison-house of language" (to use Frederic Jameson's term) also determines to a large extent how we discuss and understand issues of race, gender, and nationality. To quote Jameson, "The history of thought is the history of its models." Similarly, the history of nationalism recounts in large part how people have conceived and talked about nations.[1] Just as the reigning discourse on race and gender in the United States differed fundamentally in 1900 from the present one, so did the discourse on nationality—in effect, the categories and terms people use to think about nationality—differ in tsarist Russia from the situation presently existing in East-Central Europe and the lands of the former Soviet Union. In this chapter I aim to describe this discourse as practiced by the "Russian public" during the last decades of Romanov rule in Russia.

The term "Russian public" (*russkoe obshchestvo*) is by no means synony-mous with the entire population of the Russian Empire, or even with the

Russian-speaking part of it. Especially before 1917, this term was used to mean the educated part of the population, thus in a state where illiteracy was the rule rather than the exception, "society" comprised a small percentage of the total.[2] Furthermore, the vocal and highly educated members of Russian society—who set the tone for many others—were fewer still. However, one may argue that this small but articulate group occupied a vital place in late imperial Russia, a place quite disproportionate to its numerical insignificance.

In imperial Russia from the early nineteenth century, one is often hard-pressed to distinguish between "society" and "intelligentsia." This study is not the place to discuss the roots of the alienation between educated Russia and the ruling dynasty and bureaucracy, but we must keep in mind that, as a general rule, Russian educated society before 1917 tended to define itself in opposition to the government.[3] However, a simplistic "us versus them" model would fail to do justice to the complicated interaction existing between Russian "society" and the bureaucratic elite. After all, educated specialists were vital members of the "reformed" Russian bureaucracy after the 1860s. Certain individuals—such as professor of economics and minister of finance Ivan A. Vyshnegradskii, railway manager and statesman Sergei Witte, and even the celebrated jurist and legal scholar Anatolii F. Koni—can be cited as examples of the links between government and educated society in the late nineteenth and early twentieth centuries. Still and all, most of the voices we will hear in this chapter, particularly those of the left and left-center, must be placed in the oppositional camp. And how could it be otherwise? In a state where any sort of public initiative was viewed with misgivings, a self-confident educated class inevitably clashed with the guardians of the old order. This difference in opinion and approach to social issues between government and society arose also in regards to the understanding of the role that "nationality" ought to play in the Russian Empire.

Censorship stymied or prevented altogether any frank oppositional discussion of nationality in the years before 1905. Even rightist and nationalist writers chafed at government tutelage and at what they saw as the government's "softness" on the national question. Although some discussion did take place, the limits of allowable discourse were both narrow and unpredictable. Thus most of the sources used here come from the post-1905 period. It would be absurd to claim that Russian attitudes about nationality did not change at all between the 1860s and 1905. I would hazard to argue, however, that on the whole the Russian public did not give the issue of nationality any serious consideration until after the turn of the century. Before that time the nationality issue was far overshadowed by other social and political issues and tended to flare up only in reaction to external events, such as the Polish insurrection of 1863, the Ukrainian pogroms of 1881, or the Kishinev pogrom in 1903. After the 1905 revolution not only was the severity of censorship significantly mitigated but the national aspects of the revolutionary years 1905–1907 heightened interest in the question of Russia as a multinational state. At the same time, the crystallization of political parties, including those of the right, and a "professionalization" of nationalist-chauvinist agitation—in the form of the Union of Russian People, the Nationalist party, the Kiev Club of Russian Nationalists, and other such groups—all served to push the national question to the front of the day's political agenda.[4] Before 1905 the Russian public could ignore the empire's millions of non-Russians, optimistically imagining that somehow the national question would work itself out. After 1905 such a stance was no longer tenable: the matter of nationality in the Russian Empire had to be considered, discussed, and dealt with.

Speaking of the "discourse of nationality" that reigned in late imperial Russia does not mean that only one set view on the topic dominated unchallenged throughout Russian society. Obviously such was not the case, as attested by the clashes between Russian nationalists and the Kadets in the Duma. Perhaps it would be more precise to speak of "discourses of nationality," as several opposing stances existed. I have discerned four relatively distinct approaches to the national question, mainly from the decade before 1914 when public discussion of the national question was widespread and relatively free from the more egregious constraints of censorship. These were not the only possibilities, but they did cover the contemporary Russian political spectrum rather well. It bears mentioning that these are Russian viewpoints; and the view from "the other side" surely differed significantly, even within parallel political or social groups. My four rubrics are (1) socialist, (2) liberal, (3) national liberal, and (4) rightist nationalist. These groups are admittedly imprecise and the boundaries between them hazy and perhaps arbitrary. However, we must not be led astray by false promises of precision and exactitude when studying the thought processes of human beings or indeed when dealing with nationality in any form. At times, socialists do share certain unacknowledged premises with nationalists. Sometimes liberals and national-liberals seem to be saying the same thing. And yet, taken as a whole, I believe these four categories are valid, at least as organizing principles to assist us in understanding the ideational categories according to which educated Russia dealt with nationality—both its own and that of others—in the decades before 1914.

The Socialists

Let us start, then, with the extreme left: the socialists or social democrats. Limitations of space prevent a detailed exposition here of the differences between, say, Mensheviks and Bolsheviks. In principle, the issue of nationality should be clear for all Marxists; that is, nationality is to be subordinated to social class, and nationalism must be condemned as an attempt by non-progressive social groups (usually "the bourgeoisie") to distract the proletariat's attention from the "class struggle" by substituting a "national struggle."[5] Gellner refers to the "Wrong Address Theory favoured by Marxism":

> Just as extreme Shi'ite Muslims hold that Archangel Gabriel made a mistake, delivering the Message to Mohamed when it was intended for Ali, so Marxists basically like to think that the spirit of history or human consciousness made a terrible boob. The awakening message was intended for *classes*, but by some terrible postal error was delivered to *nations*.[6]

In practice, theory became almost hopelessly entangled with the petty but vital concrete issues of language, nationality, and social class, and the relations between these.[7] The social democrats, like any political group, had to decide such matters as how to structure the party (that is, centralized or federated) and which concrete national goals to endorse, which to ignore or explicitly reject. An independent Poland in the hands of the right-wing, anti-Semitic National Democrats could hardly be considered progressive, for example. In principle the social democrats endorsed national self-determination and, consequently, the right of national minorities to secede from the empire.[8]

Lenin also heaped scorn on "liberals" who argued that Russian must be retained at least as the lingua franca of the Russian Empire and declared: "For the workers' democracy, the solution [to the national question] is not 'national culture' but the international culture of democracy and the universal workers' movement. . . . The national program of workers' democracy is: absolutely no privileges for any one nation nor for any one language."[9] Lenin's indignant and total rejection of "national culture" is as uncompromising as it is unrealistic; it appears he was more interested in using "national culture" as a club with which to beat his Bundist opponents than in attacking Great Russian nationalists. Although attacking the dominance of any one nation (and no doubt sincerely), Lenin continued to write and agitate in Russian.

In many important respects, the Russian social democrats followed the theoretical positions on nationality developed by the Austrian social democrats, by Otto Bauer in particular. In practice, however, among Russian social democrats there was a good deal of impatience (to put it mildly) with such rabble-rousers as the Jewish Bund who demanded a federated party. Lenin's wrangling with the Bund on matters of party organization revealed that in practice the Bolsheviks would tolerate the demands of minority nationalities only as long as these did not impinge on party prerogatives and efficiency. It is more important, however, that the conflict between the Bund and Russian social democracy laid bare the optimistic illusion that any simple solution could be found to reconcile the social and the national questions in imperial Russia.[10]

The social democrats never objected to the use of local languages and even local autonomy for non-Russians. In essence, their internationalist philosophy rendered moot the issue of nationality; each national group would develop within itself the seeds of socialist democracy and would battle the bourgeois oppressors within its own national group, as Marx had urged in the Communist Manifesto. Once again, however, this seemingly clear theoretical issue often became disturbingly turbid on the local level when, for instance, local activists wondered whether to ally, even temporarily, with "bourgeois nationalists" against russifying measures.

In theory and at the highest levels of the party (for example, in Duma speeches), however, the position of the social democrats was reassuringly clear and straightforward. During the Duma period, the social democrats consistently spoke out against national chauvinism (especially Russian and Polish) and in support of the rights, both cultural and political, of non-Russians, including Ukrainians and Belorussians. This position, in theory at least, was the most radical of those considered here.[11] In the Duma, the small social democrat fraction often took the opportunity to express its views in a provocative and even outrageous (at least to more conservative Duma members) manner. A brief look at a speech by SD Duma member I. P. Pokrovskii will give an indication of the SD position vis-à-vis minority nationalities, bourgeois nationalists, and tsarist "nationality policy."[12]

Pokrovskii took the opportunity of a vote on the budget for the Ministerstvo vnutrennikh del (MVD—Ministry of Internal Affairs) to decry the ministry's policies. Pokrovskii accused the ministry of (among other things) unleashing and encouraging national hatred, keeping "Slavic peasants" in ignorance and illiteracy by hindering Polish and Ukrainian schools, and engaging in "medieval persecution of the Jews." Stolypin had formed the Nationalist party to help pursue his retrograde policies, Pokrovskii charged, and had tried to cover up violence and oppression with the "notorious national banner" (preslovutoe natsional'noe znamia). "This barbarous policy can no longer deceive anyone: pogroms were and remain the shameful pillar to which is chained, gentlemen, your politics in the national question."[13]

Pokrovskii did not limit his accusations to the MVD and its rightist allies. The liberals also, he pointed out, had in recent times become infected with national chauvinism: "And this is not all, look at our opposition, at the parties of the liberal bourgeoisie such as the Progressives and the Kadets; of late they too have begun to become infected with nationalism, moreover, with nationalism of the worst kind." The old slogan, "brotherhood of nations [bratstvo narodov]" no longer sufficed for the socialists, as the bourgeoisie had also adopted this call while in fact working to increase national hostility and strengthen international capital.[14]

Nor did the Poles in the Duma escape Pokrovskii's notice. He admonished the Poles to repent their own national crimes and misdemeanors before assuming the role of victim. While specifically defending the rights of Polish peasants to schools in their native tongue, he criticized the Polish Koło's complicity in restricting Jewish rights in the Polish Kingdom: "If you allow the persecution of Jews in your homeland [u sebia], then how do you dare protest against oppression directed at you? You sowed the wind, now reap the whirlwind!"[15] Furthermore, Pokrovskii went on, Polish policy toward Ukrainians (Ruthenes) in Galicia was anything but enlightened.

The solutions to the national problem offered by Pokrovskii were of a stark simplicity:

> Indeed, the solution of the national question in Russia, as in other coun-
> tries, is possible, first of all, only under conditions of full democracy, assur-
> ing the consistent and free development of nationalities on the basis of full
> national self-determination, and then, before anything else, [will come] that
> fusion, the unification of the proletariat of all nationalities in battle for so-
> cialism against all bourgeois, against all landowners, who are inflaming
> hatreds both national and racial.[16]

Pokrovskii made his task very easy by placing the blame for national hatreds on the "exploiting classes" and the MVD. The national question thus
became a "non-problem": with the coming of democracy and socialism, the
artificially created and sustained national hatred would disappear and all
nations would live together in peace and harmony. Although more sophisticated socialist conceptualizations of the national issue certainly did exist
in imperial Russia, the above simple scheme seemed to dominate, at least
on a practical level. By blaming national hatreds on external causes (the
tsarist government, the exploiting classes) rather than on any intrinsic difficulties of the issue, the social democrats implied that once these external
causes were removed, with the coming of democracy and socialism, the
main obstacle of national freedom and harmony would also disappear.

The Liberals

Moving toward the political center, we come to the Constitutional
Democratic party. Within this quintessentially "Russian liberal" party, I
would make a distinction between "liberals" such as Pavel Miliukov and F.
I. Rodichev and "national liberals" represented by Petr Struve. Not the personalities but their distinct views on the national question and the relations
of the Russian state and non-Russians are important here. To be sure, they
also shared a number of basic convictions. Both camps advocated national
toleration and equal rights before the law for members of all national
groups. To quote article 11 of the Kadet party program, "The fundamental
law of the Russian Empire must guarantee to all nationalities living in the
empire, aside from full civil and political equality, the right to free cultural
self-determination." The Kadet platform also endorsed broad autonomy for
Poland and Finland and equal rights for the Jews.[17]

This liberality was counterbalanced, at least in the eyes of many non-
Russians, by the Kadets' persistent emphasis on the integrity of the Russian
Empire and their hesitation, for example, to push too strongly on the issue
of Jewish rights. Article 12 of the party platform set down that "The Russian language must be the language of central institutions, the army and
fleet" (wording very similar to that of the Tsarist Fundamental Law of

1906). I do not wish to accuse the Kadets—with the possible exception of Struve—of being latent Great Russian chauvinists; many other political considerations came into play here. Most fundamentally, the Kadets were sincere Russian patriots and, although conceding administrative autonomy to the Kingdom of Poland and the Grand Duchy of Finland, remained uncomfortable with any fundamental alteration of the Russian state.

For many non-Russians, Kadet patriotism bore an uncomfortable resemblance to Great Russian nationalism. Poles complained that Russian liberal (read: Kadet) support for Polish autonomy was at best lukewarm. This view would seem to be corroborated by the stereotypical terms in which Pavel Miliukov, head of the Kadet party, later wrote about the "ethos" of Polish society: "I must admit that I did not sympathize with the Polish social system as I did with the Finnish. . . . [T]he aristocratic 'honor' and the attitude of the landowner toward the 'khlop' [Polish peasant] repulsed me." Similarly, after an initial period of pro-Kadet enthusiasm, many Russian Jews came to criticize the Kadet leaders' unwillingness to push for Jewish rights in the face of a largely hostile Duma and unreceptive government.[18]

One expression of the liberal perception of the nationality issue can be found in a collection of articles that appeared in St. Petersburg in 1910 and dealt with the issue of nationality in Russia, Austria, and Germany. The article on the national structure of Russia and the Great Russians by M. Slavinskii (from which this chapter's epigraph was taken) is particularly interesting. Slavinskii argued that the Russian state had never pursued a coherent nationality policy but had aimed always at rooting out separatism and building a unified state structure throughout the empire. As for the Russian public, it had historically not paid much attention to nationality and had accepted government policy in this area "as something normal and necessary, without protest, sometimes with sympathy, most often with complete indifference [s ravnodushnym bezrazlichiem]."[19]

At that time, however, the national issue had become recently much more topical among Russians, as witnessed by the growth of nationalist groups such as the Union of Russian People and the All Russian National Union, which demanded the "supremacy of the Russian nationality [gospodstvo russkoi natsional'nosti]." Far from blaming national intolerance exclusively on government policy, Slavinskii pointed out the frequent parallels between government policy and the attitude of Russian society. As examples of the nationalist feelings of Russian society, Slavinskii cited certain, not entirely tolerant, writings of the Decembrist Pestel, the poet Pushkin, and the literary critic Belinskii.[20] Despite the existence of chauvinistic feelings within Russian society, Slavinskii concluded, the imperial government's "policy of hatred" bore grave responsibility in exacerbating national antagonisms. Such a policy, he warned, would inevitably bear bitter fruit in the future if not changed radically. Here we have a typically liberal perception of the national question: while admitting the existence of chauvinism and national hatreds outside of government policy (in the

human heart, so to speak), the liberal Russian saw an enlightened government policy as the guarantor for the creation of a polity in which dissimilar national groups could live together peacefully.

In another essay, published the same year, Slavinskii stated his belief in
the ability of enlightened Russian society to work together with other national groups in the empire and to solve the national problem:

> The noble cooperation of the Russian intelligentsia with intelligentsias of
> non-state peoples [*nederzhavnykh narodov*] of the empire has laid the
> groundwork for a more healthy future for relations between nationalities
> in Russia. The concord between factors of state unity and national diversity
> has blazed the trail for a mighty state renaissance of the Russian Empire
> through the power of newly awakening nationalities, among which the
> Great Russian assumes the first place.[21]

This extraordinary statement goes a long way toward explaining the misgivings non-Russians felt about Russian liberals. These misgivings crystal-
lize around the "concord" between state unity and national self-determination that Slavinskii posited. For a Russian liberal, this concord was an
article of faith; for a Pole, Tatar, Lithuanian, or Jew, matters might appear
quite different. The tragedy of Russian liberals may be explained in part by
their inability to perceive that, for many non-Russians, they were Russians
above all, and liberals only in second place.

In the Duma the Kadets also spoke in favor of minority rights and
against bills that aimed to restrict these rights, such as the Finland bills and
the Kholm project. In the discussions concerning the introduction of the
zemstvo to the Western Provinces, Kadets F. Rodichev and A. Shingarev
criticized the government project as being full of hatred for Poles and interested less in improving economic conditions in the Western Provinces than
in keeping local Polish landowners from gaining any political power.[22]
Russia needed equal rights for all, not privileges for members of the Russian nationality. Rodichev argued that the use of national curiae could be
defended only by those who believed that Russians were fools (*duraki*), unable to look after their own interests. Rodichev had previously insisted that
the best way to defend the "national" interests of local peasants in the
western territory was to assure their rights as citizens, not by "renewing
old historical disputes."[23]

Particularly revealing of the mind-set of Russian liberals was Shingarev's statement that there existed two Russian "principles of state" (*gosu-
darstvennosti*). There was the progressive principle—characterized by the
law of February 19, 1861, which freed the serfs, by the zemstvo reforms, by
the decree of religious freedom, and the October Manifesto of 1905. On the
other hand there was the retrograde, repressive Russian "state principle"—
characterized by the counterreforms of the reign of Alexander III and the
devastating battles of Sevastopol, Tsushima, and Mukden, which had ex-
posed the weaknesses of the tsarist state.[24] Shingarev clearly identified

himself with the positive, progressive Russian state principle that could deal fairly with minority nationalities even while maintaining a strong Russian state.

By positing two opposing Russian "state principles," Rodichev and other Russian liberals could maintain their own patriotism while insisting that no contradiction existed between a love for Russian culture and the Russian state on one hand, and liberal ideals and fair treatment of non-Russian citizens of Russia on the other. Russian liberals thus split off the negative side of Russian history, placing russification and intolerance, so to speak, on the reactionary government's account while keeping for themselves the positive, progressive, and tolerant aspects of the Russian tradition. They refused to admit that contradictions and conflicts could arise even between their own future progressive Russian state, guided by tolerance and democratic principles, and the desires of non-Russian peoples.

The National Liberals

Liberals insisted on the benevolence of their own Russian patriotism; "national liberals" went further and made of patriotism an article of faith and a positive good. Compared with the liberals, who were gathered in the Kadet party, the Russian "national liberals" are much more difficult to define as a group. Indeed, no National Liberal party or even faction existed. I have chosen to use this phrase to describe a phenomenon linked closely with the erstwhile "legal Marxist" economist and later Kadet Petr B. Struve.[25] Although Struve's views on the national issue gained broad notoriety at the time, he did not found a faction, much less a party, to further these ideas. Still, it can be argued that Struve's ideas on the "national face" of Russia reflected views shared by broad segments of the Kadet and Octobrist parties. Here I shall use the expression "national liberals" to describe Struve and those who shared his ideas.

In a sense, the national liberals simply took the liberal conception of affirming Russian culture one step further, arguing that Russians had to develop and strengthen their own national culture in a concerted manner, just as Poles, Jews, Finns, and others were developing theirs. For liberals such as Miliukov, the national liberal Petr Struve was flirting dangerously with nationalistic sentiments that belonged more appropriately in the rightist camp. But in most respects Struve's concept of nationality differed little from Miliukov's: both emphasized a strong Russian state, both condemned forcible measures against any national group or culture, both affirmed the positive value of Russian culture not only for Great Russians but for all citizens of the Russian state. The differences were more of style and emphasis than in substance.

Struve's conception of nationality played heavily on the juxtaposition of two words: *russkii* versus *rossiiskii*. Both adjectives may be translated as "Russian," but they delineate quite distinct areas. The first, *russkii*, refers to the ethnic cultural entity, the latter to the political geographic unit.[26]

Russkii—the usual expression for Russian culture, language, and people—Struve lauded, even exalted. While praising the virtues of *russkii* culture, Struve warned of its degradation and replacement by the colorless, bureaucratic variant, *rossiiskii*. In other words, Struve feared that Russians could be losing the richness of their native culture to a feeble "cosmopolitan" mishmash, perhaps acceptable to all inhabitants of the empire as a kind of lingua franca but lacking in the vitality of a living, growing culture. Nationality, Struve maintained, was present not so much in the blood as in the soul, and Russian educated society was running the risk of losing its national soul by advocating a kind of anodyne, undifferentiated *rossiiskii* culture. And all for nothing: "But 'state' justice does not require of us 'national' indifference [*bezrazlichie*]." Russian society had not only the right but the responsibility to develop and proudly exhibit Russian national identity:

> Both I and every other Russian, we all have the right to these feelings: the right to our national identity [*national'noe litso*]. . . . In the heavy ordeals of recent years our national Russian feeling has grown and developed. It has become transformed, has gained in complexity and focus, but at the same time it has matured and gotten stronger. We must stop dissembling and hiding our national identity.[27]

Struve's words take one step further the "concord" that Slavinskii claimed to see between Russian state unity and the development of national cultures. Whereas Slavinskii had non-Russian nations in mind, Struve extended the same principle—quite logically—to his own nation. Why should Russians be expected to deny themselves something granted to all others? Struve's point may at first appear convincing, but from the perspective of a non-Russian, faced by the combined power of the Russian state and its already well-developed culture, Struve's words bore a sinister resemblance, at least potentially, to the kind of militant Russian nationalism that already threatened minority cultures.

The split between the liberals and the national liberals came into the open over the issue of Ukrainian cultural and linguistic rights. In 1908, Rodichev spoke in the Duma in favor of Ukrainian rights, specifically on the right to use Ukrainian as the language of instruction in primary schools in Ukraine.[28] Struve, on the other hand, dismissed the very idea of Ukrainian high culture and argued that, although the "Little Russian dialect" must not be forbidden or oppressed, neither should it be supported or encouraged (by being used as a language of instruction in schools or universities, for example).[29] Struve insisted that there was only one great Russian people and that encouraging the development of this "regional dialect" would only lead to stultifying particularism and separatism. In a polemic with V. Zhabotinskii, Struve pointed to

> the enormous historical fact: *the existence of the Russian [russkaia] nation and Russian culture*. Namely Russian and not Great Russian. . . . "Russian" is not some sort of abstract "medium" between [Great Russian, Little Rus-

sian, Belorussian], but a vital cultural force, a great, evolving, and burgeoning national element [*stikhiia*], a nation in the making, as the Americans say
about themselves.[30]

Struve's idea of a "positive, creative" nationalism that would fuse together
the "three branches" of the Russian people sounded to many suspiciously
similar to the official government position and was attacked as such by
many of Struve's fellow Kadets, both Ukrainian and Russian.[31] But it is important to state Struve's position clearly. His extraordinary comparison of
the Russian and American situations points to his unique point of departure. Struve apparently thought that Ukrainians and Belorussians—at
least—would willingly sacrifice their native tongues and cultures in favor
of a "Pan-Russian" culture, just as immigrants to the United States voluntarily gave up their native tongues, dress, and customs and exerted themselves to be "good Americans." It must be stressed that Struve did not support repressive administrative measures against Ukrainian culture. Rather,
he advocated that Ukrainian culture be content with a local significance,
something like Bavarian or Plattdeutsch culture within the German Empire.[32] Obviously this kind of limitation could not be accepted by nationally
conscious Ukrainians, but Struve's arguments should not be equated with
the extreme and aggressively anti-Ukrainian stance of either the government or the rightist and nationalist parties. However, in the end, one may
argue that Struve's "liberal russification" could prove even more destructive to non-Russian (and particularly Ukrainian) culture than crude government intervention.

Struve exemplified, in extreme form, the ambiguity and contradictions
inherent in Russian liberal ideology. Russian liberals saw no contradiction
or divergence of interests between a strong Russian *(rossiiskii)* state and ro-
bust national cultures. Struve differed mainly in his insistence that Russian
culture was a "nation in the making" (he used the phrase in English), a nation that embraced Belorussians and Ukrainians as much as Great Russians. By "defining away" separate Belorussian and Ukrainian nations,
Struve placed himself firmly in a Russian tradition, but in a tradition that
non-Russians could only view with suspicion and hostility.

Struve's patriotism was far from an anomaly even within the nationally
tolerant Kadet party. Kistiakovskii says as much in his letter to *Russkaia
mysl'*. The Kadets were prepared tolerate minority cultures, but when these
nationalities started to demand political rights, the Kadets began to de-
mure. In this sense Struve differed from Miliukov and Rodichev only by
degree, not by a true difference of principle. Even while defending the use
of Ukrainian as a language of instruction, Rodichev framed his argument in
terms of the interests of the Russian state, even going so far as to proclaim,
"Ukrainophilism exists only insofar as it is forbidden. I think: liberate it,
and it will be no longer." One could explain this statement as a mere rhetorical bone thrown to the more conservative Octobrists, but it seems more
likely that within the Kadet party the ambiguity and uneasiness concerning

nationality ran far deeper. The Kadets, as good liberals and good (Russian) patriots, were committed on one hand to national toleration and on the other to the preservation of the greatness of the Russian state. The attempt to reconcile these two aims made the Kadets' attitudes toward minority nationalists appear duplicitous or at least naive.[33]

The above sketch of the "national discourses" of the Kadets should not be taken as a denunciation of that party.[34] Rather, my aim is to show that even sincere liberals found it difficult to stake out a position that would both preserve the integrity of the Russian state and also allow for free development of non-Russian cultures. In practice Russian liberals (and the Kadet party was the archetypal Russian liberal party) tended to hold up Austria-Hungary as a model for the peaceful coexistence of various nationalities.[35] In hindsight, such a conception seems more than a little naive. However, we should not underestimate the difficulty of the liberal position, or glibly pretend that the problem had any easy solution, or at any rate any easy solution not repugnant to liberal ideals.

The Rightist Nationalists

For an easy, quite consistent "solution" to the nationality question, one must consult the Russian right. Here the answer was quite clear and uncomplicated: Russia existed for the Russians. Other nationalities could be tolerated only to the extent that they conformed, at least publicly, to the dominant "ruling" Russian nation. Yet even here we find contradictions and a lack of clarity. For example, what about the Jews? Of course they could not be allowed equal rights. At best Jews could be tolerated, and barely, at that.[36] Other national groups were similarly granted a grudging right to existence, but only insofar as they did not stand in the way of Russian rights and privileges.

To further complicate the picture, Russian arch-conservatives, to a greater or lesser extent, generally rejected nationalist ideology. Konstantin Leontiev even went so far as to suggest that Catholicism within Russia was a positive force, because it acted as a stimulus to the otherwise somnolent Orthodox church.[37] However, if we set aside the ideologists of the old regime such as Prince V. Meshcherskii, who looked with horror at the idea of the Russian mob, even if "true-Russian,"[38] stepping onto the public stage, we find on the right a great deal of consensus regarding the national question, particularly after 1905. Before the 1905–1907 revolution Russian nationalism as a popular movement had practically not existed, but after the shattering events of those revolutionary years both right-wing elements in society and the Russian government itself became more receptive to the conservative possibilities of Russian nationalism. Two parties, the "Nationalists" (natsionalisty) and "Rightists" (pravye) were represented and played important roles in the Third and Fourth Dumas. The following comments describe not the "program" of any one party but the overall conceptions of Russianness and the national other that underlie the programs and policies of specific parties.

The rightists' national program is summed up nicely in the title of General A. Kuropatkin's magnum opus, *Rossiia dlia russkikh: Zadachi russkoi armii* (Russia for the Russians: Tasks of the Russian Army).[39] In this peculiar work, Kuropatkin aimed to trace the tasks of the Russian army from the Kievan period to the present day. According to this account, the Russian army had united the Russian "tribe" and secured for it the territory between the Caspian, Black, and Baltic Seas. For our purposes, the most important is volume 3, *Zadachi russkoi armii v XX stoletii* (The Tasks of the Russian Army in the Twentieth Century).

In this volume Kuropatkin described the internal situation of Russia at the end of the nineteenth century and recounts in somber terms the growing weakness of Russians and the corresponding growth in foreign *(inozemnye)* influences. Although he did not claim that all foreign influences were actually baleful, Kuropatkin wrote in neo-Slavophile terms, blaming "the oppression of ministers and bureaucrats" on foreign influences introduced into Russia by Peter the Great. The negative effects of these imported ideas and practices became ubiquitous in Russia: "Bureaucratism in Russia became extraordinarily developed and significant. By substituting general European considerations for national politics in foreign affairs, also domestic matters in Russia have been pursued without taking national needs into account, without considering *above all the needs of the Russian nation [plemia]*."[40]

How could these historical wrongs be righted? In the first place, it could be done by strengthening the link between the Russian state and the Russian "tribe" (Kuropatkin and many of his fellows in the rightist-nationalist camp favored the traditional term *plemia* over *natsiia* or *narod*). Throughout the empire the rights of Russians must be safeguarded, especially in Finland and the Baltic region. Jewish rights must be strictly reduced and Jews not allowed in the army (instead they must pay a special tax). No exceptions whatsoever should be allowed to these restrictions because, "given the soft-heartedness of Russian people, a Westerner convinced of the utility of Jews or a businessman [*delets*] in cahoots with the Jewish kahal can always collect the necessary number of signatures [to obtain an exception], among which will figure persons of various positions and callings, not excluding the clergy."[41]

Here a chord is struck that is rarely absent from Russian nationalist writings: the honest, good-hearted, and (rarely stated, but ever understood) dim-witted Russian people must be protected from the conniving, sly, but intelligent and efficient, foreigner, or *inorodets*.[42] To justify his demand for special privileges for Russians and restrictions for *inorodtsy*, Kuropatkin stated: "Ideas of equality and freedom are dangerous for nations weaker in culture and advantageous for those stronger." It is clearly understood that the Russian people belongs in the former group.[43]

Kuropatkin's treatment of the Poles is also typical. Although admitting the high level of culture and bravery in battle of the Polish people, Kuropatkin is ambivalent as to the Poles' loyalty to the Russian state. Not wanting to seem chauvinistic (nearly every Russian nationalist of the era indignantly rejected such a designation), Kuropatkin allowed that some Poles, those who consider Russia their homeland and Russian their native tongue, should be accepted into the Russian nation as equals. However, those Poles who "demonstratively preserve their language," speaking it loudly in station buffets and other public places, must have their rights severely curtailed in the interests of the Russian state and people.[44] In other words, Poles who persisted in preserving and cultivating their national culture were to be regarded as inherently disloyal and anti-Russian. In trying to impress the reader with his tolerance of non-Russian high culture, Kuropatkin revealed his fundamental and profound intolerance: Poles (and, by extension, other non-Russians) ought to be tolerated within the Russian Empire as long as they accepted not only Russian political hegemony but also Russian culture. Following such a definition it is difficult to see any real difference between Kuropatkin's "loyal Poles" and Russians of Polish origin.

Like many of his contemporaries on the right, Kuropatkin scarcely differentiated between the needs of the Russian state and the needs or desires of the Russian nation. When reading his work, one is struck by the facile assumption that the "Russian tribe" (including Ukrainians and Belorussians) had immediate and concrete interests in the Great Russia described here. A contemporary reviewer of the work remarked that, for Kuropatkin, the Russian people was little more than the object of decrees and measures issued from the higher and lower administration.[45] Also characteristic is Kuropatkin's failure to offer any precise definition of the term "Russian." Apparently a Russian was what he was, and attempting to place a legalistic definition to the mystical essence of this Russianness would have be superfluous, even sacrilegious. Any attempt to set down precisely the boundaries of "Russiandom" would have severely strained—if not exploded altogether—the harmonious totality implicit in the nationalist vision of the Russian *narod*.

Running in tandem with this semi-mystical vision of the Russian people is an almost total unwillingness to allow that an individual might choose a national affiliation. The ideologues of the Russian people demanded all "for the people" but nothing "by the people." Consistently one encounters the attitude that many residents of the western borderlands perversely insisted on considering themselves Poles when their Russianness was evident, at least to nationalist writers. For certain Russian nationalists, a distant Russian ancestor quite sufficed to prove one "really" a Russian, despite several generations of Polish-speaking Catholic forefathers. For example, one nationalist describes the population of the Northwest Provinces in these words: "[there live] landowners and peasants who consider themselves Poles, although in fact pseudo-Poles [*lzhe-poliaki*], and are thus inimical to the Russian nationality and to the Russian tsar."[46] Exactly how one distinguishes real Poles from *lzhe-poliaki* is unclear, but there is no doubt that, if these deluded individuals would only realize their true (Russian) nationality, they would cease to feel seditious hatred for the Russian people and the Russian tsar.

The Polish hatred for all things Russian (*vse russkoe*) was a constant among the idées fixes of Russian nationalist discourse. Two figures stand out in the pantheon of anti-Russian Polish forces: Polish women, and the eternally plotting, "jesuitical" Catholic priest, or *ksendz*. Polish women appear in the works of Russian rightists as "particularly dangerous for Russia."[47] Even more damning is this description of the Polish gentry woman (*shliakhtianka*): "they are bad wives [and] far from exemplary mothers; caring for their children, they are concerned exclusively with developing in them a feeling of extreme patriotism, and in this respect their influence is enormous."[48] The patriotic Polish woman also figures in governors' reports to the tsar. Even the liberal governor general of Vilna, Prince Petr Sviatopolk-Mirskii, admitted that Polish women generally avoided Russian society in the region and rarely knew Russian.[49]

The *ksendz* was, if anything, an even more menacing figure. The term is a Russian garbling of the Polish *ksiądz* (Catholic priest). In Russian, quite different words distinguish not only Catholic priests from their Orthodox colleagues but also Catholic churches (*kostely*) from their Orthodox counterparts (*tserkvi*). For most practical purposes, Russian conservatives equated Catholicism with Polonism and thus with sedition, or worse. Vladimirov described Catholic churches in the Northwest Provinces as "Polish fortresses" and depicted Catholic priests in sinister terms, even inventing a new word, *ksendstvo*, to describe their evil machinations: "'Ksendstvo' is that mythical power that grows with every blow dealt it."[50] It is interesting to note that Russian anti-Semites used almost exactly the same expressions when bewailing the futility of legal measures against Jews. This is no coincidence: for the Russian right (and, as we shall see, for Russian officialdom), Poles and Jews were unmistakably the enemy.

This firm belief in the ingrained hostility of Poles toward Russians and in the essential dishonesty ("Jesuitical logic") of the Catholic church in its centuries-long embittered struggle against Orthodoxy precluded any kind of cooperation between the two peoples. To be sure, at times Russian nationalists did admit the theoretical possibility of Russian-Polish reconciliation, but they then inevitably went on to point out that "at the present time" Poles continued to persist in their hidden animosity toward the Russian people and state and hence could not be trusted. Typical is the following Russian nationalist statement, made in reaction to Count Tyszkiewicz's appeal in the liberal daily *Rech'* against the proposed Kholm guberniia: "[Before Polish-Russian cooperation is possible, it] is necessary to await the disappearance of aggressive aspirations within Polish society toward native holy Russian lands such as Kholmshchina, Belorussia, Ukraine. But this will come to pass only after a reeducation [*perevospitanie*] of Polish society in the spirit of Cyril and Methodius's legacy."[51] Such a process of reeducation would be a matter of generations, if not centuries.

The aversion expressed by figures of the Russian right toward the Catholic church highlights the importance of religion in the national self-definition of this group. Nearly always "Russian" was assumed to be synonymous with "Orthodox," even to the point that the two terms were used together as obvious equivalents. Orthodoxy was by Russian law the "reigning" religion: the tsar and his family were required to profess to the Orthodox faith, and other religions in the Russian Empire were at best only tolerated. Until April 1905, conversion from Orthodoxy to any other religion, even a Christian denomination, was strictly forbidden. The western territory had been the scene of a centuries-long conflict between Orthodoxy and Catholicism, and by the late nineteenth century this struggle was understood and remembered primarily in national terms. The abolition of the remnants of the Uniate church in the Russian Empire was merely a further step in delineating "Russian" from "Pole."[52]

Despite the unquestioned importance of religion for the Russian nationalist right, the nationalists made surprisingly little reference to the Orthodox church in their programmatic statements about the tasks of Russian nationalism. For example, in a detailed and scholarly volume entitled *Istoriia russkogo samosoznaniia po istoricheskim pamiatnikam i nauchnym sochineniiam* (A history of Russian [national] consciousness), written by a professor at the St. Petersburg Orthodox Academy, the Orthodox church receives scant attention, whereas the development of the Russian state and Russian intellectual history are described in great detail. Perhaps the importance of the Orthodox faith for Russian nationalists was so immense that no need was felt to expound on the topic. Alternately, the close ties between Russian church and state may have led to a general failure to differentiate in any strict sense between these two institutions. In any case, the significance of the Orthodox church for Russian self-definition cannot be overestimated. Although modern, secular, nationalist trends were beginning to appear in Russia after 1905, the traditional triad of Russian culture, state, and Orthodox religion remained in most respects unquestioned, at least by conservative Russians. A Catholic Russian might be a theoretical possibility, but only in individual, peculiar instances. As a general category, when "Russian" was said, "Orthodox" was understood.[53]

If the Russian right found it difficult to trust Catholic Poles, their feelings toward Russia's huge Jewish community went far beyond distrust, reaching into the realm of pathological phobias. The national mentality of the Russian right can hardly be imagined without taking into account its fundamental and profound anti-Semitism. It is not by chance that Russians played a major role in fabricating the infamous Protocols of the Elders of Zion. Indeed, even the most strident Polonophobes seem restrained and liberal compared to certain Russian anti-Semites of this period. The sense of hatred, loathing, and paranoia manifested in portrayals of Jews comes through in such extreme terms that one is at a loss to explain it on any conscious or reasonable level. Not only were Jews dangerous as economic competitors and exploiters of Russian peasants, but they presented a grave moral danger to the very essence of holy Russia. As such, they must be subjected to severe restrictions and limitations, or even ejected from the country altogether.[54]

The most extreme wing of Russian anti-Semitism claimed that Jews were plotting not only the weakening of Russia but even the conquest of the entire world. One such work bears the significant title *Evreiskoe ravnopravie ili russkoe poraboshchenie?* (Jewish equal rights or Russian enslavement?) and explicitly argued that the former would invariably bring about the latter. The pamphlet's subtitle is similarly revealing of the author's conception of the Jewish threat: "An examination of secret Jewish plans and programs aimed at the weakening and destruction of the native [*korennyi*] population and its enslavement by Jewry." These malevolent plans hinged on two factors: the organized strength of the Jews and "goyish carelessness, blindness, and defenselessness." Once again, the Russians are portrayed as simple, even lackadaisical, and the enemy as sly, efficient, diligent, and well organized. How, then, were true-Russians to defend themselves? The answer was clear: "Of course, not [by] pogroms, for these only give Jews an excuse to demand compensation from the government in the form of the extension of their rights and may give an excuse for the intervention of certain states in our internal affairs." Rather, Russians must insist on the return to the Pale for all Jews without exception, the forcing out of Jews from every kind of public institution or organization in the empire, from universities and other schools, and the exclusion of Jews from Russian political life. In essence, Jews were to be shut out as much as possible from all contacts with Russians.[55]

One finds a somewhat less hysterical tone on the Jewish question in the writings of A. Liprandi, but his conclusions differ little from those of the conspiracy theorists Demchenka or G. Butmi. Writing after 1905, Liprandi blamed the revolution of that year on the Jews, quoting approvingly a statement that "the Russian revolution [of 1905] may just as well be called a Jewish one."[56] The pogroms of 1905–1906, according to Liprandi, arose spontaneously out of the frustration and anger of exploited Christians. Scornfully rejecting accusations that pogroms had been fomented by conservative groups such as the Union of Russian People, Liprandi claimed that, on the contrary, pogroms could be explained by the very lack of such organizations. Like Demchenka, Liprandi condemned these pogroms for giving Russia a bad reputation abroad and increasing sympathy for the Jews. Instead, he recommended that Christians use economic tactics against the Jews, forming their own cooperative stores and boycotting Jewish businesses.[57] Giving Jews equal rights would spell catastrophe for Russia because of their unwillingness to be productive citizens and their penchant for circumventing the law. Liprandi also cited figures showing that Jews avoided military service 20–30 percent more than Christians. The Jewish question in Russia would be solved only when all Jews had left Russian territory. As examples of countries where the Jewish question had been solved, Liprandi mentions Japan and Finland, both of which severely restricted the entry of Jews.[58] Exactly how Russia was to rid herself of millions of Jews, however, remained unclear. Liprandi and other rightists tended to favor some kind of "absolute emigration," perhaps to Palestine, but the mechanics of this operation were never spelled out. Extreme anti-Semites such as Liprandi were caught in a corner; they wished Russia free of Jews but had no concept of how to effect this change. Although Liprandi and his fellows consistently condemned physical violence against the Jews, their insistence that Jews be segregated from Russian society, culture, and politics was manifestly but a temporary solution. The twentieth century would take the next step to the "final" solution.

One recent German study has located the origins of Russian anti-Semitism during this period in the birth pains of modern, industrial Russia and the longing for a preindustrial, rural past. This argument, although perhaps one-sided, has a certain validity, but one could also inject a more personal, psychological element, especially for true-Russian men bearing such names as Liprandi, Butmi, Puryszkiewicz, or even Savenko. In any case, it is clear that, for certain extreme anti-Semitic theorists, "the Jew" was but a symbol for the modern world of industry, parliaments, and the gold standard.[59] However, it is impossible to pursue this topic here. Suffice it to say that the right-nationalist conception of one unified and great Russia was unable to consider non-Russians as other than material to be ingested into the Russian ethnic body or as harmful matter against which the Russian people had to be protected.

The nationalist right as a political force in Russian society was born out of the political upheavals of 1905–1907.[60] Throughout the empire, but particularly in the Western and southern (mainly Ukrainian and Moldavian) provinces, local organizations such as nationalist clubs and chapters of the Union of Russian People took shape. The ideology of these organizations was in the purest sense of the word reactionary: they were reacting in shock and horror to the events of 1905. The first report of the Kiev Club of Russian Nationalists explains the raison d'être of their club in the following terms:

> Recognizing that the tempestuous revolutionary movement experienced by Russia was primarily a manifestation of national struggle, the struggle of foreign elements [*inorodicheskogo mira*] with the Russian people for sovereign rights in the state, [the club's founders] became conscious of the necessity to create such a *non-partisan* organization that, on the one hand, would by propagating the ideas of Russian nationalism awaken in Russians national feelings and would deepen their national consciousness, and on the other hand, would gather together [members of various right and nationalist groupings] around the nationalist slogan of the supremacy of the Russian people in the state.[61]

Two elements are of crucial importance in this statement: first, that the revolution of 1905 was not Russian but "alien" and, second, that the Russian people must reign supreme in the Russian state. Like the anti-Semitic voices we have considered above, the Kiev Russian nationalists blamed 1905 on outside agitators and set out to defend Russian interests against the machinations of foreigners, here understood to include not only Jews but Poles and even Ukrainian nationalists.[62] Once again the rhetoric emphasized defense, guarding the imperiled Russians from the internal enemies *(inorodtsy)* who threatened to usurp the Russian's rightful place. In this case, however, the exalted phrases calling for a restoration of Russian rights can barely veil the concrete political motivations of the nationalists whose use of the "nationalist slogan" may have been motivated in large part by rather more material causes, including their desire to increase their political influence in the empire.

We are not concerned here with explaining the psychological motivations of Russian xenophobic nationalism, but one possible contributing factor could be the overwhelming inferiority complex that seemed to permeate the Russian nationalist self-image. Again and again, as we have seen in Kuropatkin's justification for restrictions on non-Russians, nationalists at least implicitly admitted the inferiority of the Russian *narod* (*Volk*, people) in intelligence, business acumen, and general culture. Without restrictive laws, the more adept and cultured Jews, Poles, and Germans would simply devour the guileless Russian. The Russians' virtues were seen in their toleration, good-heartedness, and simplicity—precisely those traits, it would seem, that the nationalists were militating against.

The rightist self-image of the Russian state and people and their perceptions of the place of the minority nationalities within the Russian Empire also found expression in Duma speeches. First and foremost the unity of the Russian Empire and the predominance of the Russian nationality within the empire had to be safeguarded—to quote the program of the All Russian National Union: "The unity and indivisibility of the Russian Empire and the preservation in all of its parts of the supremacy of the Russian nationality [*narodnost'*]."[63] Nationalists often complained that Russians, alone among all nationalities in the empire, were denied the right to defend themselves. Pointing out that the mainly "Russian" (that is, Ukrainian and Belorussian) population of the Western Provinces was represented in the State Council by Poles, the nationalist Ladomirskii commented, "If the Vistula territory [Poland] were represented in the State Council by Russians, I can imagine what a hue and cry would be raised. . . . Russians are strictly forbidden to defend their own interests."[64]

The nationalists insisted repeatedly that they aimed not to infringe on minority rights but only to defend the Russian state and nation. The same Ladomirskii, this time in regards to the law limiting Finland's autonomy, declared, "While in no way pursuing a goal of forcible russification, we nonetheless cannot allow the political detachment [*gosudarstvennaia obosoblennost'*] of our borderlands, that our borderlands would convert into confederate states of this or the other kind."[65] Even the nationalist right had by now absorbed the idea that russification was to be condemned, even while the interests of Russians needed to be championed.

The rightist conception of nationality was propelled in great part by feelings of confusion and outrage over the changes occurring in Russian society in the early twentieth century. The tenor of these voices is one of shock combined with embittered demands that the Russian nation be "restored" its proper place within the Russian state. The rightists perceived that traditional Russia, where "Orthodoxy, Autocracy, and Nationality" once held sway, had now come under attack. At the same time, more cynical (or realistic) individuals sensed that the slogan of "national defense" could be used to win political support. Leaving aside the issue of how "national" pre-1905 Russia had been, the paucity of serious ideas and original formulations about nationality among the Russian right is perhaps its most striking feature. Caught in a web of stereotypes and ominous forebodings, Russian rightists spoke of defense when in fact they wished for destruction.

Russian rightists, as one would expect, were adamant in their support for the monarchy and the Romanov dynasty. For them the "Russian people" was inevitably linked with, and symbolized by, the Russian tsar. They seldom if ever took notice of the possible contradictions between Russian nationalism on one hand and, on the other, loyalty to a dynasty with mainly German bloodlines and to a tsar who was married to a German princess and who regularly used the English language at home. One figure symbolizes better than any other the incongruities of dynastic Russian nationalism: Prince Vladimir Petrovich Meshcherskii.

Meshcherskii was born in 1839 into an old and well-connected noble family; his maternal grandfather was the famous writer and historian N. M. Karamzin. Meshcherskii's long life spanned the reigns of five emperors; had he lived a few months longer he would have witnessed the outbreak of World War I. Meshcherskii stood firmly on the extreme right, politically, and enjoyed a degree of influence at court, despite a generally unsavory reputation. According to the diary of M. Bogdanovich, Alexander III regularly read Meshcherskii's *Grazhdanin* and urged others to do the same.[66] Hence the views expressed by Prince Meshcherskii in his many publications are of more than personal interest.

For Meshcherskii, the foundations of the Russian Empire were to be found in the solid and unquestioned authority of the autocracy, in a tradition-bound nobility imbued with a sense of duty, and in a strong respect for the Russian nationality. To his mind, ever since the reforms of Alexander II's reign, all these elements had unfortunately come under serious attack both from liberal elements within the government and from Russian society. The behavior of minister of internal affairs P. A. Valuev after the Polish uprising of 1863 and his intrigues against Vilna governor general M. N. Muraviev symbolized for Meshcherskii the combination of weak liberalism and cosmopolitan decadence that was all too prevalent even at the highest levels of Russian officialdom. Meshcherskii characterized Valuev's attitude toward the Polish question as "strange," adding, "This strangeness consisted in that he as minister of internal affairs was considerably more hostile toward the *Russian* party, whose representatives at that time were Muraviev and Katkov, than toward the Poles [who had recently risen in rebellion against the Russian authorities]."[67]

Only in Russia, Meshcherskii lamented in his memoirs, were men criticized and disadvantaged for being "overly Russian": "Already from the early years of my activity in government service and as a writer I had noticed with a kind of heavy astonishment that the most difficult thing in Russia for a state or societal figure is—to be *Russian.*" Precisely what this would entail, however, Meshcherskii did not explain. He did express admiration for such patriotic figures as Muraviev and M. Katkov, editor of the chauvinist *Moskovskie vedomosti,* but he also criticized certain figures such as interior minister N. P. Ignatiev for an exaggerated antipathy toward Jews.[68] Although one may explain some of these apparent inconsistencies by personal affinities and dislikes, overall Meshcherskii's ideology is of a whole. Its contradictions may be explained as inherent in any attempt at combining a dynastic patriotism based on the conservation of a strictly stratified social order with certain elements of modern nationalism.

Among Meshcherskii's bêtes noires were the nationalist newspaper *Novoe vremia,* its editor A. Suvorin, and after 1905 the nationalists in the Duma and Prime Minister P. Stolypin. For Meshcherskii, Suvorin was a "socialist"—clearly the two men's distinctive brands of "nationalism" bore little in common other than the word itself.[69] Meshcherskii set down his objections to the nationalism of *Novoe vremia* in a short article entitled "O patriotizme" (About patriotism). Meshcherskii's point of departure was an article by one Novikov in *Novoe vremia* that extolled patriotism, condemned chauvinism, and called for a bridging of the gap between intellectuals and the people. Meshcherskii called into question not only the opinions stated in this article but its very assumptions. Meshcherskii pointed out that patriotism is indeed "love for the motherland [*rodina*]," but this "motherland" could hardly include more than a small corner of any given state. In Russia, natives of Riazan' and Kaluga hardly regarded each other as fellow countrymen *(zemliaki).*[70] In any case, patriotism was the very opposite of rationality—reason would dictate that any corner of civilized Switzerland would be preferable to backward Russia. "No, Mr. Novikov, in patriotism (especially Russian), if it is sincere and not driven by empty phrases, there is less, far less, rationality than in your article! And for that very reason it is dear to us."[71]

Predictably, Meshcherskii objected to Novikov's call to efface the differences between peasants and educated classes, arguing that the most sincere patriots were to be found in the village, not among the educated classes. He also rejected Novikov's facile distinction between patriotism and chauvinism, pointing out that, according to Novikov's terms, the Russian patriots Minin and Pozharskii, who rallied the Russians against the Polish invaders at the end of the Time of Troubles, could also be called chauvinists. Particularly interesting is Meshcherskii's account of the origins of patriotism:

> Patriotism of the nation developed [out of three fundamental principles]: geography, ethnography, and ethics. Nations [*narody*] came to perceive *themselves,* to love and defend *themselves,* when they became closed off within geographical limits, induced by similarity [*odnoobrazie*] of customs, language, and faith. The more firmly these limits stood out, the stronger the patriotism of the nation.[72]

Thus for Meshcherskii, patriotism's strength and legitimacy derived from its historical development, and it mattered little that this patriotism could easily lead to clashes with other nations. Attempts like Novikov's to present an anodyne "reasonable" patriotism were not only false but even dangerous in their social implications.

Meshcherskii was suspicious of anyone who tried to make national feeling into a political issue.[73] Perhaps this explains his unrelenting hostility to Stolypin and the Nationalist party after 1905. Already in the autumn of 1905 he published an article severely criticizing attempts to russify Russia's borderlands. Such policies could only increase hostilities toward the government and weaken the Russian state: "The borderlands' question is a critical, burning question and there is no need to exacerbate it even further. All Russian subjects, regardless of their nationality or faith, must be allowed to live unrestrained and free under the canopy of the Russian eagle, and only under such circumstances will the solution of this question become possible." These words did not come from Meshcherskii's pen, but he published them without any commentary, which suggests he shared the sentiments. He had previously published similar comments of his own on more than one occasion.[74]

For Meshcherskii nationality was a given, much like faith or social class. His own patriotism consisted of respecting Russian traditions (including autocracy and the existing social order) and loving the Russian land. But any attempts to harness nationalist feelings to a political cause or to pressure non-Russian peoples to accept the Russian nationality were just as repugnant to him as calls for sweeping changes in the Russian Empire's social structure. For Meshcherskii, even Stolypin and such conservative nationalists as V. Shulgin and V. Purishkevich smacked of socialist leveling and revolution.[75] Perhaps better than they, he sensed that the potential danger of any kind of "national politics" in a state like the Russian Empire far outweighed possible benefits. Meshcherskii—and quite possibly many other Russians on the traditionalist right—longed for a simple, unchanging Russian state, led by a strong emperor and peopled by strictly segregated social groups, each content with its own lot. In the same way, each of the empire's national groups would accept its position within the state and would accept Russian culture, if at all, on the basis of its attractiveness and utility, never from outside pressure. To be sure, Meshcherskii did not formulate his views on the national question in any clear form (clarity was never his strong point), but the desire to wish away the national question by positing an idyllic harmony of nations was hardly limited to him alone. We shall see similar views when we examine official Russia's statements on nationality.

❖   In this chapter we have focused on the national views of Russian society, that is, the small, educated, articulate segment of the Russian public. But what about the millions of Russian peasants, townspeople, and small merchants who made up the bulk of the Russian people? Each of the political groupings we have considered claimed to be speaking for the Russian nation as a whole. The socialists saw in the working classes the healthy core of the nation; liberals perceived the nation in the growing ranks of educated Russians; conservatives extolled mainly the peasants; and dynastic reactionaries such as Meshcherskii espied the nobility as the caste most properly fit to set the tone for and to lead the Russian nation. All of Russian society denied that anti-Semitism and chauvinism were intrinsic to Russian attitudes toward the national other. Pogroms were blamed either on Jewish provocation (by rightists) or on government machinations (by leftists). In both cases, the Russian nation itself was absolved of responsibility but simultaneously became not the subject of history but a passive pawn, devoid of its own opinions, goals, and actions.

Any attempt to fix precisely the contours of Russian national thought is doomed to failure. Both sources and methodologies are inadequate to the task. Nonetheless, certain pervasive stereotypes do appear among large segments of the Russian population. Despite the repeated denials of the liberals and leftists to recognize the fact, anti-Semitism—at least in the sense of distrust and fear of the Jewish "deocides"—does seem to have been widely present among the Russian masses, and nearly universal (in greater or lesser form, to be sure) among the Christian population of the Pale of Settlement.[76] This topic obviously deserves far more detailed study than can be given here, but one indication that Russian popular feeling toward the Jews—even in the Central Provinces—was hardly neutral may be found in Turgenev's story of the nobleman Chertopkhanov in *Zapiski okhotnika* (Notes from a hunter's album). When Chertopkhanov comes upon a peasant mob beating a Jewish merchant and asks a peasant woman why her fellows attack the Jew, she replies, "I don't know, your honor. A piece of business, it seems. And why not beat him? After all, your honor, he crucified Christ!"[77]

In official documents, broad anti-Semitic feelings are similarly often attributed to the peasant masses. For example, after the 1881 pogrom wave in the Southwest, a government investigation into the causes of these disturbances stated openly that the "simple people" considered "beating up the Jew" *(bit' zhida)* a normal and even praiseworthy activity: "To beat Jews is not sinful, but on the contrary a very good thing [for Ukrainian peasants], for the simple man has heard from his youngest years from his father, from his grandfather, from the peasant commune [*gromada*] that Jews always and everywhere have always been beaten and hence, they should be beaten [*tak i sleduet bit'*]." Clearly this is a controversial topic. It goes without saying that literary and official sources can hardly "prove" the level of popular anti-Semitism.[78] On the other hand, denying its existence also fails to do justice to this complex issue.

Quite possibly Prince Meshcherskii was correct in stating that regional consciousness was stronger in Russia than "national" feelings. One would also expect that Orthodoxy played a central role in popular Russians' understanding of their national identity. In any case, most contemporaries claimed that the level of national self-consciousness remained low in the Russian countryside. These are, of course, but hypotheses and conjectures. Some recent scholarship has begun to deal, albeit indirectly, with the issue of national identity among the Russian masses during this period, but these studies have barely scratched the surface of this important topic.[79]

In the first decades of the twentieth century, Russian society was undergoing important changes in its national self-image. Whereas the socialists could still confidently predict that the fall of the old order and the establishment of a free, socialist, and democratic state would sweep away national antagonisms and prejudices, the feelings of most educated Russians on the notorious national question were far more ambivalent. Liberals championed the positive worth of Russian culture and a strong Russian state, and some, like Petr Struve, refused even to countenance the possibility of Ukrainian and Belorussian cultural development. After 1905 Russian liberals suffered a crisis of conscience that crystallized into a small book of essays entitled *Vekhi: Sbornik statei o russkoi intelligentsii* (Signposts: Collection of essays about the Russian intelligentsia). Here, too, the "national idea" found expression. In his essay, "Geroizm i podvizhnichestvo" (Heroism and asceticism), Sergei Bulgakov wrote, "The national idea rests not only on ethnographic and historical foundations, but above all on religious and cultural ones. It is based on religious and cultural messianism, in which, by necessity, any conscious national feeling is cast."[80] Bulgakov was anything but a Russian chauvinist, but his words (like those of Petr Struve discussed earlier) indicate a subtle but momentous change in the self-image of the Russian intelligentsia. Attitudes toward the "national" (or at least "patriotic") waxed increasingly positive, whereas the currency of the "cosmopolitan" dipped ever lower.

In sum, one may discern several different, if at points overlapping, attitudes toward nationality in late imperial Russia. The far left refused to consider nationality as an enduring problem, foreseeing an end to national antagonisms and struggles simultaneous with the coming collapse of the old order. The liberals argued that with an enlightened policy, non-Russians could and would be enticed into full citizenship within the Russian state. Others, mainly to the right of the political spectrum, rejected this argument and insisted that Russia belonged first and above all to her subjects of Russian nationality and that, although people of other ethnicities might be allowed to live unmolested within the boundaries of the Russian Empire, they must always remember that the "reigning" nationality was, is, and ever more would be, the Russian.

Whereas concepts of Russian national identity and the mission of the Russian state differed widely, the growing importance of the national issue was conceded by people of all political persuasions. Particularly after 1905 no one could any longer ignore Russia's status as a multinational empire, nor could even the most benighted Russian nationalists honestly believe that the empire's national problems would somehow work themselves out naturally. The increasing level of national self-consciousness among non-Russians was paralleled in Russian society by a feeling that relations between the "ruling" Russian nation and the other nationalities of the empire had to find more specific and consistent form, not only in the empire's legal code but in the hearts and minds of Russians. In nationality matters, as in so many other areas of political and social life, the Russian Empire and Russian society were faced by unfamiliar, disturbing, and even threatening events, ideas, and movements. The often confused and unrealistic views expressed on Russianness and nationality in the Russian Empire by Russians of various political stripes were but an attempt on their part to deal with this uncomfortable new situation.

Talking about Nationality

Official Russia and Non-Russians

The Russian State is one and indivisible. . . .
The Russian language is the common language of the
State and is compulsory in the Army, in the Navy, and
in all State and public institutions. The use of local
languages and dialects in State and public institutions
is determined by special laws.

—*Fundamental State Laws of the
Russian Empire (1906)*

❖   The Russian government's national psychology was rather less clear-cut than that of the true-Russian patriots. Of course, an entire bureaucracy could hardly be inflamed by the ideological passions (not to say manias) of the anti-Semite Butmi or the ultra-patriotic Kuropatkin, but a subconscious national ideology did reign in the halls of Russian officialdom. This is not to say that this implicit "official nationality" was identical to that of the xenophobic Russia-for-the-Russians nationalism examined in the previous chapter. Indeed, a huge multinational state cannot afford such ideological extremism: somehow a modus vivendi must be reached whereby various nationalities may live together, perhaps not equal in rights or entirely separate from one another, but according to some kind of legal arrangement—either understood or explicit—to regulate intercourse between the various peoples. Or such would be the theory; practice, as usual, appears much more complex and contradictory. All in all, despite its many and varied nationalities, the Russian imperial state did manage to hold together with relatively little serious (that is, immediately threatening) national agitation until 1917.

Speaking of "official Russia" or of the "Russian bureaucracy," one inevitably falls into generalizations, some of them no doubt unwarranted. Russia's ruling classes did reflect to some extent the diversity of the empire they administered, and in such a large and disparate group, differences of approach and opinion always arise. Yet, we should not overemphasize the differences that separated these men (women did not figure at all within this group). A certain shared feeling of purpose must have motivated these men to join the ranks of the empire's preservers and defenders. Furthermore, ties of education, background, and even family connections often existed between these men.

In a recent study of the highest rank of imperial Russia's ruling class, D. Lieven has stressed that, even during the final decades of Romanov rule, scions of old aristocratic families were still represented in large numbers among his "target group" (men appointed by Nicholas II to the State Council, 1894–1914).[1] Shared educational and service experiences also linked these men, even when there were significant differences in political outlook. There is no reason to doubt that similar shared experiences helped form the political and national mentalities of the men whose voices will be considered in this chapter, though most of them could not boast the high connections and aristocratic backgrounds found so often among the men Lieven describes. There is some overlap (in the case of Prince P. Sviatopolk-Mirskii, for example), but on the whole the administrators considered here—for the most part provincial governors—made up the second echelon of imperial Russia's administrative aristocracy. Most of these men held the rank of privy councillor (*tainyi sovetnik*, rank 3) or actual state councillor (*deistvitel'nyi statskii sovetnik*, rank 4), corresponding respectively to the military ranks of lieutenant and major general. Several of the governors held not civilian rank but the military rank of general. Among the governors we find many names hinting at non-Russian roots, such as Vatatsi, Utgof, Rosenschild-Paulin, and at the highest level, the governor general of Warsaw (1905–1914) G. Skalon and the governor general of Vilna, later minister of internal affairs, Prince P. D. Sviatopolk-Mirskii, who, though himself Orthodox, was by origin closely related to Polish and Catholic magnates of the Grand Duchy of Lithuania.[2] The foreign origin of these men's families did not, however, play any role either in their careers in government service or (as far as I can ascertain) in their conceptions of nationality. This in itself is of prime significance and should alert us to the large difference in conceptions and assumptions regarding nationality that exists between ourselves and the figures under consideration here.

How did official Russia conceive of nationality as a sociological or political category? and What kind of relation was envisioned between the ruling classes of the Romanov state and these non-Russian peoples? These are the fundamental questions to be investigated here. I have already argued in chapter 1 that not russification but, rather, state preservation was the primary goal of the Russian government between 1863 and 1914. Even given this admittedly debatable thesis, we have yet to consider how executors of government policy conceived of members of individual nationalities. Certain national groups (particularly the Jews and the Poles) were tarred irretrievably with the brush of "unreliability," but even this did not prevent diverging views in official policy on how these peoples were to be treated. Other groups such as the Lithuanians were seen as harmless or even "friendly," though usually this friendliness was most apparent in reference to the common Polish enemy. Finally, the numerically largest national groups (from the present-day point of view)—Belorussians and Ukrainians—are barely visible at all in the official record. For official purposes, these mainly peasant populations were simply Russian; minor local differences from the Great Russian standard scarcely concerned local or central administration. When these groups do appear as something other than Russian, it is almost always in one of two contexts: as dangerous separatists (here it is usually the Ukrainian intelligentsia that is mentioned) or as victims of Polonization (most often the Belorussian Catholics). As we shall see in the final three chapters of this study, the basic conception of these national groups in the official mind was to play a significant role in forming policy for the Russian Empire in its final years.

In memoirs, especially those written after the 1917 revolution, former Russian officials make scant reference to the nationality issue. By that time, their minds were concentrated on one point: how the revolution came to pass in their native land. Just to take one particular, egregious example, in reading the over five hundred pages of former minister of finance and premier Count V. N. Kokovtsov's memoirs, one would be hard-pressed to realize that the state administered by Kokovtsov and his colleagues was peopled by dozens or hundreds of diverse national groups; nationality simply does not appear, whereas St. Petersburg intrigues, conflicting personalities, and court politics most certainly do.[3]

Nationality does appear here and there in these works. Erstwhile assistant to the minister of the interior and architect of the Kholm project, S. E. Kryzhanovskii does mention the Jewish question—mainly in reference to Stolypin's support for an easing of the legal restrictions on Russia's Jews and Nicholas II's firm rejection of any such policy—and describes the ultranationalist Union of the Russian People as a "prototype of the union of fascists [in Italy]."[4] Another high-ranking official, Prince Serge Urusov, devotes a great deal of his *Memoirs of a Russian Governor* to the Jewish question and anti-Semitism (as might be expected of the governor appointed to Bessarabia Province after the horrendous Kishinev pogroms of 1903), but again, other nationalities (Ukrainians, Bessarabian Romanians, and so on) do not appear.[5]

In the perhaps most celebrated single memoir of the pre-revolutionary period, by minister of finance and later premier Count S. Iu. Witte, nationalism and nationality are mentioned here and there, in various contexts. Witte writes approvingly of the "nationalism" of Alexander III, all the while insisting that the late tsar would have hated the extremely chauvinist figures who had appeared on the Russian political scene since 1905, in particular the notorious ultra-patriotic Judeophobe V. Purishkevich. Several figures are described as "completely Jewish types" (a description, it should be noted, that was not always meant in a particularly derogatory way). Following another reigning stereotype, Witte portrays the aristocratic Count Potocki as a "typically" haughty Pole. In other words, even in volume 1 of his memoirs where he recounts his experiences in the mainly non-Russian Southwest Provinces, Witte seldom goes beyond stereotypes, jocular references to national "types," and anodyne remarks condemning "narrow" nationalism. Once Witte moves on to St. Petersburg, references to nationality become even less frequent, except when linked with Witte's effort to denounce and discredit his hated rival and successor, Peter Stolypin.[6] The relative lack of interest in the national question reflected in memoirs is no quirk. Official Russia preferred to ignore or minimize the importance of that issue and took notice of national frictions and potential conflicts only when these difficulties became so intense as to make some kind of response unavoidable.

V. I. Gurko

As a general introduction to the issue of Russian officialdom and the national question, I would like to present two extremely diverse, even opposing voices. One belongs to Prince P. Sviatopolk-Mirskii, mentioned above as the scion of a long-established Lithuanian magnate family; the other belongs to Vasilii I. Gurko, son of the notorious "russifying" governor general of Warsaw of the 1880s, Iosif Vladimirovich Gurko. The Gurkos, like the Sviatopolk-Mirskii clan, traced their nobility back to the days of the Grand Duchy of Lithuania, to the year 1539. The Gurko family was well established in the Belorussian area and in its political and national orientation leaned strongly toward Russia and Orthodoxy.[7] Mirskii and Gurko resembled each other in several ways: both came from long-established noble families based in the Northwest Provinces; both had made successful careers in government service (Mirskii in the military, Gurko in the civilian branch); both were committed to the autocracy, the Orthodox church, and Russian nationality. Yet despite these strong similarities in background and even in outlook, Mirskii and Gurko came to opposed views as regards the national question on Russia's western borders. Mirskii, well known for his liberal sympathies, predictably advocated a soft line toward the Poles and other nationalities in the West. Gurko, on the contrary, argued against any conciliatory measures and emphasized the importance of Russia's mission in the western territory: to protect, defend, and strengthen Russian culture and political power there.

An anonymous work appeared in 1897 under the title *Ocherki Privislian'ia* (Essays on the Vistula territory). The author hiding behind the pseudonym V.R. was quickly revealed to be V. I. Gurko. This is clearly a work by a knowledgeable Russian administrator evaluating the results of some three decades of russification. Gurko draws a detailed portrait of

Russian Poland, the social groups and nationalities that populated it, their political and economic interests, and the interests that should guide the imperial government and its administration there. As a work by a strong Russian nationalist, this book is significant as an expression of the conservative, "russianist" camp within the Russian bureaucracy. But even Gurko denied any interest in russifying the Poles. The Russian government should pursue, rather, the more modest goal of keeping the Poles (and Jews) in check while assuring that Russian state interests (including military considerations) were not neglected in this strategically important area. Yet his description of Russia's goal in the Vistula country in this "final stage" after 1883 sounds suspiciously close to a call for total assimilation of the Poles: "In a word, since 1883 Russian policy on the Polish question has entered the final—but the most difficult—period of its final solution: by means of impassive but constant pressure on the Polish nation to eradicate in it those peculiarities which separate it from Russia, gradually bringing into the Russian family. . . ."[8]

What were for Gurko the goals pursued in Poland in the decades after 1863 and to what extent were they achieved?[9] The hard core of Russian policy is reflected in the epigraph with which the book starts: Du mußt herrschen und gewinnen / Oder dienen und verlieren / Leiden oder triumphieren / Amboß oder Hammer sein (You must rule and win / Or serve and lose / Suffer or triumph / Be either anvil or hammer). The ultimate aim of Russian policy after 1863, in Gurko's view, should be to ensure that Russians played the role of the hammer, Poles that of the anvil ("should" because this aim was not ever fully realized, according to Gurko's view). Why this should have been so the author explained primarily as a function of Polish character weaknesses: the Polish ruling classes loved conspiracies and intrigue and were unwilling to share power with the broader masses of Polish society. The description of the szlachta (Polish gentry) was particularly negative: "Vanity, frivolity, inconstancy, a tendency for deception and lies . . . there you have the main outlines of the moral character [nravstvennyi oblik] of the Polish szlachcic."[10]

Given these character flaws of the Polish ruling class, coupled with Poland's strategic location as Russia's real "window to Europe" (and to the Western Slavs), the Russian government must adopt a kind of mission civilisatrice vis-à-vis the Poles. The Russian government neither could nor should attempt to convert Poles to Orthodoxy, nor did Russian officialdom have anything against Polish culture or language per se.[11] Rather, Poles must merely accept the role of the "state language," using Russian for many official and public purposes while retaining Polish for home and private use. The author, like many other conservative Russian officials, seemed to imply that the Baltic German barons should serve as a model for the Poles, all the while ignoring that the Germans enjoyed a good deal more autonomy in their home provinces after 1863 than did the Poles. In short, Gurko advocated a paternalistic policy that would turn the Poles into good subjects of the tsar but stopped short of linguistic or religious russification in a broader sense.

If the Polish ruling classes were untrustworthy and immoral, whom could the Russian government depend on in Poland? Gurko's answer comes as no surprise: "Without a doubt, the peasantry forms the most trustworthy element for Russia in the country [*krai*]." To be sure, the Polish peasants were sluggish, taciturn, servile, and sly *(khitrye)*, partly because of their long history of oppression at the hands of the szlachta, but even more because of "tribal peculiarities" *(plemennye osobennosti)*, as was evident when one compared Polish and "Little Russian" peasants. Still, they remained the most likely group in the area to respond favorably to Russian policy. For this reason Gurko advocated the abolition of *serwituty* in favor of the peasants, in essence bribing the peasants and punishing the szlachta at the same time.[12]

According to Gurko, workers in Poland—unlike their Russian counterparts—were true proletarians, having lost all links with the land. As such they were much more vulnerable to changes in the financial climate and most especially to "the Jew [*zhid*]—the most malignant [*zleishii*] enemy of the Polish worker." Besides exploiting workers, Jews controlled the Warsaw press, encouraged socialism, and in general were the masters of the country: "In a word, the Jews resolutely hold all classes of the population of the Vistula land in their hands." Summing up Gurko's view of the inhabitants of the Vistula land, we have a frivolous and deceitful upper class; a middle class made up of foreigners (mainly Germans) and pernicious Jews; an exploited industrial proletariat, highly susceptible to socialist propaganda; and sullen peasants. With such an unattractive population, it is easy to see why stern "educational" measures needed to be enforced by the Russian government.[13]

Such measures were unfortunately never applied consistently and efficiently by the Russian administration: "The main cause for the failure of Russian policy in the country is to be found in [the policy's] inconsistency [*nepostoiannost'*]." As Gurko saw it, after 1866 and especially in the 1870s and early 1880s, St. Petersburg was distracted by "nihilists"—that is, socialist revolutionaries—and thus neglected to follow a strong policy in the empire's western borderlands, much to the detriment of all involved.[14] Only with the arrival of General I. V. Gurko as governor general of Warsaw was a consistently strict policy again pursued, if not always achieved. Gurko implies that his father's policy was stymied by Polonophiles in St. Petersburg and circumvented by corrupt and inefficient Russian bureaucrats in Poland itself. He concludes that, to solve the Polish question, St. Petersburg must implement a strong, consistent policy in the Vistula lands, grant the Warsaw governor general very broad powers, and pursue this policy with efficiency and determination.[15]

Ocherki Privislian'ia is clearly the work of a polonophobic, anti-Semitic Russian nationalist. For all that, many of Gurko's prejudices, usually in muted form, were present throughout Russian officialdom, particularly the mistrust of Poles, the fear that the Jews were taking over, and a total inability to recognize the contradictions inherent in a policy that explicitly claimed not to be russifying, while dismissing cooperation with Poles as impossible because of their "untrustworthiness."[16] On the other hand, one must keep in mind that Gurko's aims stopped short, at least consciously, of forcible denationalization and russification, laying much emphasis on the seeming inability of the Russian government to pursue a firm and consistent policy.

P. D. Sviatopolk-Mirskii

The views of Prince P. D. Sviatopolk-Mirskii on the national issue opposed Gurko's in nearly every respect. Where Gurko saw the need for tough measures, Mirskii advocated concessions. Where Gurko demanded severity and consistent pressure, Mirskii suggested that a more measured, nuanced, and conciliatory policy might better serve Russian state interests. Yet, ultimately, Gurko and Mirskii aimed at a similar object: to pacify discontent and to strengthen the position of the Russian government in the western regions. A cynic might be tempted, in Mirskii's case, to speak of a "kinder, more gentle russification." Such a comment would, however, be both unfair to Mirskii and unreasonable, given the obvious need (from its own point of view, of course) for the Russian state to protect its interests and to inculcate among its people or peoples a feeling of "oneness" with the state. Mirskii's approach might be described as the attempt to create a supranational Russian (emphatically *rossiiskii*, not *russkii*) patriotism. Such a patriotism would allow subjects to be loyal both to the Russian state and to the cultural nation of their birth. That such a patriotism did not develop in the Romanov Empire—unlike, for example, the pro-Habsburg feelings among Jews in Austria—does not discredit the ideal but may call into question the feasibility of its realization.

The most important source for Mirskii's political program may be found in his voluminous annual report as governor general of Vilna for 1902–1903. Here Mirskii described the nationalities that inhabited the six Northwest Provinces, discussed the goals and results of government policy since 1863, and set down his own proposals for future policy. The report was printed with a lengthy informational paper (*spravka*) put together by the chancellery of the Committee of Ministers, an indication of the importance St. Petersburg lent to Mirskii's words. Clearly, the government saw in his report an important proposal for future policy in the western territory.[17] Had the revolution of 1905 not intervened, Mirskii's report might have formed the basis for reforms in the region.

Mirskii was appointed the governor general of Vilna on September 15, 1902, and submitted his report some eighteen months later in May 1904. The report began, inevitably, with a reference to the insurrection of 1863 and its "lessons" for the Russian government:

> The events of 1863–1864 convinced the government that the population of the northwest territory, despite the Russian origins of the masses there, was led by individuals foreign [*chuzhye*] to it both by nationality and by

way of life. . . . Thus [after 1863] the most immediate tasks of the government in the northwest country were: preserving the area in the spirit of devotion to the throne and of consciousness to the local and abiding Orthodox church and the ousting of the Polish element from exerting influence on the peasant masses.[18]

We have seen this "program" outlined before; it should come as no surprise. Mirskii, like his predecessors in Vilna, continued to insist on the Russian origin of the peasant population in the Northwest, to ignore the Lithuanians, and to stress the importance of the Orthodox church as a fundamentally Russian institution. Mirskii's outline of the government's most vital tasks after 1863 echoed Uvarov's famous trinity, differing mainly in the order of the tasks mentioned: (1) devotion to the throne (autocracy), (2) increasing "consciousness" of Orthodoxy, and (3) lessening Polish influences (nationality). Here the governor general was merely rephrasing statements of policy issued before him, but he did not challenge its basic assumptions; he merely questioned the effectiveness of the measures adopted.

Mirskii admitted that the law of December 10, 1865, forbidding Polish purchases of land in the Western Provinces had been a failure. The main reasons for this failure, he claimed, lay in the exceptions the government made for Poles not involved in the "mutiny" of 1863 and in the purchase by Russians of lands for purely speculative purposes. Since 1887 foreigners had been forbidden to buy land in the region, and anyone wishing to acquire an estate there had to obtain first a certificate from the governor general attesting to the buyer's political trustworthiness and non-Polish origins. Mirskii complained that the governor general's chancellery lacked the means to investigate the applicants for such certificates and that, in the midst of these various restrictions and bureaucratic measures, one lost sight of the fundamental goal of government policy, which was to establish an economically strong, local Russian landowning class, without reference to its social origins.

Here Mirskii put his finger on a sore spot of the imperial nationality policy: how to reconcile class or estate and nation. In 1863 the Poles dominated landowning in the West and in the early twentieth century remained the single largest group of private landowners in many areas of the Northwest. The Russian government had failed to establish a local Russian landowning class in the two generations following 1863, and Mirskii explained this failure in terms that stressed national over social factors. The restrictive laws since 1863 defined "Polish" too narrowly and "Russian" too broadly, preventing Catholic peasants from purchasing land but giving Baltic German nobles privileges as "persons of Russian descent." Mirskii stated that as Vilna governor general he had refused to issue certificates to would-be land purchasers of non-Russian descent, including Baltic Germans, and had opposed the sale of Russian estates to non-Russian peasants.[19] Here Mirskii's conception of nationality seems quite modern: no longer were considerations of estate to confuse the issue of nationality. Henceforth nationality was to become the most important organizing factor in this region.

Mirskii's proposals to increase Russian landowning in the Northwest Provinces included the selling of some state lands to Russian peasants; immigration of peasants from central Russia to the Northwest; and even the encouragement of Polish szlachta (in this context, impoverished Polish nobles now essentially indistinguishable from peasants) to emigrate to Asian Russia.[20] The main bulwark of Russian policy in the Northwest, however, had to be the local Belorussian peasantry. Mirskii admitted that the Belorussian language ("constituting, according to the latest research, a particular dialect [podrechie] of the Great Russian language") exhibited certain Polish influences, but he denied that Belorussians—whether Catholic or Orthodox—felt kinship with the Polish nationality. (As we shall see, this opinion was not always shared by Mirskii's colleagues in the Belorussian provinces.) Mirskii did not, however, explicitly state that Belorussians felt any stronger kinship with the Great Russian nation.

Mirskii's primary concern with the Belorussians involved government policy toward the Catholic church. In order not to alienate Belorussian Catholics, the imperial government should treat the Catholic church with as much leniency as possible, insofar as this was possible without injuring the prestige and status of the Orthodox church. The use of Belorussian should be allowed in Catholic churches (rather than Polish, as was presently the case), and more Catholic priests of Belorussian background should be trained. In general, the government must cease equating "Catholic" with "Polish" as it had nearly always done since 1863; such an identification of religion and nationality only helped the Poles to the detriment of the Russian cause.[21] Here again Mirskii exhibits a conception of nationality more "modern" than had hitherto predominated in government circles. Not religion, but language and culture, would be the primary determinant of nationality.

And yet precisely here, in the disputed territory between religion and nationality, Mirskii failed to be consistent. Whereas the government should not equate Catholicism and Polonism, it could also not remain indifferent to the progress and development in the Orthodox church. In other words, while explicitly rejecting the equation "Catholic equals Pole," Mirskii implicitly recognized and advocated the related proposition "Russian equals Orthodox." One offhand sentence—one may even speak of a *lapsus* in this case—glaringly reveals Mirskii's inability to free himself from this fundamental assumption about the nature of Russianness. Although never advocating the conversion of Belorussian Catholics to Orthodoxy, his own discomfort with the idea of Catholic Russians comes through in the following words: "At the same time, I cannot help but express my certainty that in time, as the Belorussian tribe imbues the consciousness that it is a Russian tribe, it will by itself return to the bosom of the Orthodox church."[22] Even for Prince Sviatopolk-Mirskii, despite his explicit desire to separate religion from nationality, the idea of Catholic Russians seemed absurd, and in the end literally unthinkable.

Mirskii's remarks about the Catholic church are similarly stereotyped, speaking of its "Jesuitical" tendencies and methods and painting a generally negative picture of the Catholic clergy and hierarchy: "One of the most important principles of the Catholic church is the struggle for world domination." It is significant that this observation appears not in the section on Catholicism but in that devoted to the Orthodox church. The Catholic church represented for Mirskii, and for nearly all his colleagues, an implacably anti-Russian institution. And, in their defense, one must recognize that the Catholic church was indeed closely identified with the Polish nation and was sharply opposed to many government policies, particularly in the religious sphere. On the practical level, however, Mirskii came to rather different conclusions than, say, M. N. Muraviev. The Russian government could not hope to destroy the Catholic church through repressions; thus a policy of leniency and reconciliation—within strict limits—would bring the best results. In effect, the Russian government should allow Catholic rituals such as processions, the erecting of roadside crosses, and the like, while striking quickly and severely against any instances of religious propaganda among Orthodox believers, mockery of the Orthodox religion, or conversions. The government should adopt a kid-glove policy toward the Catholic clergy while keeping an eye on them: "Of course, speaking generally, the Roman Catholic clergy remains an element that must be kept under vigilant surveillance." Only a long-term policy to avoid conflicts with the Catholic clergy could hope eventually to improve relations between the Catholic and Orthodox faithful in this land. "Mutual distrust, insincerity, and lies—these are the typical characteristics of relations between the two leading Christian denominations [in the Western Provinces]."[23]

For Mirskii, the Lithuanians of the Northwest represented a minor factor for government policy. "There is not, to my mind, the slightest basis for perceiving in the process of Lithuanian [national] development a danger for the state interests of Russia." Among Lithuanians a feeling of loyalty to Russia remained strong, despite Polish influences. However, the government's policy of forbidding the use of Latin letters in Lithuanian publications was a grave error, serving merely to antagonize Lithuanian sentiment toward the government and to strengthen the hand of Polish nationalists. The government should allow Lithuanians to publish in Latin letters, as had been done throughout the history of that language. In any case, Mirskii did not see much of a future for the Lithuanian language and culture. Because of the small number of Lithuanians and their lack of a "historical tradition," Mirskii predicted that they would sooner or later "be absorbed into the general population of Russia" (this exceedingly vague phrase reads in Russian *voiti v obshchii sostav naseleniia Rossii*). Mirskii did not explicitly state that Lithuanians would soon become completely assimilated to the Russian language, but this is precisely what he seems to predict when he remarks that the complete russification of schools in the area would soon render moot the question of "restrictions on the Lithuanian language."[24]

If the Lithuanians represented a "non-problem," the same could not be said for the Jews. Jews made up a higher percentage of the population of the Northwest Provinces than nearly anywhere else in the Russian Empire. Here, as throughout the Pale, Jews were subject to the Temporary Laws of May 3, 1882, which forbade them to settle outside urban districts. Mirskii described the effects of that measure as "a mass of misunderstandings, often linked with abuses." While not denying the "harmful influence" and "exploitation" of peasants by Jews, Mirskii observed that the restrictions of May 1882 had not improved the situation in the Pale and should be abolished. Indeed, a general review of laws pertaining to Jews should be undertaken. For Mirskii, the solution to the Jewish problem could be found only in education and assimilation. Hence he opposed Zionism and periodicals "in Jewish languages" and emphasized that "At the present time the Russian language is known, one may say, to nearly all Jews of the country entrusted to me." Although Jews did figure prominently among those engaged in revolutionary activity, the government should adopt not only repressive measures against these movements but should also combat the root causes for discontent among workers.[25] As regards the Jewish question, Mirskii's proposals seem remarkably similar to those advocated by Russian liberals: abolition of restrictive laws, assimilation, "normalization."

Mirskii ended his report by expressing regret that, although conditions in the Northwest Provinces had changed significantly in past decades, government policy there had not kept up with the times:

> In the past half century, social life has made great strides forward. New forms of social activity have appeared, new forms of labor, new demands on life. All of this has created problems previously unknown. Meanwhile local administration has not developed in tandem with the development of life. On the contrary, by lagging behind, the administration has merely lost its authority.[26]

Sviatopolk-Mirskii's proposals for reform, although based on relatively liberal principles, may not have satisfied the local non-Russian population any better than the policy of previous governor generals. Although emphasizing the need to conceive nationality outside of religious and social considerations, Mirskii was himself unable to escape the national mentality of his environment. For him, a Catholic Belorussian could only be a kind of transitional figure toward true-Russianness, and Lithuanians and Jews would soon be absorbed into the general population of Russia. Looking more directly at the issue of nationality than most of his colleagues, Mirskii was nonetheless unable to fathom the strength and explosiveness of this factor. And in this respect he remained a man of the old regime.

The Poles

Thus far we have considered the perceptions of two specific men concerning Russia's role in Poland and the Western Provinces. How typical were these two voices? I believe that the opinions and perceptions expressed by Gurko and Mirskii—although unique in many respects and reflecting the background, personality, and experiences of these two men—were by no means unusual or extraordinary. The extent to which these perceptions were shared by broad segments of the top Russian administrators in this region will be the concern for the rest of this chapter.

In its everyday business of administering the empire, Russian officialdom on the periphery came into constant contact with non-Russian peoples. How were these groups perceived and evaluated by the Russian administration? One source for the expression of such attitudes are the reports submitted annually by provincial governors. To be sure, these reports were written according to strict form, and the national issue per se was seldom discussed in depth. Nonetheless, individual nationalities were frequently mentioned and their activities evaluated.

In governors' reports one encounters Poles mainly as fervent Catholics and unredeemed enemies of all things Russian. With little exaggeration one may say that, for official Russia, the Poles on the western frontier were Public Enemy Number One. As in Prince P. Sviatopolk-Mirskii's 1902–1903 report, the Catholic clergy provided a special target for governors' complaints and was often portrayed as a "state within a state," not at all friendly to Russian state interests. The governor general of Vilna in his 1898 report blamed the Catholic clergy for failure of "our system," that is, the use of restrictions on Poles and Catholics in the Western Provinces in order to reconcile Poles with the Russian state. Among other things, the Catholic clergy spread false rumors, opposed Russian schools, and worked together with Catholic women who are described as "a tool to carry out the ideas [of the clergy]." The Catholic clergy operated as a "status in statu," steadfastly opposing efforts to increase Russian cultural influence in the area. The church hierarchy and bishops were particularly hostile to the Russian administration, consistently transferring or defrocking any priests who failed to exhibit the proper enthusiasm for the Polish cause. Such a situation would not be tolerated "in any European state," the governor general exclaimed, warning that a religion could only be tolerated insofar as it obeyed state laws and did not oppose "the cherished tasks of the state."[27]

Many other local administrators concurred in this negative description of the Catholic clergy. In his 1910 report, the Mogilev governor complained that priests carried out religious and political propaganda and tried to convert local residents of Orthodox faith. In the same year the governor general of Kiev made reference to "Catholic propaganda aimed at the broadest possible polonization of the country."[28] Concern about such activities was not limited to local authorities. Around this time the Ministry of Internal Affairs (MVD) in St. Petersburg drew up a "Memorandum about the activities of the Catholic clergy, aimed at the subjection of the population of the Western territory to Polish influence, and about measures to combat these influences."[29] Once again we see in this title the equating of Catholic with Polish in the government mind.

Distrust—even fear and loathing—of pernicious Polish Catholic influences in the Western territory had a long pedigree among Russian officialdom. One of the most strident expressions of this distrust may be found in the report drawn up by Vilna governor general I. S. Kakhanov in 1885 entitled simply "On the question of the Roman Catholic clergy in the Northwest Territory." Kakhanov begins the account with a striking description of his subject: "The Roman Catholic clergy, having brought together Polish political ideas with the Catholic religion, has created, so to speak, a new Polono-Catholic faith and works to fanaticize the local population and then to subordinate it to [Polish Catholic] influence." To be sure, the restrictions introduced since 1863 and particularly the break with the Vatican have forced the local clergy to behave "in superficial actions . . . more cautiously," but fundamentally little has changed. The hierarchy—Vilna Bishop Griniewicki in particular—worked to prevent any Russian (or Belorussian) influences from penetrating into the clerical sphere.

For Kakhanov the government's position was clear: although it would not be appropriate to restrict the Catholic faith, Russian state interests demanded the lessening of Polish influences within the Catholic church. For instance, Kakhanov called on the government "to eliminate from divine services the use of Polish, which as a symbol of a hostile nationality cannot be tolerated in the church." To take its place, Russian must be allowed and encouraged at all levels of the church, most particularly within the Catholic seminary. Only in this way could the Russian government hope to carry out its mission of reestablishing its cultural domination in the land. "The elimination of the Polish language from Catholic services in a country where Poles constitute only 15.58 percent of the total Catholic population would be [an act of] supreme justice . . . besides which it would be a measure in complete accord with the government's continued efforts to destroy Polish influence in the area."[30] Here, as so often, the hundreds of thousands of Catholic Lithuanians disappear from the government perspective, and Catholic Belorussians appear only as the passive object of either Polish or Russian influence.

One governor pointed out that the word "Pole" referred less to a nationality than to a political stance, a sort of inbred opposition to the Russian government: "In general at the present time [1907] the term 'Pole' in Vilna Province has lost its ethnographical character and has become almost exclusively a political term." Even in the considerably more "Russian" Podolia Province, the governor remarked that the local Poles, though making up only 8 percent of the population, because of their extensive landholdings continued to exert significant influence on the local peasantry, an influence all the more pernicious in that "it acts and is carried out through Jews," that is, through the Jewish stewards and employees of the Poles.[31] Among the Poles, the most disloyal element was to be found among the "half-educated petty nobility," that is, the so-called szlachta, described as "in general very inclined to political intrigues [politikanstvo], to the hatred of all things Russians and to separatism."[32] This conception of Poles as ipso facto anti-Russian was to play an important role in the western zemstvo debates after 1905.

In official documents—and in Prime Minister Peter Stolypin's speeches—one often finds the western territory portrayed as a battlefield between Polish and Russian influences. Shortly after the turn of the century the governor of Vilna Province wrote, "Everywhere are visible the vestiges of that sharp battle between Russian and Polish influence that raged for centuries in the Northwest country and has left its indelible imprint on all aspects of the region's [social, economic, political] order." And yet (the governor continued), by this time certain indications pointed to the possibility of a new, less hostile relationship between Poles and Russians.[33] Slowly but inevitably local Poles were giving up their dreams of a Poland "from [Baltic] sea to [Black] sea" and reconciling themselves to a future within the Russian state. One finds such sentiments not infrequently in governors' reports and other official documents around the turn of the century (especially before 1905), but this optimism about the possibility of Polish-Russian reconciliation was nearly always tempered by expressions of caution and misgivings about the presence of influential "fanatical" elements among the Poles. Predictably, after the events of 1905–1906 such optimism diminished considerably.[34]

On the other hand, one group of Poles—the peasantry—enjoyed a benevolent reputation among Russian officials. Polish peasants were generally portrayed as loyal to the tsar, despite their devotion to the Catholic church. One specific element of Russian policy after 1863 was to favor the peasant, both in the Polish Kingdom and the Western Provinces, in an effort to create a social class loyal to St. Petersburg. Governors made frequent reference to the allegiance of Polish peasants to the Romanov throne. In 1894 the governor of Kielce Province reported that peasants appreciated the land and self-government that they had received at the hands of the Russian government and that this appreciation "has rooted in them respect toward Russian authority and a reverential devotion to Russia." A similar note is struck in the Siedlce Province report for 1899: "among the rural population . . . feelings of loyalty, love, gratitude, and devotion to their Monarch are indissolubly linked with, and equally strong as, love for the Highest Creator."[35]

Once again, after 1905 certain cracks appear in this comforting representation of adoring and devoted rural folk, and yet even as late as 1913 a governor could write that Polish peasants exhibited "trust in the strength of Russian state power."[36] Official Russia's lack of a truly "national" attitude is revealed in these rhapsodies about the loyal Polish peasant. Since the very aftermath of the 1863 uprising, the Russian government had strived to cultivate good relations with this class of the Polish population. Even into the twentieth century, when the falseness of this ideal was becoming all too apparent, official Russia clung to it doggedly. The alternative—that all of

Polish society was united in its antagonism to Russian power (not that this conception was any closer to reality than that of ultra-loyal peasants)—would have been too painful to countenance.

And yet the official Russian perception of the Poles was somewhat more nuanced than has been suggested so far. Whereas the stereotypes of fanatical Catholic priest cum Polish patriot, loyal but passive peasant, and radically anti-Russian szlachta continued to prevail in official documents, other less predictable notes were also struck. At times, particularly in provinces where relatively few Poles lived, governors reported that national discord *(rozn')* between Poles and Russians had diminished almost to the point of disappearance. In 1894 the governor of Mogilev Province remarked that the local Poles, making up a minute percentage of the total population, because of the influence of the surrounding Orthodox population did not exhibit "that intolerance and fanaticism that is peculiar to the majority of Poles" and could safely be allowed a greater role in local administration, particularly in the economic sphere.[37]

The governor general of Kiev agreed. In his report for 1900 he stated that Poles no longer presented a danger to Russian interests in the three Southwest Provinces. He based this opinion on statistics showing the decline in Polish population and landholdings in the region since 1863. He did not, however, hazard a judgment as to any improvement in actual political reliability of local Poles. Still, he considered their numbers and economic influence sufficiently diminished as to allow for the introduction of elective bodies of rural self-government, or zemstva, there.[38]

Other governors concurred that the Poles no longer presented a significant danger. The governor of Volhynia stated in 1894 that the Polish question had ceased to threaten his province, which had taken on an increasingly Russian character. Similar reports from Minsk and Podolia emphasized the loyalty of the Polish upper classes and suggested a broader role for Poles in local affairs. Given the contemporary events in St. Petersburg and Warsaw, it is remarkable that in 1912 the Mogilev governor could write, "no national or political groups were observed, no frictions arose" in the nearly formed zemstvo there.[39] Clearly at least some Russian officials felt that Poles, particularly those of the upper classes, could now be regarded as loyal elements, deserving of government favor. And yet even among such Polonophile administrators, a cautious note is nearly always present: Poles should be allowed a greater measure of participation in local affairs, but mainly in economic matters and not at the highest levels. No governor proposed a total elimination of the restrictions on Poles wanting to enter government service in the Western Provinces and the Kingdom of Poland.

The official voices calling for a more moderate policy toward the Poles remained in the minority, and in most cases were restricted to those provinces with the smallest percentage of Poles among the general population.[40] Their arguments were based, for the most part, not on a recognition of strong pro-Russian feelings among Poles but rather on the feeling that

Poles had come to terms with Russian predominance and could not pose a threat to Russian power even had they wanted to. Most officials, however, remained skeptical. The governor of Grodno Province pointed out in 1907 that Duma election campaigns had divided up "almost exclusively on national lines" and that, while all Christians opposed the Jews, this did not translate into closer relations between Russians and Poles. Around the same time, the police chief of Warsaw expressed the view that Polish society remained saturated with ideas of separatism and continued to dream of political independence and to flirt with socialist schemes.[41] Despite certain voices to the contrary, and with the exception of the idealized "loyal peasant," views of the Polish nationality expressed by official Russia remained deeply suspicious throughout this period.

The Jews

Along with the Poles as a fundamentally disloyal element, and often appearing in official documents hand in hand with them, were the Jews. The nine Western Provinces all belonged to the notorious Pale of Settlement; Jews had made their home in this region for centuries. In the time of the Polish-Lithuanian Commonwealth *(Rzeczpospolita)*, Jews had often served as the bailiffs and managers for Polish nobles and magnates, and the local peasant population thus often regarded them with suspicion, or worse. This suspicion was shared by Russian administrators. Although the direct connivance of government officials in fomenting pogroms appears to have been a rare occurrence, it seems equally clear that the Russian government did not feel at ease with Jews as individuals or with the Jewish question in general.[42] This unease finds expression in official documents, but (perhaps remarkably) the solutions proposed by local officials differed widely.

The legal and economic situation of Jews in the ten Polish provinces differed significantly from that in the Pale. Here Jews enjoyed quasi-equal rights with the rest of the population and were not subject to the "temporary regulations" of May 1882. In reports from these provinces, Jews were often mentioned in connection with growing Polish anti-Semitism, particularly after 1905. In most respects, however, the official view of Jews did not vary greatly between the Polish and the Western Provinces: in both cases we observe the same discourse at work, chiding socialist and separatist tendencies, praising progress in learning Russian, and advocating measures to neutralize Jewish nationalism, all the while feeling less than comfortable about the idea of "Russian Jews" in any context.

Because of their peculiar legal status, Jews figured frequently in governors' reports. According to the Temporary Laws of May 3, 1882, Jews in the Western Provinces were not allowed to take up residence in rural areas except for short periods of time and under special circumstances. Judging from the governors' reports, however, these laws were almost universally circumvented. In his report for 1910, for example, the governor of Grodno Province pointed to the practice of Jews falsely claiming artisan status (which provided an exception to the law) in order to move to rural areas. The governor of Podolia went even further, seeing the Jews of his province as causing "the greatest difficulty" for local administration, "always inclined to deceitful activities in order to circumvent laws," avoiding taxes and other obligations, and on the whole behaving in a way most "immoral" from the government point of view.[43]

The governor general of Kiev acknowledged that the 1882 laws did not succeed in lessening Jewish exploitation of the rural population. On one hand, this was attributable to the "clumsy wording of the law," on the other, to "Jewish wiliness." In any case, the governor general complained, it was impossible to enforce the law forbidding Jews from residing in rural areas because the Senate—at that time in effect imperial Russia's supreme court—had specifically allowed the "temporary" residence of Jews in rural areas for the purpose of trade or industry. In practice, such temporary stays could last for years. Furthermore, the letter of the law forbade Jews from entering into written agreements to manage estates; thus landowners simply hired Jewish managers on the basis of oral contracts.[44] Judging from this report, one gets the impression (surely false) that Jews easily avoided all legal restrictions placed on them. It is interesting that the governor general placed the blame for this situation less on the Jews (one may even detect a hint of grudging respect for them) than on the imprecise and clumsy legal apparatus of imperial Russia. He did not take the next logical step and call for a wholesale revision of Jewish restrictions, but his remarks clearly lead in that direction.

The figures of the Jewish merchant and (closely related to it) Jewish exploiters of hapless peasantry appeared frequently in governors' reports. Jews made up the majority of the middle class in the Western Provinces and were prominent in small-scale trade throughout the region. A recurrent charge was that Jews speculated in land or rented estates illegally and then exploited them so ruthlessly that the land was laid waste. The dominant position of Jews in the region's cities and in urban commerce and industry was also often mentioned.[45]

Most important, however, were contacts between Jews and the local peasantry, usually subsumed under the rubric "exploitation." The laws of 1882 aimed specifically at limiting this exploitation by denying Jews access to the countryside, but, judging from official accounts, to little avail. At the turn of the century the governor general of Vilna noted the impossibility of setting up any kind of business in the Northwest Provinces without the participation of Jews and mentioned frequent petitions from peasants who complained of Jewish exploitation.[46] A similar sentiment was expressed around the same time by the "liberal" governor general of Warsaw, Prince A. Imeretinskii. In reference to a 1891 law restricting Jewish access to peasant land in the Polish provinces, Imeretinskii tartly commented, "It would seem that the goal of the government in this country should consist not of protecting Jewish rights, which are in any case strong here, but in guarding that estate [soslovie] which thus far has been most loyal to the government [that is, the peasantry]."[47] In the official mind, restriction of energetic (but untrustworthy) Jews was, among other things, a function of the protection of backward (but loyal) peasants.

Governors often complained that Jews avoided military service and that it was impossible to collect the fines levied on Jewish draft dodgers. The Vitebsk governor wrote of a "systematic evasion by the Jews of military service." A colleague in Suwałki agreed: "The evasion by Jews of military service both in Suwałki Province and in other provinces with Jewish population constitutes a usual occurrence that repeats itself year after year."[48] By law, anyone failing to appear for military service was subject to a 300 ruble fine, and if the actual offender could not be located, his family was liable. In practice, however, it appears that local authorities were often unable to collect these fines from impoverished families.[49] In the Polish provinces, moreover, not only Jews but also the Christian population often tried to avoid military service, even going to the extremes of self-mutilation. Obviously one cannot uncritically accept the view presented by Russian officials of Jews as almost genetically averse to military service, but one should also not attempt to deny that for various good reasons many Jews did attempt to avoid service in the Russian army, and this fact—no doubt exaggerated in the official mind—simply corroborated the already accepted image of the Jew as scofflaw.[50]

Jews, especially of the younger generation, were persistently linked with the socialist movement. The view expressed by the Vitebsk governor in 1894 was shared by many: "The Jewish population, particularly the younger generation which has received middle and higher education, represents politically the most unreliable element and demands constant and vigilant observation." Especially in the revolutionary years 1905–1906 governors reported that Jews circulated political pamphlets, organized the workers' movement, spread revolutionary propaganda, and generally behaved in a "provocative" manner.[51] In most cases, however, a clear divide was seen in the Jewish population between the revolutionary youth and the indifferent or even law-abiding older generation. After the revolutionary events of 1905 and 1906 the governor of Radom Province wrote, "the greater part of the Jewish population took no part in the revolutionary movement, with the exception of an insignificant part of the Jewish youth." Whereas few governors portrayed the Jews in such a favorable light, nearly all could agree with the statement of Łomża governor that "Jewish society in its attitude to events of social and political life is sharply split into two camps: the older and younger generations."[52] Despite the broad recognition of this split within Jewish society, one rarely encounters in official documents a proposal to woo the "loyal" older generation and thereby perhaps win over the less radical youth. Instead, the fact of radicalism among young Jews seems to have been accepted as a given, against which the Russian government was powerless to act.

Jewish nationalism and separatism was roundly condemned by officials both in St. Petersburg and in the provinces. To be sure, Russian bureaucrats seldom looked with favor on any non-Russian national movement and even felt frequent discomfort with Russian nationalists. In the Jewish case this official distaste for separatism was exacerbated because both Zionist and non-Zionist Jewish movements in the Russian Empire were closely linked with socialist currents. One governor lumped revolutionaries, Zionists, and fighters for Jewish equal rights together in a remarkable amalgam and warned, "Such a movement must be considered dangerous because every Jew is essentially a revolutionary for, having neither land [*pochva*] nor a past and always living off the labor of others, he easily takes up with any sedition [*smuta*], in the hopes of extracting some profit for himself."[53]

Before 1905, Jewish nationalism was not perceived as a significant threat to Russian interests. In 1898 the governor general of Vilna (by no means a friend of the Jews) could write that "from the political point of view . . . such a phenomenon as the Jewish population [*evreistvo*] does not as yet present a large danger because Jews do not pursue national aspirations."[54] This was not to say that the Jews lived in close contact with their gentile neighbors. One year later the same official complained that Jews lived closed off from the rest of society, and he urged measures to break down this isolation. His description of "the Jew" states explicitly characteristics often alluded to indirectly:

> For centuries the Jew has been brought up by his religion and, thanks to this religious isolation, has taken on certain peculiar moral notions that differ from ours. . . . [T]o this very day he has retained untouched his distinguishing racial traits which are already mentioned in the Bible: a striving for profit, toward exploitation, indifference, to say the least, for the surrounding population, a rebellious spirit, and so on.[55]

Few Russian officials in the Polish and Western provinces would have denied these three main characteristics of the Jewish population: greed/exploitation, indifference to the fate of non-Jews, and "rebelliousness" or an ingrained lack of respect for law and state authority. Jews were inherently "different" from "us," from Christians. But more interesting than the presence of this pervasively anti-Jewish sentiment in the halls of Russian officialdom (it would have been remarkable in that time and place had Russian officials not distrusted the Jews) are the different answers to the practical question of how to deal with the region's Jewish population.

What was to be done? Predictably, there were calls for stricter measures and a tightening of already existing restrictions. This attitude found detailed expression in the report of MVD official E. K. Sivers in 1876. Sivers argued that the "history of the past hundred years" proved conclusively that only strict measures toward the Jews would bring them in line with government interests. Sivers's stated goal was assimilation of Russia's Jews, that is, complete and total assimilation: "Of course, a Jew, as long as he remains a Jew [*evrei*], will not be a Russian." In a similar vein the governor of Kovno Province maintained that the Pale should be upheld, disputing claims that if the Jewish population were distributed throughout the empire it would lose its negative characteristics: "Spread across Russia they would learn to speak Russian better and would extend the sphere of their activities, but they would not become Russians." Other governors insisted that the hostility felt by Jews toward Russians (and indeed all non-Jews) had not lessened and in certain respects was even gaining in strength.[56] In the opinion of these officials, although the eventual assimilation of the Jews—transforming them into useful and loyal citizens—could possibly occur in the long run, for practical purposes of the present generation the negative characteristics of Russia's Jewish minority would remain. Indeed, the sometimes mild statements about the "eventual" possibility of assimilation expressed by Russian administrators would seem to be belied by their intransigent hostility toward Jews as Jews.

Some governors, however, attributed the negative characteristics of the local Jews to the legal restrictions placed upon them. This argument among Russian officials, stressing "nurture" over "nature," can be traced back at least to the early 1860s when governor generals of the Western Provinces argued in favor of lessening restrictions on Jews. Even before the 1863 Polish uprising, the governor general of Kiev argued in a long memorandum that Jews were intrinsically less disloyal than Poles and that the Russian government should open government service to qualified Jews, allowing them to participate in elective city government and generally encouraging a feeling of solidarity between the Russian government and the Jewish minority. Obviously, this solidarity would be aimed quite explicitly against the Poles. Around the same time, the governor general of Vilna called for reforms and a loosening of restrictions with the aim of improving the "pitiful" economic situation of Jews.[57]

Many governors pointed out that the artificial concentration of Jews in urban areas, exacerbated by the 1882 laws, translated into poverty for the Jewish masses and negatively affected the development of the region's cities. Some went so far as to advocate the abolition of the Jewish Pale of Settlement, pointing to the material and moral destitution that the concentration of Jews in this one region had caused. Others were less radical, wishing merely a relaxing of regulations—for instance to allow Jews to open factories in the countryside. In the wake of the 1905 disturbances, the Vilna governor general proposed to eliminate the 1882 regulations and to allow Jews to purchase land in the Western Provinces.[58]

As these instances show, it would be wrong to see in Russian officialdom a monolithic bloc, invariably opposed to any extension of Jewish rights. Various contradictory opinions vied with each other as to the character of the Jewish population in the area, and regarding policy toward it. Whereas on one hand provincial governors certainly expressed anti-Semitic arguments about Jewish exploitation and lack of productivity, on the other hand they usually saw the solution to the Jewish question in the gradual assimilation of Jews into the Russian body politic, especially by education.[59] On the whole, however, even those officials who advocated reconciliatory policies toward the Jews were seldom motivated by feelings of admiration or respect. Rather, the loyalty of the Jewish population was seen as an important weapon against the most dangerous foe in the region: the Poles. In any case, the proposed "total assimilation" that figured so recurrently in these reports was so divorced from the realities of turn-of-the-century Russia that one may term it utopian, a desire to "eliminate" the Jewish question by dissolving the Jews in a Russian sea.[60]

Ukrainians and Belorussians

As for Ukrainians and Belorussians, they were almost entirely ignored by the imperial government. That is, the two ethnic groups were considered merely "branches" of the Russian nation. Both Belorussians and Ukrainians were seen as "ethnographic raw material" by St. Petersburg *chinovniki* and their local representatives. When considering in early 1905 the needs of local education in the Western Provinces, the Committee of Ministers stated that schools should be allowed to use Polish and Lithuanian, but "the little Russian and Belorussian dialects are so close to the Russian language that the teaching of both together is not necessary. Furthermore regarding the Belorussian language, since it lacks its own literature, it can hardly even be taught on its own."[61] Even linguistically official discourse subsumed Ukrainians and Belorussians into the Russian nation. In official (and Russian nationalist) parlance, the term *ukrainskii* was seldom or never used, and when referring to the peasant population of the "Belorussian" provinces (Vitebsk, Vilna, Grodno, Mogilev), officials often spoke simply of *russkie*. Neither of these ethnic groups were seen per se as a problem. On the contrary, the Russian government ostensibly based its policy in the Western Provinces on strengthening these peasant populations and protecting their interests, not coincidentally against those of local Poles and Jews.

Only when educated Ukrainians (nota bene: not peasant masses) were perceived as separatists does one encounter them at all as an object of specific government policy. For example, in 1909 the Siedlce governor reported that at the city high school (*gimnaziia*) it had been discovered that several students belonged to an anti-government, separatist Ukrainophile circle. Little importance was attached to this event, and the report dwelled in far greater detail on the political pretensions of the local Polish population and the need to protect the province's "Russians" from Polish influences. During the revolutionary year 1905 the Podolia governor mentioned that brochures calling for agrarian strikes and boycott of the government had been distributed "in the local little Russian language," but his concern was aroused not by the language of these flyers but by their seditious content.[62]

The government position on the "Ukrainian question" was set down in unusual explicitness in a memorandum written by minister of public enlightenment A. N. Shvarts in response to a Duma bill calling for elementary schools that would use Ukrainian as the language of instruction. Shvarts protested strongly at the Duma project's use of the terms "Ukrainian language" and "Ukrainian people," insisting that "Great Russians, Little Russians, and Belorussians form, historically speaking, parts of one and the same Russian people [*narod*]." Five pages later, Shvarts went on to protest that "the aspirations of a certain part of the Little Russian intelligentsia to recognize Little Russians as a separate 'Ukrainian people' . . . totally lack historical foundation." Certainly, the minister admitted, there existed various minor differences between individual expressions used in Great Russian areas and Little Russia, but these presented no major difficulty for mutual comprehension. Shvarts concluded with a broadside aimed at the individual political pretensions of Ukrainian nationalists: "Little Russia does not need the introduction of instruction in the Little Russian dialect. This novelty is necessary exclusively for those Ukrainian separatists, and not for the Little Russian people, which cherishes the knowledge of general-Russian [*obshcherusskii*] literacy and aspires to gain such knowledge."[63] Shvarts's dichotomy of virtuous Little Russian peasants and pretentious, demanding, and ultimately corrupt and treacherous Ukrainian intellectuals was one that can be found in more or less explicit form in official Russia's discussions of the Ukrainian issue.

The government's conception of Ukrainians and their place in the Russian state—a conception moreover shared by significant numbers of educated Russians—was revealed with particular clarity in the deliberations over the formation of the Kholm Province. No one denied that the "Russians" who were to be protected from polonization by the formation of this new province belonged, in fact, to the *malorusskii*, that is, Ukrainian ethnicity, but neither did any of the forces in favor of the creation of the new province seem to find this at all significant. Most commentators, Russian and Polish, agreed that Ukrainian national feeling was minimal in the Kholm area. In any event, the issue from the official standpoint was *Russians* (of any "branch") against Poles (see chapter 6).

To the end, the Russian government seemed convinced that the Ukrainian national movement was a chimera, interesting only a few disgruntled intellectuals and lacking broad support among the "loyal Little Russian peasantry." Although the tsarist police did investigate the Ukrainian national movement, this does not seem to have been a major government priority, and the very existence of Ukrainian nationalism was passed over in silence by annual governors' reports. After the outbreak of World War I, the tsarist government began to take the threat of Ukrainian separatism more seriously. The Ukrainian cultural organization Prosvita was closed in 1915, and official reports began to express concern over the potential danger of Ukrainian separatism—perhaps fueled in part by the not entirely positive experiences during the Russian occupation of Austrian Galicia.[64]

Although generally considered to be at a lower level of national self-consciousness than the Ukrainians, Belorussians were the subject of more government interest than their brethren to the south. The reason was simple: Polish influences, especially those of the Catholic church, were far stronger in the Belorussian provinces, and significant numbers of Belorussians professed the Catholic faith. Local officials and the MVD in St. Petersburg considered efforts to protect Catholic Belorussians from polonizing influences particularly vital for Russian state interests. When official documents mentioned Belorussians, they appeared as objects of polonization; Orthodox Belorussians practically never appeared.

As so often, the real object of government disquiet in the West was the Polish nation. The Belorussians were merely a pawn in the game. In the midst of the political, agrarian, and national disturbances of 1906, the governor general of Vilna wrote to St. Petersburg, militating for a more active policy to capture the hearts and souls of the region's Belorussians. These peasant folk remained unconscious of their ethnic identity, somewhere between Poles and Russians: "The Belorussian tribe, which predominates in Grodno and Vilna Provinces, by language and customs [nravy] represents something midway between native [korennye] Russians and Poles." The Poles were doing all they could to exert energetic influence on the "uncultured, downtrodden, impoverished Belorussians," and the Russian government must counter these efforts with similar energy. Because restrictive measures on the Poles had not been effective, the government should adopt a more active role in encouraging the development of Belorussian national consciousness, including the establishment of schools using Belorussian as the language of instruction and of churches (including, one must suppose, Catholic churches) using Belorussian, and helping local Belorussians to acquire land.[65] The governor general clearly did not perceive any danger in Belorussian separatism and felt, on the contrary, that educated Belorussians would naturally gravitate toward Great Russian culture.

After 1905, official Russia became increasingly—even obsessively—concerned with Catholic influences on Belorussians. When saying "Catholic," Russian officials automatically thought "Polish." Explicitly, however, they were compelled to deny and even denounce this mental association in order to retain Catholic Belorussians for the Russian nation. In 1907 the governor of Vilna Province pointed out that, despite the influence of Catholic clergy over local Belorussian peasants, these remained loyal to "Russia." Still, he continued, official measures must encourage the development of Belorussian consciousness, and Belorussian should be used in Catholic churches and in religious instruction in schools. Similar sentiments were expressed in other reports after 1905.[66] Already at this early stage, however, local administrators noted that the fledgling Belorussian intelligentsia was already "infected with socialism." They complained about a new kind of rural teacher who "in words [expressed] a fiery nationalistic patriotism and loyalty to the historical foundations of our state [gosudarstvennost']" but in practical matters was openly hostile to large landowners of any nationality.[67] Unfortunately for the Russian Empire, national, social, and economic elements were all too often inextricably intertwined.

A similarly irritating complexity plagued government efforts to woo Catholic Belorussians away from the Poles. As we have seen, local administrators argued against equating "Catholic" with Poles, but the same official quoted above to this effect—Vilna governor D. N. Liubimov—admitted that the strength of Polish culture in the area was such that a Catholic Belorussian peasant with pretensions to "bettering himself" immediately identified with the Polish nationality.[68] But how to combat this phenomenon? Official Russia could do little more than repeat the same litany: replace Polish with Belorussian (or Russian) in Catholic churches, encourage the publishing of popular works in Belorussian or Russian (again, the language of these documents is not always clear), increase the patriotic Russian content in local elementary schools, encourage patriotic Russian clubs and societies, and (most important of all) keep strict tabs on the Poles and restrain their influences on the peasant population.[69] It goes without saying that none of these proposals were particularly new, and in any case a lack of organization (and especially funds) precluded a truly militant pro-Belorussian policy.

It would have been impossible for "official nationality" to admit the existence of Ukrainian or Belorussian nations distinct from the Russian. Such an admission would have fatally upset the nationality calculus, not only in the West but in the empire as a whole. With Ukrainians and Belorussians considered a part of the Russian people, it was possible to speak of a majority (nearly two-thirds) of the empire's population as being "Russian."[70] Without Ukrainians and Belorussians, this proportion would fall below half. In the nine Western Provinces, the situation would be even more fatal for Russian nationalist pretensions (see the statistics in the next chapter). If the government had admitted that Belorussians and Ukrainians were separate from the Russian nation, its prime argument for anti-Polish and anti-Jewish policies in the West—"protecting the Russian peasant"—would have lost all validity.

The Lithuanians in the Northwest Provinces enjoyed a kind of shadow existence in official discourse. That is to say, they appeared now and again, but their presence in the area seldom aroused significant interest on the part of local administrators, much less in the central offices of the MVD in St. Petersburg. Lithuanians clearly enjoyed, on the whole, more confidence from local authorities than did the Poles or Jews. On the other hand, they were also seen as less important. Governors referred to Lithuanians most often as diligent agriculturalists and ardent patriots.[71]

Since the Lithuanians' national aspirations were directed less against the Russians than against local Poles, the Russian authorities could regard them with relative benevolence. Before 1904 the prohibition on the use of Latin letters in printing Lithuanian was often mentioned, and most officials argued for the abolition of this prohibition.[72] After the turn of the century Polish-Lithuanian relations became increasingly antagonistic, and one governor advocated encouraging the Lithuanians' anti-Polish feelings: "given the starkly evident lack of incompatibility of Polish aspirations with Russian state principles, the Polish-Lithuanian struggle should be used as a weapon in the struggle with Polish influence." However, this sort of activism does not seem to have found support, and the governor never proposed it again. Another report strongly warned against encouraging the Lithuanians against the Poles, pointing out that a similar policy in the Baltic provinces (pitting Estonians and Latvians against Germans) had backfired in 1905.[73] The conflict between Poles and Lithuanians received considerable attention in annual reports, but intervention on either side on the part of the Russian administration was not seriously considered.[74] The Lithuanians were to be left to themselves and, it was hoped, would in the end weaken Polish influences and quite possibly become assimilated themselves into the Russian nation.

❖   By the turn of the century, nationalist movements were gaining strength throughout Europe. Even in states ruled by nondemocratic elites over multinational populations, such movements made themselves felt. Nationalist feelings were growing in Russia after 1905. Rightist organizations rallied around tsar, Orthodoxy, and the Russian nationality while even liberal Russia—most remarkably in the figure of Petr Struve—evinced interest in preserving and strengthening its own Russian nationality. The attitude of the tsarist bureaucracy lay somewhere between these two extremes. While generally rejecting overt nationalist appeals, the tsarist bureaucracy also felt itself to be Russian and considered it natural that Poles, Jews, and others defer to the Russian nationality and use the Russian language for most public functions.

In most respects, official Russia's national world was not clearly expressed or even conceived. After all, the term "Russian" was not even defined as a legal concept under the old regime. Most basically, one may say that imperial Russia did not wish to think or speak in precise national terms and did so only when political circumstances dictated measures for the defense of state interests. Inevitably, however, this state and its interests were linked with the Russian nationality and the Orthodox church. Russian officials conceded that the terms "Russian" and "Orthodox" were not congruent exclusively when attempting to cast the net of Russianness as broadly as possibly, most particularly in order to include Catholic Ukrainians and Belorussians. But even in these cases, officials betray their own unease with the concept of "non-Orthodox Russians" by stating their hope that in the end these individuals would find their way back to the maternal Orthodox church.

The subconscious, pervasive understanding that the Russian Empire should naturally be dominated by the Great Russian language and Orthodox faith was coupled with a stereotypical division of non-Russians in the West into hostile and friendly (or at least neutral) camps. Into the latter came "Little Russians," Belorussians, and (with certain reservations) Lithuanians. For the most part, official Russia ignored these ethnicities except as objects of influence, usually either Russian or Polish. The two hostile nations in the region were the Poles and the Jews, but the influence and activity of these two ethnic groups were so distinct as to preclude a comprehensive Russian policy toward the two. Instead, official Russia treated them separately, even while aiming to isolate both groups from the local peasant masses.

Official Russia did not perceive nationality as a historical principle to be cherished in its own right. To be sure, they regarded their own national language, culture, and religion in these terms, but they found similar pretensions on the part of Belorussians or even Lithuanians absurd and even seditious. In this respect imperial Russia's administrators were men of the nineteenth century: the triumphant march of history dictated that Russian culture would survive and flourish while Yiddish and Belorussian would dwindle and disappear. But these men also recognized the historical viability of Polish culture; perhaps for this reason they opposed Polish influences all the more strongly. Imperial Russia did not aim to crush non-Russian cultures and to amalgamate all of Russia's peoples into one undifferentiated mass. And yet Russian officialdom did hope that the attraction of Russian culture would exert itself on the dark, uncultured masses—whether they were Lithuanian, Ukrainian, or even Jewish. In this sense—of a natural process helped along by a certain amount of state benevolence—they were unrepentant "russifiers." Whether this mentality and this process can without qualification be called russification, the reader can decide.

Four

West of Russia

Land, Nations, Economy

Quant à l'action, elle se passe en Pologne, c'est-à-dire
Nulle Part. (As for the action, it takes place in Poland,
that is to say, Nowhere.)

—*A. Jarry, à propos his absurdist play,*
Ubu Roi (1896)

❖ Nationality policy is not formed and implemented in a void. It would
be more correct to say that in the Russian Empire no such thing as "nationality policy" existed per se: one finds only some specific political, administrative, or local needs involving regions of mixed or (in the present case)
non-Russian population. Administration and education, or rights to reside,
be employed, purchase land: these were but a few of the areas in which
one's nationality determined one's rights in the Russian Empire.[1] Most directly affected were the members of certain non-Russian nationalities, in
particular the Jews, who were forbidden to live in most areas and were
subject to myriad other restrictions and exclusions. But, as in the distorting
mirrors of an amusement park, the government's own perceptions of nationalities and of local needs were themselves to a large extent formed in
advance by past policies, expectations, and prejudices. Thus one might say
that the imperial government became the captive of its own nationality
perceptions.

To complicate matters, St. Petersburg could not deal with one nationality at a time; restrictive measures aimed at one nationality necessarily had effects—some foreseen, indeed planned; others unexpected and undesired—on the other national groups living in the same area.[2] Thus, for example, by forbidding Poles to acquire landed property in the Western Provinces in the aftermath of the uprising of 1863, the imperial government unwittingly encouraged German colonists to settle in this area.[3] Similarly, the anti-Jewish "temporary laws" in the interior of the empire had the effect of encouraging Jews to move to the Kingdom of Poland, where Jews had enjoyed quasi-equal rights since 1862. It was inevitable that Jews would be attracted from the restrictive, economically backward Pale to the Kingdom of Poland, where they enjoyed in a large measure civil equality and where economic opportunities existed.[4]

Livelihood, administration, daily life—all were both formed and affected by the nationality issue. Hence it is necessary to have some idea of the peoples who inhabited the region under study here and of the role that each played in the local economy. In the present chapter I aim to present just such a sketch of nationality, economic realities, and administration of the nine Western Provinces and the ten provinces of Russian Poland during the final decades of the Russian Empire. Of course, I can make no pretension to completeness here; this chapter has the more modest aim of anchoring, as it were, the discussions of national ideology in the previous chapters and the arguments about government policy in chapters to come in some semblance of concrete reality. After all, "nationality" and "policy" are but abstract, pale words behind which living people struggled for existence in the face of complex economic, social, and political realities. With more insight into the tangible realities behind national relations in the area, one can surely better understand and appreciate the reasons for the government's apparently contradictory actions.

Theoretically, at least, the imperial government pursued very different policies in the nine Western Provinces on one hand and the Kingdom of Poland on the other. The Western Provinces were considered historically, ethnographically, and religiously Russian and Orthodox. To be sure, official sources did not deny the presence of various alien elements here, but these were viewed as small in number and, historically speaking, as elements that had come in from outside. Later in this chapter we shall consider some statistics that do not, on the whole, support these views. In the first place, official Russia consistently spoke of the "rooted Russian" peasant population of the nine Western Provinces. This was only possible if one denied separate ethnic and linguistic status to Ukrainians and Belorussians. Furthermore, the hundreds of thousands of Lithuanian peasants who resided in the Northwest Provinces were often simply omitted in broad statements about the region's ethnic makeup.

The government's fundamental and explicit line of policy in the Western Provinces after the 1863 Polish insurrection was set down by M. N. Muraviev (see chapter 5). For Muraviev, and for Russian officialdom after him, the basic issue in the Western Provinces was the liberation of the local

"Russian" population from Polish oppression. In a memorandum presented to Tsar Alexander II in 1864, Muraviev stated his fundamental concern in the form of a rhetorical question:

> Is it possible for the higher government authorities to allow a country in which ⅚ of the population is completely Russian, professing the Orthodox faith, to be ever [kogda-libo] considered Polish? Can it be permitted, as it was for many decades, for the Polish element there to develop itself, an element completely alien and allowed there only due to our lack of foresight and a failure to respect our own nationality?[5]

Obviously, to Muraviev's mind, the Russian Empire could not afford to continue a policy that strengthened the historical enemy and betrayed the Russian majority in the land.

In Muraviev's statement we find the expression of several assumptions about the western territory that appear again and again in official and Russian nationalist accounts regarding the area. First of all, let us take the dubious statistic of overwhelming Russian numbers in the provinces. Even if one could agree that Belorussians and Ukrainians were really Russians (obviously an unacceptable opinion), the figure of ⅚ of the total population is clearly exaggerated: Jews alone made up nearly one-sixth of the population of these provinces. We have previously noted the pervasive and hardly conscious equation of Orthodox and Russian, repeated here. Then there is the division of the local population between "rooted," historically justified people (usually peasants and, of course, nearly always "Russian") and "newcomers" such as Jews and Poles. That these "newcomers" may have resided in the area for centuries made no difference to this ideology: Russians were there first. We are obviously dealing with mythohistory here, but this ideology was no less potent for being historically inaccurate. Finally, one notes in Muraviev's description of the Northwest Provinces an almost total absence of Lithuanians. This large national group simply did not fit into his politico-national calculations. So he just left it out.

The historical and ethnographic situation of the Kingdom of Poland contrasted significantly with that in the West. The overwhelming majority of the population was of Catholic faith and Polish ethnicity, which even Russian officialdom could not deny. It was perhaps of equal importance that the Polish state had existed as a historical unit for many centuries. Hence Polish culture in these provinces, unlike the western territory, enjoyed a kind of historical justification. Thus the aim of Russian official policy was never explicitly to crush Polish culture here; instead, the stated aim of Russian rule in the Polish provinces was to reconcile the continued existence of this culture with Russian rule. This statement, admittedly, vastly simplifies a maddeningly complex and inconsistent set of Russian attitudes and policies toward the Poles. At this point, however, it is more important for us to emphasize the stated explicit difference in Russian policy toward the Western Provinces on one hand and the Kingdom of Poland on the other.

This difference was expressed quite clearly in a speech by Premier Peter Stolypin to the MVD Sovet po Delam Mestnogo Khoziaistva (Council on Matters of Local Economy) comparing the government's aims in introducing zemstva to the Western Provinces and in extending elected municipal government to Poland: "If thus in the Western region [*zapadnyi krai*] the Ministry strove to create a Russian-tinged zemstvo [*po okraske russkoe*], in the cities of the provinces of the Kingdom of Poland, on the other hand, we expect to see Polish self-government merely subordinated to the Russian [*russkii*] state idea."[6] We need not take the premier's words too literally. After all, just how is one to interpret "subordination to the Russian state idea"? Nonetheless, in theory especially, but also in reality, the difference between the western region and the Polish Kingdom remained a key point of government policy.

The final aim of government policy in the Western Provinces was complete fusion *(sliianie)* with the surrounding "Russian" population, whereas in Poland it would suffice for a Pole to "subordinate himself to the Russian state idea" while retaining his own culture and, to a certain extent, a few vestiges of previous autonomous institutions. This, at any rate, was the stated policy. On the practical level it makes more sense to regard the above principle as a minimum demand from the government's viewpoint. At the very least, the safeguarding of Russian state interests, however interpreted, remained the government's foremost demand. At the same time, however, the government remained extremely suspicious of allowing Poles, even within the Polish Kingdom, to participate in local government or to form their own cultural associations, such as the Macierz Szkolna or Sokol.[7] So here we have a Russian government admitting, in principle, the right of Poles to be Poles (especially within the Polish Kingdom itself) but at the same time doing its best to keep the Polish element from positions of administrative power and authority, and even hindering Poles from forming their own private social organizations. (It must be kept in mind, however, that before 1905 even Russian social organizations were closely monitored and restricted by government authorities.)

So far the discussion of government policy in the West has been dominated by the Russian/Polish nexus. This is no coincidence. Historical memory among Russian officialdom reached far back and recognized in the Pole the centuries-long enemy of Russians and Orthodoxy. In more concrete terms, the 1863 uprising had convinced Russian officials that Polish culture still represented a threat to the Russian state. The suspicion felt by Russian officials toward Poles continued almost unrelieved until 1914.

As for the other nationalities in the area, they were of less immediate concern to the government. The Jews were seen as a problem sui generis. We have already considered some specific, even stereotypical, references to Jews in official documents. They presented not so much an immediate threat to the government (unlike the Poles) as a feared foreign influence that was believed to have detrimental economic and moral *(nravstvennyi)* effects on the surrounding population. Governors frequently pointed out the role of Jewish youth in socialist agitation, especially in the Bund.[8] The Lithuanians, a mainly peasant people before World War I, were largely ignored by the government except for occasional efforts to free them from Polish influence (exercised especially through the Catholic church) or even to elicit them as allies against the Poles. Belorussians and Ukrainians (*malorossy*) were seen as local variants of Russians and thus not as minority nationalities at all. Finally, the various other small ethnic groups in the area (Czechs, Tatars, Germans) played a relatively minor role in the government's nationality calculations, though certain publicists and local officials expressed concern at the growing number of German colonists settling in the region.[9] To sum up, tsarist policy in the Western Provinces and Poland had two prime aims in mind: to restrain the separatist longings of the Polish population and to inhibit presumably negative Jewish influences and exploitation.

❖   The Western Provinces and the Polish Kingdom were administered according to laws and institutions that differed significantly from those in place in central Russia. These diverse administrative and legal structures reflected the region's history as a former part of the Polish-Lithuanian Commonwealth, incorporated into the Russian Empire by the Polish Partitions of the late eighteenth century and assuming final shape at the Congress of Vienna after the Napoleonic Wars. The Polish constitution granted by Tsar Alexander I in 1815 was thrown out by his successor, Nicholas I, after the November Insurrection of 1830. The decades between the 1830 and 1863 uprisings witnessed a more or less continual process, within the Russian Empire, of limiting Polish autonomy and cultural institutions.[10] The repressive measures taken after 1863 were to cap this process. In many respects, the western territory and Russian Poland bore the marks of a conquered land, sternly kept in line by governor generals and restrictive laws.

Looking more closely at the western region, we observe a form of administration that appears not very different from the rest of European Russia: large provinces (*gubernii*) with a governor at their head, divided into districts (*uezdy*; in Polish, *powiaty*) that were often of enormous size. For example, the Obruchskii district of Volhynia Province covered 9,274.5 square versts, an area representing nearly one-third of the entire territory of the Kingdom of Belgium. Here, as in most of European Russia, the municipal statutes of 1892 were in force, which meant that there were elected city councils (dumas) in Kiev, Minsk, Vilna, and other centers. Unlike the majority of provinces in European Russia, however, zemstvo institutions had not been introduced here, and the administrative order of the West was characterized by certain other local peculiarities.

Most striking, the governors in most of the Western Provinces were not masters in their own house. Overshadowing their position and authority was the institution of the *general-gubernatorstva*, located in Kiev and Vilna.[11] These governor generals divided the nine Western Provinces into three

THE KINGDOM OF POLAND AND THE NINE WESTERN PROVINCES

0   50   100   150 Miles

BALTIC SEA

N

GERMANY

KOVNO

VITEBSK

VILNA

SUWAŁKI

MOGILEV

PŁOCK

ŁOMZA

GRODNO

MINSK

WARSAW

KALISZ

SIEDLCE

PIOTRKÓW

RADOM

LUBLIN

VOLHYNIA

KIELCE

KIEV

AUSTRIA

PODOLIA

K. J. Carr, 1996

groups: the Western or Belorussian provinces (Minsk, Vitebsk, Mogilev), which were not subordinated to a governor general (in 1869 and 1870 these provinces had been removed from the jurisdiction of the governor general of Vilna); the Northwestern or Lithuanian provinces (Vilna, Grodno, Kovno), subordinate to the governor general of Vilna; and the Southwest or right-bank Ukrainian Provinces (Kiev, Podolia, Volhynia), subordinate to the governor general of Kiev.[12]

In point of fact, however, the subordination of governors to governor generals was—as so often in the Russian Empire—not strictly ordered, and the governors themselves, while complaining bitterly of the diminution of their prerogatives by the governor general, in fact enjoyed broad discretionary powers.[13] Furthermore, throughout this period it was debated whether to abolish the institution of the governor generalship, which some believed was no longer appropriate. The institution had been introduced in the aftermath of the 1863 rebellion, but after forty years of calm, opponents argued, it had outlived its usefulness and only complicated administration and added to red tape.[14] The Vilna general governorship was finally abolished on July 1, 1912.

All nine of the Western Provinces fell within the Pale of Jewish Settlement (*Cherta evreiskoi osedlosti*) and, according to one Polish statistician, the majority of Russian Jews (a total of nearly five million in 1907) lived in these nine provinces.[15] As we shall see below, Jews made up a significant percentage of the urban population in the West. For various reasons, both historical and geographical, trade and commerce in this region tended to be carried out by Jews, a fact that local governors never tired of bewailing. The large numerical presence of this non-Christian element was a constant concern of both administrators and "society" in these provinces. It is no coincidence that after 1905 the western region became a stronghold of the nationalist and rightist parties, both of which professed strident anti-Semitism, as well as pronounced polonophobia.[16]

Besides Jews, the western region was home to one other large non-peasant nationality: the Poles.[17] Poles were especially numerous in the Northwest, particularly in the "Lithuanian" Provinces of Vilna, Grodno, and Kovno. More important than their numbers, however, was the economic and cultural strength of the Poles. Despite the restrictions placed on them since 1865, Poles retained a good deal of landed property in the region, even after the turn of the century, and made up a large percentage of the indigenous local intelligentsia. It is significant that the Polish national poet could address Litwa, not Polska, as "my fatherland" (*ojczyzno moja*).[18] Mainly because of the Polish economic and cultural predominance in the area, organs of local self-government such as the zemstva had never been introduced in the western region, despite the frequently admitted need for such institutions. The absence of zemstva also made administration in the nine Western Provinces differ sharply from that in central Russia. Almost exclusively non-local bureaucrats—ignorant of local conditions—administered the provinces, and consequently local needs and demands were less likely to be satisfied. Poles were kept out of all government positions but the most lowly in the Western Provinces.[19]

The economy of this entire region was to a large extent still determined by the land's physical aspect. That is, the area on the whole had not yet progressed into the industrial era. This was far truer of the Western Provinces than of the Kingdom of Poland, which encompassed such massive industrial centers as Warsaw and Łódź. Because of these significant differences in industrial development, the following discussion of land and economy will be divided into three sections: the six Northwest Provinces, the three Southwest Provinces, and the ten provinces of the Kingdom of Poland.

The Northwest Region

The northwest region, made up of six provinces, encompassed an area of some 266,978 squared versts, that is, an area considerably larger than many European states. The area of Vitebsk guberniia alone exceeded that of Switzerland (38,649.5 square versts to 37,293), for example. This area is characterized by low, often marshy land, a damp climate, and clay or sandy soils.[20] Almost no large-scale industry was to be found in these provinces. The only factories mentioned in the Brokgauz-Efron encyclopedia's articles produced matches or vodka (spirt). Governors' annual reports also mention the lack of large-scale industry in the area and emphasize the link between most local industry and agriculture. To quote the governor of Podolia Province: "A significant majority (on the average around 90%) of industrial enterprises in the province are engaged in processing agricultural products."[21] The great majority of the area's inhabitants lived from agriculture or orchard-keeping; among the Northwest's major crops were flax, rye, and fruit.

Commerce in the region was not highly developed and was, by all accounts, dominated by Jews. Jewish merchants were significant among traders in lumber, agricultural products, and industrial goods. Similarly the majority of the region's artisans were Jews, and it is significant that such names as Portnoi (tailor) and Plotnik (carpenter) came to be seen as Jewish.[22] By the early twentieth century, Jews in significant numbers were also entering the local intelligentsia, using their own Yiddish and Hebrew languages as well as (and increasingly) Russian.

At the beginning of the reign of Nicholas II, the landowning class was mainly Polish. Restrictive measures placed on local Polish landowners after 1863 attempted to create a solid class of Russian landowners in the Northwest, but even officials admitted that these measures failed. Although the percentage of total land owned by Poles did fall, it was not Russian nobles but local peasants who extended their landholdings. As late as 1909, Polish influence was felt to be so strong in the three Lithuanian provinces that plans were scrapped to introduce zemstva there, even with national curiae that severely discriminated against Poles.[23]

Throughout the western territory, but most especially in the Northwest, the economic effects of the Temporary Laws of May 1882 made themselves felt. Forbidden to settle in rural areas, the Jews of the western territory found themselves crowded into urban areas and towns (*mestechki, shtetlekh*), where the already poor economic situation was further strained by demographic pressures. The poverty, crowding, and poor sanitation of the Jewish neighborhoods were noted by many at the time and used as one argument in favor of the abolition of the Jewish Pale. To quote one contemporary writer:

> Jews constitute 31.4 percent of those engaged in industry, 72.8 percent of those in trade [in the Pale as a whole]. The northwest territory is particularly noticeable in this respect. There Jews make up 52.3 percent of those engaged in industry and 88.6 percent of those in trade, 20.9 percent of those in transport and communications, and 19.3 percent of those of unproductive and indeterminate professions.[24]

These latter would be the large group of Jewish indigents known in Yiddish as *luftmentshn*, people who live on air.

Industry in the area was small and underdeveloped. In 1911–1912 the industrial production of the six provinces averaged 10.6 rubles per capita, much less than in the Kingdom of Poland, where the figure was 60.8 rubles. The largest industry in the region was distilling; in this branch the Northwest outproduced even the Kingdom of Poland. Probably the sole "industrial city" in the entire region was Białystok (Belostok), where a booming textile business had given rise to related trades such as the production of chemicals and dyes, and a well-developed credit and finance system. A visitor in the late 1880s wrote of "boisterous, rich Belostok."[25] Białystok was a predominantly Jewish city, and much of the industry in all six Northwestern Provinces were in Jewish hands. Only in Vitebsk Province was the percentage of Jewish ownership of factories under 25 percent.[26] To be sure, nearly all of the "factories and plants" that figure in the statistics were small affairs indeed, more like artisanal workshops than industrial enterprises.

To sum up, the Northwest was a largely agricultural, underdeveloped region where to a great extent nationality was coterminous with a specific social class. At the risk of simplification, one may characterize the ethnic and social structure of the Northwest as follows. The large landowners were sometimes absentee Russians, but more often resident Poles. The intelligentsia drew mainly from the Polish and Jewish populations. The urban population tended to be heavily Jewish; indeed, the term *shtetl* (Yiddish for "small town") can be applied to nearly all settlements of the region larger than a village and smaller than a city.[27] Officials, including teachers, were ethnic Russians from the Russian interior and tended to be very isolated from local conditions and society.[28] Finally, the peasant masses belonged to the Lithuanian and Belorussian ethnicities, with Latvians and Ukrainians in certain border areas.

To be sure, this nationality/class nexus was changing during the last decades of the nineteenth and the first decades of the twentieth century, partly because of government policy (against Polish landowning, for example) and partly in spite of it (in the case of Jewish workers). The development of a considerable body of Russian-speaking Jewish *intelligenty* in the region, especially after 1905, significantly altered both national and professional balances. As early as 1894 the Minsk governor remarked, "I am happy to report the progress that the Jewish population makes in Russian. Knowledge of Russian is regarded in Jewish society as a sign of education."[29] Despite industrial development, changes in landowning, and the rise of modern nationalist movements, even in 1914 the categories—Belorussian and Lithuanian peasants, Polish gentry or intelligentsia, Jewish merchant or artisan—remained much more than just stereotypes.[30]

The Southwest Region

In many respects the three Southwest Provinces resembled the Northwest. Here, too, agriculture was the main livelihood of the population; industry and commerce were underdeveloped; and social and occupational categories were often dominated by members of a certain nationality. On the other hand, the differences between the two regions were at least as important as the similarities. In such respects as climate, crops, economy, national makeup, and historical consciousness, the Southwest Provinces differed strikingly from the Belorussian-Lithuanian region.[31]

Here the climate was much drier than in the Northwest; grains, sugar beets, and even tobacco figured among the major crops of the region. Especially after the turn of the century, capitalist agriculture in the form of large latifundia for sugar beet production played an increasingly important role.[32] As in the Northwest, orchards were also important. The ethnic mix of the area was considerably more homogeneous than the provinces to the north, with "Russians" (that is, for the most part Ukrainians) making up over two-thirds of the population in all three provinces.[33] The Polish influence in the Southwest, both economic and cultural, was considerably weaker than in the Belorussian and Lithuanian provinces, but Polish economic strength, especially in the agricultural sphere, should not be underestimated. Even in 1909, Poles owned nearly half of all the privately owned land in the Southwest.[34]

Agriculture in the Southwest was relatively advanced when compared to other regions of the Russian Empire, including the Northwest Provinces. Unlike regions to the south and east, grain for export did not occupy an important place in the local economy. That place was taken up by sugar beet, which was also usually refined within the confines of the three Southwest Provinces. Agricultural machinery was not extensively used, to a great extent because of the availability of cheap local labor. Sugar beets and the refining of sugar made up the backbone of the local agricultural economy, but the profits from this enterprise remained in the hands of the middle and large landowners and the refiners themselves. On their lands the larger landowners often possessed a distillery or a sugar refinery, or both.[35] Peasants made up the bulk of day and seasonal laborers both in the fields and in the refineries but otherwise benefited little from this industry. The economic situation of the peasants actually deteriorated, mainly because of demographic pressures and the continually decreasing size of the average peasant holding.[36]

Compared to the Northwest Provinces, the Southwest enjoyed considerably more and larger industry. To quote Witold Kula, a Polish economic historian, describing industrial development during this period, "compared to backward Lithuania and Belorussia, Ukraine represented a land flowing with milk and honey." These large factories were nearly exclusively engaged in agriculturally related production such as the refining of sugar from sugar beets and the distilling of alcohol. Most of the large industrialists in the Southwest were of Great Russian nationality, although Jewish capitalists—such as the almost mythical sugar magnate I. Brodskii—were also important. Jewish ownership and entrepreneurship in the Ukrainian sugar industry was considerable. Regarding the situation in Ukraine just prior to World War I, A. Kahan wrote, "About one third of the sugar mills belonged to Jewish owners and produced about 52 percent of the refined sugar." In the words of Petr Struve (to be sure, not necessarily the most objective witness), in Ukraine "capitalism speaks and will speak Russian, and not Ukrainian [po-malorusski]."[37]

The Kingdom of Poland

The administration of the Kingdom of Poland (*Tsarstvo Pol'skoe* in Russian; *Królestwo Polskie* in Polish) differed greatly from that of either the Western Provinces or Central Russia. This region went under several names, and the choice among these names often depended on the speaker's nationality and politics. Officially, the Kingdom of Poland had ceased to exist after the uprising of 1863, and true-Russians made a point of using the term *Privislinskii krai* (Vistula country), thereby reducing the area to a mere geographical entity within the Russian Empire. Poles usually referred to the region as *Królestwo Polskie, Kongresówka* (Congress Kingdom), or even, in the Russian context, as *Polska*. The official Russian usage varied, and even after 1905 one finds the term *Tsarstvo Pol'skoe* in official documents. Here we will follow common usage and speak of the "Kingdom of Poland," even though this term is not strictly correct.

Russian Poland was divided into ten small provinces, the governors of which were subordinate to the governor general of Warsaw, a much more powerful figure than his counterparts in Kiev and Vilna. When the position of viceroy (*namestnik*) was allowed to lapse upon the death of F. Berg in 1874, many of the tasks of this office devolved upon the governor general.[38] The Polish Kingdom—a peninsula of "Russian" territory surrounded on three sides by Austria and Prussia—was rightly regarded as a potential battlefield in case of war with Germany or Austria. Consequently, military considerations were never far from the minds of local administrators.[39] The memory of 1863 and the possibility of future Polish "mutinies"—possibly in alliance with Poles across the borders in both Prussia and Austria (Galicia)—lived on in the minds of Russian administrators in the Vistula country and helped stifle suggestions for broader local participation in administration. The two largest nationalities living in the Kingdom were Poles and Jews, both "untrustworthy" groups, making up nearly 90 percent of the total population in 1913.[40]

The lack of "reliable" (blagonadezhnye) local elements and the foreign danger combined to make the Polish Kingdom possibly the most bureaucratically administered area in the already very bureaucratic Russian Empire.[41] The zemstvo reform had not been introduced to Poland and the gmina, sometimes touted as a kind of Polish zemstvo, was dominated by arch-conservative elements and was tightly supervised by local (Russian) authorities.[42] The municipal reform of 1892 had not been extended to Poland, so at the beginning of the twentieth century, Warsaw—the third largest city in the Empire and the eighth largest in Europe—was administrated by a strictly appointive council and mayor (prezydent) whose powers were tightly circumscribed by the MVD in St. Petersburg.[43]

Besides the strictly bureaucratic administration, the inhabitants of Russian Poland had to endure a much stricter censorship than the population of central Russia, especially before 1905. This strictness sometimes took on ludicrous forms, such as when Warsaw newspapers were forbidden to even reprint articles that had already appeared in the Russian press.[44] Because of the extra-strict censorship in the ten provinces ruled over by the Warsaw governor general, the best and most open Polish journal published in the Russian Empire before 1905 was the St. Petersburg weekly Kraj.[45]

The ten provinces of the Kingdom of Poland differed sharply from the western region in their economy and ethnic composition. On the whole, Russian Poland had more industry (especially textiles) than the western territory, was more urbanized, and had a significantly higher population density. The most urbanized and most populous Polish province, Warsaw, had over 40 percent urban inhabitants in 1897. In the second most urbanized province, Piotrków (Petrokov), over one-third of the population lived in urban centers at that date. The average population density among the ten Polish provinces in 1912 was 108.7 inhabitants per square verst, a figure reached in no Western Province, where, at the time, only Kiev and Podolia provinces had population densities of above 100 inhabitants per square verst.[46] In industrial production, especially of textiles, the two major centers of the Kingdom—Warsaw and Łódź—were rivaled in importance only by the Central Industrial Region and St. Petersburg in the Russian Empire.[47]

At the same time, Warsaw and Łódź should not be taken as typical of Russian Poland as a whole.[48] Outside these two cities, the bulk of the population (well over 80 percent in all eight provinces aside from Warsaw and Piotrków) lived on and from the land. In Płock, Siedlce, Łomża, and Suwałki

Table 1. Population of the Kingdom of Poland by Religion, 1897

	Orthodox	Catholic	Jewish	Protestant
Kielce	1%	87.9%	10.8%	0.3%
Radom	1.4	83.5	13.9	1.1
Kalisz	1.1	82.8	8.6	7.4
Płock	3.1	81.1	9.1	6.6
Łomża	5.4	77.5	15.7	1.2
Suwałki	6.1	76.2	10.9	6.4
Piotrków	1.6	73.0	15.8	9.5
Warsaw	5.5	71.6	18.1	4.7
Lublin	21.8	62.4	13.2	2.4
Siedlce	22.0	60.5	15.8	1.5

Source: Zygmunt Gloger, ed., *Królestwo Polskie* (Warsaw, 1905), p. 202, table 7.
Note: Figures are in percentages.

Provinces (to name the least industrialized), less than 1 percent of the population was engaged in factory work around the turn of the century.[49] In these provinces, one of the greatest economic problems was rural unemployment and the increasing parcelation of agricultural land.

The nationality situation in the Congress Kingdom was rather less complicated than in the Western Provinces. The Polish nationality formed a decided majority in nine of the ten provinces (as the statistics found in tables 1 and 2 will attest). The Polish nationality formed a large majority of the total population in nine of the ten provinces, exceeded only in Suwałki Province by Lithuanians. In all ten provinces without exception, by far the largest religious group was Catholic. Jews were present in significant numbers throughout Russian Poland, but Orthodox believers were to be found only in eastern Lublin and Siedlce Provinces, which bordered on the mainly Ukrainian Volhynia. Here the official statistics are somewhat misleading; these "Orthodox people" are the ex-Uniates of the Kholm and Podlasie region, many of whom were Orthodox only by grace of being registered officially as such. It was to "protect" this population that the Kholm Province was finally formed in 1913.[50] Germans lived throughout this area, both as peasants in isolated, self-contained settlements and as town people and industrialists, most importantly in Piotrków Province, which included the industrial center of Łódź.

It is interesting to note that, when the 1897 census results for nationality in the Polish Kingdom were finally published in 1905, they showed a considerably higher percentage of Russians in every Polish province except for

Table 2. Population of the Kingdom of Poland by Nationality, 1894

	Russians	Poles	German	Lithuanians	Jews
Warsaw	0.4%	74.5%	7.2%	——%	17.9%
Kalisz	0.1	80.4	9.3	——	10.2
Kielce	——	89.4	0.4	——	10.2
Łomża	——	82.0	2.0	——	16.0
Lublin	19.2	63.7	2.8	——	14.3
Piotrków	——	73.1	13.4	——	13.4
Płock	——	81.0	7.8	——	11.0
Radom	——	83.1	2.1	——	14.6
Suwałki	3.1	19.0	6.1	57.7	14.0
Siedlce	21.9	57.3	2.2	——	18.6

Source: *Ezhegodnik Rossii* 1 (St. Petersburg, 1904), pp. 87–88.
Note: Figures are in percentages.

Siedlce.[51] This discrepancy can probably be explained by the high numbers of Russian bureaucrats and soldiers stationed there who would normally not be included under the rubric of "residents." In general one must be alert to the tendency of official statistics to exaggerate numbers of Russians living in border areas.

As is evident from the statistics cited, Jews made up a large portion (nearly 15%) of the total population in the Kingdom of Poland.[52] As in the western region, Jews tended to be concentrated in cities and towns. Unlike the Jews in the Pale, however, the Jews of the Kingdom were not legally forbidden to reside outside urban areas.[53] Despite this lack of formal legal interdiction, Jews in Poland, as elsewhere, remained largely urban dwellers (see table 3), and this high percentage of Jewish urban population was to have a considerable effect on discussions after 1905 regarding the introduction of elective municipal government in Poland.

Of the ten Polish provinces, seven had urban populations on the whole more Jewish than Polish. It is significant, however, that the two provinces with the lowest percentages of Jews among urban dwellers were precisely those provinces that boasted the Kingdom's two largest cities, Warsaw and Łódź, and in general the highest amount of urbanization. Still, the percentages and absolute numbers of Jews living in "Polish" cities were high, and this was disturbing to many Poles. To look at the figures another way, of the 116 "cities" of the Polish Kingdom in 1909, 73 had a population more than half Jewish.[54] Taking the total city population of a dozen of the largest of these cities in 1910, we find the following percentages of Jews: Warsaw

Table 3. Jews as Percentage of Total Population by Province, 1892–1893

	Cities	"Osada"[a]	Rural
Warsaw	36.5%	44.0%	2.7%
Kalisz	42.3	34.6	0.6
Piotrków	31.4	37.8	3.2
Płock	50.4	44.7	1.8
Kielce	53.8	47.4	2.8
Łomża	58.0	61.4	3.8
Radom	59.1	47.9	2.7
Lublin	48.4	55.3	1.6
Suwałki	57.2	53.5	4.4
Siedlce	65.4	54.3	2.5

Source: Gloger, *Królestwo Polskie,* pp. 210–12, tables 10–12. For more detailed statistics on the Jewish population of Congress Poland, see Dr. Erich Zechlin, *Die Bevölkerungs- und Grundbesitzverteilung im Zartum Polen* (Berlin, 1916), esp. pp. 25–28; Bohdan Wasiutyński, "Ludność żydowska w Królestwie Polskiem," *Ekonomista* 11, no. 2 (1911), pp. 75–173, *idem., Ludność żydowska w Polsce w wiekach XIX i XX* (Warsaw, 1930), and Szyja Bronsztajn, *Ludność żydowska w Polsce w okresie międzywojennym: Studium statystyczne* (Wrocław, 1963), pp. 47–67.

Note: [a] The term "osada" can be translated as "town" or "settlement." The *osady* lacked the legal status of "city" but were not agricultural colonies.

39.4, Kalisz 35.3, Kielce 36.4, Lublin 50.7, Chełm/Kholm 44.5, Łomża 44.6, Piotrków 37.0, Łódź 22.7, Płock 39.2, Radom 43.1, Siedlce 55.0, and Suwałki 54.9 percent.[55]

To sum up, in the Kingdom of Poland we find a region with great contrasts in urbanization and economical development. Different national groups made their homes here, with significant numbers of Lithuanians and Ukrainians on the Kingdom's eastern borders and German settlements along the western border with Prussia. On the whole, however, Poles made up a large majority of the total population, especially in rural areas, while in urban areas the Jewish element tended to be strong or even predominant. The existence of this large urban Jewish population was to play a primary part in the growth and intensification of Polish anti-Semitism after 1905.

The Western Provinces

Returning to the Western Provinces, some statistics will back up the general comments offered above. As we have seen, religious affiliation constituted one of the most important indications of nationality in late imperial Russia. Indeed, one may argue that, in administrative practice, the imperial government inevitably defined "Russian" as "Orthodox," and "Catholic"

Table 4. Religious Groups in the Western Provinces, 1897

Province	Total Pop.	Orthodox	Old Believers	Catholics
Volhynia	2,989,482	2,106,521	8,282	298,110
Podolia	3,018,299	2,358,497	18,849	262,738
Kiev	3,559,229	2,983,736	15,843	106,733
Vilna	1,591,207	415,296	25,673	935,847
Grodno	1,603,409	919,346	504	386,519
Kovno	1,472,564	46,514	32,940	1,108,303
Minsk	2,147,621	1,558,264	15,860	217,959
Vitebsk	1,489,246	825,601	83,022	357,309
Mogilev	1,686,764	1,402,161	23,349	50,159
Total	19,557,821	12,615,936	224,322	3,723,677

Table 4—*Continued*

Province	Protestants	Jews	Muslims	Other
Volhynia	175,439	395,948	4,877	305
Podolia	3,876	370,636	3,460	243
Kiev	15,610	434,055	2,931	321
Vilna	4,643	205,262	4,375	111
Grodno	12,687	280,499	3,731	123
Kovno	69,619	212,869	1,920	399
Minsk	5,777	345,031	4,619	111
Vitebsk	46,888	175,678	661	87
Mogilev	6,923	203,958	184	30
Total	341,462	2,623,936	26,758	1,730

Source: Edward Czyński, *Etnograficzno-statystyczny zarys liczebności i rozsiedlenia ludności polskiej* (Warsaw, 1909), table 36, p. 91.

as "Polish." Table 4 provides data on the numerical strength of various religious groups in the western region at the turn of the century.

The Orthodox religion in the Russian Empire was professed mainly by Russians, Ukrainians, and Belorussians. Thus we see that in the Western Provinces these three nationalities were indeed predominant, with the

Table 5. Nationalities in the Western Provinces

Province	"Russians"	Poles	Jews	Lithuanians	Germans
Vilna	61.2%	8.2%	12.8%	17.6%	0.2%
Vitebsk	66.3	3.4	11.7	17.9	0.5
Volhynia	73.7	6.2	13.2	——	5.7
Grodno	71.2	6.2	17.4	0.2	0.6
Kiev	85.3	1.9	12.2	——	0.4
Kovno	7.3	9.0	13.8	68.3	1.4
Minsk	80.4	3.0	16.0	0.1	0.2
Mogilev	86.1	3.0	12.1	0.6	0.1
Podolia	84.3	2.3	12.3	——	0.1

Source: *Ezhegodnik Rossii* 7 (1910), pp. 65–67.
Note: Figures are in percentages.

exception of the mainly Lithuanian Kovno (Kaunas) Province and neighboring Vilna (Wilno, Vilnius) Province. The situation in Vilna Province was complicated further because many local Belorussians had adopted the Catholic faith. The Old Believers in the West were mainly settlers from the Russian interior who had fled to this area from religious persecution in the seventeenth and eighteenth centuries. As in the Polish provinces, Jews resided throughout the region and again made up a large percentage of the urban population. German settlers were present in significant numbers, as attested by the high figures for Protestants in Kovno, Vitebsk, and particularly Volhynia Province.

Another indication of nationality is language. The statistics in table 5 reflect the relative strengths of national groups in the region, as reported in the 1897 census. The determining factor there was "native tongue" (*rodnoi iazyk*) and here, as in most official sources, "Russian" includes Great Russians, Belorussians, and Little Russians.[56] It must be emphasized that these figures cannot be considered free of error or tendentiousness. But it is vital to keep in mind that these are the figures that guided the Russian government in perceptions and policy regarding the western territory.

To repeat, these figures were derived from the government statistics gathered in 1897 during the first general census of the population of the Russian Empire. Compared with previous statistics, the results of the 1897 census were solidly based on carefully gathered data. Even so, especially as regards nationality, many deficiencies remained. Quite aside from any conscious effort to skew the figures, contemporary observers criticized the 1897 census as being not entirely consistent with contemporary statistical methods. Despite these generally justified criticisms, the data provided by

Table 6. Privately Held Land, by Province

Province	Polish	Russian
Kovno	75%	14.3%
Vilna	73	20.5
Grodno	53.6	40.8
Minsk	49.7	41
Vitebsk	40.6	42.3
Volhynia	47.9	45.4
Mogilev	33	63
Kiev	——	59.3
Podolia	48.3	49.8

Source: Kraj 18 (May 6/19, 1905), *dodatek*, p. 2. It is unclear from which year these figures are taken.
Note: Figures are in percentages.

the 1897 census give us a good general idea of the relative numerical strength of the various nationalities in the area.[57]

Also important, especially during the debates on the introduction of zemstva in the western region, is the relative strength of Polish and Russian landholdings in the area. The relative percentages of privately held land in 1905 are reflected in figures taken from a May 1905 issue of *Kraj* (shown in table 6).[58] Here only private landholdings are reflected. Thus the mainly peasant holdings of local Lithuanians, Ukrainians, and Belorussians are not included (Belorussians and Ukrainians, of course, fell under the general heading "Russian"). Clearly, even in 1905, although two generations had passed since laws were enacted to reduce Polish landholdings and encourage Russians to settle in the area, the Poles retained a great deal of land and economic power in the Western Provinces.[59]

Similarly, despite long years of restrictive laws on Jews, a significant percentage of the property in the Western Provinces still belonged to Jews. The available statistics unfortunately do not allow us to distinguish between rural and urban property. However, the statistics found in table 7, gathered by the MVD after 1905 as part of the preparation for the western zemstvo project, presumably concentrated on rural holdings. Thus it would seem that, despite the restrictions of over two decades, Jews were frequently able to retain and even increase their landed property. On the other hand, only in Grodno Province (probably because of the presence there of the rich city of Białystok) did the percentage of landed wealth owned by Jews equal their percentage of the local population.[60]

The western territory was not a highly urbanized area. Indeed, according to the census of 1897, the percentage of the total population that lived

Table 7. Jewish Landholding in the Western Provinces

	Jewish Holdings	Total Holdings	Percentage Jewish
Vilna (without Vilna city)	6,814	129,843	5.25%
Vitebsk	26,659	243,556	10.95
Volhynia	33,560	566,840	5.92
Grodno	41,035	218,626	18.77
Kiev	56,794	797,155	7.12
Kovno	16,579	189,894	8.73
Minsk	23,807	223,561	10.65
Mogilev	17,428	248,856	7.00
Podolia	38,108	641,583	5.94

Source: RGIA, f. 1278, op. 2, 1910, d. 1171, ll. 149–52.
Note: Figures are by value, in thousands of rubles.

in urban centers exceeded 15 percent in only Grodno Province. And even here, the high urban percentage (15.9 percent) may be explained by the presence of the atypical industrial city of Białystok at the western edge of the province.[61] Moreover, the urban population usually differed sharply in ethnic composition from the surrounding countryside; so much so that certain writers, particularly those representing the rural nationalities, simply dismissed the urban population as "inconsequential" in drawing up total percentages of nationalities living in a given area.[62] The ethnic composition of the largest cities in the region shows this peculiarity (see table 8).

Most striking is the large percentage of Jews in the major cities of the area. This is hardly surprising, to be sure, when one considers the restrictions placed on Jewish residency in rural areas and the legal inability of Jews to purchase or to lease land in rural areas.[63] The ethnic composition of the cities was also determined by the traditional occupations of certain national groups. Russians held bureaucratic positions; Poles were specifically excluded from government service in the area.[64] Poles predominated among local society and intelligentsia, whereas Jews predominated among artisans and in trade and commerce. As the Western Provinces became more industrialized, the importance of these ethnic or occupational categories became gradually weakened, but this process was far from complete by 1914.

Several distinct nationalities made their home in the Kingdom of Poland and Western Provinces (see chapter 6). But we should not ignore entirely the smaller groups also present here: Germans, Czechs, and Tatars.[65] All three ethnicities lived for the most part on the land, Germans and Czechs mainly as prosperous peasants and Tatars as small landowners. Although these three groups taken together did not make up more than a few percentage points of the total population of any given province, their presence

Table 8. Ethnic Composition of Major Cities, Western Provinces

	"Russians"[a]	Poles	Jews
Kovno[b]	15.5%	18.9%	46.5%
Vilna[c]	22.9	28.6	39.8
Vitebsk	40.9	11.3	43.2
Mogilev	38.6	5.0	55.4
Gomel'	47.5	1.8	50.5
Minsk	43.0	11.4	43.3
Belostok	29.2	2.9[d]	64.9
Zhitomir	37.0	16.9	45.6
Kiev	73.8	10.8	11.7
Berdichev	17.2	10.8	77.0
Kamenets-Podolsk	36.8	13.9	48.4

Source: Goroda Rossii v 1910 g. (St. Petersburg, 1914), pp. 90–93, 554–57.

Note: Figures are in percentages.

[a] "Russian" includes Ukrainian and Belorussian. But contemporary accounts generally agree that the majority of these "Russians" in cities were generally either Great Russians (*chinovniki,* intelligentsia) or russified locals.

[b] Of Kovno's population, 17.6 percent is listed as "other"—almost certainly Lithuanians.

[c] There also lived 6.1 percent "Finns" in Vilna.

[d] This is undoubtedly an error. Białystok had a large Polish population, as shown by the following percentages given by a Polish statistician using data from the 1897 census: Poles 18, Germans 5, Belorussians 2, Russians 6, and Jews 66 percent. Czyński, *Etnograficzno-statystyczny zarys,* table 38, p. 95.

here among Ukrainians, Poles, Jews, and others is just one more indication of the complex national (that is, "ethnic") situation of the area.

Most important, both numerically and from the military standpoint, were the Germans, who lived in considerable numbers in Volhynia Province as well as in certain Vistula provinces. German settlers tended to live in scattered, self-contained communities and did not mix with the Slavic population. They were admired as efficient, model farmers. Leon Trotsky, for one, noted the difference between the rather slovenly agricultural methods of local peasants and the neat, productive German colonies near his family's small farm in Kherson Province.[66]

The political reliability of these settlers was often questioned by local authorities. The Grodno governor, for example, in 1901 demanded strict restrictions on German and Austrian citizens who wanted to settle in the area, arguing that they could help the German or Austrian general staff in case of war.[67] Dietmar Neutatz, in a recent detailed study of German colonies in the Black Sea area and Volhynia Province, has shown that the Russian government came to see these settlers as a potential security risk only from the final decades of the nineteenth century. Indeed, already during the reign of

Alexander III certain publicists warned of a "peaceful conquest" of Russia's western borderlands by German settlers.[68] These fears were only to grow in the ensuing decades, but on the whole the government continued to regard German colonists as, at the most, a minor problem.

After the Germans in numbers, came the Czechs, sometimes referred to as *gusity* (Hussites). The Czech colonists lived mainly in Volhynia and were concentrated in a few districts. Czechs also lived in Kiev and Płock Provinces. Many of these peasants had been invited into the region by the tsarist authorities at the end of the 1860s, in the rather fantastic belief that they would provide a counterweight against Poles in Volhynia. Unfortunately for the Russian authorities, the Czechs in the "Hussite movement" soon split into various factions, did not pose a significant counterforce to Polish influences in the province, and generally held themselves apart from the local population, avoided government schools, and retained their Czech language and culture. By encouraging Czech immigration in the 1860s the government simply complicated an already difficult situation in the area.[69]

Finally, some twenty thousand "Tatars" lived in the Northwest Provinces, especially in Grodno and Vilna Provinces.[70] These Tatars—who preferred to be called Moslem nobles *(shliakhta musulmane)*—had lived in these parts for centuries. They traced their history back to the days of the Lithuanian Grand Duchy, when Grand Duke Gediminas had allied with Tatar khans against the Muscovites. Their presence in the Polish-Lithuanian Commonwealth and later Russian Empire posed an interesting anomaly of non-Christians who were specifically allowed to own land on which Christian serfs resided. This privilege was explicitly confirmed by a special law in 1840. Although they retained their Moslem faith, their knowledge of Arabic was severely limited, and even in their prayers they used local languages (to quote one source) "according to their social standing, that is, landowners and nobles [spoke] Russian and Polish, and simple farmers Belorussian."[71] In the period after 1863, the Lithuanian Tatars' status as landowners was again reconfirmed, and they were not subject to the special land taxes levied on Poles.[72] Despite their Moslem faith, the Lithuanian Tatars were seen as loyal subjects and were thus privileged over their Catholic neighbors.

❖   This quick excursion through the nineteen provinces of Russian Poland and the western region has given some idea, however sketchy, of the economic, social, and ethnic conditions of the area. This was a region where, to greater or lesser degrees, "modernity" had not yet arrived. That is to say, the overwhelming mass of the population lived on the land, and social distinctions were still strong and to a great extent considered "natural." Thus the fact that social categories often overlapped with national and religious ones also comes as no surprise. In the late nineteenth century the Polish Catholic gentleman *(Pan)*, Ukrainian peasant, Russian official, and

Jewish merchant were all figures that were readily recognizable to the inhabitants of this area. But the old world was beginning to come undone precisely during these decades. Polish landowners saw their estates dwindle and their cultural influence wane; Jewish merchants sent their sons and daughters to obtain an education in distant towns and were astonished and horrified when they returned looking for all the world like Russian revolutionaries; well-to-do Lithuanian peasants sent their sons to seminaries and were gratified, if perhaps surprised, to see their offspring join the nucleus of a strong national movement that challenged the traditional hegemony of Polish culture in local Catholic churches.

We have seen some of these changes reflected in the statistics cited above. For the most part, the figures do little justice to the incipient revolution in national relations. It bears repeating, however, that for most Russian administrators the old stereotypes died very hard indeed. Although some recognized the presence of national movements in the area, most remained wedded to old conceptions and continued to view the Poles and the Jews with almost unrelenting suspicion, while ignoring the growing strength of the Ukrainian, Belorussian, and Lithuanian national movements. In any case, the complexity of ethnic relations in the region could hardly be dealt with according to any simple formula. The policy, adopted by the Russian government, of denying national rights to any but the Russian ethnicity was perhaps the worst that could have been followed. The "logic" of this policy and its consequences will be the subject of the rest of this study.

Five

East Meets West

Russification and Coexistence

I approve neither of Polish rebels nor of Polish dream-
ers, but I cannot sympathize with those
Russophiles who, under the pretext of russification,
want to settle peasants in the landlord's mansion as representatives of the Russian nationality. Putting down the
revolt [of 1863] does not mean destroying traditions and
civilization, regardless of what
nationality they might be.

—*Prince V. P. Meshcherskii (1897)*

❖   Thus far we have spoken much of "nationality" and the various dominant perceptions among Russians concerning the diverse national groups
inhabiting the western lands and the Kingdom of Poland in the final
decades of Romanov rule there. In concentrating so heavily on nationality,
however, we have neglected another key element of Russian attitudes and
government policy in this region—history, particularly the history of two
large and hostile states, the Polish Commonwealth and Muscovy. It may
seem nonsensical to bring up the Polish Rzeczpospolita—a state that had
been declining since the seventeenth century and that had disappeared entirely at the end of the eighteenth—in a discussion of events occurring several generations after the final partition of Poland in 1795. But however absurd it may seem, any understanding of Russian attitudes and "state
interests" as perceived by contemporaries is impossible without an appreciation of the historical lessons lurking behind Russians' perceptions of
their role in these lands.

From the Russian point of view, the western territories were indisputably Russian. Kiev—the "mother of Russian cities" and site of the "Christening of Rus'"—was located here. Grodno, Vitebsk, Mogilev, and other towns also had a long "Russian" history. Only after the Mongol invasion of the mid-thirteenth century did the position of Russian sovereignty weaken, and in the following centuries the region came under Polish rule. From the Russian point of view, the several centuries of Polish rule over these lands had disastrous results for the local population.[1]

Local elites, previously "Russian" (Ukrainian, Belorussian), became polonized, often accepting the Catholic religion along with Polish culture. The founding of the Uniate church in the late sixteenth century as a way of bringing Orthodox peasants into the Catholic fold was only one of many nefarious (from the Russian viewpoint) Polish schemes to root out Russian culture here. Russians also emphasized the miserable conditions under which "Russian" serfs lived during these centuries, never failing to mention that the Polish lords considered their peasants not even human but mere *bydło* (cattle). Jews were employed by Poles as stewards and served as their agents in the oppression of the local "Russian" peasantry, thereby gaining the peasants' lasting enmity.[2] Thus political, social, religious, and national questions went hand in hand. Even after this territory had "returned" to the Russian state in the late eighteenth century, Polish elites continued to dominate, in many ways up to and beyond the 1863 rebellion.

When Peter Stolypin and others spoke after 1905 of "two state principles" at war in this region, they meant that the memory of the powerful Polish state remained strong and that, for Poles, the boundaries of the Polish state included the western territory. This is not the place to dispute such contentions; suffice it to say that for official Russia—and for significant parts of the Russian public—the Western Provinces were a contested region, claimed both by Poles and Russians.[3] Hence the primary goal of the Russian government needed to be the defense of the Russian and Orthodox element here and, conversely, the strict limiting of Polish Catholic influences. What Poles might justifiably see as repression remained for Russians simple defense. Both conceptions are on their own terms justifiable, and from a present-day point of view equally repugnant. But these were the predominant political and national stereotypes of the day. Either Polish or Russian: a third choice did not exist.[4]

Whereas the events of distant centuries—the Union of Brest at the end of the sixteenth century and the Khmelnytsky insurrection some fifty years later—were surprisingly often present in the minds of Russian administrators in the Western Provinces, the Russians did not have to delve so far back in history for examples of Polish perfidy. The examples of the Polish uprisings of 1830 and 1863 were much closer at hand.[5] Once again, the simple choice of words to describe these events revealed politics and, very often, national feelings. Russians, and particularly those in official positions, nearly always spoke of the mutiny *(miatezh)* of 1863; Poles and more liberal Russians referred rather to the insurrection *(powstanie)*. Speaking of mutiny, the Russians stressed the traitorous, disloyal action of the Poles. Choosing to speak of insurrection, Poles described instead the just rebellion of oppressed subjects against a despotic power. No matter which word was used, however, the specter of 1863 haunted both the western lands of the Russian Empire all the way to 1914. In Warsaw and Lublin—no less than in Kiev, Vilna, or Minsk—the effects and aftermath of 1863 did much to create the political, legal, and even social order in which all nationalities of the region lived. Hence, to appreciate the national situation of late imperial Russia's western borderlands one must go back repeatedly to the 1860s.

Reform and Revolt

In the western lands and the Kingdom of Poland, one may well say about attitudes and mentalities at the end of the nineteenth century that "all roads lead to 1863," or perhaps to a few years earlier, to Marquis Aleksander Wielopolski's aborted attempts at reform. So we start our prehistory in the early 1860s, the two prime players being Emperor Alexander II and Marquis Wielopolski.[6] Alexander, as is well known, aimed both to reform Russia and to retain his own power; that is, he desired social and economic development in order to finance the military and administrative reforms needed if the empire were to retain its great power status. Wielopolski seems an obvious ally of Alexander in such an effort: a basically conservative magnate, of impeccable aristocratic lineage, at home in the courts of Western and Central Europe. Wielopolski, like Alexander, realized that the "Metternich system" (or, in Russian, the system of Nicholas I) had outlived its time, and any hope of averting major social upheavals could be based only on some sort of political and social reform. Therein lay the rub: what kind of reform?

In the Kingdom of Poland, as throughout the Russian Empire, the reign of Alexander II began with high hopes and a good deal of social ferment, not to say anarchy.[7] The death of the hated Nicholas I, who had crushed the 1830 uprising with great brutality and put an end to many elements of Polish autonomy, could only be welcomed by the Poles. Many hoped that the new tsar would restore at least some degree of Polish autonomy; some aspired, indeed, to a restoration of the 1815 constitution that had been cast aside by Nicholas I after 1831. The status of the western territories was also an item on the Polish agenda: hopes were raised for their return to a newly autonomous Kingdom of Poland within the Russian Empire. It was clear that winds of change were blowing from St. Petersburg.

The man in charge of ushering in the new order in Russian Poland was Aleksander Wielopolski, a magnate with an impressive pedigree, but with the outward appearance (to quote one longtime Russian resident of Warsaw) of a "German Burger." Wielopolski stood for a conservative but nonetheless extensive reform, dictated from above for the good of all, something like the Prussian reformers of some half century before.[8] Relations between lord and peasant were to be modernized, with the abolition of compulsory labor duties *(panszczyzna)*. (Polish peasants, unlike their Russian brethren, had been legally emancipated since 1807. However, the continued existence of *corvée [barshchina,* in Russian] meant that the Polish peasantry in Russia remained for practical purposes enserfed until the 1860s. The 1807 "liberation" did not grant land to the peasants.) The Jews were to receive equal rights, and in general the estate-bound social order was to give way gradually to a class-and money-driven system. Such were the ideals that guided the Wielopolski reforms.[9]

On the Russian side of the equation, Alexander II was not steadfastly opposed to change in the Kingdom of Poland, but he wanted this reform to take place in a calm orderly manner. He refused to countenance a return to the Constitution of 1815, or "personal union" of the Congress Kingdom with the Russian Empire. On a visit to Warsaw in May 1856 he emphasized the need for sober thinking, admonishing the assembled marshals of the Polish nobility: "C'est à Vous, Messieurs, de me faciliter ma tâche, mais je Vous le repète, point de rêveries, point de rêveries" (It is up to you, Sirs, to help me with my task, but I repeat, absolutely no daydreams, no daydreams).[10] Alexander's words mirror his cautious desire to reach a reconciliation with the Polish nobility as well as his fear of the notorious Polish tendency for idle and dangerous political dreaming.

One should not disparage Wielopolski's accomplishments. In his few years at the head of the civil government in Warsaw, he helped introduce several important reforms. The Polish State Council, moribund since 1831, was resurrected, thereby restoring to the Congress Kingdom some measure of the autonomy it had lost in 1815. A separate Polish educational council was reestablished, with Wielopolski at its head. Legal restrictions on Jews were abolished by the law of May 24, 1862. Peasant *corvée* was converted into cash payments as the first step toward emancipation. In certain respects (in particular the legal situation of the Jews), the Polish provinces could be seen as exemplary for the entire empire. It is certainly not the case that the 1863 insurrection was set off by a specific refusal of St. Petersburg to take Polish needs and demands into consideration.[11]

Unfortunately, these reforms did nothing to quiet the growing unrest in Russian Poland. On the contrary (following Tocqueville's classic scheme), the lessening of repression led not to satisfaction and calm but to demands for further concessions. Minor incidents and confusion led to armed clashes, which led to patriotic funeral demonstrations, which in turn led to further bloodshed. Efforts on the part of both Wielopolski and the Russian authorities to defuse tensions proved fruitless. Martial law was declared in Warsaw on October 2, 1861. When the Grand Duke Konstantin Nikolaevich arrived in Warsaw some nine months later to take up his duties as viceroy *(namestnik),* he was shot and wounded by the Polish worker Ludwik Jaroszyński.[12] By the end of 1861, one Polish historian had written, "all hopes for a change of course in Russia appeared extinguished"; the "Wielopolski system" had come to an impasse, and violence seemed inevitable.[13] An ill-advised attempt to draft some ten thousand troublemakers into the Russian army proved the drop that made the glass overflow, and open rebellion exploded in early 1863.

The specific events of the rebellion, admirably described in great detail by S. Kieniewicz, concern us less than its general contours and, particularly, the "lessons" learned by the Russian government.[14] The rebellion started in Warsaw and soon spread throughout the Kingdom of Poland and into the Western Provinces. The insurgents promised peasants an equitable land settlement, but on the whole the peasant masses remained indifferent to the uprising. Particularly in the non-Polish provinces, few peasants aided the insurrectionists, and many actively opposed them and helped the Russian forces crush the uprising.[15] In Warsaw, Jews and Poles joined together to oppose the Russians, but this Jewish-Polish fraternity (which was to take on the trappings of myth in the ensuing decades) was neither universal throughout the Polish provinces nor deeply rooted in either society.[16] The cooperation between Jews and Poles did, however, confront the Russian government with a frightening prospect of united opposition to Russian rule.

The eruption of the Polish rebellion caught Russia at a sensitive moment. The edict liberating the serfs had been issued two years earlier but in most areas had not come into effect. The Russian army was still smarting from the bloodletting of the Crimean War. On the international scene, the recent defeat of the Austrians in northern Italy by combined Piedmontese and French armies had increased French prestige, leading many to think that Emperor Napoleon III would use his combined military and political power in defense of the Poles. In the end the Western European powers limited themselves to a few diplomatic protests, but at the time the prospects of major war to many seemed very real indeed. The Poles had found the Russian Empire's Achilles' heel; the Russian government was determined they should never be in a position to do so again.

With the outbreak of insurrection or mutiny (depending on one's views and nationality), the Polish fate was sealed. True enough, a reform would come, but it would be a reform aimed directly at crushing Polish freedoms, designed to split the Polish elite—szlachta and magnates—from the broad masses of the Polish population. The Russian government exerted considerable efforts to mitigate Polish separateness (odrębność) and to undermine the economic and cultural supremacy of the Polish intellectual and social elite, especially in areas populated by "Russian" peasants. Even in the Polish Kingdom, however, Russian policy after 1863 aimed at putting an end to autonomous institutions, tying the Polish provinces more tightly to the Russian center both politically and economically, and in general strengthening Russian power.

Post-1863 Repressions

In the Western Provinces stern measures were taken—usually associated with the figure of Count M. N. Muraviev—to undermine and root out Polish culture in that region.[17] As the insurrection gained strength in the Northwest Provinces in the spring of 1863, Alexander II begged Muraviev to take charge of the area and to save "at least" the Lithuanian (and Belorussian) provinces for Russia. The extreme agitation expressed in the tsar's words reflected the alarm felt in official circles over the uprising. Muraviev (if we are to believe his memoirs) reluctantly accepted the post of governor general but, once having taken up the position, acted energetically to crush the Polish rebels. The situation in the Northwest at this moment was, in his words, critical:

> I found the country in a state of extreme anarchy. . . . Thus we were faced with the task not only of crushing the open rebellion, but with the need to forbid criminal schemes and to do away with the very possibility of continuing the mutiny and, on the other hand, to promote to the greatest extent of our powers the unification of the country with the rest of Russia.[18]

Here we have Muraviev's program in a nutshell: crush the uprising; force local Poles to realize that any future rebellion would be fruitless and suicidal; and strengthen Russian cultural, political, and economic power. In general terms, this remained the government's explicit policy in the Western Provinces until the end of the Russian Empire. In that sense one may draw a direct line from Muraviev to Peter Stolypin.

The brutality of Muraviev's short tenure as governor general of Vilna cannot be denied; it is not for nothing that he has gone down in Russian and Polish history as Muraviev the Hangman. Nor did he or any of his many supporters deny the brutal measures taken. Rather, they insisted that decisive measures were needed to cow the local rebels, who were themselves engaging in acts of revolution and terrorism, and to demonstrate to any wavering locals (including the large Jewish community) that resistance to the Russian authorities would be futile. This kind of resolute policy also found broad support, at least initially, in St. Petersburg and among the Russian public.[19] And one should not underestimate the amount of prestige that Muraviev enjoyed among patriotic Russians and officialdom even after his departure from Vilna in 1865 and his subsequent death. After all, the Russian government never repudiated Muraviev's policy and even erected a monument in his honor in Vilna in 1898. Perhaps the cautious words of the *Military Encyclopedia* best sum up the diverse views on this figure, pointing out that his "extraordinary energy" prevented the explosion of open rebellion in the Northwest Provinces, particularly by deterring local peasants from aiding the Poles, while, on the other hand, "he earned the intense hatred of the Poles and their friends, who to this day cannot forgive Muraviev his severe, but completely expedient, considering the circumstances of this day, repressions and his russifying policies." One may question the expediency of measures that caused so much hatred even generations later, but certainly Muraviev's importance remains beyond question.[20]

Repression and punitive measures made up the most striking part of Muraviev's policy, but he did not limit himself to such measures. Particularly after the immediate danger of rebellion had been stifled, Muraviev recognized the need to win over the peasant masses in the area. He described his primary concern as being the prosperity of the rural population. In particular the government needed to strengthen the economic position of the peasants who, along with local Old Believers, constituted the only loyal group in the area. As for the nobility and Catholic clergy *(shliakhta, pany i ksendzy)*, "they were and always will be our enemies." The Russian government should abandon any effort to woo these groups and work instead toward "the definitive affirmation of peasant property and [thus] establish on firm foundations the principle of Russian nationality and Orthodoxy." To this end the government must eliminate the economic dependence of Orthodox peasants on Polish landlords, build more Orthodox schools, and expand the number of Russian schools in the area, "not only among Christians, but also among Jews," bringing in teachers from the central Russian provinces and keeping the Catholic clergy under close surveillance.[21] In order to lessen Catholic and Polish influence over Lithuanians, Muraviev advocated the teaching of "Sarmogitian" *(zhmudskii,* that is, Lithuanian) using "Russian letters."[22] To sum up, all government efforts were aimed at weakening the Poles and strengthening the Russian and Orthodox cause.

One of Muraviev's lieutenants saw the most important legacy of those years as the achievement that "this land was above all recognized to be Russian; our press helped in the strengthening of its Russian character." Although significant numbers of Catholics would remain here, even they would be forced to admit that the land itself was "Russian" and "Orthodox."[23] According to this line of argumentation, before 1863 Russia had not fully recognized its mission in the Western Provinces (particularly in the Belorussian and Lithuanian area). The Polish threat posed in 1863, however, awakened both the Russian government and Russian public feeling to the need to reclaim these lost Russian provinces from impending polonization. It was under the banner of such a reclamation that Russian policy was to be formed and carried out in the ensuing decades.

The point of departure for post-1863 imperial policy was, naturally enough, to prevent any further uprisings. The best way to do this appeared to be by weakening the two groups most directly implicated in the uprising: the szlachta (Polish gentry) and the Catholic clergy. Thus many estates were confiscated (often sold or awarded to Russians), monasteries were closed, restrictions were introduced forbidding Poles from purchasing land in the Western Provinces, priests were exiled or forced into monasteries, and educational institutions were taken out of the hands of the Poles and russified. Poles were eliminated from most employment in government administration and education in the area; it became easier for Poles to make a bureaucratic career outside the Congress Kingdom and the Western Provinces.[24]

As the above comments have made perhaps excessively clear, the one nationality targeted for repression in the post-1863 years was the Polish, and most specifically the Polish intelligentsia, Catholic clergy, and szlachta. One need not look far to find the reasons for this. In the Congress Kingdom, of course, Poles were numerically, economically, and culturally predominant. But even in the western territory, especially in the six northwest Lithuanian and Belorussian provinces, Poles constituted the hegemonic cultural influence and the strongest economic group.[25] In the mid-nineteenth century, elite and intelligentsia in this area tended to be Polish by birth or education or both. In the West, Polish magnates and szlachta owned more than 60 percent of the manorial estates in the three Lithuanian provinces and nearly half in the Belorussian provinces.[26] The ruling class in the entire region, both in the Polish Kingdom and in the West, was of Polish nationality, and it was this group that the Russian government set out to master.

The most important measure taken to break the economic hold of the Poles on the western region was the interdiction of Poles to purchase land in these nine provinces, set down in the decree of December 10, 1865.[27] Persons "of Polish descent" were not allowed to purchase land in the Western Provinces again until 1905, and even then they were permitted to acquire landed property only from other Poles, not from Russians.[28] At the same time, many Polish estates both in the West and in Poland that had belonged to participants in the insurrection were sold off at bargain prices to Russians.[29] Polish landowners were also subject to a special tax on their lands, which further exacerbated their economic condition and encouraged them to sell their lands. All of this could not help but weaken the Polish economic position in the West. Nonetheless, even in 1905 Poles continued to hold a majority of the private land in the Lithuanian provinces and a goodly amount in Belorussia, which did much to deter the government from introducing zemstva in this area.[30]

On the cultural front, government measures were also harsh and specifically aimed at breaking Polish cultural hegemony. The lands of Catholic monasteries were confiscated, and the rights of priests, especially in education, were severely circumscribed. Polish teachers lost their positions and were replaced by pedagogues from the Russian interior. Catholic priests disappeared from local schools, which led to the absurd situation whereby Catholic religious classes were sometimes taught by Orthodox or Lutheran teachers. In general, the Polish language was reduced to a barely tolerated status in the Western Provinces.[31]

The most obvious symbol of Polish culture was the Polish language. Russian policy aimed quite ruthlessly to eliminate the use of Polish in education during the decade or so after 1864. At the same time Russian replaced Polish for practically all official and public uses. To quote a modern historian on the situation in the Western Provinces, "The Polish language was eliminated from all official correspondence, the educational system, and civil registry records. Even Polish shop signs were not allowed." Contemporaries noted that even conversations in Polish in public places were frowned upon and could have unpleasant consequences.[32]

The situation in the ethnically Polish provinces was somewhat different. Here the government could not claim, as it did in the West, that this territory was merely returning to Russia after a period of foreign domination. The Russian government respected, albeit grudgingly, Polish culture and did not, at least explicitly, connive to destroy it altogether. Nonetheless, the political supremacy of Russian had to be impressed upon the Poles, and any signs of separatism had to be rooted out once and for all. At first, it appeared that political reforms in the Polish provinces would be relatively mild, at least in the cultural sphere. But the "logic" of the harsh anti-Polish measures taken in the Western Provinces soon spread to this area as well.

The cornerstone of Russian reforms in the Polish Kingdom was peasant reform. Before the rebellion had even been totally crushed, a team of three Russian high officials headed by N. Miliutin embarked on a journey through Poland to determine the nature of local peasant needs.[33] As in the Western Provinces, though perhaps with even less justification, the Russian government saw in the peasantry the only reliable social class. Since the upper classes were seen (for the most part, justifiably) as the main instigators of the rebellion, the government hoped to bring the peasant masses over to the Russian side by favorable treatment.

The peasant masses thus profited, at least initially, from the reforms. Here the Russian government could kill two birds with one stone: by liberating the Polish peasants with generous allotments of land, the tsarist administration could both weaken the untrustworthy szlachta and (so it was hoped) establish a benevolent relationship between the Polish peasantry and the emperor. Unlike their counterparts in Russia proper, Polish peasants obtained their land without being burdened with redemption payments. Polish landowners, conversely, lost a good deal more by the terms of the peasant emancipation than did the Russian gentry.[34] As a result of this demagogic reform, St. Petersburg hoped to secure the loyalty of Polish peasants. Until the very end of Romanov rule in Poland, this ideology remained still intact, if rather tattered: the only indigenous group in the Vistula region on which St. Petersburg felt it could depend was the peasantry.[35] In a sense, the Russian authorities defined "Polish," at least in the political sense, as congruent with the upper classes of the Polish nation. Here, as so often, we see the pre-modern character of tsarist conceptions of nationality.

As for education, at first the Russian administrator N. A. Miliutin rejected a completely russified educational system in the Polish provinces, advocating instruction in various languages for the different ethnic groups. Soon such a liberal approach fell by the wayside, however, and the Statute of 1866 established a firmly Russian curriculum. In 1869 the Polish Szkoła Główna was transformed into a Russian university, and in the ensuing decade the educational system in the Kingdom of Poland became almost purely Russian, run by teachers from the interior of the Russian Empire who were noted for their contempt for all things Polish.[36]

Parallel to this official system of schooling there arose many illegal underground schools (both Polish and Lithuanian), which had to operate under extremely unfavorable conditions, always overshadowed by fear of discovery by the Russian authorities. One result of the Russian educational policy was that, even at the turn of the century, two-thirds of the population of the Vistula land was illiterate.[37] As in the Western Provinces, so too in Warsaw and other ethnically Polish provinces, Russian was the language used in courts, government offices, even on shop signs. True enough, Polish was also allowed on these signs, but it had to be written in smaller letters and after or below the Russian version. (The requirement to translate all Polish signs had the amusing effect of encouraging shop signs in French [Coiffure, Café], which needed no Russian translation.) In short, everything was done in the decade following 1864 to make educated Poles feel themselves foreigners in their own land.[38]

One of the few aspects of Wielopolski's reforms that was left untouched after 1863 was the Jewish statute of 1862. Whereas laws on Jews in the Kingdom of Poland and the Pale of Settlement had never been coordinated, before 1862 the Jewish legal situation was actually more onerous in the Polish provinces than in the Pale.[39] With the promulgating of the 1862 law, Jews in the Kingdom of Poland suddenly saw the situation reversed: now they enjoyed significantly broader legal rights than their brethren outside the Polish provinces. After 1863, despite several attempts to set back the clock, Jewish quasi-equal rights in the Vistula region were never abolished.[40] As restrictions on Jews in the Pale of Settlement were tightened, especially after 1881, and with the economic opportunities in the Polish provinces, thousands of Jews from the Lithuanian, Belorussian, and Ukrainian provinces predictably migrated to the cities of Warsaw and Łódź. This influx of "Russian" Jews, the so-called Litwaks, was to exacerbate already tense Polish-Jewish relations (see chapter 8).

In the decades following 1863, as Russian commentators never tired of pointing out, economic development in Poland had been most impressive. The customs barrier between the Congress Kingdom and the rest of the Russian Empire had been abolished in 1851, opening the enormous Russian market to Polish manufactures. The decades between the crushing of the uprising and the death of Alexander III may be rightly called the formative years of Polish industrialization; their literary reflection can be seen in such works as Bolesław Prus's *The Doll* (1887–1889) and Władysław Reymont's *The Promised Land* (1899). To quote a recent study, "A combination of these factors [Russia's protectionist policies, a slump in agriculture, railroad construction] produced, in the decades following the January Insurrection, a veritable industrial revolution in Congress Poland. To all practical purposes this revolution was completed by 1890." Russian public opinion was unanimous in its belief that tsarist policy in Poland had exerted a positive effect, at least on the Kingdom's economic development.[41] One may also observe the simultaneous growth of the sugar industry and the railroads in the Southwest Provinces. On the whole, the economic development of the region, even when the relative stagnation of the North-west Provinces is taken into account, compared favorably with the economic growth in the Russian Empire as a whole.[42]

At the same time, most of the political reforms of Alexander II's reign were preempted in this area because of the uprising. The zemstvo reform, despite initial hesitation, was shelved indefinitely, and whereas the municipal reforms of 1870 and 1892 were implemented (with certain amendments) in the nine Western Provinces, the cities of the Polish Kingdom remained without elective governments. Similarly the Polish legal system, although reformed in 1875, did not provide for juries as in Russia proper. In a sense, Russian Poland and the western territory (to a lesser extent) missed the first, liberal stage of Alexander II's reign. In these areas the "post-1866 reaction" began three years earlier.[43]

By 1875, the legal framework of restrictions was pretty well established. The autonomy of the Kingdom of Poland, along with its very name, had been officially abolished by this time;[44] the Szkoła Główna in Warsaw had been turned into the russifying Warsaw University; and Poles were forbidden to purchase land in the Western Provinces and were subjected to special land taxes designed to encourage the sale of land—to Russians, of course. From elementary education to the courts to the highest level of administration, Poles in both the Western Provinces and in the Vistula lands could only feel themselves to be a defeated and barely tolerated minority.

The restrictions on the Poles were paralleled in various ways by laws and administrative orders aimed against other nationalities. For example, the notorious Valuev circular of 1863 forbade the publishing of works in Ukrainian and declared that the Ukrainian language "did not, does not, and cannot exist [*Nikakogo osobennogo malorosiiskogo iazyka ne bylo, net i byt' ne mozhet*]."[45] Printing in the Lithuanian language was allowed only in Cyrillic script, a restriction unacceptable to most literate Lithuanians that led to an almost complete cessation of publishing in that language in the Russian Empire.[46] For the Jewish residents of the western territories, the edifice of repression was crowned by the Temporary Laws of May 1882, destined to remain in effect until 1917. In short, the decades after the uprising of 1863 were a difficult time indeed for the nationalities of Russia's western borderlands.

Another significant indirect by-product of the 1863 rebellion was the final elimination of the Uniate church in the Russian Empire. After the 1839 conversion of the Belorussian Uniates to Orthodoxy there remained only a small Uniate community in the empire, concentrated in the Podlasie area just west of the Bug River in the Polish provinces of Lublin and Siedlce. Because of the participation of certain Uniate clergy and monasteries in the 1863 rebellion, the Russian government looked upon the remnants of that church with deep suspicion. A series of measures aimed at "purifying" Uniate rituals from Catholic influences led to peasant unrest, administrative repression, and finally to the absorption of the local Uniate church into Orthodoxy in 1875. For Russians, at least officially, this "reunion" of Uniates and Orthodoxy was the expression of local desires to free themselves from polonizing influences. For Poles—and for many former Uniates, as the following decades were to show—the elimination of the Uniate church was an act of administrative brutality and a violation of religious toleration.[47]

❖   The discussion in this chapter has been dominated by the question of Polish-Russian relations and government repressions aimed at Poles, particularly the non-peasant classes, after 1863. This emphasis is by no means accidental: from 1863 to the outbreak of World War I, the Russian Empire's "nationality policy," at least in this region, was directed primarily against local elites who could present a possible separatist threat to the empire. The ideology of peasant loyalty remained strong, though not entirely unshaken. In a sense, the Polish enemy was limited, by definition, to the educated classes and the Catholic clergy. As for the other nationalities in the area, they were less directly the targets of policy after 1863, though often affected indirectly, as in the case of the Lithuanians mentioned above. As for the Jews, on the whole the 1860s and 1870s were decades of expanding, not contracting, rights (relatively speaking, of course). Only with the assassination of Alexander II and the ensuing pogroms did the legal situation of Russia's Jewish community begin once again to worsen.

A listing of repressive laws and administrative orders can hardly do justice to the actual situation in this region, particularly when one takes into consideration the great gap in the Russian Empire between law and reality. Whereas the repressions of the 1860s and 1870s certainly had a great influence on the daily life of the region, restrictions and prohibitions were only one part of the story. This was also the time of significant cultural and political development among the nationalities of this region (see chapter 6). But the actual interpretation and carrying out of restrictive measures in the region also depended greatly on local administrators and the overall situation in the empire.

Immediately upon Muraviev's departure from Vilna, a change was noted in the local administration. In his memoirs Muraviev complained bitterly that his successor only pretended to continue the hard anti-Polish line, while in fact showing a good deal of sympathy to the local Polish gentry class. Similarly, Muraviev's erstwhile lieutenant, A. Mosolov, wrote that the new governor general was more interested in pedantic administrative detail than in firmly anchoring the Russian cause there.[48] Perhaps even more ominously for this cause, Mosolov and Muraviev both described intrigues in St. Petersburg that were aimed against Muraviev's policy, fueled both by Polish magnates and by Russian bureaucratic hatred of the vigorous governor general. Meshcherskii wrote that the minister of internal affairs P. Valuev found reprehensible both the man Muraviev and his repressive policy. Besides personal animosities, social fears fueled opposition to Muraviev. His program was based on concessions to the "Russian" peasantry against the Polish landed class, and it was this social element that many conservatives in St. Petersburg found difficult to stomach. The class sympathy between Russian administrators and Polish landowners may have somewhat mitigated the carrying out of anti-Polish measures, but it hardly amounted to a change in policy. Rather, Russian administrators could help Poles to make land purchases, for example, by defining these purchases as being necessary for consolidating estate boundaries or by simply considering the land purchaser "Russian"—after all, there were no firm legal characteristics that differentiated "Russian" from "Pole." On the other hand, such small concessions to the Poles were more than overweighed by a tendency that soon became universal, to define "Pole" as "Catholic" and thereby to extend restrictions even to peasants, including Lithuanians and Belorussians.[49]

The situation was similar in the Kingdom of Poland. Count F. F. Berg took over the position of viceroy in 1863 and proceeded in the next years to implement a program very similar to Muraviev's, even to the levying of special taxes *(kontributsii)* on the inhabitants of Warsaw and the rest of the Polish provinces. Although some Russians questioned the ability of Berg, a Baltic German, to defend Russian state interests in the Polish provinces properly, his years as governor general were anything but conciliatory toward the Poles. When Berg died in 1874, the position of viceroy was abolished, but most of its duties were transferred to the new governor general of Warsaw, P. Kotzebue, who held this position for the rest of the decade.[50] Thus, for the entire period during which the administrative autonomy of the Kingdom of Poland was dismantled and distinctively Polish political, social, and educational institutions were abolished, Baltic Germans held the supreme military and administrative position in the Kingdom of Poland—or, to speak officially, the Vistula land.

The latter half of Alexander II's reign, and particularly the 1870s, was a difficult time in Russian history. These years saw the development of the "nihilists," the growing popularity of radical thought and socialism among Russian youth, and the beginnings of Russian revolutionary terrorism.[51] The fear of revolution at the center lessened vigilance on the periphery or, at least, shifted the Russian government's attention away from the Poles in Warsaw and Vilna and toward the nihilists in Moscow and St. Petersburg. The international situation—particularly growing tensions in the Balkans— also occupied the government's attention. This was the heyday of Panslavism, and after the danger of rebellion in the Polish provinces had been crushed, many Russians began to see a reconciliatory policy toward Poland as one step toward the healing of this greatest wound in the Slavic body politic. Thus by the late 1870s, official Russia saw its most immediate tasks in the curbing of revolutionary tendencies at home and, on the internal scene, in defending Russian and Orthodox interests in the Balkans.[52] To quote a contemporary:

> At the beginning of the second half of the 1870s, government and [Russian] society were completely engrossed in the events taking place on the Balkan

peninsula [and by the ensuing Russo-Turkish war], and immediately following the end of that war the villainous assassination attempts carried out
by nihilist bands distracted the government from any other issues.[53]

Thus, this writer continued, the Russian government neglected its task of
narrowing the distance between the borderlands and the Russian interior.
One might also attribute the lessening ardor of restrictive measures in the
1870s to simple inertia: by this time calm and order had been restored in
the region, neither Poles nor any other national group appeared in any way
ready for rebellion, and the government was faced with more pressing issues. Various legal restrictions remained in force and continued to stymie
the cultural and economic growth of the region, but neither new measures
nor stricter enforcement of old laws were forthcoming.

After many failed attempts, the nihilists finally achieved their goal in
early 1881, putting an end simultaneously to the life of Alexander II and to
an era in the history of the Russian Empire. The new tsar, Alexander III,
harbored none of his father's liberal sympathies. He soon embarked on a
program of harsh reaction and increasing limitation of non-Russian rights
and institutions in the borderlands. The summer of 1881 witnessed the
worst wave of pogroms yet seen in the Russian Empire. The government's
response to this crisis was indicative of its approach to nationality issues as
a whole. In effect, the so-called Temporary Laws of May 3, 1882, blamed
the pogroms on Jewish exploitation of peasants and thus restricted Jews
from settling outside of urban areas in the Pale, disallowed the purchase or
leasing of rural land by Jews, and forbade Jews from doing business on
Sundays and Christian holidays. Although the word "temporary" is repeated twice in the text of this short law, it was fated never to be super-
seded.[54] The law's essence was to narrow and restrict the "injurious" activities of Jews, and speaking in general, this approach was to characterize the
policy of Alexander III's reign toward all non-Russians.

A Russian historian of nationalist tendencies was later to term Alexander III "Tsar-Nationalist." Although Alexander was hardly a modern nationalist, he was a patriotic Russian and worked to strengthen the Russian
state, not only in the sense of crushing revolution in the center but also by
restricting local privilege on the periphery. His russifying policies in the
Baltic provinces and Finland and his anti-Semitism, coupled with his commitment to political reaction, have earned him a decidedly negative historical profile.[55]

In the Western Provinces and Kingdom of Poland, Alexander's reign
brought with it increased pressure against local nationalities. From the perspective of Warsaw, anti-Polish measures of the 1880s are associated with
two names: I. V. Gurko, governor general of Warsaw from 1883 to 1894,
and A. Apukhtin, head (*kurator*) of the Warsaw educational district (which
covered the whole of the Vistula territory) for nearly a generation from 1879
to 1897. Gurko was the faithful executor of Alexander III's repressive policy
toward any liberal or socialist trends, crushing the first Polish socialist

party (Proletariat) in the 1880s. A conservative Russian source summed up Gurko's policies in the following words:

> Even now [the period of the 1880s] is known as "the time of Gurko," so strong was the mark left by his personality and activities there. For the foreign [*inorodch.*] population of the western territory [*sic*] Gurko was a true representative of strong authority, a formidable [*groznyi*] but just power firmly linking the borderland with the center of the empire.

Poles, naturally enough, took a more negative view of the "reign of Gurko." Many were offended by Gurko's refusal to allow Polish nobles and Catholic bishops to speak French in his presence, and the governor general seemed to go out of his way to offend Polish sensibilities.[56]

Similarly Apukhtin is linked with a dark period in Polish culture—"the Apukhtin night [*apuchtińska noc*]." Under his leadership, pupils were forbidden to speak Polish even among themselves, spying was encouraged, and slight infractions of rules could lead to draconian punishments. Russians, on the other hand, praised Apukhtin's activities as helping strengthen Russian culture and political loyalty among the youth of the Vistula land. To quote one of his colleagues and admirers:

> Aleksandr L'vovich Apukhtin's services will remain for Russia ever remembered. His activities are of historical significance, and for his firm character, unbending will, and unwavering persistence in his efforts toward the implementation of general-state principles [*obshchegosudarstvennye printsipy*], for loyalty to throne and fatherland Aleksander L'vovich Apukhtin is worthy to assume a place along with the outstanding statesmen and public figures of the Russian land.[57]

The 1880s were a decade of repression throughout Russia. On the empire's peripheries, however, the general repression was exacerbated by an attack on non-Russian cultures (the trend represented in Warsaw by Apukhtin and Gurko). But the anti-Polish actions of these two men should not blind us to the fact that no new policy was inaugurated during these years. Indeed, Apukhtin assumed his post some two years before Alexander III ascended to the throne. Although both Apukhtin and Gurko worked steadily (and, one must say, sincerely) to strengthen the position of Russian power and culture among the Poles, no new laws or change in policy was necessary for their activities. The general line laid down since 1863 was merely continued, albeit with a degree of harsh and brutal consistency that had been absent for most of the 1870s. In the Western Provinces even less of a change in policy—except for the strengthened repressions against the Jewish community—can be detected during Alexander III's reign. On the whole the specifically new and aggressive anti-German measures introduced in the Baltic provinces did not find a precise parallel in the Polish and Western provinces.

Nonetheless, the years of Alexander III's reign were grim ones for all non-Russians. It comes as no surprise that his demise went unmourned in the western borderlands and that Poles greeted the new tsar, Nicholas II, with high hopes. One of the leaders of the Polish "conciliators" *(ugodowcy)*, Erazm Piltz, wrote of a "turning point in Russian-Polish relations."[58] The hopes of the Polish and other non-Russian communities were paralleled by similar sentiments in Russian society, which were symbolized by the famous letter of the Tver zemstvo to the new emperor, speaking of aspirations for a greater public voice in government affairs. Liberal Russians and non-Russians alike were unfortunately to be disappointed by the response from Nicholas II, who dismissed these "senseless dreams" and vowed to continue the policies of his father.

Whereas Nicholas II refused to embark on any specifically reconciliatory policy on the borderlands, he and the empress did visit Warsaw in 1897, a move interpreted as at least a moral concession to Polish feelings. Governor general Gurko was replaced by the more agreeable A. Imeretinskii, and Apukhtin retired from his position as head of education in the Polish provinces. Soon after Nicholas's ascent to the throne, the long dormant issues of elective municipal government in the Polish provinces and of zemstva in the western land were raised both in the press and in official circles in St. Petersburg. Thus, even though Nicholas did not consciously embark on a new policy on the borderlands, new currents began to make themselves felt, and long-delayed reforms were once again considered. To take just one example, by 1894 it was abundantly clear, even to Russian administrators, that the old system of bureaucratic rule was unable to cope with the problems of a rapidly developing region. Education, medicine, roads, sanitation—the miserable conditions in all these areas had become a matter of public outrage. Clearly, the only way to improve the situation would be to open up possibilities for the "public" (meaning the educated, politically reliable public) to participate in governing the area. The most obvious institution to effect this kind of societal opening would be the zemstvo, already in place for three decades in most of European Russia (we shall consider the government's attempts to find a way of fitting the zemstvo institution to the largely non-Russian region of the Western Provinces in chapter 7).

The revolution of 1905 formed a major caesura in the reign of Nicholas II. It ushered in a new semi-constitutional and semi-parliamentary government in Russia, significantly eased censorship, allowed for the first time true religious freedom, and brought (at least initially) important concessions for non-Russian languages and cultures.[59] The disturbances of 1905 were particularly intense on the empire's western borderlands, including the Baltic region and the industrial centers of the Polish Kingdom. Here social, political, and national movements amalgamated, making a strict differentiation of "national" and "social" demands impossible. One historian has gone so far as to speak of the "Springtime of Non-Russian Nations" in 1905–1907.[60] While the revolutionary years did bring about significant political concessions for non-Russians, the events of that turbulent time also reconfirmed official Russia's distrust of non-Russians, most particularly

Poles and Jews. After 1905 any concessions in the Polish and Western provinces could be opposed not only on the basis of 1863 but also with arguments from the more recent "mutiny" of 1905.

In the years after 1905, the Russian Empire struggled desperately to cope with social, political, and national problems that ultimately proved beyond its powers.[61] (Three of the most important government projects for reform in this region are considered as case studies in the following chapters.) In general terms, it is possible to see a parallel between the Russian Empire's uneasy political position between autocratic and constitutional government in its no less precarious balancing between Russian nationalism and dynastic "cosmopolitanism" during this period. The crisis of conscience that the Russian Empire was undergoing after 1905 also affected its self-image as a multinational state. On one hand, the predominance of the Russian nationality and Orthodox church had to be maintained, as before; but on the other, the religious freedom granted in 1905, more open press (in a variety of languages), and the need to deal with public opinion confronted the imperial government with new tasks and burdens that had no analogy in previous decades.

❖   To sum up, for the Russian government at the end of the nineteenth century, when regarding the Western Provinces and Poland, memories of 1863–1864 overshadowed any considerations for political reform and liberalization. The specter of 1863 continued to haunt the region—and St. Petersburg—throughout the reign of Nicholas II. Opponents of political reform in the area or of improved relations with the Poles would point to 1863 as an example of Polish perfidy and treachery. Within Polish society, the advocates of reconciliation (*ugoda*) would insist that the Poles had learned their lesson after 1864, that the Polish romantic revolutionary of the early nineteenth century had perished in that senseless and bloody struggle.[62] Only those who completely rejected the possibility of reform within the framework of the Russian state—the socialists, for example— did not feel compelled to take a stance on 1863.[63] In one respect, however, all agreed: the year 1864 marked the beginning of a new era for Poles both inside the Russian Empire and outside its borders as well as for Polono-Russian relations. We should add that it was a new era for the other inhabitants of the Kingdom of Poland and the western region as well.

What we find, then, on the western borderlands of the Russian Empire in the period after 1863 are various non-coordinated policies aimed against Poles and Jews, or, to use the government's own rhetoric, "to protect local, 'rooted' Russians," and most especially to preserve the Orthodox church against the Catholic. This "policy" (the word seems hardly appropriate for this amalgam of different laws and administrative orders) ran in fits and starts. It was especially oppressive, at least on paper, in the decade or so after 1863 and then again during the 1880s, but it was never consistently and efficiently carried out.[64] The gap between law and reality was huge, a con-

stant subject of discussion and complaints both in government and in public circles during the period.[65] One should keep in mind that, for members
of national minorities such as Poles or Jews, government inefficiency and
corruption often provided paths to circumvent, at least for a time, restrictions and exclusionary laws.

During the reign of Nicholas II, this general picture was further complicated by two factors. The first was the increasing strength of nationalism
among minority nationalities. To be sure, neither Zionism nor Ukrainian
separatism, nor even the newly militant Polish National Democracy Party,
presented a real and immediate threat to the integrity of the empire at that
moment, but their movements certainly had great potential for disruption,
and this potential did not remain unnoticed by imperial officials.[66] The second was the new semi-constitutional order ushered in by the October Manifesto that made it imperative for the government to take its case to the
people, thereby opening the way for a more overtly Russian-nationalist
policy, usually associated with the figure of Premier Peter Stolypin. Just
how much Stolypin deserves this reputation as arch-nationalist is another
question, and one that will be considered in reference to the specific issues
discussed later. But it cannot be denied that contemporaries saw the post-
1905 period as more restrictive and oppressive toward minority nations
than the first half of Nicholas's reign.[67]

In this chapter I have attempted to sketch out a narrative describing in
broad terms the Russian government's policy in the Western and Polish
provinces. The actual population of this region has appeared here only as a
shadow, the object of repressions and restrictions. In fact this half century
was a crucial time in the cultural, political, and even economic development of the peoples inhabiting the western borderlands of the Russian Empire. This was, after all, the era of Sholom Aleichem, Isaac Loeb Perets,
Lesia Ukrainka, and the Nobel prize–winning Henryk Sienkiewicz. During
these decades Lithuanian and Ukrainian national movements came of age,
modern political Zionism was born, and the first signs of Belorussian nationalism emerged. A detailed account of the political and cultural development of these nations would explode the framework of this volume, but
it is important to consider the changes that these decades wrought within
the various nationalities. In the following chapter I shall attempt to outline
those developments.

National Awakenings

The Peoples of the Western Provinces and the Kingdom of Poland

1863–1914

We are living at a time of extreme animation of
national and nationalist feelings among all
peoples inhabiting the Russian Empire.

—*M. Slavinskii (1910)*

❖   The second half of the nineteenth century was a period of national
and nationalist ferment throughout Europe. Between 1848 and 1914, Germany and Italy were united as nation-states; Romania, Bulgaria, and Serbia
were liberated from the Turkish yoke; and in the far West, Irish nationalists
demanded home rule for their island nation. This ferment was nowhere
stronger than in the multinational Habsburg and Romanov Empires. Particularly after 1863, with the relative decline of Polish cultural and economic domination in the western borderlands, cultural and political movements among Lithuanians, Jews, Belorussians, and Ukrainians developed,
gained strength, and by the second decade of the twentieth century, were
beginning to challenge not only Polish but even Russian cultural and political hegemony in the region. At the same time, new forms of Polish and
Russian nationalism took shape in response to new political circumstances
and, not least of all, in order to counter the threat of minority nationalisms.

In recent decades, historians and social philosophers have sketched a
theoretical model to explain the emergence of nationalist movements. We

have already considered the works of Ernest Gellner and Benedict Anderson when discussing the theoretical complications of the terms "nation" and "state" and their interaction in the modern world. In certain respects these rather abstract models may also be applied to the burgeoning national movements of this region. We have hitherto concentrated on government and Russian perceptions of the "national problem"; in this chapter we shall attempt to show, in brief, the other side of the story.

A recent discussion of the formation of national elites, a vital precondition for any national movement, points out some of the terminological and conceptual difficulties in any such study. Kappeler, in *The Formation of National Elites,* compares such diverse national groups as Catalans, Macedonians, Poles in the Grand Duchy of Poznań, and Ukrainians in the Russian Empire. He notes the importance of educational institutions in the formation of national elites, pointing out that urban centers are much more likely to be the foci of national agitation, and discusses the various modes of communication that could link up members of a national group, including print culture, the press, and even the performance of dramatic works by roving troupes.[1]

More specifically pertinent to our region are the theoretical works by M. Hroch and J. Chlebowczyk, who in various monographs have attempted to come to grips with the why, when, and how of national movements in Eastern Europe. Miroslav Hroch locates the origin of modern nationalism among the smaller peoples of Europe in the strivings of educated urban residents for a more equitable, and for them more advantageous, political system. Although it is impossible to accept Hroch's reified concept of the nation as an eternal entity waiting for centuries to be awakened or revived (and one may question the validity of some of his broader conclusions, given the limited data upon which they are based), his work does represent a major contribution to the theoretical and substantial understanding of the foundations of nationalism. Particularly suggestive is his periodization of national movements. Hroch divides the development of national movements into three discrete phases: "Phase A (the period of scholarly interest), Phase B (the period of patriotic agitation), and Phase C (the rise of a mass national movement)."[2] In the Western and Polish provinces of the Russian Empire, several diverse and often antagonistic national movements passed from Phase A to Phase C during the three generations between the January Insurrection of 1863 and the outbreak of World War I.

The Polish scholar Józef Chlebowczyk wrote extensively on the development of national consciousness among minority nations in Eastern Europe. Unlike Hroch, Chlebowczyk recognizes that a "nation" is not a given; on the contrary, it develops and is created by historical circumstances. In several works he outlines the processes by which "nations"—particularly in the Habsburg lands—differentiated themselves, organized themselves into cultural and political movements, and eventually began to demand cultural, economic, and even political rights. Chlebowczyk correctly points out that, in Western Europe, unified states helped mold unified languages, which then gave rise to national unity. One thinks, for example, of the French, English (or even British), Dutch, and Spanish examples. East of the Elbe, on the other hand, the formation of national movements moved in the opposite direction, and linguistic unity (of sorts) developed into feelings of national unity, which then ignited specifically political demands for a national state.[3] This typology does not fit all the national groups resident in the Western and Polish provinces, of course. Most especially, the Polish nation could hark back to its own powerful medieval and early modern state.[4] But Chlebowczyk's remarks do alert us to the very different historical and social processes taking place in this region as the concept of nationality developed here.

The Poles

The period after 1863 appeared a dark one for Poles in the Russian Empire. Their legal and political situation was certainly not to be envied. But this negative portrait fails to do justice to historical reality: after all, the political rights of all subjects of the Russian Empire during this period were in many ways restricted, and yet, culturally and politically, great strides were taken in these decades. Although it appears that literacy among Poles as a whole may have actually declined between 1863 and 1905, this was also the period of intense cultural work, literary development, and artistic creativity.

Polish political ideas underwent a similar transformation and deepening during these decades. Polish romantic messianism died as a political alternative in 1864. To quote Andrzej Walicki, the leading specialist, "The very term 'political Romanticism' began to be used [after 1863] in a pejorative manner, as a synonym for idealistic daydreaming and irresponsible actions, leading, as a rule, to national disaster."[5] Out of the ruins of this destroyed ideal arose a new ideology, usually described as positivism. The Warsaw positivists of the period between 1864 and 1905 rejected the Polish heroic tradition of Kościuszko and Mickiewicz and turned to a more modest but also more practical philosophy of small deeds, gradual change, and economic self-betterment, so-called organic work *(praca organiczna)*. In a sense, the positivists were the Fabians of Polish nationalism: they did not necessarily reject the ultimate goals of the previous struggles, but they most certainly condemned the methods and the unbridled passion that had accompanied those struggles. Also unlike the romantics, the positivists stressed economic development and eventually came to be seen, though not always fairly, as neglecting political progress in favor of base self-enrichment. It is perhaps not unfair to call positivism a quintessentially rational, unemotional, bourgeois, nineteenth-century movement.[6]

In 1866 a group of Warsaw intellectuals founded the journal *Przegląd Tygodniowy*, which was to become something like the official organ of the Warsaw positivists. In the words of one Polish historian, "Practically the entire intelligentsia of the city [Warsaw] grouped itself in this camp." Among the luminaries of Warsaw positivists one finds Aleksander Świętochowski and Bolesław Prus, whose political skepticism, liberal meliorism, and distrust of revolutionary methods did much to set the tone of the intellectual milieu of Russian Poland for several decades after the 1864 defeat. Warsaw positivism (as the trend came to be known) must be seen as a Polish version of European liberalism, which arose under the circumstances of the shock administered to Polish society in the Russian Empire by the defeat of 1863 and the severe anti-Polish policies followed thereafter. Positivism, especially in its beginnings, stressed economic and educational development, seeing therein the future for the Polish nation. Thus the positivists came to be seen as apologists for capitalism and were attacked as such by both the right and the left.[7]

Running parallel with the positivist trend was *ugoda* (in English, agreement or reconciliation), or the belief that Poles could be loyal and productive citizens of the Russian state, and conversely, that the Russian state should recognize this and grant Poles the cultural rights and national dignity they deserved. To be sure, it would be misleading, even wrong, to overemphasize the similarities between the two movements. Positivism arose out of the ashes of the 1863 defeat and turned away from politics, not because of loyalist sentiments but out of sheer necessity. Ugoda, on the other hand, was an avowedly political and not economic trend, based on a firm belief in the unassailable might of the Russian state and desiring to reach a modus vivendi with the Russian authorities.[8] A contemporary opponent of ugoda, the Cracow journalist and litterateur Wilhelm Feldman, considered ugoda to be based on "the unshakable belief in Russian power, the conviction that outside of Russia no future for the Poles existed, that all attempts to achieve independence led only to national catastrophes and that only loyalty and legality could save the Polish nation." In a sense, Wielopolski may be designated the founding father of ugoda.[9]

By the 1880s, when memories of 1863 had faded somewhat and the Polish intelligentsia was feeling increasingly dissatisfied with mere economic, apolitical, positivist progress, a new version of ugoda appeared among the Poles of Russia. This new, improved ugoda (to simplify somewhat) aimed to combine positivist economics with the gradual opening of the political sphere to Poles who had proved their loyalty to Tsar and State. Perhaps most important, the leaders of this movement were not nobles and landowners but intellectuals and journalists. The two main figures among the new generation were Włodzimierz (Vladimir) Spasowicz and Erazm Piltz, who both resided in St. Petersburg during the first decade of Nicholas II's reign and published in the Russian capital the weekly liberal "conciliatory" journal, *Kraj*.[10]

For a time—during the first years of Nicholas II's reign, especially during preparations for his visit to Warsaw in 1897—ugoda achieved a relatively high level of support and prestige among the Polish educated classes.[11] Once it became clear, however, that Nicholas had no intention of significantly improving the lot of Poles within the Russian Empire or of granting Russian Poland any sort of autonomy, ugoda's stock took a large loss among the Polish public. Still, one should not underestimate the continued influence and importance of the conciliators (reorganized as the "realists" from 1905). This conservative, loyalist group continued to play a role in Polish-Russian relations until the end of Nicholas's reign.[12]

Already in the late 1870s, socialism was making its appearance on the Polish scene. The enormous growth of industry in Łódź and Warsaw produced a large proletariat in Poland for the first time, and the simultaneous atmosphere of political and national oppression enticed disaffected youths to embrace socialism as the most satisfying response both to economic distress and to political repression.[13] Whereas it would be wrong to overemphasize the importance of socialism in Russian Poland before the turn of the century, one can also not deny that, by the 1890s, two well-organized Polish socialist parties were active both within the Russian Empire and abroad. This movement was to provide an alternative for young Poles dissatisfied with the meliorist program of the positivists and repelled by the chauvinist and anti-Semitic agenda of the Polish National Democrats.

The reign of Alexander III, and the almost exactly contemporaneous regime of I. V. Gurko and A. L. Apukhtin in the Kingdom of Poland, did much to discredit ugoda and the ideology of positivism.[14] By the 1890s Poles had, for longer than a generation, been expiating their guilt for the uprising of 1863, but despite this lengthy and grueling penance, absolution seemed as far away as ever. The younger generation, seeing in the passive apoliticalism of their fathers a self-abasement that had brought little or no positive results, turned to more active political behavior. This struggle between positivists and activists was described as a "battle of 'the old' with 'the young'" by a Russian contemporary, sympathetic to Polish aspirations. The turn toward activist (and, by definition, oppositional) politics usually took one of two ideological forms, either socialism or nationalism (though most Polish socialists also supported the restoration of the Polish national rights, or even independence). Whatever their differences, what the nationalists and the socialists both had in common was a rejection of the philosophy of small deeds preached by their positivist and conciliator elders.[15]

To put matters simply, in the final decade of the nineteenth century we see three major currents—positivist, socialist, and nationalist—competing in Polish cultural and political life. Although the heyday of positivism was now past, the tendency remained visible on the political scene throughout our period in the guise of ugoda, and after 1905 as the Realist party.[16] At the same time, the socialists showed their strength during the uprising of 1905–1907; and the nationalists, grouped around the figure of Roman Dmowski and his National Democrats, dominated Polish legal politics in the Duma period. One may sum up the period between 1863 and 1894 in a simplified dialectical scheme: the political nausea brought on after 1863 led to a rejection of romanticism and the birth of positivism. A generation later, the stagnation and apparent lack of concrete results achieved by the positivists begat the activist nationalists on one hand and the socialists on the other. By the turn of the century, the era of political acquiescence by Polish society in Russia was passing away, and a new confrontation seemed imminent.

The new forces building up in Polish society in the two generations since 1863 exploded onto the political scene in 1905. News of the events of Bloody Sunday in St. Petersburg rapidly spread throughout the Kingdom of Poland, and strikes soon broke out in Warsaw, Łódź, and the Dąbrowski Basin. Students at the University of Warsaw and the newly inaugurated Politechnicum joined workers' strikes, and the entire Congress Kingdom was rapidly engulfed in strikes, disturbances, and terrorist acts. Even in rural areas peasants refused to pay rents and participated in rural strikes. The Russian authorities responded by placing first Warsaw, then all ten Polish provinces under martial law. Terrorist acts and street fighting still continued.[17] By late 1905, the Russian government appeared helpless in the face of massive protests, strikes, and popular violence.

Not all Poles viewed the revolutionary events unfolding around them with approval. Roman Dmowski, head of the National Democrats, warned that any attempt to take advantage of the Russian government's temporary weakness would inevitably lead to catastrophe for the Polish people. Dmowski went so far as to travel to Tokyo in order to dissuade Japanese officials from lending active support to the Polish socialists in their struggle against Russian hegemony. At home, the National Democrats opposed socialist-led strikes and terrorist acts and only slowly began to organize their own workers' circles and other actions. As one would expect, more conservative elements viewed the popular uprising with horror, calling for the reestablishment of order. But even conservatives recognized that fundamental reforms were needed in the Polish Kingdom, and by late 1905 the demand for Polish autonomy was nearly universal among Poles of all political stripes.[18]

Alas, as so many times before and since, the expectations for reform were disappointed. Although local self-government was promised for the provinces of Russian Poland, the promise was never realized. The religious freedom allowed by the decree of April 17, 1905, was soon confined within narrow administrative boundaries. Polish representation in the First Duma was considerable: thirty-four representatives from the Congress Kingdom were joined by nineteen others from the Western Provinces. The electoral law of June 3, 1907, severely reduced this number, however, and in the Third and Fourth Dumas one finds a scant dozen representatives for the Polish provinces and only a handful of Poles from the Western Provinces.[19]

After the crushing of the 1905 revolution, and particularly after the appointment of Peter Stolypin as minister of internal affairs, Poles felt themselves to be, in the words of Roman Dmowski, "second-class citizens." The unfavorable electoral law, the closing of the Macierz Polska and other educational and cultural institutions, and the failure of the Russian authorities to deliver on promises of local self-government meant that for Poles the years between 1907 and 1914 meant not the beginning of a new era of freedom but the return to the atmosphere of cultural restriction and political oppression that had existed before the revolution.[20] Although the government did not explicitly reject or abolish the concessions granted during the crisis years, the new freedoms were interpreted as narrowly as possible. The interests of order and the Russian nationality were placed far above those of any non-Russian group.

Still, not everything returned to normal after 1905. The press continued to enjoy, on the whole, far greater freedom than in the pre-revolutionary era; social and cultural organizations were allowed to form, albeit subject to a certain degree of government supervision; and, possibly most important of all, Polish politics were allowed legal, if limited, expression. The Polish National Democratic party dominated the scene in these years, and the Polish Duma club—the Koło—was composed exclusively of members of this party. During this period Roman Dmowski, head of the National Democrats, argued that Poland's future lay in close cooperation with Russia against the common German enemy. Dmowski's refusal to countenance active opposition to the Russian government led to a rebellion (the so-called *fronde*) against him within the ranks of the National Democrats and increased the animosity felt toward him by the Polish socialists. The socialists found themselves split between the Piłsudskite PPS-*frakcja*, which vowed to continue the armed struggle against tsardom, and the PPS-*lewica*, which advocated underground propaganda and educational efforts rather than active military opposition. And one should not forget that also, despite electoral defeat, the liberals of Russian Poland—organized in the various incarnations of the Progressive party—continued to take their message to the people.[21]

The year 1905 raised high hopes for political and national reform, hopes that were crushed along with the military repression of 1906 and 1907. The bitterness felt by the Poles was vented, in part, against their Jewish neighbors. Polish-Jewish relations had deteriorated steadily since the heady moments of Polish-Jewish brotherhood in 1863, but it was not until after 1905 that Polish anti-Semitism came to be accepted at almost all levels of Polish society.[22] By 1912 anti-Semitism had become ubiquitous throughout Polish society (with the exception of the socialists and, to a certain extent, the far right). Polish anti-Semitism of the immediate prewar years reflected not only anger at Jewish pretensions to their own national culture but in equal measure the frustration felt by the failed promise of 1905. In this sense, the social and national situation in the Polish provinces—and, to a slightly lesser degree, in the Western Provinces—was strained to the point of explosion in the years before 1914. And this was the situation in which the Russian government attempted to carry out the reforms described in the next three chapters.

The Jews

For the Jewish community of the Russian Empire, as for the Poles, the half century between 1863 and 1914 was a period of political repression, intensifying national antagonism, and socioeconomic change, but also one of rapid cultural and political growth.[23] In the political and legal sphere under Alexander II, Jews did see certain improvements of their situation, but high hopes for a solution of the Jewish question in Russia were dampened by the unwillingness of the tsar's government to go beyond meliorative measures, which merely divided the Jewish community into "useful" privileged groups and the impoverished Jewish masses, condemned to a life of penury within the boundaries of the Pale of Settlement. The disappointment already present before 1881 turned to despair when, following the assassination of the "tsar-liberator," a wave of brutal pogroms swept the Ukrainian provinces. The edifice of repression was capped by the notorious Temporary Laws of 1882. One of the few bright spots on the political horizon was the political liberation of Polish Jews, which, despite much controversy and many attacks, was not abolished in the ensuing years of reaction.

The Jews of Russian Poland received quasi-equal rights (równouprawnienie) in 1862. Thus Polish Jews were not subject to the extremes of police arbitrariness suffered by their brethren in the Pale. The position of Jews in the Vistula provinces was hardly an enviable one, however, caught as they were between the hardly judeophilic Polish peasantry and the distrustful Russian overlords. The Russian authorities acted with particular hostility toward any rapprochement between Jewish and Polish communities. In particular, the use of Polish in the synagogue was strictly forbidden, though it appears that this prohibition—like so many others—was often ignored by local authorities. In any case, the number of reformed synagogues (on the German model) in the Polish provinces was minuscule; the Jewish masses remained Orthodox and hardly inclined toward assimilation with the Poles.[24]

The subject of Polish-Jewish relations is a complex one that cannot be treated here. Suffice it to say that relations deteriorated steadily throughout this period and, after 1905, were on the brink of explosion. Many Poles felt themselves to be an incomplete nation—lacking a solid middle class because of the Jews—and came increasingly to attack the Jews resident in the cities of Poland as an element harmful to the interests of the Polish nation.[25] These agitators argued not only that the Jews in Poland had usurped the rightful place of a Polish bourgeoisie but also that recent Jewish immigrants from Russia, the Litwaks, had acted as a de facto russifying force.[26] Indeed, many Poles regarded the influx of Russian Jews to Polish cities as a deliberate depolonization tactic by the Russian authorities. Some of this ill feeling can be attributed, directly or indirectly, to the policies and actions of the Russian administration in the provinces, but on the whole, the brunt of the responsibility for the situation must fall on changing economic and social conditions, as well as on the growth of national feelings among both Poles and Jews.[27]

Even in the Kingdom of Poland Jews were not secure in their legal status. Already in the 1860s there was a movement to extend various restrictions on the Jews to the Polish provinces, and early in the following decade the Komissiia po Ustroistvu Byta Evreev po Tsarstvu Polskomu (Committee for Reforming the Jewish Way of Life), which met in Warsaw throughout the 1870s, complained of Jewish exploitation of Polish peasants and suggested that restrictive laws might be in order. In 1885 the governor general of Warsaw, I. V. Gurko, advised Alexander III to apply the May Laws of 1882 to Poland.[28] Luckily for the Jews of Poland, this advice was not accepted. The overall Russian policy vis-à-vis the Polish Jews was determined by a hope that the Jewish problem would just go away, that is, that Jews would gradually be assimilated into the general population and lose their distinctiveness. Unfortunately, this general policy was inherently self-contradictory: the Russian government opposed the transformation of Jews into Poles, and it would be absurd to hope that Jews in Poland, surrounded by Polish language and culture, would become assimilated into the Russian people. Moreover, there were numerous stridently anti-Jewish voices, such as that of the anonymous author of *Evrei v privislinskom krae*, a tract bearing the imprimatur of the Ministry of Internal Affairs (MVD), which alleged the deleterious effect of Jews in the Vistula lands and advocated legal restrictions on them.[29]

In the early 1890s the MVD, led by V. Plehve, made serious efforts to abridge the legal position of Jews in Poland. In the end, however, *równouprawnienie* remained in force for Polish Jews, mainly for three reasons. First, there was no immediate cause to take such a radical step. Second, Russian officials in Poland could not agree among themselves on the proper policy. Third, and possibly most important, the government feared the negative economic effects that would ensue from renewed restrictions.[30] To these factors I would add the persistent bureaucratic inertia that reigned within the administration of the Russian Empire. Thus the legal position of Jews in Poland remained relatively unscathed in the period 1863–1914.

The same could not be said of the situation of Jews in the rest of Russia. The last half century of Romanov rule was for the tsar's Jewish subjects one of the most tragic of their history. Besides the legal restrictions already mentioned and the increased severity of enforcement, Russian Jewry was traumatized by the pogrom wave of 1881 and the indifference (or worse) of local officials to the destruction of Jewish lives and property.[31] At the beginning of Alexander II's reign Jews, like so many other of Alexander's subjects, were filled with hope for improved legal and economic conditions. Many looked forward to a modernization of Jewish life under the banner of Haskalah (Enlightenment).[32] But no hopes or dreams could survive the pogroms and oppression of the 1880s.

The 1880s began, as is well known, with the revolutionary activity that culminated in the assassination of Alexander II. In the wake of the assassination, the first major wave of pogroms exploded over Russia. The following year, with the pogroms barely over, Russian Jews were hit by the Temporary Laws of May 1882, which further limited their legal rights. The law of May 3, 1882, contained four short articles. "As a temporary measure and until a general review, according to the established order, of laws on Jews," the first article forbade further settlement of Jews outside of cities and towns *(mestechki)*. The second article forbade, "temporarily," the purchase and renting of rural property by Jews. The third article forbade Jews to carry on business on Sundays and twelve major Orthodox holidays *(dvunadesiatye khristianskie prazdniki)*. The final point set down that these rules applied only to the provinces of the Pale of Jewish Settlement.[33]

To investigate the "Jewish question," a commission headed by Count Pahlen was set up to investigate the Jewish question. The commission deliberated from 1883 to 1888 and finally arrived at the conclusion that the Pale should be eliminated and Russian Jews be given legal equality. By this time, however, Alexander III's reactionary politics were firmly in force, and any liberalization of Jewish rights was unthinkable. Far from getting better, the Jewish legal position steadily worsened. In 1887 percentage norms were established at Russian universities: 10 percent inside the Pale, 5 percent outside, and 3 percent in the two capital cities. Jews living outside the Pale were subjected to increasingly stringent controls and harassments, the most egregious of which was the wholesale expulsion of thousands of "illegal" Jewish merchants and artisans from Moscow in 1891. Quite aside from the immediate suffering caused by this measure, the Moscow expulsion was to have a fateful long-term effect. Many of the Jews expelled from Moscow settled in Russian Poland, especially in the cities in Warsaw and Łódź, which further exacerbated the strained relations between Poles and Jews. Although one cannot say that the Litwak problem started with the Moscow refugees (the word *Litwak* in Polish and Yiddish actually refers to Jews from the Lithuanian area), this influx of Russian Jews to the Congress Kingdom did much to make Polish public opinion aware of the issue.[34]

Despite pogroms, legal restrictions, and economic difficulties, however, Jewish life in the Russian Empire developed and even flourished in these years. The pogroms of 1881 made necessary a fundamental rethinking of Jewish priorities. If in the 1870s a Jewish writer, such as I. Orshanskii, could have pleaded for an end to legal restrictions and could imply that, with the "disappearance" of Jews per se from Russia's legal system, the Jewish problem would also vanish, such a sanguine attitude could hardly survive the events of 1881. In the final decades of the nineteenth century, the massive emigration of Jews from the Russian Empire began, and within the empire the forces of secularization and nationalism began even within conservative Jewish communities.[35] Jews in Russia polemicized against accusations of moral turpitude and economic exploitation. For example, I. S. Bloch and Henryk Natanson sent a memorandum to the governor general of Warsaw in 1886 to counter Gurko's opinion that the legal status of Polish Jews should be restricted. A few years later Bloch published a study arguing that Jews, far from exploiting the surrounding population, significantly increased its economic well-being.[36]

While the "enlightened," assimilationist Jewish community in Russia was shaken by the pogroms of 1881, we should not be too hasty in proclaiming the death of assimilationist beliefs or processes. Even if the ideal of total assimilation into the Russian (or Polish) nation was discredited, many Russian Jews still cherished the ideals of Europeanization—in this case, usually through the medium of Russian language and culture.[37] During this time, several periodicals were published for "enlightened" (that is, Europeanized and assimilationist) Jews, such as *Izraelita* in Warsaw and *Voskhod* in St. Petersburg. Hebrew journals such as *Ha-Magid* and *Ha-Tsfira* found readers among Jewish intellectuals both traditional and "enlightened." A thoroughgoing reform of the Hebrew language became an integral part of new Jewish national thought, symbolized in many respects by the figure of Asher Ginzburg, better known under his pen name, Ahad Ha'Am.[38]

Parallel with the revitalization of Hebrew as a modern medium of communication, during these decades Yiddish was transformed from a despised dialect of the masses into a respected language with its own literature and press. Some Yiddish journals did appear in Russia before 1905, but they were quite rare and short-lived. As Orbach's study shows, obtaining permission to open a Yiddish journal or newspaper was far from easy. The Russian government shared more general prejudices against the Yiddish tongue, seeing it as a jargon of Germanic and Hebrew elements. The breakthrough for the Yiddish press came in 1903, when the first Yiddish daily in Russia, *Der fraind,* appeared in St. Petersburg. Whereas Yiddish periodicals were severely discouraged before 1905, these same years saw the beginnings of modern Yiddish literature in Russia. Mendel Mokher Sefarim's classic *Travels and Adventures of Benjamin the Third* was written in the 1870s, Sholom Aleichem's first story appeared in 1883, and Sholem Asch's *Dos shtetl* was first published in 1904. It is indicative of the growing respectability of Yiddish that Asch, who published his first story in Hebrew, switched to Yiddish on the advice of the great Hebrew and Yiddish writer, Isaac Leib Perets.[39]

Along with cultural developments came new political trends. To simplify greatly, one may speak of the previous assimilationist ideology (represented by *Voskhod* and perhaps, to name one figure, Judah Leib Gordon) as being challenged by the more activist (and nationalist) Zionist and Bund ideologies. Here the situation in certain respects paralleled that found among the Poles: both Polish positivists and Jewish "enlighteners" propagated a universalist and liberal creed, which by the last decades of the nineteenth century seemed no longer adequate, at least to the impatient younger generation. Restless and energetic Jewish youth found an outlet for their political energies in the Zionist and socialist movements.[40]

The Zionist ideal has always played a part in Jewish religious consciousness, but the translation of these age-old religious longings into a modern, secular political movement was the work of the late nineteenth century. The beginnings of modern Zionism in Russia are inextricably linked with the outrage and profound disappointment felt by Russia's Jewish community—and particularly the "enlightened" minority—in the wake of the pogroms of 1881. The pogroms and the ensuing Temporary Laws of May 1882 cast severe doubt that Russia's Jewish community might ever follow a "normal" course of assimilation into a progressively more enlightened Russian nation. The works of Perets Smolenskin, Moshe Leib Lilienblum, Leo Pinsker, and Ahad Ha'Am—all active in the Black Sea seaport of Odessa—helped pave the way for a Jewish national movement in Russia. Herzl's *Judenstaat* was first published in early 1896, and in an important sense the modern Zionist movement dates from that decade. By 1910 at least eight legal Jewish parties were in existence, and most of these were explicitly Zionist or socialist, or both. This high degree of politicalization was probably unparalleled by any other national group in the empire.[41]

Thus by the early twentieth century one perceived in Russia a well-educated but politically disaffected Jewish intelligentsia, writing in Russian, Hebrew, Yiddish, and Polish. The political discontent of this group found expression in specifically Jewish political movements such as the Bund and Zionism, as well as the broad participation of Jews in the Russian socialist movement. As with the Poles in the Russian Empire, so also for the Jews, the time of patience and acquiescence was coming to an end, and an era of organization, protest, and upheaval was close at hand.

The Lithuanians

For the Russian government, the two major problem nationalities in the Western and Polish provinces were the Poles and the Jews. The other nationalities living in this region received less attention and were usually mentioned in official discourse mainly as possible allies with the Russians against the Poles or as objects of Jewish exploitation. In the Western Provinces, members of these nationalities made up the bulk of the peasant population. For the most part these were "Russians," that is, Ukrainians and Belorussians, but in the northwest region and in the northeastern corner of the Kingdom of Poland, particularly in Kovno (Kaunas) and Suwałki Provinces, the bulk of the rural population belonged to the Lithuanian nationality.[42]

The Lithuanians at this time were a peasant nation, in the early stages of developing national self-consciousness, and were not perceived by the imperial government as a major threat. Lithuanians lived in significant numbers only in two provinces of the Northwest—Vilna and Kovno—where they made up a good part of the peasant population, along with Belorussians and a small number of Latvians. Before the 1863 uprising, ethnographers tended to distinguish between Lithuanians and Samogitians (*zhmudy*), but this distinction was fading by the late nineteenth century. A contemporary and quite sympathetic Polish commentator described the Lithuanians as a "completely peasant" people. The few educated Lithuanians tended to be Catholic priests, who played an important role in the development of Lithuanian culture and national self-consciousness during this period.[43]

As Catholics, the Lithuanians were suspect from the Russian government's viewpoint, which had traditionally seen Lithuanian Catholics as potential allies for the rebellious Poles. To lessen the Polish influence on the Lithuanians, the Russian government forbade the use of Latin letters in the writing of Lithuanian, an interdiction that lasted for forty years from 1864 to 1904 and did much both to embitter Lithuanian feelings against the central government and to stymie Lithuanian cultural development. By the turn of the century, however, the absurdity of laws forbidding the printing of Lithuanian in Latin letters had become clear, even to the local administration. Many local officials pointed out that the restriction did nothing to increase Russian prestige in the region and merely antagonized the Lithuanian population.[44] The interdiction on printing Lithuanian in Latin letters was finally lifted by imperial decree *(vysochaishee povelenie)* on April 24, 1904.

Lithuanian periodicals were smuggled in from Tilsit, in East Prussia, and tended to be antagonistic to Russians and to Poles equally. A Polish commentator wrote that the Lithuanian periodical *Ausztra* (published in Tilsit) considered Poles and Russians enemies of Lithuanianism *(litewskość)* and went on to complain: "Senseless attacks on Poles and 'Polonism' [*polskość*], fighting against the liberation movement and a furious Lithuanian chauvinism—these are the most evident characteristics of the first Lithuanian periodicals published within the Russian state."[45]

Lithuanians had cause for resentment against the two dominant nationalities in their homeland. Russian law limited their rights, and as Catholics they were subject to various forms of harassment on the part of local authorities.[46] From the point of view of Lithuanian peasants, the Poles were not the downtrodden victims of Russian oppression but the rich landlord and class enemy. From the point of view of the Lithuanian nationalists, there was much to be feared from the Poles, who enjoyed a strong position in the Catholic church and whose culture remained predominant in Lithuania. In the years between 1905 and the outbreak of World War I, the Lithuanian-Polish antagonism in the religious sphere took on such alarming and even violent forms as to become something of a public scandal.[47]

The national revival of the Lithuanians in the late nineteenth century looked back to the historical greatness of the vast Lithuanian state of medieval times and implicitly blamed the Poles for its downfall. More prosaically, Lithuanian intellectuals worked to spread literacy in their native tongue and to combat earlier prejudices that tagged Lithuanian a peasant tongue. During the 1905 revolution, Lithuanian groups organized an "all-Lithuanian conference" in their historical capital, Vilnius, and agitated for national rights in schools and the local Catholic church. Inevitably, the attempts by Lithuanians to gain rights for their own language led to clashes with Poles and to accusations that the Lithuanians were acting in tandem with the Russian authorities to wipe out Polish culture. Thus by the early twentieth century the Lithuanians had established themselves as a legitimate national group that could no longer be ignored either by their Polish neighbors or by the Russian government.[48]

The Ukrainians

For the Ukrainians, the generation after 1863 was marked by restrictions and repressions on one hand, and by increasing national self-consciousness and the building of a national intelligentsia on the other. Already in 1862, as the eminent historian Mykhailo Hrushevskyi pointed out, the Peterburgskii Komitet Gramotnosti (Petersburg Committee on Literacy) had petitioned for Ukrainian to be used as the language of instruction in the elementary schools *(narodnye shkoly)* of Ukraine. Local officials in Ukraine as well as their masters in St. Petersburg remained suspicious of the separatist potential of Ukrainian culture and language and opposed any slackening of restrictions on Ukrainian. Only a decade and a half earlier, as St. Petersburg well remembered, a conspiratorial group of intellectuals—the Brotherhood of St. Cyril and Methodius—had been discovered in Kiev. However innocuous this group may have been, the government of Nicholas I took the threat very seriously and meted out severe punishment to the conspirators, including the Ukrainian poet Taras Shevchenko.[49]

Mistrust toward any resurgence of separatism had not faded by the early 1860s and was further aggravated by the Polish uprising of 1863. Although the Little Russian peasants did not join in the uprising and even helped the Russian authorities to capture their mutinous masters, St. Petersburg was morbidly sensitive to the possible alliance between Ukrainian intellectuals and Polish szlachta. The Polish slogan "Za naszą i waszą wolność" (For our freedom and yours) could only be interpreted by the tsarist authorities as a direct threat to the integrity of the empire—which, of course, it was.

In July 1863 minister of internal affairs P. A. Valuev came out with his infamous circular against Ukrainian literature, denying the very existence of a separate "Little Russian" *(malorossiiskii)* language. Even the Bible could not be printed in Ukrainian. This act was further strengthened in the following decade by the Ems Ukaz of May 18, 1876, which forbade the printing of books, brochures, even musical lyrics in Ukrainian, as well as prohibiting the performance of plays in that language.[50]

The imperial government failed to make a clear distinction between Russian, Belorussian, and Little Russian in its own understanding of nationality. However, even the government admitted the existence of the Belorussians and Ukrainians (seldom, however, using those words) as ethnic groups using dialects of Russian. Thus in the census of 1897 we find figures for Ukrainians and Belorussians under the category "native language" *(rodnoi iazyk)*. According to these figures, significant numbers of Ukrainians lived in four Western Provinces: Kiev, Podolia, Volhynia, and Grodno. These people were nearly all peasants and lived predominantly in rural areas. The urban dwellers in right-bank Ukraine (that is, the three Southwest Provinces) were predominantly Jews, Poles, and Russian officials.[51]

Criticisms of the Ukrainian national movement came from both Russians and Poles. Russians often claimed that Ukrainian (for them, always "Little Russian") was a dialect of the "all-Russian" tongue, and Ukrainians were a branch of the Russian people. According to this scheme, Ukrainian activists (usually referred to as Ukrainophiles) were depicted as political intriguers, much more interested in pressing forward their own political programs than in any actual benefit for the Little Russian people. Such Russian writers usually claimed that the Ukrainian language was an artificial creation and that peasants of, say, Poltava Province understood Russian far more easily than the Ukrainian language cooked up by intellectuals in Lvov.[52] This dogged refusal to concede the existence of Ukrainian as its own language and culture not only characterized Russian conservatives and officialdom but, as we have seen in the case of Petr Struve, was present even within Russian liberalism.

Poles in the Russian Empire were on the whole less hostile toward the Ukrainian movement. Russians of an anti-Ukrainian stripe sometimes claimed that the movement was a Polish-led political plot against the Russians. In Austrian Galicia, however, Polish-Ukrainian relations were very tense by the turn of the century. This tension spilled over into the Russian Empire also, and Polish National Democrats such as Roman Dmowski expressed hostility toward Ukrainian national pretensions. Still, few Poles (unlike the Russians) denied the very existence of the Ukrainian people.[53]

At the turn of the century, the Ukrainian national movement was gaining strength both in the empire and across the border in Galicia. Mykhailo Hrushevskyi began to publish works on Ukrainian history and culture in the 1890s and taught Ukrainian and "universal" history in Lviv from 1894. At the same time, belletrists such as Ivan Franko and Lesia Ukrainka were producing essays, plays, poems, and works of fiction. In Galicia, the Ukrainian language enjoyed the status of one of that autonomous province's official languages. A Ukrainian university (or, more precisely, a Ukrainian section at the previously Polish university) existed in Lviv (Lwów to the town's Polish inhabitants), with Hrushevskyi holding the chair of Ukrainian history there. By the first decades of the twentieth century, Ukrainian culture, though still barely recognized by the Russian public, possessed a solid and growing body of literature and scholarship.[54] This was perhaps as yet merely a culture in the making, but only a seriously biased observer (such as S. Shchegolev, mentioned above) could claim that Ukrainian language and culture were only a production of the overly fertile minds of a few intellectuals in Lviv and Kiev.

Still, Ukrainian national consciousness as a mass political movement remained quite limited before 1905. After all, in none of these three provinces in 1897 did the level of literacy reach even 20 percent. This was a peasant society, as yet little concerned with larger political and cultural issues. Even much later, after the absorption of Ukraine into the Soviet Union, the mainly peasant composition of the Ukrainian nation was to be reflected in the high percentages of Russians and Jews in the Ukrainian Communist party.[55] To put it another way, the *longue durée* in Ukraine did not really come to an end until 1905. After that date the long-term efforts of nationalist Ukrainian intellectuals began very rapidly to bear fruit.

The level of national self-consciousness among the rural population of the Southwest is difficult to gauge. From an admittedly limited data base, it would seem that these peasants were seldom conscious of their Ukrainian national identity. That is, they did not, on the whole, see themselves as Ukrainians as opposed to Russians. They were more likely to see themselves as Orthodox "locals" as opposed to Catholic Poles, or Jews.[56] This is obviously a controversial subject; but I have found little evidence that would show the peasant masses in the Southwest to have been nationally self-conscious before 1914. The example of the Kholm controversy (see chapter 9) revealed relatively little Ukrainian national feeling among the local population.[57]

This is not to say that there was no Ukrainian national movement before 1905. On the contrary, the "rebirth" of the Ukrainian nation dates back at least to the 1840s and to the Cyril and Methodius society. In the 1860s the Ukrainian historian Nikolai Kostomarov pointed out in a famous essay the existence of "two Russian nationalities."[58] In the following decade M. Dragomanov wrote on the complicated relations between Poles, Jews, Russians, and Ukrainians in the Southwest Provinces. Still, at the end of the reign of Alexander III, the Ukrainian national movement remained in a fledgling state, in good part because of the repressive measures taken against it by the tsarist regime. As Leon Wasilewski wrote in his Ukrainian memoirs, the nationally aware Ukrainians he knew as a young man in St. Petersburg scarcely spoke Ukrainian, even among themselves.[59]

During the years preceding the outbreak of World War I, however, a significant upsurge in Ukrainian national feeling took place. One associates this movement especially with the renowned historian Mykhailo Hrushevskyi (Grushevskii), whose works in Russian and Ukrainian did so much to further the Ukrainian national cause.[60] When the prohibition on publications in Ukrainian was lifted, a large number of Ukrainian journals and newspapers came into existence. Many of these were short-lived, to be sure, but this phenomenon was hardly limited to the Ukrainian press. Several Ukrainian parties also took shape in the post-1905 years, ranging from the liberal center to the revolutionary left. By 1917 the Ukrainian question had taken on grave, even fatal, significance for the Russian government.[61] However, the Ukrainian movement during Nicholas II's reign remained more a potentiality than a real threat to the imperial government. Although the Klub russkikh natsionalistov (Russian Nationalists Club) in Kiev never tired of denouncing the dangers of "separatism" and "Ukrainophilia" *(ukrainofil'stvo)*, the government itself failed to take the "Ukrainian danger" very seriously.[62] Russian bureaucrats in St. Petersburg and in the Southwest continued to see the Little Russians not as a national minority but as potential allies against the Poles and Jews.

The Belorussians

The Belorussian national movement was considerably less developed than the Ukrainian.[63] While Ukrainians lived in a large area and had a cultural center, including certain departments at a university, in Lwów/Lviv, the Belorussians were a much less numerous people and lived in significant numbers in only five provinces.[64] Furthermore, these provinces lacked even the agriculture-based industry present in the Southwest Provinces. Belorussians, even more than Ukrainians, labored nearly exclusively on the land and, when educated, tended to shed their Belorussian ethnicity and become absorbed into the Russian or Polish cultures. About the Belorussian national dilemma a Polish poet born in the region wrote, "This formless rural society lacked those elements of crystallization that were so manifest among the Balts. Hence, perhaps, their readiness to accept such elements from the outside. One thing is clear: the Byelorussians never fared very well. They were simply given the choice of jumping into the frying pan or the fire, Polonization or Russification."[65]

The Belorussians did present one major difficulty for the tsarist administration: many of them were Catholic.[66] Despite the embittered efforts of certain activists to establish the possibility of Catholic Russians, Catholic Belorussians continued to suffer legal discrimination, at least until 1905. Religion clearly played a much stronger role in both the official mind and local perceptions than did ethnicity. In any case, Belorussians presented no serious challenge to the dominant Russian ideology and, unlike Ukrainians, did not possess a strong enough national movement to be perceived as a threat by the central government or by true-Russian patriots: "the Belorussian movement of national self-determination began late in the nineteenth century. Its beginnings were vague and uncertain. . . . Indeed, Polonized on the one hand, Russianized on the other, the Belorussians 'were as if they did not exist at all as a people.'"[67]

Even among the Belorussians certain indications of national awakening could be perceived before 1914, however. An organization for the propagation of the Belorussian language was founded in St. Petersburg in 1902, and in the following years Belorussian radical parties arose, with specifically socialist programs. As befits the representatives of a mainly peasant people, the first Belorussian parties called for land reform and aid to impoverished peasants. After 1905, Belorussian newspapers, journals, and primers began to appear, and a Belorussian printing house opened in Minsk.[68] Although the cities of the region continued to be dominated by Jews, Poles, and Russians, the Belorussian national movement was slowly but surely gaining strength.

Great Russians

The Russians (or rather, Great Russians) in the West and in Poland were mostly officials or landowners. The landowners were often themselves former officials who had taken advantage of the government's policy of encouraging transfer of landed property in the region from Polish to Russian hands. In the Western Provinces, especially in the Southwest, these Great Russian landlords made up the backbone of the Nationalist Party as well as the Rightists (*pravye*) in the Third and Fourth Dumas.[69] Two of the leading

Nationalists were A. I. Savenko from Kiev and P. N. Balashov from Podolia. Some of the best-known, not to say notorious, Rightists also hailed from the empire's western borderlands, such as G. G. Zamyslovskii (Vilna guberniia), V. M. Purishkevich (Bessarabia), V. V. Shulgin (Volhynia), and Count A. A. Bobrinskii (Kiev Province). Generally speaking, however, the bulk of Russian landowners in the West and in Poland did not live on their properties but in the capital cities or abroad. In both the Western Provinces and Poland, the Russian population exceeded 6 percent of the total only in one province (Vitebsk), and that is according to the probably inflated official figures of the 1897 census.[70]

Despite their numerical weakness, however, the political strength of these Russians, especially during the Duma period, should not be underestimated. Throughout the Duma period the government had to rely on the Nationalists and the Rightists for support, and these groups had the strongest bases in the Western Provinces. After 1905 these patriotic Russians became increasingly well organized politically, as the activities of the Kiev Klub russkikh natsionalistov will attest. (For some of their activities, see their publication, *Sbornik kluba russkikh natsionalistov*.) Given the government's suspicion of the Poles and its ideology that Ukrainians and Belorussians were but Russians in the making, it was only natural that St. Petersburg should seek its political allies, both before 1905 and after, from this milieu.

Looking at the representatives from the nine Western Provinces to the Third Duma, we find a preponderance of Rightists and Nationalists. The large Jewish community in the area sent one representative (N. Fridman from Kovno Province), and both Polish and Lithuanian representatives also figured among the several dozen delegates from these nine provinces. However, the lone Jewish representative was far outnumbered by Orthodox churchmen, including Bishop Mitrofan from Mogilev Province and parish priests from nearly every province. The peasant representatives from this area were in nearly all cases affiliated with either the Rightist or the Nationalist parties. Despite the relatively small percentage of Russians in the western region, this was the very center of Russian nationalist politics, including the Union of Russian People.[71]

Besides bureaucrats and landowners, a sizable number of the Russians in the six Northwest Provinces were Old Believers who had fled to these regions in the seventeenth century, in response to Nikon's church reforms. These Russians tended to live in relatively self-contained colonies, equally hostile to Poles and to tsarist officials but fervently devoted to the tsar. The largest colonies of Old Believers in the western region, according to the 1897 census, were in Vilna, Vitebsk, and Kovno Provinces.[72] Although the Old Believers tended to stay away from politics, Russian nationalists hailed them as a russifying force on the western frontier and pointed out that the Old Believers had fought against the Poles in 1863. Aside from the Old Believers and officials, a certain number of Russians had settled in the area after the 1831 and 1863 uprisings, taking advantage of the government's advantageous terms for Russian colonizers in the region.[73]

In the Kingdom of Poland, the situation of Russians was rather different. Here the Russians were almost exclusively either officials or professionals attracted by the benefits of a career in Poland. There were many enticements for Russian officials to pursue their career in Poland: every three years of service here counted as four toward a pension, and for teachers, twenty years of service counted as thirty-five.[74] Russian officials in Poland were also entitled to special travel money and "supplements" (dodatki) to their normal salaries. To give just one concrete example, in 1896 the Lublin governor's normal salary was 3,500 rubles, plus 3,500 rubles food allowance (stolovye). To this were added 600 rubles travel costs and a supplement of 1,226 rubles. One can see why one contemporary Polish publicist referred to the Polish Kingdom as a California for Russian officials (Beamtenkalifornien).[75]

Although their numbers were small, there existed a certain number of Russian landowners in the Vistula country. These Russians had bought the large estates available in Poland at a bargain price in the decades after 1863 or had been granted estates, known as maioraty, for loyal service. By the turn of the century, however, many of these de facto landowners and potential russifying elements preferred to live in St. Petersburg or Warsaw and lease their lands out, often to Jews.[76] Sales of formerly Polish maioraty continued even after 1905, and plans were mooted in St. Petersburg to encourage even Russian peasants to settle in Poland, one of the empire's most overpopulated areas, despite the opposition of governor general G. Skalon.[77] In the end, however, this plan, like so many others during the history of the Russian Empire, came to naught.

Naturally enough, the largest concentration of Russians in the Kingdom of Poland was found in its capital, Warsaw.[78] These Russians tended to keep to themselves and were not welcomed into Polish society; nor did most of them desire any such connections.[79] The Russian community in Warsaw lacked its own theater, a cause of much indignation on the part of Russian patriots, but the Polish capital could boast a large Orthodox cathedral (sobor) downtown, built at the cost of over three million rubles.[80] After 1907, members of the Russian community in Warsaw had their own political representative in the Duma. They sent Sergei Nikolaevich Alekseev, a nationalist who achieved notoriety for his anti-Polish Duma speeches.[81]

According to the terms of official Russia, another group of "Russians" lived in the Kingdom of Poland. These were the former Uniates who resided in the eastern districts of Siedlce and Lublin Provinces. We would consider them not Russians but Ukrainians; however, the Russian government—and the right-wing Russian parties—insisted on their Russian identity. This insistence led to the formation of a separate province to "protect" these Russians from Polish or Catholic intrigues (see chapter 9). Even before the formation of the Kholm Province, however, the Russian government acceded to local demands (stemming, it would seem, mainly from

Orthodox clergy in the town of Kholm) for specific representation of these local Russians (in the end, defined specifically as "Orthodox"). Thus the approximately 300,000 Orthodox residents of Siedlce and Lublin Provinces had their own Duma representatives, Bishop Evlogii in the Second and Third Dumas and his colleague A. Budilovich in the Fourth.[82]

❖   The pan-European phenomenon of nationalism around the turn of the nineteenth to twentieth centuries did not pass Russia by. During the decades between the Crimean War and World War I, national feelings, self-consciousness, and the not entirely unrelated phenomena of chauvinism and anti-Semitism grew steadily. The spread of nationalist sentiment not only affected previously dormant nationalities such as Ukrainians, Belorussians, Lithuanians, and (in certain ways) Jews but also transformed the political ideologies of Poles and Russians. Poles in the Northwest Provinces, for example, could hardly remain indifferent to the prospect of militant Lithuanian nationalists in league with the Russian authorities, squeezing out Polish culture from two directions.[83] Similarly, Russians in the Southwest Provinces often reacted furiously at even timid pleas from local Ukrainians for the use of their native tongue in schools and other cultural institutions.

As the national landscape was transformed by the growing strength of the less dominant nationalities (neither Polish nor Russian), the simple binary national choice implicit in Russian government policies (that is, either Polish or Russian) became increasingly irrelevant to the present conditions. The alternative was no longer a simple Us versus Them; each of the region's nationalities demanded consideration for their own linguistic and cultural heritage and refused to be pigeonholed as either pro-Russian or pro-Polish. It is predictable that these new attitudes—requiring greater understanding, tolerance, and tact—infuriated many members of the formerly dominant national cultures. Indeed, the Russian government and its allies in the Rightist and Nationalist Parties in this region consistently refused to admit even the existence of a new national landscape, continuing to be held captive by their own, now sadly outdated, national conceptions.

In one respect, however, official Russia did recognize the power and significance of nationalism. Persisting in its view of Poles and Jews as the enemies in this region, the Russian government acknowledged the need to mobilize national feelings among local Russians. Although this mobilization took on the ugly form of encouraging groups such as the Union of Russian People (URP), this was at least a logical—if repugnant—policy for the hard-pressed empire to take.[84] And yet even here the support was far from universal, and most commentators agree that, in the years after 1907, groups like the URP waned in membership and authority. The imperial government could not help feeling uncomfortable with "popular" groups that, in one form or another, demanded their rights. Such demands, from the official viewpoint, inevitably took on social, even socialist, overtones. Thus during the last decades of Romanov rule, and particularly in the period after 1905, the Russian Empire found itself hemmed in between insoluble social and economic exigencies, which inevitably demanded a new, more flexible outlook on the national issue. The failure of the Russian government to develop such an outlook will be documented in the following three chapters.

Seven

Rural Administration and Nationality

Western Zemstvo

If we introduce this measure [the zemstvo] tomorrow
in the Western Provinces, the results will be striking,
and I am sure that in a few years the region
will be unrecognizable.

—*P. Stolypin to the State Council,*
February 1, 1911

❖   The zemstvo institutions are frequently cited by historians as the
seedbeds of Russian democracy. Many of the political figures of the post-
1905 semi-constitutional period began their political activity within these
modest organs of rural self-government. Russian liberal society recognized the zemstvo as a step, however small, toward an expansion of political rights in the empire and cherished the zemstva accordingly. To be
sure, there were some dissenting voices that complained of the taxes
levied by these bodies and predicted darkly that only evil could come of
institutions so clearly contrary to the spirit of autocracy. Indeed, the famous call of the Tver zemstvo to Nicholas II—asking that public bodies be
given a greater role in government—seemed to corroborate these conservative fears. However, the general consensus remained clear: in the first
decades of their existence, the zemstva had proved their worth, improving
sanitary conditions, building roads and bridges, and increasing literacy.
By the last decades of the nineteenth century, most government officials
realized the worth of the zemstvo in the economic sphere, even though

wary of the potential threat to bureaucratic prerogatives that these elected local councils presented.[1]

Before we turn to the history of the imperial government's attempts to fit zemstvo institutions to the multinational Western Provinces, it may be in order to give a short description of the zemstvo and its history from 1864. When the zemstvo was created in 1864, the institution was first extended to thirty-three provinces of European Russia.[2] Zemstva were not introduced to peripheries that lacked a strong Russian nobility such as the far North (Arkhangelsk Province), Siberia, the Don region, and the Caucasus, or to the western borderlands, that is, the Baltic, Polish, and Western provinces. There was an obvious and specific reason behind the failure to introduce zemstva in the latter two areas: the Polish uprising of 1863. Although the State Council had planned to introduce the zemstvo reform to the nine Western Provinces even after the outbreak of the rebellion, the governor general of Vilna, M. N. Muraviev, succeeded in persuading St. Petersburg that this reform would significantly endanger his efforts to pacify the northwest region.[3] The original plans to include the nine Western Provinces and the Polish Kingdom in the 1864 reform law were thus thwarted by the rebellion, which convinced Alexander II and his advisors that the time was not ripe for the introduction of local government in any form in this Polish-dominated territory.[4] During the decades following 1864, plans to extend the zemstvo reform to these provinces were often mooted, but they never assumed serious form until the reign of Nicholas II.

Without delving into the details of zemstvo structure and prerogatives, it is important to sketch these organs briefly in order to contrast the original zemstva with the bodies later introduced in the western region. The 1864 statute created two levels of zemstvo self-rule in the empire: the provincial and the district. The primary function of these bodies was, according to the first article of the law, to administer and manage matters of "local economic welfare and the needs of each province and each district." At both provincial and district levels the zemstvo organization consisted of an assembly (*sobranie*), which was entrusted with decision making (*rasporiaditel'naia vlast'*), and an executive board (*uprava*), which carried out the assembly's decisions. The assemblies at the district level were chosen in a tripartite electoral procedure. The district assemblies, in turn, chose delegates to the provincial assemblies. The executive boards for province and district, which carried out the zemstva's everyday operations, were also chosen by the respective assembly.[5]

Leaving aside the exact mechanisms of election, the key aspect to note here is that zemstva deputies (*glasnye*) were "elected representatives of the local population." The electoral principle (*vybornoe nachalo*) constituted the cornerstone of the zemstvo, at least in the mind of liberal Russia, and this principle (or rather, its absence in the new western zemstva) provided one of the most trenchant arguments of Russian liberals against the "zemstvo" institutions introduced in the Western Provinces in 1903.

The jurisdiction and competence of the zemstvo must also be considered here. McKenzie lists fourteen areas in which the zemstvo was allowed to act, ranging from public health, education, veterinary care, and scrutiny of food supplies to collecting taxes for zemstvo needs and communicating local grievances and desires to the central government.[6] Administering fire insurance, building roads and bridges, encouraging trade and industry also fell within the purview of zemstvo activities. The areas in which the zemstvo was empowered to act were often not clearly delineated, and frictions between zemstvo and local administrative organs arose constantly, to a greater or lesser extent, throughout this period.

The more essential issue at hand in zemstvo versus administration squabbles involved the differing conceptions of the role these bodies of self-government *(samoupravlenie)* were to play within the Russian state.[7] For many liberals, the zemstvo constituted but a first step toward a constitutional regime, and the electoral principle and autonomous zemstvo activities—unfettered by tsarist bureaucrats—were seen as essential for the proper development of local self-government.

On the other hand, the central government and especially the MVD both in St. Petersburg and in the provinces tended to regard the zemstvo institutions as at best rivals for local power and at worst dangerous centers for opposition to the autocracy. According to this view, if the government was to tolerate them at all, the zemstva must content themselves with the relatively passive and nonthreatening role of implementing central directives at the local level, especially in matters such as public health, construction and maintenance of infrastructure, and primary education. Perhaps the most brilliant development of the structural contradiction between autocracy and local self-government may be found in Witte's famous essay of 1899, *Samoderzhavie i zemstvo.* On one issue, however, both administration and "society" were agreed: that "politics" should play no role in the zemstvo. At least, this was the line taken up by zemstvo liberals in public utterances. In reality, it was inevitable that "politics," however defined, would creep into any publicly elected bodies in an autocratically ruled state. In the words of Roberta Manning, "Very early in the history of the zemstvo, this local institution of local self-government began to concern itself with the direction of state affairs, engaging in deliberate attempts to shape and influence national policies and political structures."[8]

❖   The original zemstva were introduced only in the provinces of central Russia, that is, in provinces where the Russian nationality predominated. As usual, the government was concerned primarily with the nobility and intelligentsia in the area. Here, as always, it did not distinguish Great Russians from Ukrainians or Belorussians, so zemstva were introduced to Chernigov, Ekaterinoslav, Kharkov, Kherson, and Poltava Provinces, where the peasant population was primarily "Little Russian" by language.[9] In the nine Western Provinces, however, the property-owning class in 1864 was overwhelmingly Polish. The Russian authorities took the recent rebellion as clear proof that entrusting Polish landowners with local self-government would be inadvisable, even foolhardy, from the viewpoint of Russian state interests.[10] The remainder of Alexander II's reign was played out under a dark cloud of anti-Polish suspicion that precluded any societal opening in the Western Provinces. Under Alexander III the position of Poles in the empire improved not at all. Any hopes for a relaxation of this negative attitude toward Polish participation in local government, including the introduction of zemstva in the West, would have to wait for the reign of Nicholas II. And after 1894, in fact, indications that the zemstvo reform would soon be extended to the West were not slow in coming.

In 1896 *Vestnik Evropy* reported that the State Council had officially requested the MVD to review the agricultural and economic situation in the non-zemstvo provinces and recommend to the State Council on the advisability of introducing zemstva in these areas, as well as on the form that such zemstva should take. The State Council further requested that this review be done and recommendations offered before the end of the present fiscal period, that is, within three years.[11]

Vestnik Evropy's reaction to this announcement is not hard to guess: the liberal journal welcomed the prospect of the extension of local self-government to the peripheral areas of the empire but warned that the new zemstva should not differ fundamentally from the "spirit and letter of the law of June 12, 1890." In 1864, *Vestnik Evropy* admitted, the volatile situation in the Baltic, Poland, and the West had made it impossible to set up zemstva in these areas. But, the article continued, "Since that time the situation has changed completely. In the West (not excluding the Vistula provinces) profound tranquillity reigns, and alongside the nobility and urban estate there has developed a free peasantry, which owes its economic independence [*samostoiatel'nost'*] to the Russian government."[12] This statement acknowledges a certain residual distrust of the urban and noble segments of society in the West but attempts to counterbalance it with a putatively loyal peasantry. Such a view of the social situation in the West and in Poland was not limited to Russian liberals, though their insistence that even Polish nobles and burghers could be trusted separated them from the conservatives, and from most of Russian officialdom.

Vestnik Evropy and its liberal readership also differed from conservatives and official Russia in their relative disinterest in the national mixture of peripheral regions of the empire. Liberals primarily concerned themselves with the zemstvo itself, with its extension throughout the empire, and with the preservation of its role as the organ of local society. Indeed, the short article quoted above announcing the State Council's communication to the MVD devoted but one page to the issue of zemstva in the periphery and followed this with three pages of polemic against the archenemy of Russian liberaldom, the reactionary daily *Moskovskie Vedomosti*. Liberal Russia's discussions of the western zemstvo tended to emphasize the noun "zemstvo" (that is, the introduction of organs of self-government without major alterations), whereas the government deliberations stressed the adjective "western" (that is, how to mold the institution to fit the situation in the Polish-dominated West). In keeping with the liberal mind-set on nationality, liberal Russia deemed it insignificant that a large proportion of the zemstvo members would be of Polish and not Russian ethnicity. Official Russia saw matters quite differently.

The leading Polish journal in the Russian Empire, *Kraj*, also welcomed the introduction of zemstva in the West. Like *Vestnik Evropy*, the Polish liberal-conservative organ argued that self-government in the Western Provinces was absolutely essential for economic development and would pose no threat whatsoever to Russian interests. At the same time, *Kraj* took great pains to point out that Polish dominance in the Western Provinces had diminished significantly since 1863. Hence, Poles would not enjoy unchallenged hegemony in the new organs of self-government. In the many articles published in *Kraj* after 1896 on the western zemstvo, there is a constant emphasis on three issues: the economic desirability of the zemstvo, its political innocuousness, and the falseness of the arguments in such official or right-wing periodicals as *Varshavskii Dnevnik, Vilenskii Vestnik,* and *Moskovskie Vedomosti* that Poles would take over the new zemstva.[13]

The view looked somewhat different from the chancelleries of the MVD in St. Petersburg and in the governors' offices in Vilna, Minsk, Kiev, and other provincial capitals in the West. Here, arguments tended to center around two key issues: how to minimize the influence of Polish landowners and maximize that of "loyal Russians"; and how to retain all real political authority in the government's hands while allowing for a certain amount of local administrative power in economic matters to pass into the hands of the zemstva. It is interesting to note that the Jewish question played little or no role in deliberations about the western zemstvo. As primarily urban dwellers, the Jews figured little (if at all) in the government's calculations on the wisdom of allowing zemstva in this area. When the Jewish question came up at all in this context, it was usually assumed that Jews would not be allowed to participate in these institutions. From the first, the MVD had in mind only one main threat to the security and well-being of zemstva in the West: the Polish landowning class.

The initial impetus toward the western zemstvo legislation apparently came from a comment by the Mogilev governor, Nikolai Alekseevich Zinoviev, in his annual report for 1893, to the effect that an improvement in meeting local needs could be achieved only by reforming rural *(zemskie)* institutions and allowing the participation of "representatives of the local population" in such bodies. The governor hastened to point out, however, that such a reform would be impossible at the present time, in view of the "significant numbers of Polish landowners in the province." Although not openly antagonistic to government aims, the Poles could in no case, according to Zinoviev, be considered entirely trustworthy *(vpolne blagonadezhnye)*. Thus, he concluded that increasing Russian landholding in the West presented not merely a political but also an economic necessity.[14]

Zinoviev's remarks contained a certain contradiction. On one hand, local needs could be satisfied only by increasing local participation in administration; on the other hand, the loyalty of the local population in question seemed far from assured. The solution: change the national makeup of the local population by importing Russians. The tsar was apparently taken by Zinoviev's comments and marked on the report: "Predstavit' ob"iasneniia [Submit explanation]," thereby setting the bureaucratic wheels of the MVD in motion. By mid-1895 the ministry was engaged in collecting the necessary information, opinions, and statistics upon which to base a reform project to introduce zemstva to the West.[15] Among the administrative opinions collected were two 1894 discussions of the need for western zemstva, one from the Kiev governor and one from the Volhynia governor.

The Kiev governor, L. P. Tomara, pointed out that the lack of zemstva institutions meant "the province's material riches and the personal energies of the well-to-do and educated part of the population" were going to waste.[16] Unlike his colleague in Mogilev, Tomara found no reason to fear Polish influence in the future zemstva. Polish landholding in Kiev Province had decreased significantly in the past decades, he emphasized, and only in two districts of the province (Berdichev and Lipovetskii) did Polish landowners make up more than half the total. With the predominance of Russian landlords, the almost exclusively "Russian" peasantry, and the safeguards afforded by governor's and governor general's supervision of the institutions as provided in the 1890 law, the Kiev governor concluded, the introduction of zemstvo institutions to his province presented no political danger whatsoever.[17]

The governor of neighboring Volhynia Province, Sergei P. Sukhodolskii, agreed. In his report for 1894, Sukhodolskii dismissed the "Polish danger" as nonexistent in his province and came out in favor of zemstva in Volhynia. "The introduction of zemstvo institutions would bring Volhynia a double benefit," wrote Sukhodolskii. The zemstva would increase the well-being *(blagosostoianie)* of the population and would bring Poles and Russians together in a sober, working atmosphere, which could not help but further understanding between the two peoples. The Volhynia governor went so far as to state that the zemstvo would serve as the "best school for Russian civil education" for the Poles of the province. The success of the "Polish Jewish" city governments in the Southwest and the lack of complaints about Poles' serving as jury members, Sukhodolskii concluded, corroborated his opinion that zemstva in the Southwest would present no danger to government interests or stability.[18]

We have, then, two very positive assessments of the need and feasibility of zemstva in the Western Provinces, or at least in the Southwest. Nor were these the only official figures who argued in favor of the introduction of zemstva in the West. In these provinces, with their relatively homogenous populations of Russian (that is, Ukrainian) peasants and a comparatively strong presence of Russian landowners, the introduction of rural self-government seemed possible and even desirable. Had all governors responded so favorably, the western zemstvo would most likely have become reality much sooner than 1911 and in a much different form.[19]

Many MVD officials, both in St. Petersburg and in the West, expressed serious doubts about the advisability of such a step. These doubts and fears came out most clearly in a series of meetings of the governors of the Western Provinces held in March 1898 to discuss the possibility of zemstva in this region.[20] All nine governors agreed that the present economic situation suffered from the inadequate and outdated system of local administration. Similarly, all agreed that the solution to this problem must include the introduction of some sort of zemstvo. But the form that the western zemstvo should take remained a point of contention.

The meetings began with the governors of Kiev, Volhynia, and Kovno provinces recommending the immediate introduction of zemstva without any special restrictions in their regions. Sukhodolskii—now governor of the Northwestern, mainly Lithuanian Kovno (present-day Kaunas) Province—stated his case in strong terms: "Zemstvo institutions can be introduced without restriction in Kovno Province. The special political situation of the region can not serve as an obstacle to this, just as it did not hinder the introduction already twenty years ago of the municipal government law [*gorodskoe ustroistvo*]." Sukhodolskii's opinion is particularly striking when one considers that his province, Kovno, contained the smallest percentage of Russians in any of the nine Western Provinces.[21] If the full and unrestricted zemstvo law of 1890 would work in Kovno Province, then clearly it could be introduced in all nine Western Provinces without difficulty.

Many of Sukhodolskii's colleagues, not surprisingly, disagreed with his assessment. The governor of Mogilev Province, N. A. Zinoviev, argued that, even in Mogilev, the most Russian province in the western territory, the 1890 zemstvo law could not be introduced without certain changes:

> [A] close acquaintance with local conditions convinces me that even in this province the introduction of zemstvo institutions to their full extent is impossible. After a long period of stagnation [*dolgii zastoi*] to rouse social life simultaneously at the provincial level as well as in the districts would be dangerous.[22]

Thus the government should not rush to introduce the entire zemstvo reform but rather should limit itself to a more modest reform, such as introducing provincial zemstva alone.

Several officials spoke out against underestimating the strength of the Poles in the West. The director of the MVD Economic Department, I. I. Kabat, warned against trusting statistics that indicated Russian majorities in certain areas. "Even among the local nobility of such provinces as Kiev and Mogilev the moral preponderance [*nravstvennyi pereves*], which is incomparably more important than the numerical, will indubitably be on the side of the Poles." The Poles, as longtime residents and the well-organized traditional ruling class in the area, would carry the day even against a putative

Russian majority. As Kabat and others pointed out, even when Russians lived on their estates and attended meetings (which was far from usual in the area), the Poles' organization and solidarity would make it nearly impossible for Russians to succeed in defeating Polish proposals. The governor of Grodno Province, D. N. Batiushkov, pointed out that in zemstvo meetings "Poles will turn out to be a huge majority even in areas where according to statistical data one would expect a predominance of Russians."[23]

The governors were thus caught in a bind. They recognized the need to reform local rural administration and admitted that the zemstvo had shown its worth in this respect in other provinces of Russia. However, fears of the Polish landowning classes prevented most of them from agreeing to an introduction of the 1890 zemstvo law without change. Serious differences in opinion existed, based apparently more on vague suspicion and misgivings than on any concrete statistical or factual data. In the end, caution and the fear of a vague Polish menace carried the day. The majority of the governors voted in favor of limiting the western zemstvo to the provincial assembly with non-deliberative bodies (ispolnitel'nye zemskie organy) to carry out the decisions of the provincial assemblies in the districts.[24]

As it transpired, this well-meaning project of 1898, sponsored by minister of internal affairs I. L. Goremykin, encountered opposition not only from the governors of the Western Provinces, but also from the formidable minister of finance Sergei Witte, and the project ended up being shelved indefinitely. This episode was but one in a series of battles between the two most powerful ministries of the day, Witte's Ministry of Finance and the MVD. The failure of Goremykin's project had much less to do with nationality, or the specific situation in the Western Provinces, than with the rivalry between the two ministries and Witte's desire to retain or even increase his own power within the bureaucracy. Even though the project did not come to fruition, its progress in the MVD presents a revealing picture both of how this ministry worked and of the various national judgments, prejudices, and fears at work within it.

From the very start of the deliberations in 1896, it was clear that the government planned to modify the zemstvo statute of 1890 more or less severely before introducing it to the Western Provinces. One finds many references in the press of the time concerning rumors as to the form that the western zemstva were to take. For instance, in December 1898, Vestnik Evropy reported that, two months earlier, the reactionary press had "rejoiced" at the news that only land captains (zemskie nachal'niki) were to be introduced in the West.[25] In the event, this rumor turned out to be without foundation.

However, the ostensible "zemstva" proposed by the MVD for the West in 1898 bore faint resemblance to the organs of self-government introduced elsewhere in the 1860s.[26] The proposed zemstva entirely lacked assemblies at the district level, and the deputies in the provincial assembly were nearly all appointed by the government. All members of the executive boards (upravy) at both province and district level were to be appointed by the government and did not even need to be landowners from the area. All deputies were required to know Russian fluently and to be literate in that language, a requirement common to all zemstva.[27]

Vestnik Evropy was quick to point out the inadequacies of this project. First of all, the journal criticized the appointive executive boards: "Proper cooperation between the deliberative [*razporiaditel'nyi*] and executive [*ispolnitel'nyi*] organs of the zemstvo is only conceivable when there exists between them the internal link of a common method of selection." The article criticized the lack of district assemblies: "Against the setting up of district zemstvo assemblies only one argument may be raised: that of the difficulty of surveillance over them." Such an argument, the article continued, could not be seriously maintained. Even if district boards were to be entirely in the hands of Poles, existing laws and local representatives of the MVD would ensure that the district assemblies remained well within the bounds of legality. In general, the district assemblies were completely unsuitable for any "oppositional" activity: "The district is a patch of land less suited than anything for tendentious undertakings and more than anything propitious for simple, unpretentious, humdrum work on the development of general prosperity; for 'politics' there is here decidedly no place." This statement is typical of liberal argumentation that downplayed, rather ingenuously, the role of politics in the zemstvo while militating for the extension of zemstvo activities and prerogatives.[28]

Apparently the arguments offered by *Vestnik Evropy* did not convince the government, as the district committees—not only in the Goremykin project, but later in the 1903 "margarine [*Ersatz*, fake] zemstvo" law—remained little more than the local executors of the decisions made at provincial level. However, the deathblow to the 1898 western zemstvo project came, in the end, not from arguments regarding details such as the specific form of the new zemstvo or even from national fears but from the wholesale critique of the zemstvo as such issued by minister of finance Witte.

❖   Besides the difficulty of instituting local self-administration in nationally mixed areas, discussions regarding the introduction of zemstva to the Western Provinces inevitably raised the more fundamental question of the role of self-government within the autocratic Russian Empire. Perhaps the most interesting examination of this question is to be found in the bureaucratic battle between minister of internal affairs Goremykin and minister of finance Witte, touched off by the original deliberations on the western zemstvo and culminating in Witte's essay *Samoderzhavie i zemstvo*.[29] Although Witte's essay was not primarily concerned with the national aspect of local self-government, its arguments reveal one persistent and widespread attitude of the Russian bureaucracy toward popular participation in local administration. That proposals to change the administration in the peripheral regions of the empire should set off a discussion touching on the very principles and fundaments on which the Russian Empire stood is in and of itself highly significant.

The exchange began when Goremykin expressed the opinion that the introduction of zemstva into non-zemstvo provinces was both necessary and nonthreatening to social order in those regions or in the empire as a whole. Witte, in five points, sums up the arguments Goremykin based his conclusions on: (1) "the system of local administration does not depend on the political order of the state"; (2) organs of self-government do not differ essentially from bureaucratic organs; (3) legal and historical studies do not recognize a link between local government and constitutionalism; (4) comparisons between western and Russian history are inappropriate as "all germano-romanic states developed on historical and material [*bytovoi*] soil completely distinct from the Slavonic-Russian world"; (5) "Russia is the country of local government par excellence."[30]

The weakness in Goremykin's arguments was readily obvious, and Witte spared no time in demolishing them one by one. We need not linger long on Witte's specific arguments. The central theme of his memorandum is that the zemstvo in its very essence represented a first step toward constitutionalism and as such was incompatible with autocracy.[31] Goremykin's rather astonishing claim that Russia had enjoyed a long history of self-government Witte dismissed with references to Anatole Leroy-Beaulieu and Pavel Miliukov, both of whom regarded Russia as a fundamentally centralist state.[32] Witte then goes on to note that one could speak of Turkey as a "state of self-government par excellence" in Goremykin's sense, but that this stemmed from Turkey's weakness, which Russia did not share: "The difference lies therein, that Turkey never had the capability of assimilating the foreign [*inoplemennyi*] part of its population—it was further hindered by Islam in this respect—whereas Russia possesses such a capability in the highest measure."[33] Although one may question the validity of this statement, the implied point that Russian "decentralization," such as it was, stemmed mainly from weakness, not out of any liberal principle or especial fondness for self-government per se, is well taken.

As to the specific idea of introducing zemstva in the Western Provinces, Witte rejected such a measure entirely, insisting on the "complete unsuitability" of zemstva in that territory. Goremykin had presented three arguments for the introduction of zemstva to the West:

> 1. The Western territory is the cradle of the Russian nationality [*narodnost'*], the Russian state [*gosudarstvennost'*], language and faith; 2. Zemstva are needed to strengthen Russian influences in the region; 3. Introducing zemstva will give rise to the possibility for local Russian self-government to develop in the region into a specific and conscious societal force.

Witte dismissed all three of these points. First of all, he pointed out that the Poles, too, regarded this area (for them, the *kresy*) as the cradle of their nationality. But, more important, Witte continued,

> In state affairs, it is necessary to deal not with those times when the nation was still in the cradle, but with the actual situation existing at present in

the region, which shows rather vividly which elements, instead of "Russian nationality, state, language, and faith," have settled in this cradle, especially in its northwest part.

Witte, unlike Goremykin, had no toleration for the romantic strain of Russian nationalism, preferring to base his arguments on concrete statistical or economic data rather than on "historical destiny." Or, just as likely, the metaphors used by the men should not be taken too literally: the whole episode was, after all, an example of interministerial rivalry, in which Goremykin's conservative Russian-national stance paralleled his position as an arch-bureaucrat opposing Witte's "revolutionary" policies of industrialization.[34]

Regarding the "strengthening of Russian influences" in the area, Witte noted that Polish landowners dominated the area, while Russian landowners in the Western Provinces represented a hodgepodge of various social elements, devoid of any unity. The situation was complicated by the large numbers of Jews residing in the area and by the "separatist daydreams of the Ukrainophiles." On a more fundamental level, Witte argued, it would make no sense to introduce self-government for Russians in a Polish-dominated area, because self-government can work only when it is manned and run by those elements who have a real interest in the area—in the West, obviously the Poles. To back up his position, Witte quotes Konstantin Pobedonostsev's negative view of zemstva in the West: "it is not difficult to imagine the harm that will come from this measure for the Russian cause [*russkoe delo*] and for the essential interests of Russian power in the North-West and Southwest territory."[35]

How should we interpret Witte's essay? It is interesting to note that Witte's position is understood in utterly opposing ways by the introductions to the two editions of the work that I have used here (Stuttgart 1901 and St. Petersburg 1908). The 1901 introduction lambasted Witte's hypocrisy and conservatism and pointed out that the "Witte system" was itself built on a contradiction that found expression in this work. "The Witte system presents a historically irresolvable, self-contradictory task: to provide the country with rapid and continuous cultural progress and to maintain and strengthen autocracy."[36]

The author of the 1908 introduction, however, maintained that Witte meant his work primarily as an attack on Goremykin (this much, I think, cannot be denied) and that he did not advocate the abolition of zemstva but rather opposed "the introduction of some faint semblance of a zemstvo [*chto nibud' pokhozhoe na zemstvo*] in the western territory." Arguing dialectically, the author described Witte's logic as follows: "It is impossible to destroy the zemstvo, it is irreconcilable with the 'old order,' hence the old order must fall. . . . Thus, even unequipped with a special introduction, Witte's work is a clear and strong pamphlet aimed against absolutism." Witte would, no doubt, have objected strongly to such an interpretation, but the logic is not so far-fetched. Witte was concerned primarily with efficient administration—

and with furthering his own career. If the zemstva could be incorporated into a smoothly functioning constitutionalist Russian government, it is likely that he would not have raised any major objection to them.[37]

In any case, Goremykin's stance on the zemstvo per se differed but little from Witte's. In his own memorandum Goremykin took pains to point out that the zemstva must be integrated into the general administration of the state, to become in effect the lowest level of state bureaucracy.[38] It becomes clear that such a zemstvo, as an integral part of the empire's bureaucratic administration, could not be oppositional, hence could not present any political danger to the state: "To think that the zemstvo, city, township [volost'] or Cossack settlement [stanitsa] can oppose the Highest will means to affirm that our system of government [obraz pravleniia] is not an autocratic system." Goremykin advocated a rather old-fashioned, Slavophile approach toward government in general: "In our country there have never been indications of any sort of mistrust, much less animosity, between the people and ruler." And this approach applied also toward non-Russian nationalities in particular: "No state on earth includes within its boundaries such a diversity of tribal and local particularities, as Russia. Under such conditions the system of self-government was always not only the sole practical possibility, but also the most effective method of governing."[39] The liberals' cherished view of the elective zemstvo as an autonomous, societal (obshchestvennyi) organ, separate from and indeed often in opposition to the state bureaucracy, was as alien to the career bureaucrat Goremykin as it was to Witte.

More important than the personal viewpoints of Witte and Goremykin, however, is the fundamental contradiction pointed out by Petr Struve. Not only Witte but the entire Russian government had to face the dilemma of encouraging economic and "cultural" development (a process that demanded a loosening of state tutelage and encouraging greater popular initiative at the local level), while maintaining control over the land under a thoroughly antiquated political system, headed by a stubborn and inflexible autocrat. Keeping a balance between these contradictory givens was difficult enough in the ethnically Russian territories, but in the periphery, the additional frictions of national and ethnic considerations continually jammed the administrative machinery. This is perhaps nowhere more evident than in the compromise reached in 1903 on the western zemstva issue, the "margarine zemstva" introduced by the legislation of April 2, 1903.[40]

In 1894, the governors of Kiev and Volhynia Provinces had spoken in favor of the introduction in the western territory of elective zemstva on the 1890 model. Goremykin then reduced the proposed reform to elective provincial assemblies instead, with executive boards in the districts to carry out their decisions, as the western (especially northwestern) governors themselves had requested in 1898. Even this proved too radical a measure for most of the governors of the Northwest Provinces, and by 1901 the minister of internal affairs Dmitrii Sipiagin declared that it would be "premature" to introduce elective zemstva of any kind in the West, suggesting instead a reform that would keep administration entirely in government hands, while bringing local people into the new organs by government appointment.[41] Despite some opposition to this purely appointive zemstvo (one MVD official pointed out that appointed delegates would not enjoy the trust of the local population, thus the "best people" would refuse to accept such positions), Sipiagin's truncated zemstvo won out over a more liberal reform. The following year Sipiagin's successor, V. Plehve, reduced the scope of the reform to the nine Western Provinces only, and it was in this form that the reform project was discussed in the State Council.[42]

In the State Council, too, voices were raised against the project's distrust of Polish landowners and against its appointive character. Sixteen members of the State Council spoke against the MVD project on the grounds that it overemphasized the danger of Polish-inspired disorders in the West and thus needlessly restricted the scope of the zemstvo there. The majority, on the other hand, agreed with the late Sipiagin's opinion that elective bodies could not be introduced in the West without endangering Russian state interests.[43] Even these members agreed, however, that the MVD project was in many respects inferior to the 1890 version. The minister of internal affairs, they noted, had stated that perhaps these bodies would soon be superceded by true elective zemstva of the 1890 type. Thus, even before the margarine zemstvo law was passed, even its supporters—led by the minister of internal affairs—admitted that this reform presented only a half step toward improved administration and that from a purely administrative viewpoint it was in many respects inferior to the 1890 zemstvo law.[44]

Nearly a decade passed between the first stirrings of the bureaucratic monolith and the tentative western zemstvo law of 1903, which introduced an institution that was immediately christened the margarine zemstvo. The final form of the law not only incorporated the elements criticized by *Vestnik Evropy* in 1898 but further restricted public participation in the western zemstva.[45] This half-hearted hybrid of bureaucratic and public principles immediately won the enmity of both the educated classes, whose role in these institutions was severely circumscribed, and the masses, who were obliged to pay higher taxes to support these zemstva. Nor did the local bureaucracy embrace the margarine zemstva wholeheartedly.

In effect, the law of April 2, 1903, gave the Western Provinces the worst of all possible worlds. The new institutions were entirely appointive and completely at the mercy of the local governor and the minister of internal affairs. As the legal expert V. D. Kuzmin-Karavaev argued in a slightly different context, the new organs would remain in the hands of MVD bureaucrats and thus would only add to the stifling bureaucratic rule in the Western Provinces: "Other than a similarity in names," he asserted, "there is nothing in common, from an analytical point of view, between zemstva institutions [that is, those of 1864–1890] and these [new] organs of local [*zemskii*] administration."[46]

Thus even before the margarine zemstva were introduced, their inadequacy as organs of self-government had been widely recognized. Even the timid, conservative *Kraj*, although greeting the reform as a step in the right direction, pointed out, "Naturally [the margarine zemstva] cannot compare with [genuine] institutions of self-government, cannot call forth, as they do, societal initiative [*ruch spoleczny*], or act with their independence or energy." In a similar vein, W. Spasowicz criticized the reform as "completely bureaucratic [*splosh' biurokraticheskoe*]" and argued that the new law went against Russian state interests by further differentiating administration in the West from the rest of Russia.[47]

Most of liberal Russia felt much less sanguine about the law, seeing it not only as inadequate for the Western Provinces but as an attack on the elective zemstvo as such. It would be only a slight exaggeration to say that for most Russian liberals the main significance of the 1903 western zemstvo law was as an ominous harbinger of further restrictions on zemstva in the rest of the empire. To quote the leading historian of the zemstvo movement, Boris Veselovskii, "And who knows whether it would not have come to a general zemstvo reform in the spirit of the law of April 2, 1903, had not the development of reaction been interrupted by the events that soon followed." The "events," of course, were the Russo-Japanese war (which broke out some eight months after the margarine zemstvo law) and the ensuing revolution of 1905. These events indeed turned public and government attention away from the problems of zemstvo reform in the West.[48] As social tensions mounted in 1904, the government tried to placate liberal society with the decree *(ukaz)* of December 12, 1904, which promised (among other things) "to grant zemstvo and municipal institutions the broadest possible role in the management of various aspects of local social services [*blagoustroistvo*]" (article 2).[49]

Soon after the publishing of this decree, the MVD set to work drawing up plans for elective zemstva in the Western Provinces. The 1903 zemstvo law had been but a half measure, and when put into practice it satisfied nobody and antagonized all.[50] Even before the project had been passed into law its main author, minister of internal affairs Sipiagin, had stated his hope that soon this "quasi-zemstvo" would be replaced by real, elective zemstva. The moment for this transition came somewhat earlier than Sipiagin may have imagined. In 1905, using the previously gathered opinions and statistics, the bureaucrats once again set to work.[51] Both the inadequacy of the margarine zemstva and the new political situation inaugurated by the ukaz of December 12, 1904, and the October Manifesto of the following year forced the imperial bureaucracy to concede that some sort of elective organs of self-government were needed in the western lands. By 1906, as the smoke of revolution was beginning to clear, the MVD was putting the finishing touches on a new project for real, elective zemstva in the Western Provinces.

In late 1906 the new minister of internal affairs, Peter A. Stolypin, presented a project to the Council of Ministers that foresaw introducing elective zemstva to the nine Western Provinces with little change from the 1890 law. Citing the urgency of the need for local reform of rural institutions, the minister urged the introduction of this reform by article 87 of the fundamental law, thereby circumventing Duma and State Council and avoiding lengthy legislative deliberations.[52] This project aimed to protect the rights of the Russian minority by holding elections "according to the principles of proportionality [of nationalities]," with at least a half of the hired zemstvo positions reserved for Russians, and with only the Russian language permitted in zemstvo gatherings and correspondence. It is not surprising that this project was immediately criticized by the Poles for its anti-Polish character. The Council of Ministers, ever cautious, did not support Stolypin's request to put through the reform administratively (that is, under article 87). Thus the western zemstvo bill began its long trek through the newly formed parliamentary bodies of the Russian Empire.[53]

One must bear in mind that over three years went by between the original MVD western zemstvo plan (November 22, 1906) and the MVD presentation *(predstavlenie)* to the Duma on January 20, 1910.[54] During this period many fundamental changes were made in the original project, nearly all of them to the detriment of non-Russians.[55] Perhaps the greatest change involved the deleting of three provinces, the so-called Lithuanian provinces (Vilna, Kovno, Grodno), from the project. In this area, the numbers of Russian landowners were so insignificant that no manner of electoral gerrymandering could guarantee a Russian majority.[56] Furthermore, rather than holding elections based on proportional representation, the final MVD project introduced national curiae in which Russian landowners were blatantly favored. Orthodox priests were also specifically included in the new zemstva. Finally, the western zemstvo law did away with the estate *(soslovie)* element that had been basic to the 1890 law. The latter modification aimed not to democratize the zemstvo but rather to counterbalance Polish landowners with "Russian" peasants.[57]

The final years of the western zemstvo saga were complicated by the new political situation in Russia produced by the events of 1905–1906, which opened the way, however cautiously, for greater political freedoms and broader public participation in government. After 1905, the western zemstvo project was dominated by the figure of prime minister Peter Stolypin, whose political fate became inextricably entangled with the fate of this law. Indeed, in much of the historiography the significance of the western zemstvo project seems to be measured principally by its effect on Stolypin's career.[58] To be sure, Stolypin played a key role in this project, and his views on local self-government and specifically on the western zemstvo are certainly of interest here. It has been argued that Stolypin advocated greater freedom for local self-government, including an all-class *volost'* zemstvo, but without a diffusion of political power, which would have amounted to a squaring of the circle.[59]

Be that as it may, there can be no doubt that Stolypin desired the introduction of zemstvo institutions in the West, though in a form that would safeguard the interests of the local "Russian" population. The future prime minister had grown up in that region and had served as Marshal of the

Nobility *(predvoditel' dvorianstva)* in the mainly Lithuanian Kovno Province.[60] So Stolypin was no stranger to this territory and its national complexity. It would be a distortion to portray him as a reactionary, chauvinistic, "black-hundred" minister, desiring to crush anything non-Russian and to build Great Russia on the bones of vanquished minority nationals.

The reality was far more complex and ambiguous. On one hand, Stolypin favored a lessening of anti-Jewish restrictions and went so far as to argue this point with Nicholas II.[61] He also expressed respect for Polish culture and insisted that the government did not aim to oppress the Poles in the West but wanted only to defend the rights of the Russian natives *(urozhentsy)*. On the other hand, Stolypin emphasized that always first and foremost in his mind was the good of the Russian state, the Russian people, and the fulfillment of the "historical tasks" of Russian autocracy and Orthodoxy in the West. "[A] state such as Russia can not and may not without injury *[beznakazanno]* relinquish the carrying out of her historical tasks."[62] Stolypin's attitude toward the Poles and Russia's mission in the West came out clearly in a speech he gave before the State Council on March 3, 1911: "I have always openly stated that I consider Polish culture a valuable contribution to the general treasury of human endeavors *[sovershchenstvovanie chelovechestva]*. But I know also that this culture in the West has for centuries waged war *[vela bor'bu]* against another culture, nearer to me, more dear to me: Russian culture."[63]

Stolypin's advice to the Poles made his position abundantly clear: "First of all take up our point of view, admit that the highest good is to be a Russian *[russkii]* citizen, bear this title as proudly as Roman citizens once did when they called themselves first-class citizens, and you will receive all rights." Such a statement could only be greeted with bitter irony by Poles, given their present situation in the Russian Empire.[64] Still, it should be noted that Stolypin's attitude allowed—at least potentially—for cooperation and peaceful mutual work between Poles and Russians. Such cooperation and coexistence was ruled out, however, by such powerful and influential groups as the Nationalist party and the Kiev Club of Russian Nationalists who tended to see Poles (not to mention Jews) as evil and perfidy incarnate.[65] Compared to these zealous defenders of Russiandom, Stolypin appears almost liberal. But Stolypin's Duma majority was based on an alliance with the Octobrists and with the nationalists too, and he was therefore obliged to take the nationalist point of view into account lest the government's projects be blocked in the Duma. One should not underestimate the organization and lobbying power of the nationalists and other rightists. Stolypin could also not help but be aware of Nicholas II's susceptibility to nationalist and Orthodox appeals and slogans.[66]

Stolypin found his extra-governmental or "public" counterpart in the Duma. Within the Duma, to put his measures through, he tended to rely on the Octobrist party in conjunction with the rightists and nationalists. So it was with the western zemstvo project. The Duma committee on the project was headed by the nationalist D. N. Chikhachev, and arguments for and against the project ran for the most part along political lines, with the Polish Koło and the Left (including some Octobrists) opposing the bill, while the majority of the Octobrists and the nationalist rightist camp supported it.[67]

Speaking against the project, Duma members concentrated on refuting the government's contention that the Russian cause in the western territory needed special protection and on pointing out the negative economic effects of past government restrictions on Poles.[68] It was also argued that the government's real motive in the bill was to assure the election of Russians to the State Council by establishing Russian zemstva in the area.[69] One conservative Duma member from Vilna Province denounced the project in detail, pointing out that at each stage in its development the restrictions on Poles had increased and concluding, "The most severe analysis could not discover disloyal activities on the part of the Polish rural element in the western territory. . . . Standing firmly on the ground of the Russian state idea [*russkaia gosudarstvennost'*], Poles desire only to be equal in rights with the rest of the area's population."[70]

Arguments from the other side of the Duma were not less impassioned. The Nationalist deputy from Mogilev Province, N. Ladomirskii, declared that national curiae were absolutely necessary to prevent the polonization of rural self-government in the region. Ladomirskii saw no possibility of compromise between Poles and Russians: "Whatever may be, whatever may happen, Poles will always be opponents of the Russian state idea and neither with concessions nor with bounties will you succeed in buying them." The Rightist V. V. Shulgin warned that to introduce zemstva in the West without national curiae would unleash a "national struggle" among all "cultured elements" in the area. Finally, Bishop Evlogii of the Kholm region reduced the entire western zemstvo controversy to one simple question: "What kind of country is this [*kakoi eto krai*], Russian or Polish?" Answering his own question, Bishop Evlogii bewailed the fact that "even the Poles themselves refuse to admit that this country is Russian." The local Russian population, he continued, was intimidated, oppressed, and servile from the long years of Polish dominance. Thus the restrictions on Poles in the new zemstva were a matter of sheer survival for the Russian peasantry of the region.[71]

The embittered arguments for and against the western zemstvo law occupied the Duma for the entire month of May 1910. When the measure came to a vote, the measure passed by 165 votes to 139. Although one should not overestimate the cohesion of the nationalist-rightist-Stolypin alliance, in this case Stolypin's allies in the Duma carried the day: the western zemstvo bill was passed by that body on June 1, 1910.[72] But the project's legislative trek was far from over. The fierce opposition it was to encounter in the State Council would precipitate one of the gravest crises of Stolypin's tenure as prime minister.

Given the multifarious sources of opposition to Stolypin and his western zemstvo project, it is hardly surprising that the project eventually ran up against major opposition. After a good deal of parliamentary give and take, the Duma finally passed the western zemstvo bill, but then, to everyone's surprise, the bill was obstructed and finally rejected by the conservative State Council, which objected particularly to the inclusion of national curiae.[73] The State Council also objected to the lowering of the property qualification *(tsenz)*, seeing in this the danger of a democratization of the zemstvo. Witte, on the other hand, defended the peasantry of the region, saying that in the area tens of thousands of peasants could be found who were at least as competent for zemstvo service as the landowners of the region. Witte objected principally to the national curiae, which he regarded as contrary to the spirit of the unity of the Russian Empire.[74]

The combination of these two factors—the specter of democratization and the distaste for national curiae—came together to defeat the bill in the State Council. Stolypin was faced with a major crisis. The defeat of the western zemstvo bill was, in effect, a vote of no confidence for his government and could not be passed over lightly. Stolypin reacted in a characteristically active and aggressive manner, threatening to resign unless the tsar agreed to prorogue the State Council and Duma for three days. At the cost of gravely offending both the tsar and all Duma members (including his allies on the right and among the Nationalists) Stolypin pressed on, and the project became law in an extra-parliamentary manner. With both Duma and State Council "recessed" from March 12 to 15, 1911, Stolypin was able to have the western zemstvo bill promulgated using the emergency powers of paragraph 87 of the fundamental law.[75]

The western zemstvo law passed by paragraph 87 differed significantly from the zemstvo statute passed in 1890, and even from the original project put forward by Stolypin to the Council of Ministers in 1906. The most striking feature was that zemstva were introduced in only six of the nine Western Provinces. Apparently the government shared the fears of the Kiev Nationalist Club that setting up zemstva in the three Lithuanian provinces would indeed entail a devouring of this Russian country by voracious Poles. And even in the six Ukrainian and Belorussian provinces, specific measures were provided in the western zemstvo law to "protect" Russian rights, that is, to guard against Polish hegemony.[76]

First of all, there were the national curiae, which had provided Witte and other members of the State Council with a conveniently unpopular issue with which to attack Stolypin. The national curiae were divided, essentially, between Poles and non-Poles. Depending on the district, the first curia *(otdelenie)* selected delegates from "persons of Russian descent" *(litsa russkogo proizkhozhdeniia)* or among those "not belonging to the number of persons of Polish descent [*ne prinadlezhashchie k chislu lits pol'skogo proiskhozhdeniia*]."[77] The difference between these two descriptions may not be readily obvious. The significance lies in whether electors of other nationalities would vote with the Russians or with the Poles. It was feared that, in certain districts of Vitebsk Province (Dvinskii, Liutsinskii, and Rezhitskii), Catholic Lithuanians might side with the Poles against Russian and Orthodox interests. Whatever the logic, in this respect the law was a marvel of complexity, an obvious result of attempts at ethnic gerrymandering in this region. As for the executive boards *(upravy)*, at both the district and provincial levels these were to be manned by a majority of Russians or, specifically, with members of the first curia. Jews, predictably, were excluded from voting altogether: "Jews, until such time as existing laws concerning them are revised [*vpred' do peresmotra deistvuiushchikh o nikh uzakonenii*], are not permitted to participate in zemstvo elections and may not be elected as zemstvo deputies."[78]

In all districts and provinces, the great majority of elected delegates *(glasnye)* belonged to the first (Russian) curia. For example, in Vitebsk district of Vitebsk Province, the first curia sent sixteen deputies, the second sent four, and peasant communities *(sel'skie obshchestva)* were represented by only ten. Of the fifty-five delegates to the Vitebsk provincial zemstvo, only ten were members of the second, "non-Russian" curia. These numbers were arrived at by taking the arithmetic mean between the percentage a national group made up of the total population in the area and the percentage of (private) land this group owned. Thus, if in a certain district or province Poles made up 5 percent of the population and owned 35 percent of the private land there, they would be entitled to 20 percent of the deputies. Of course, the official statistics on nationality used in these calculations were themselves not devoid of error or tendentiousness.[79] In any case, the total number of representatives allotted aimed to ensure that Russians would dominate in the new zemstva. For this reason, local Polish attitudes toward the new zemstva were far from enthusiastic.

Immediately after the publishing of the western zemstvo law on March 14, 1911, the government marshaled its forces to set up the new zemstva as soon as possible. According to the Fundamental Law of the Russian Empire, any measure passed by article 87 had to be ratified by the legislature within six months.[80] Thus Stolypin was at pains to present the Duma and State Council with a fait accompli that would discourage any further attempts at opposition. Measures were taken to dismantle the old "quasi-zemstva," and elections were scheduled for July 1911. *Russkie Vedomosti* reported that during the course of July the form of the new zemstvo throughout the region would be established. *Vestnik Evropy* explained the government's haste:

> [The government aims to ensure that] when the Duma and State Council come together in the autumn they will see that the new zemstva have already put down strong roots in the population and they will realize that destroying these zemstva would be a difficult, painful, and unprofitable [*ubytochnyi*] operation for the population.[81]

The MVD rushed to set up the zemstva in the West. According to regulations *(pravila)* sent out in March 1911, preliminary electoral lists were to be published by May 1, the elections held by mid-August, and the zemstva were in place by mid-October 1911. In the Southwest, at least, specific instructions were sent out to local governors stating that, in general, Catholics should be placed in the Polish curia and that baptized Jews were not to be allowed to participate in zemstvo elections. Polish landowners tended to adopt a low profile in the zemstvo elections, though generally did not boycott them altogether. Similarly in Mogilev Province, the governor reported, the national issue played little role in the elections.[82]

The Nationalists saw these elections as a major opportunity to extend their political influence, but on the whole their hopes were disappointed. In Volhynia, the Nationalists—allied with Orthodox Archbishop Antonii—led a campaign against the Volhynia Czechs, to little avail. In several districts the first curia was dominated by Czechs who refused to be intimidated by the Nationalists and the Union of Russian People. It was also reported that provincial governors worked hand in hand with the Nationalists during the elections.[83]

In the end, however, despite the combined efforts of "Russian Committees," Orthodox clergy, and government officials, the general level of interest in the elections remained low, and suspicion toward the Nationalist government candidates remained high. When the MVD collected information about the political affiliation of zemstva executive boards and their chairmen *(predsedateli)* in these six provinces, it found that, in the district zemstva, 56 percent of members were Rightists *(pravye)*, 5.4 percent Russian Nationalists, 24.1 percent moderates, 10.4 percent nonparty, and 2.9 percent leftists *(levye)*. In the provincial zemstva, Rightists made up 48 percent of the members, Russian Nationalists 8 percent, and moderates 36 percent, with 4 percent (one member) each for leftists and nonparty.[84]

Meanwhile, no zemstvo of any kind had been introduced in the three Lithuanian provinces of Vilna, Grodno, and Kovno. The margarine zemstvo of 1903 had never been implemented in this region, and these provinces had been excluded from the western zemstvo project in 1910. Hence in these areas pre-reform rural administration continued to be in place even after 1911. In 1913 the MVD Sovet po delam mestnogo khoziaistva (Council on Local Economy) deliberated the introduction of the 1903 zemstvo in this area. These plans never came to fruition, to a large extent because of national antagonisms and the outrage of Poles that the universally scorned margarine zemstvo should be extended to this area. Once again, the government's fear of local nationalities prevented reform. Rather than reducing tensions between center and borderlands, the paralysis of Russian policy—expressed in the lack of reform in the Northwest—served only further to discredit the tsarist government in the eyes of the local populace.[85]

Once in place, the western zemstva did not live up to the hopes of those Russian nationalists who saw them as potential centers for nationalist agitation. On the contrary, these zemstva were in general more interested in the local economy, improving medical care, and building schools than in more overarching and ambitious causes. A contemporary observer described the initial meetings of the Kiev provincial zemstvo:

> And, listening to their businesslike speeches, one felt somewhat embarrassed for the wavers of the nationalist banner *(stiag)* who so bellicosely

and with such pretentious fervor have tried and continue their attempts to influence the form of the zemstvo in the western territory. That banner hung all alone in the air. And according to all appearances and the convictions of local old-timers (*starozhil*), in the future the same fate awaits it.[86]

At least in the short period to 1914, the "Russian" western zemstvo appeared to lack interest in furthering the "Russian" cause in the region. Perhaps the situation might have changed had the Russian Empire survived longer, but in the event, the victory of Stolypin and the Nationalist party in the western zemstvo affair turned out to be a hollow triumph indeed.

CHAPTER Eight

Poles, Russians, and Jews in Conflict

City Government Reform in the Kingdom of Poland

Ho, patriotismo, patriotismo, kiam fine la homoj
lernos kompreni ĝuste vian sencon? (Oh, patriotism, patriotism, when at last will the human race correctly understand your meaning?)

—*L. Zamenhof, creator of Esperanto (1910)*

❖   The introduction of zemstva in the Western Provinces both set off a
chain reaction of nationalist fervor and released pent-up national fears,
mainly on the part of Russian nationalists and fearful government officials.
Even more violent were the nationalist passions unleashed by plans to introduce elective municipal government in Poland, on the model of the 1892
municipal law. Aside from the eternal problem of Russian distrust of Poles,
efforts to introduce elective city government to the Polish Kingdom were
complicated by the high percentage of Jews dwelling in the Kingdom's
cities. Government distrust of both Poles and Jews was compounded by increasing tension between the Polish and Jewish communities in the Kingdom of Poland, and especially in its two largest cities, Warsaw and Łódź. It
was not the Russian government but Polish anti-Semitism and the intransigent Russian reaction in the State Council that prevented the introduction
of elective city governments in Russian Poland.

After an initial attempt to avoid taking a stand on the issue, Polish nationalists, led by the National Democrat (ND or "endek") Party, expressly

rejected proposals to allow all town dwellers equal representation in future self-government. They adamantly refused to consider any plan that would allow Jews to dominate town government anywhere, even in those (many) urban settlements with a majoritarian Jewish population. Whereas Polish anti-Semitism had been apparent before the city government project reached the Duma in 1910, during the Duma debates on this subject the vehemence of Polish anti-Semitism embarrassed would-be Polonophile Russian liberals and made Polonophobe Russian Nationalists, themselves no Judeophiles, crow with delight at the Poles' double standard.[1] In effect, the fervor caused by the city government bill showed all too vividly that the Russian government and Russian reactionaries held no monopoly on nationalist chauvinism and intolerance.

Before turning to the mechanics of the administration of Polish cities we need to examine the laws according to which Russian cities were governed. The contemporary system of administration in Russian cities, like the zemstvo reforms, originated with a reform during the period of the Great Reforms of the reign of Alexander II and had then been modified to ensure greater bureaucratic control during the reign of Alexander III.[2] Although the current system of urban government satisfied neither "society" nor the government entirely, it did at least permit some measure of public participation in the day-to-day affairs and administration of the empire's cities.

The original municipal statute of 1870 created in each municipality a city council *(gorodskaia duma)* and an executive board *(uprava)*. The vote was given to men at least twenty-five years of age who paid some kind of city tax or fee. As voting was divided into three curiae (as in the zemstva), the more affluent city dwellers had a disproportionate influence in the elected city governments. These residents concerned themselves, much like the zemstva, with public health, utilities, maintaining public markets, and other services.

The 1892 law lessened the independence of municipal self-government by giving local officials the right to intervene and nullify the city council's decisions if these were found inexpedient. The 1870 statute had allowed such interference in city affairs only when the city self-government's actions were deemed illegal. The curial system of voting was abolished in the 1892 law, but at the same time suffrage was narrowed so that only a few particularly affluent city residents could participate in these bodies at all.[3]

The parallels with the zemstvo reform are obvious. The original form of self-government, already limited to the wealthier and better-educated classes, was then further restricted by a nervous government in the early 1890s, when it seemed that even these modest organs of local self-government could serve as centers for independent action against, or at least not "with," the central government. Also, as in the case of the zemstvo reforms, the imperial government did not extend the municipal statutes to the Kingdom of Poland, though the original statute of 1870 contained a footnote stating that texts of the statute had been sent out to all governor generals, to the viceroy in Poland, and to the Uchreditel'nyi v Tsarstve Pol'skom

Komitet (Constituent Committee in the Kingdom of Poland), apparently to get the opinions of these officials as to the feasibility of extending this reform to their region.[4]

The statutes of 1870 and 1892 were, however, extended to the Western Provinces. In fact, the supposed domination of the Minsk city government by Poles was used by Russian conservatives as an argument against the introduction of zemstva in the area.[5] Governors from these nine provinces often complained that local city governments were inefficient, corrupt, and full of "uncultured" elements. Still, the economic and hygienic situation of these provinces' cities was on the whole better than in the Polish Kingdom, where despite several false starts in the ensuing decades the municipal reform was never introduced.[6]

While the system of municipal government in the empire clearly left much to be desired, the cities of Russian Poland lacked elective government entirely.[7] The Vistula land was occupied territory, and Warsaw was the headquarters of this occupation. In Warsaw the city government consisted of *magistraty*, named by the government, headed by a city president. The president was appointed from St. Petersburg and often had little or no knowledge of Poland or things Polish prior to his appointment. (This was the case even with Sokrates Starynkevich, the most famous of Warsaw city presidents.) All decisions by the magistrates and city president occurred under the tutelage of the governor general and the Warsaw chief of police *(oberpolitseimeister)*. Furthermore, major expenditures by the city (over 30,000 rubles) had to be approved by the minister of internal affairs. This system of administration, in place since 1818, admitted no public participation.[8] Moreover, due to the strict rules against Poles' holding government positions in the Kingdom of Poland, the bureaucrats running Polish cities were nearly all outsiders, poorly acquainted with the cultural and economic needs of the local population.

During the early years of the reign of Alexander II, elective city government had been introduced in Russian Poland. The decree of June 18, 1861 (new style), granted elective self-government in twenty-eight cities and thirty-nine districts of the Kingdom of Poland. The campaign for elections to the Warsaw city government in the summer of 1861 gave rise to considerable controversy, and although the elections took place as scheduled in late August, the declaration of martial law soon after prevented the elective city governments from actually getting down to work.[9] The outbreak of the January uprising sealed the fate of the essentially stillborn city government reform in Russian Poland. In the wake of the uprising, the administration of Polish cities reverted to the old bureaucratic system that had existed before 1861.[10] This cumbersome arrangement was to remain in place nearly to the end of the Russian Empire.

Long before the reign of Nicholas II, administrators in Russian Poland had recognized the need for a reform of city government there. In 1870 viceroy F. Berg had called for the introduction of elective city government to the provinces of the Polish Kingdom. Toward the end of the decade, an

KINGDOM
OF POLAND

Provincial Capitals
and Principal Towns

0   25   50   75 Miles

N

BALTIC SEA

Kovno
Province

KOVNO

VILNA

Mariampol

Vilna
Province

SUWAŁKI

PRUSSIA

Augustów

GRODNO

Białystok

ŁOMŻA

Grodno
Province

Mława

Włocławek   Ciechanow

Sokołów

PŁOCK

WARSAW   SIEDLCE   Białystok

Brest-Litovsk

Konin

Łódź

Lubartow

Volhynia
Province

KALISZ

Chełm

PIOTRKÓW   RADOM   LUBLIN

Częstochowa

Hrubieszow

KIELCE

Biłgoray   Zamość

Tomaszow

PRUSSIA

AUSTRIA

K. J. Carr, 1996

MVD study on city administration in the Polish Kingdom cautiously suggested that the cities of the area were ready for elective self-government. A few years later, in 1881, newly appointed governor general P. Albedinskii wrote to minister of the interior N. P. Ignatiev, requesting that the "lawful desires [*zakonnye zhelaniia*] of the inhabitants of the Vistula country" (including the introduction of the 1870 municipal statute) be fulfilled. Ignatiev answered in typical bureaucratic fashion, stating that, although he agreed with Albedinskii's desire to introduce the city government law, the government must act with extreme caution in order not to awaken Polish hopes for further political concessions.[11]

At the beginning of Alexander III's reign in 1881, however, plans were already being mooted for a major revision of the 1870 law. These considerations precluded any further development of projects for elected municipal government in the Congress Kingdom until after 1892. By this time, the inadequacies of the system of urban administration in Russian Poland and public dissatisfaction with it had become obvious, even to the Russian occupiers, and in the summer of 1895 governor general Prince A. K. Imeretinskii indicated that he favored the introduction of the 1892 statute to Poland.[12]

Polish conciliators (of whom Adolf Suligowski was one) greeted Imeretinskii's suggestion with enthusiasm. The *Kraj* group saw elective city government in the Polish Kingdom, and especially in Warsaw, as an opportunity for creating a space for Polish society within the administrative structure of the Congress Kingdom. Once the Russian government admitted that elective city governments in Poland posed no danger to Russian security (the argument went), a general reconciliation between Polish society and Russian government might be possible. From late 1895 several articles appeared in *Kraj* pointing out the deficiencies of the present administration of Polish cities and arguing for the introduction of elective city governments.

Typically for *Kraj*, a good part of these articles was made up of quotations from the Russian press. On November 2/14, 1895, *Słowo, Birzhevye Vedomosti,* and even *Grazhdanin* were quoted as favoring the introduction of the 1892 statute to Poland. The conservative *Słowo* pointed out that the present favorable condition of Warsaw was attributable to the former city president, Sokrates Starynkevich, thereby insinuating that under a new president the city might not fare as well.[13] Moreover, *Słowo* continued, now Polish cities should take up the example of the cities of the empire (that is, where the 1870 and 1892 statutes were in force), where "after obtaining the new statute, funds were raised for public needs in amounts exceeding those previously possible and [the cities] were thus enabled to deal more zealously [*gorliwiej*] with public education, thereby fulfilling the Most High Will as it has been expressed upon several occasions." *Słowo* concluded that the tasks of city government such as education, public health, and provisioning could all be better carried out by a system based on "the participation of the most concerned elements," that is, the wealthier burghers of

Warsaw, not quite coincidentally, the readers of *Słowo*.[14]

The conservative and loyalist arguments encountered in the *Słowo* article were typical of the language used on the Polish side in favor of concessions from the Russian government. Indeed, the issue of municipal reform in Poland was completely dominated before 1905 by the *ugodowcy* or conciliators such as Adolf Suligowski, Erazm Piltz, and Włodzimierz Spasowicz. Before 1905 both the PPS and the ND parties remained committed, at least rhetorically, to Polish independence and thus were not particularly interested in half measures such as a city government project that in any case would have given the vote to only a small percent of the city's wealthiest citizens. This left the conservative *Kraj* group to argue the case for elective municipal government in Poland.[15]

In the same article, the St. Petersburg daily *Birzhevye Vedomosti* was quoted in order to back up one of ugoda's favorite themes—that much had changed in Polono-Russian relations since 1863:

> The plan to apply the municipal statute to the Kingdom [of Poland] bears witness to the fact that the past thirty years have not passed without a trace. The extension of the municipal statute, and of other reforms, to our borderlands [*kresy*] creates the moral link between Russia and her non-Russian [*roznorodnye*] nationalities, and this link is significantly more durable than any external measures.

The article went on to cite the example of city government in the mixed-nationality area of the Western Provinces, where this reform brought nothing but benefits for the local population.[16] In other words, *Birzhevye Vedomosti* supported the central supposition of ugoda: that Poles had learned a lesson since 1863 and could now be entrusted with administrative and public responsibilities within the Russian state. Even the reactionary *Grazhdanin* was quoted as saying that the 1892 reform must be extended to Poland, "if for no other reason than to eliminate that striking difference that now exists in city administration within one and the same state." The only dissenting voice in this chorus of support for the reform of city government in Russian Poland came, predictably enough, from *Varshavskii Dnevnik*, which was quoted as opposing the reform of the present administrative system in the Vistula lands.[17]

The *Varshavskii Dnevnik*, official organ of the Russian government in Poland, denied that an extension of the 1892 law to Poland was even being considered. The paper also expressed its belief that the existing system of city government successfully carried out its tasks and was in no need of reform. This view is hardly surprising, since the *Dnevnik* reflected the opinions of the Russian authorities who presently held the reins of power in the region.[18] According to this group, the prosperity and order to be found in Warsaw proved conclusively the wisdom and efficacy of the city government there. To quote an 1897 visitor, Nicholas II, "Warsaw is in excellent condition, I know that and saw it myself."[19] (They seldom mentioned any other Polish cities.) The agitation for municipal reform, they insinuated, was no more than a Polish grab for power. Concurring with the Warsaw daily, the reactionary *Moskovskie Vedomosti* warned that self-government in Poland would only fan the fires of separatism, insisting that "urban well-being [in Poland] leaves nothing to be desired." *Kraj* indignantly rejected these claims, making the counter-accusation that *Varshavskii Dnevnik*'s preference for the "archaic magistrate administration" only reflected a selfish desire to shut out public involvement, which "better corresponds to modern needs and the demands of a proper municipal administration."[20]

In the end, it would seem, the Warsaw daily carried the argument over the St. Petersburg weekly. In any case, despite repeated complaints in *Kraj* and elsewhere about the deficiencies of city administration in the Kingdom of Poland, no measures were taken to change the situation until after 1904.[21] The reasons for this were many: the most important was general bureaucratic lethargy, exacerbated by the lingering suspicion that Polish-dominated city governments would complicate the lives of Russian administrators in the region. Furthermore, general conditions in Warsaw were far superior to those of nearly any city in the interior of the empire, so local Russian officials failed to perceive any pressing need for reform.[22] Then, as later, Russian administrators compared the Polish situation favorably with conditions at home in the central Russian provinces, whereas Poles compared the existing administrative order unfavorably with that current in Vienna, Berlin, or Paris.[23] And, as always, one should not underestimate the almost morbid caution and inertia that reigned within the tsarist administration. Without a major and compelling cause for reform (the catastrophes in the Crimea or in Manchuria, or the revolution of 1905, for example), the prevailing tendency was to leave well enough alone.[24]

Reform of Polish municipal administration, like so many other reforms, had to wait until public unrest compelled the imperial government to issue its ukaz of December 12, 1904. As we have seen, article 2 of this proclamation promised "to grant rural [*zemskii*] and urban institutions the broadest possible participation in the management of local well-being [*blagoustroistvo*]."[25] This decree was correctly taken as a pledge to extend elective municipal government to Poland.[26] Rather like the situation in the late 1850s and early 1860s, much of Polish society saw the present time as quite possibly the beginning of a new era in Russian-Polish relations or, at the very least, a propitious moment to demand concessions from the weakened Russian government.

In early April 1905, *Kraj* reported, the Committee of Ministers had discussed the issue of city administration in the Kingdom of Poland and had come to the conclusion that it was necessary to introduce both municipal and rural self-government. In considering the application of article 7 of the December 12, 1904, decree to the Kingdom of Poland, the Committee of Ministers remarked:

the zemstvo and city statutes were not introduced within the Kingdom of
Poland; its cities are administered on the basis of extremely antiquated
laws . . . . The absence of the societal element in the administration negatively affects the well-being and prosperity of the Vistula land: schools,
medicine, and social welfare remain significantly worse than in the internal
provinces of Russia.

The committee went on to mention that a draft project for zemstva in the
Polish Kingdom had been sent to the governor general of Warsaw and expressed the desire that the problem of self-government in Poland, both urban and rural, be solved with all possible haste.[27]

A month later, *Kraj* published an article describing spirited public discussion of the issue. Already the Polish anti-Semitic press had come out
against the participation of Jews in "Polish" organs of self-government,[28]
demanding that participants should be only those who were literate in the
Polish language. Not only anti-Semites such as National Democrats demanded restrictions on Jewish participation in city governments. Even the
conciliator Suligowski—who cannot be termed anti-Semitic for this place
and time—held that the town councils would properly be led by the Poles
and advocated indirect methods of ensuring this. The Towarzystwo Hy-
gieniczne (Hygienic Society), on the other hand, issued a list of nine demands, foreseeing zemstva and city governments with broad autonomous
powers based on universal suffrage without curiae and without distinctions based on religion or class.[29] Thus Polish society was not unanimous in
its conception of the exact form future city institutions should take.

Despite certain disagreements about specifics, all of educated Polish society, like its Russian counterpart, looked forward to broader participation
in political life, at least at the local level. However, the more modest original desire for self-government *(samoupravlenie, samorząd)*, predominant in
Polish society in late 1904, had a year later been supplanted by demands
for autonomy or even independence. There existed even more radical demands for severing the Polish Kingdom's links with Russia, especially during the revolutionary months of late 1905 and early 1906. Nonetheless, despite differences in tactics and philosophy, by the end of 1906 all Polish
political parties were united in their demand for autonomy, variously interpreted, for the ten provinces making up Russian Poland. Freely elected
municipal governments were to form an integral part of the new system of
autonomy.[30] The central government also seemed to recognize the need for
municipal self-government in Poland. Just after Prince P. D. Sviatopolk-
Mirskii assumed the position of minister of internal affairs (following Plehve's assassination on August 26, 1904), he was visited by a delegation
from the Warsaw Stock Exchange. These men warned Sviatopolk-Mirskii
that mass unemployment threatened Russian Poland and that disaster
could be averted only by entrusting "society" with a greater role in governing the Kingdom. Similarly, many Polish public figures petitioned the new
minister of the interior, urging the end of restrictions on Poles and asking

that Russian-Polish relations at last be allowed to progress beyond the punitive post-1863 mind-set.[31] Until the very end of 1905 and the declaration of martial law in the Vistula provinces, the government assumed a relatively benevolent but noncommittal attitude toward Polish petitions for self-government and autonomy, possibly out of weakness but arguably because of the realization that efficient administration required a greater amount of participation on the part of local elites.

In a Special Journal *(Osobyi zhurnal)* approved by Nicholas II on June 6, 1905, the Committee of Ministers recommended the introduction of the 1892 municipal statute to the Kingdom of Poland, and on October 24 of the same year a commission was summoned in Warsaw to work out the details of the new municipal law.[32] At the same time, the office of the Warsaw governor general was making advances toward Polish figures regarding the shape of future city government in the Polish Kingdom.[33] A subcommission headed by Adolf Suligowski drew up two projects: one for Warsaw and Łódź, by far the two largest cities in the Kingdom, and the other for the remaining cities in Russian Poland.

Some years later, Suligowski wrote that among the principles guiding the council that drew up this project, two were of particular importance. First of all, the council wished to open city government to representatives of all social classes, nationalities, and religions though with a special place for educated people *(ludzi wiedzy)*. Equally vital from their point of view was the use of "the local Polish language [*język miejscowy polski*]" in the city governments, with special rights for the use of Lithuanian in city governments in northern Suwałki Province and Ukrainian *(maloruski)* in eastern Lublin and Siedlce Provinces. Suligowski defended the division of the electorate into two curiae and the denial of suffrage to illiterates as essential for the proper functioning of urban self-government in this region where, for so many years, the population had been deprived of any influence over local administration. What Suligowski and his colleagues foresaw was in fact a modest, conservative, but essentially Polish, system of municipal government.[34]

For our purposes the differences between the two projects are insignificant, so I will limit my comments to the Warsaw/Łódź project.[35] The language of the municipal governments was to be Polish, although correspondence with the Russian authorities would be composed in Russian (article 19). City government would consist of four organs: a city council *(rada)*, city administration *(zarząd)*, city president, and a supervisory committee *(komisya rewizyjna)*. As for voting rights, all male members of the city commune *(gmina)* over twenty-five years of age could vote, as long as they were literate in Polish and had resided in the city for at least one year. Voters were divided into two curiae. The first was to be made up of wealthier citizens and professionals: people paying over 50 rubles annually in city taxes; owners of enterprises; and honorary citizens, including clergy, rabbis, and mullahs. The second curia was to consist of everyone else.[36] Since both curiae elected an equal number of representatives, city governments would obviously be weighted in favor of the most prosperous, "cultured" citizens.

Clearly, this was no radically democratic project. Although universal manhood suffrage was to be introduced, the literacy requirement coupled with the requisite one-year residency would have probably deterred many potential voters from the poorest classes from participating in elections. Similarly, though no national curiae were foreseen, many of the potential Jewish and Russian voters would be deterred by the requirement to be literate in Polish. Still, the project was far more democratic than the 1892 statute, and infinitely preferable (from both democratic and national points of view) to the later projects proposed and discussed in the Duma and State Council.[37]

In any case, the project put forth by Suligowski and other members of Polish "society" was not allowed to develop beyond draft form. In October 1906 the governor general of Warsaw, G. Skalon, rejected this project as not sufficiently protective of Russian interests. In a long letter to minister of internal affairs Stolypin, Skalon warned that the Polish intelligentsia aimed at the broadest possible autonomy from Russia and that these strivings were informed by a hatred of Russia and the Russian government: "The introduction of zemstvo and urban self-government is exceedingly desirable from the point of view of the Polish intelligentsia in general, and for local politicians in particular, since this reform will untie their hands." The use of Polish in these bodies could not be allowed: "it would not be in keeping with the dignity and interests of the state to allow the conducting of business in zemstvo and urban self-government in any language other than Russian." By allowing the use of Polish, he maintained, the government would not only encourage the centrifugal tendencies of the worst elements of Polish society but would also antagonize the Jews and Lithuanians in the Congress Kingdom, who would then demand that their languages be given proper recognition in these bodies. The governor general then forwarded to St. Petersburg another project, which he had drawn up without the participation of Polish "society." This project, in various permutations, was to remain under consideration within the MVD for nearly four years.[38]

In late 1906 a special conference (*osoboe soveshchanie*) was called in St. Petersburg to discuss the introduction of self-government to Poland. This body included Poles such as Adolf Suligowski as well as zemstvo figures and MVD officials. Already at this point the Jewish question was raised, and Suligowski pointed out that by requiring deputies to be literate in Polish, many Jews would ipso facto be excluded. Another Pole—Roman Zaremba, the mayor (*prezydent*) of Lublin—disagreed with Suligowski, saying that more specific restrictions were needed, and he gave the example of Lublin where, if suffrage was limited to payers of city taxes (*gorodskie nalogi*), Jews would certainly dominate the city government.[39] As the conference constituted only an advisory body, no conclusions were reached on this perplexing issue.

When the members of the special conference returned home, they expected that elected city government in Poland would not be long in arriving.[40] To quote Suligowski, "We left St. Petersburg convinced that in the course of 1907 zemstvo and city government bills would pass the Duma and that in 1908 these would be introduced [in Poland]." Such expectations were to be sadly disappointed. After 1906, the Polish city government project disappeared into the bowels of the MVD, not to resurface for nearly three years. Finally, in October 1909, a revised project was considered by two separate commissions, one consisting of selected members of Polish society along with zemstvo representatives and MVD officials (the so-called Vybornaia Komissiia) and the other a special committee within the MVD (Osoboe Prisutstvie Soveta po Delam Mestnogo Khoziaistva). As we might expect, some of the most embittered arguments had to do with the Jewish question and with which language to be used within the bodies of urban self-government. In the end, the Poles lost on nearly all points. Suligowski remarked that the most violent Polonophobes were not the official figures but the zemstvo activists. The use of Polish in the internal workings of the city governments was further restricted, and Jews who had embraced Catholicism were placed in the Jewish, and not Polish, curia.[41]

Finally, in April 1910, the Council of Ministers discussed the project drafted by the MVD Council on Local Economy. This project, "O preobrazhenii upravleniia gorodov v guberniiakh Tsarstva Pol'skogo," was discussed in the Council of Ministers on April 6 and 27, 1910. Shortly thereafter, in July, the project was forwarded to the Duma.[42] For the Poles, this bill constituted a great step backward from the Suligowski project of 1906. As we have seen, the Polish project of 1905 had set down Polish as the language of the city councils, although correspondence with the Russian authorities would be in Russian. The government project, by contrast, extended the use of Russian and, although it did not shut out Polish entirely, gave the impression that Polish would be merely "tolerated" within urban self-government in the Vistula provinces. All official communication had to be composed in Russian, even when in response to a Polish petition. All queries or petitions made in Russian had to be answered in that language. The internal documents, protocols, and minutes of city government were to be kept in Russian. During the meetings of the city council, however, speakers could use Russian or Polish as they wished. Finally, laws and announcements of the city government were to be written in Russian, though a parallel Polish translation might be given. All council members were required to know Russian.[43]

The national curiae set down by the government project also discriminated against the Poles. The city councils were to be divided into three curiae—Russian, Jewish, and "other." Even though the third curia exceeded the other two in size, one can well imagine the reaction of Polish patriots at being relegated to the category of "none-of-the-above" in the city governments of their own country. And, as we have seen, Catholic converts of Jewish origin were to be included not with the Poles but in the Jewish curia.

Taking the example of Warsaw, we find that out of 160 city council members, 27 would be elected from the first (Russian) curia, 16 from the second (Jewish), and 127 from the third (other). Looking at these numbers we must keep in mind that, in 1908, according to official sources, Catholics (for the most part Poles, of course) made up 56.65 percent of Warsaw's population, Jews made up 36.93 percent, and Orthodox (nearly all Russians) 3.66 percent.[44] Thus the real losers of the curia system were the Jews, who made up nearly 40 percent of the city's population but received only 10 percent of the town council members. One should also keep in mind that, in many of the smaller cities in the Kingdom of Poland, Jews made up an even larger percentage of their community's total population, whereas Russians formed a minuscule minority. One can also imagine the difficulty of conducting all business in the Russian language in the town councils of such places as Szydlowiec, Radom Province, where 6,433 of the 8,597 inhabitants were Jews and, of the 30 council members, 24 were to be Polish and 6 Jewish.

Article 29 of the project set down the rule that in those cities where Jews made up more than half of a city's population, their curia was to receive 20 percent of the seats in the town council, otherwise the second curia was to have at most 10 percent of the total seats.[45] Russians in Warsaw, as one would expect, gained most from the government project; for the most part they were temporary residents, making up under 4 percent of the city's population, but they enjoyed nearly 17 percent of the representatives. From the Polish point of view this preferential treatment was all the more outrageous when one took into account that these Russians often lived in Warsaw for a short period of time, had interests quite foreign to those of permanent residents, and already enjoyed various advantages over the Polish—or Jewish—locals.

The total electorate was minuscule, in any case. In Warsaw, suffrage would have been limited to only about 23,000 voters, or under 3 percent of the total population. However, Suligowski says that the project would give the vote to nearly the "entire intelligentsia of the city." One of the few more progressive aspects of the voting scheme set down by the government project was its inclusion of renters, not just property owners.[46] In addition, the project lessened the amount of power that the local governor could exercise over the organs of city government. Apparently it was felt that the curia system, the narrow electorate, and other "guarantees" for Russians provided adequate protection for government interests. In this respect the project resembled the original 1870 municipal statute more than the 1892 counter-reform. For all that, the inadequacy of the project was apparent to all, especially to Poles and their elected representatives in the Duma. The government project was seen by Poles as a direct challenge and insult to their national honor, and Duma debates on this issue reflect the high level of outrage felt by Polish society.[47]

The project was first sent to the Duma Komissiia po mestnomu samoupravleniiu (Commission on Local Self-Government), which dedicated eleven sessions to discussion of the reform. The commission regarded this reform as particularly important since it was widely seen as a prototype of a future municipal statute for the cities of the empire. After this detailed consideration, the commission recommended several changes. First, the strictures against Polish were to be slightly lessened for the internal workings of the city councils, though Russian remained obligatory for any documents that might be reviewed by Russian authorities. The commission also recommended that the area of competency of the city governments be considerably broadened, and that the suffrage be somewhat extended.[48]

The project was introduced to the Duma plenum by the Nationalist P. V. Sinadino. In his initial speech, Sinadino defended the introduction of elective city government on practical grounds, pointing out that since 1870 several of the governor generals of Warsaw had supported the reform of city administration there. Sinadino defended the national curiae as being inevitable in a region of mixed population such as Russia's Polish provinces. He even went so far as to call the establishment of a Jewish curia "a gigantic step forward [*giganticheskii shag vpered*] toward the general solution of the Jewish question." And although correspondence with the central authorities would have to be composed in Russian, that the Polish language was allowed at all represented a significant concession to the empire's Polish subjects: "Here for the first step the possibility and right is recognized for those persons wishing to speak publicly, using Polish in a public gathering." Sinadino hastened to add that a translation in Russian would be provided for any persons wishing it.[49]

The Polish parliamentary club, the Koło, did not immediately oppose the project. Noting its deficiencies, Koło member W. Grabski recognized that city government in the rest of Russia was also not without defects and saw the project as in any case an improvement on the present bureaucratic administrative order. With these considerations in mind, Grabski stated his belief that the bill should be passed without significant amendments, which would only further delay the introduction of elected city government to the provinces of Russian Poland.[50] Beside their stated motives, the Koło no doubt wanted to avoid lengthy discussion of the project, which could only exacerbate nationalist feelings on the part of Jews, Poles, and Russians alike.

Grabski's views were not shared by Russian liberals and leftists in the Duma. The Lithuanian delegate A. A. Bulat, representing Suwałki Province, explained the acquiescence of the Koło by pointing out that its members all belonged to the "urban bourgeoisie" favored in the project. Effective city government, Bulat affirmed, would require universal suffrage and the use of local languages, including Polish and Lithuanian, in all aspects of city government. In a similar vein, the Kadet N. N. Shchepkin from Moscow dismissed the project as a "surrogate of what we need." By putting up limitations on the suffrage for the poor, the women, and the Jews, the project significantly reduced the possibilities of local self-government. As to the suggestion that this project might be a prototype for reforming city government in the Russian interior, Shchepkin exclaimed, "God save us from such a prototype!" The Duma delegate from Kovno

Province, N. Fridman (one of only two Jewish members of the Third Duma), also condemned the project. The restrictions on the Jews represented a serious violation of the principle of Jewish equal rights that had existed in Poland for nearly fifty years. Furthermore, the example of Galicia (where city governments existed without national curiae) showed that even in nationally mixed areas, elective urban self-government could function without recourse to such restrictive measures.[51]

Some Duma members found, however, that the bill included too many concessions to the Poles. Sergei Alekseev, delegate for the Russian population of Warsaw, argued that allowing speeches in Polish in the city dumas constituted a violation of the fundamental law, which stated that Russian was the language of all administrative organs of the empire. Alekseev and his allies helped reject many of the "liberalizing" amendments that had been introduced by the Duma commission for local self-government.[52] Not only did the plenum reject any broader use of Polish by the town councils, but, led by Alekseev, it further restricted the Polish language, causing a contemporary observer to exclaim, "The Duma was less tolerant of the Polish language than the very author of the project, Stolypin."[53]

The issue of language was soon overshadowed by another aspect of the project, the Jewish question. Although Jews made up a large percentage of the urban population in the Kingdom of Poland, unlike their co-religionists in the interior of the empire they enjoyed, in principle at least, quasi-legal equality within the Polish provinces. The national curiae proposed in the city project aimed primarily at the "protection" of Russian rights but, at the same time, severely abridged the representation of Jews. This kind of blatant national discrimination could hardly scarcely go unnoticed by Russian liberals, who had previously supported Polish national demands.[54]

Unfortunately for the relations between Russian liberals and Poles, the Polish representatives in the Duma refused to relinquish their support for Jewish restrictions, all the while insisting that limitations on Polish rights must be abolished. When Koło member W. Jaroński vociferously attacked Jewish pretensions to proportional representation in future Polish city government, the Poles found themselves totally isolated within the Duma.[55] Their erstwhile allies, the Kadets, refused any support of Poles against Jews, while the extremely polonophobic right within the Duma leapt at the chance to pontificate on the general hypocrisy of the Poles who demanded national rights for themselves while denying them to others.[56] The final break came after a speech by the Kadet Fedor Rodichev, criticizing the Polish deputies' actions. In his rebuttal to this speech, Koło member Jan Harusewicz bid farewell to the Poles' political liaison with the Kadets, quoting Lermontov: "The love was without joy, the parting will be without sorrow [*Byla bez radosti liubov', razluka budet bez pechali*]."[57]

The issue was further complicated and considerably exacerbated by discussions of the Kholm project, which occupied the Duma at the same time.[58] Indeed, one of the arguments presented by supporters of the Kholm bill was that the introduction of city government in the Polish provinces made the formation of a new, non-Polish province out of the eastern parts of Lublin and Siedlce Provinces inevitable (see chapter 9). The reasoning ran that, if the government were to introduce local self-government to the Polish Kingdom, the Poles would dominate the zemstva and city governments. Hence, it would be necessary to separate the "Russian" population of the eastern regions of Lublin and Siedlce Provinces from the Kingdom. The Polish city government project and the formation of the Kholm Province were thus inextricably tied together in their legislative fates. Both projects came to be seen (and rightly so) as prejudicial to Polish interests, and it is probable that the combination further antagonized the Polish nationalists of the ND party, who were then that much less willing to compromise on the Jewish question.

The question of Jewish-Polish relations immediately assumed a central place in discussions of the city government project. Already in November 1910, just two months after deliberations began in the Duma plenum, one commentator complained that the many weaknesses of the project were being completely ignored in the outrage over Jewish restrictions. The majoritarian Polish view held that no ground could be ceded in this question, as Jewish domination over Polish city governments could absolutely not be allowed. On the other hand, Polish socialists and *ugodowcy*, now known as realists, both rejected Jewish restrictions as repugnant and harmful for Polish national interests.[59]

Already at the end of 1910, then, Polish-Jewish relations were extremely strained. Indeed, signs of growing antagonism between Poles and Jews had long been noted. Already in the spring of 1905 one Russian official of long service in the Polish Kingdom submitted a report to the MVD in which he stated that the abnormally rapid growth of Łódź and the many Jews and Germans there provided a rich soil for disorders. He pointed to the large immigration of Jews to the Polish provinces from the Russia interior and noted that Jews controlled nearly all trade in the Congress Kingdom. Kirilov warned that these conditions could give rise, "and in the near future," to serious political complications.[60]

Kirilov's predictions were rapidly realized in the years after the crushing of the 1905–1907 revolution. The hitherto latent (or at least unobtrusive) anti-Semitism in Polish society, most pointedly in the ND party, intruded increasingly onto the public scene. Here was a prime example of one nationalism (Russian against Poles) serving as a catalyst to exacerbate a second (Poles against Jews). Polish society became practically united against the Jewish intruders, and the most bitter reproaches were hurled at the Litwaks, Russian Jews who had settled in Polish cities since 1881.[61] According to the Poles, these Jews acted as a russifying element, arrogantly refusing to learn Polish and demanding that Poles speak to them in Russian. Many Poles went so far as to suggest that the imperial government had dispatched these Jews to Poland as a deliberate russifying measure.[62] Whether seen as an intentional plot by the Russian authorities or as the natural outcome of the economic opportunities available to Jews in Poland, the Litwak

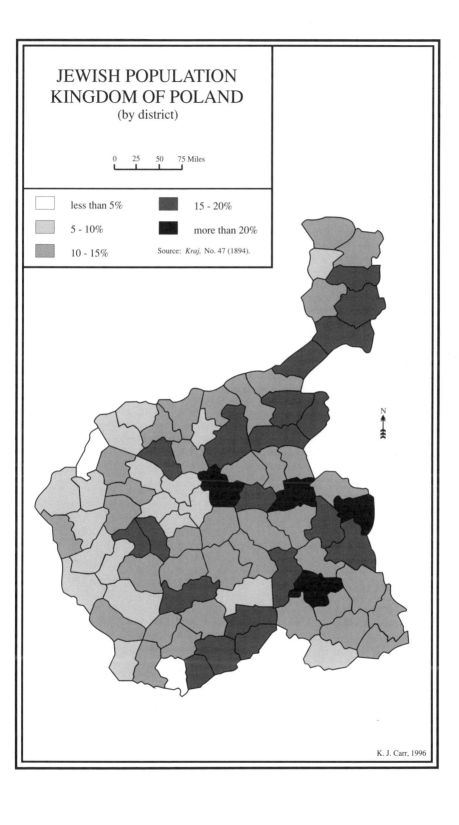

JEWISH POPULATION
KINGDOM OF POLAND
(by district)

0   25   50   75 Miles

less than 5%   15 - 20%

5 - 10%   more than 20%

10 - 15%   Source: *Kraj,* No. 47 (1894).

N

K. J. Carr, 1996

question served further to antagonize Polish-Jewish relations.

Although it is difficult to understand and impossible to justify the rise of anti-Semitism in Russian Poland during the first decade of this century, certain factors must be kept in mind. First of all, if one necessary condition of nationalism is truly, as Isaiah Berlin has suggested, "the infliction of a wound on the collective feeling of a society, or at least of its spiritual leaders," then Poland and Poles certainly had cause to be nationalists in the early twentieth century.[63] Poles in the Russian Empire felt themselves under attack from the central government, which restricted use of their native tongue, closed down private Polish educational institutions such as the Macierz Polska, and conspired to deprive the Polish Kingdom of its eastern marches by forming the Kholm Province. At the same time, within the Jewish community in Poland and throughout the Russian Empire the first stirrings of nationalism could be witnessed at this time. Polish commentators saw the Litwaks as zealous propagators of this new movement in Poland.[64]

Added to these purely national and emotive factors was the Jewish economic position in Russian Poland. Although the majority of large capitalists and industrialists were not of Jewish origin, Jews made up a very significant percentage of petty merchants, artisans, and the like in the Polish Kingdom. To quote a recent study, "Anti-Semitism of the kind engendered by the clash between an entrenched Jewish commercial and industrial class, from which the secular elite emerged, and a rising native middle class was probably greater here [in the Congress Kingdom] than anywhere else in Poland [that is, in the Austrian and Prussian partitions]."[65] The combination of emotive and economic factors poisoned Polish-Jewish relations in the post-1905 years to an unprecedented extent.

The nadir of Polish-Jewish relations was reached in 1912, during the elections to the Fourth Duma. Under the prevailing electoral system the city of Warsaw elected two delegates, one from Warsaw's Russian population and the other from the remaining voters.[66] Because of peculiarities in the electoral system, Warsaw Jews found themselves in the embarrassing position of controlling the votes needed to elect the non-Russian Warsaw delegate. The National Democrats, in a show of national bravado, put up the anti-Semite Roman Dmowski, head of the party, as their candidate. As a recent study states, "The main slogan put forth by Dmowski was 'an open battle against Jews.'"[67] When the Jewish electors asked that a compromise candidate be found who would at least support Jewish rights within Poland, the endeks refused.

Dmowski dropped out of the race when he failed to place among the winning electors in the first round of voting. The National Democrats then switched their support to the candidate Jan Kucharzewski, who was certainly less committed to anti-Semitism than Dmowski. But even Kucharzewski declared his support for restrictions on Jewish participation in Polish city government and declined to support Jewish rights in public.[68] Hence the Warsaw Jewish electors sent not a Jew (they feared that this would be too provocative) but the Polish socialist Jagiełło to the Duma.[69]

The Polish press—particularly those organs of a nationalist bent—were outraged at what they interpreted as a further example of Jewish presumptuousness. The call for a national boycott raised in the anti-Semitic morning newspaper *Gazeta Poranna-2 Grosze* was soon taken up by other, more moderate, newspapers and journals. The boycott spread quickly under the slogan "Swój do swego" (in English, roughly, "Keep to your own kind") and served to poison relations between Jews and Poles, not only to 1914 but long afterward.[70]

Thus a simple project for reforming city government gave rise to—or, rather, revealed and greatly aggravated—the enormous national tensions existing in tsarist Poland. (This bill also brought forth demands from the Lithuanian-speaking residents of Suwałki Province for language rights for Lithuanian in the city governments of that area.) Back in St. Petersburg, the project, with additional restrictions on the use of the Polish language, passed the Duma on February 6, 1912, and was sent along to the State Council. Here, as with the western zemstvo project, the bill encountered stiff opposition.[71]

The State Council delayed action on the project until the end of the 1912 session, when the Third Duma, along with the session, came to an end. Thus after the recess, the State Council was able to treat the bill as a completely new project. The State Council then rejected the Duma amendments and significantly increased the level of taxation necessary to participate in city government elections—for Warsaw up to 560 rubles, a quite significant sum.[72] Clearly, the State Council wished to prevent the passage of the bill and would not shy away from a collision course both with the Duma and with the government itself.

Having rejected Duma amendments and increased the *tsenz* (that is, the amount of wealth required to qualify for suffrage), the State Council proceeded to attack various details in the bill—particularly those allowing Polish to be used in city council debates—and subjected these articles to vociferous criticism in lengthy and impassioned speeches. This assault found its leaders primarily in two figures: V. I. Gurko (whose *Ocherki Privislian'ia* we have considered above) and A. S. Stishinskii (like Gurko a longtime employee in the MVD but unlike Gurko appointed, not elected, to the State Council). The pugnacious anti-Polish speeches in the State Council infuriated the governor general of Warsaw, who sent off a scathing letter to the emperor denouncing Gurko and Stishinskii as representatives of an outdated and thoroughly discredited system of russification *(obrusenie)*. According to Radziszewski, the State Council argued that it would be impossible to grant the Kingdom of Poland a better system of city government than that existing within the empire proper.[73]

Gurko and Stishinskii insisted that the use of a "local language" (Polish) had no place in any administrative body of the Russian state, including city councils in the Polish Kingdom. Indeed, the very shrillness and complete rejection of compromise formulae manifested in the State Council lead one to the conclusion that this group aimed not to reform the Polish city government project but to obstruct extension of elected city government to the Polish provinces entirely. Apparently, for them any kind of concessions to the Poles would pose a grave danger to the integrity of the Russian state.

The form in which the State Council "passed" the Polish city government bill was so different from the Duma project that the project was returned to the Duma in April 1913. The Duma, predictably, refused to accept all the State Council's changes and returned the bill, again in altered form, to the upper house, where, on November 29, 1913, the Council promptly rejected it.[74] A committee was formed to reach a compromise between State Council and Duma, but the State Council's dogged refusal to budge caused assistant minister of internal affairs S. E. Kryzhanovskii to give it up as lost on May 12, 1914.[75]

It is interesting to note that once again, just as in the case of the western zemstvo, the government's desire to reform administration in the West was blocked by the most conservative house of the Russian legislature, the State Council. That the government and the MVD wanted the Polish city bill passed into law is beyond doubt. Among other things, we have the evidence of the letter mentioned above from the governor general of Warsaw, Skalon, who warned that the State Council's intransigence on the language question would serve only to antagonize the very people with whom the Russian government must necessarily construct a viable city government in the region. (The State Council's amendments to the project essentially excluded Polish from deliberations in town councils.) This sort of old-style russification, Skalon insisted, had long since outlived its time.[76] Thus, even the highest Russian official in the Polish provinces conceded that some kind of modus vivendi and common language had to be found between the Russian government and the inhabitants of the Vistula land.

In a similar vein, the minister of foreign affairs, S. D. Sazonov, complained that the polonophobic storm in the State Council was bound to have negative effects on Russian relations with the Slavic states in the Balkans.[77] The imperial government found itself once again in the irritating position of finding its desires for reform (such as they were) blocked not by liberals or the left but by reactionary elements within the State Council. On May 12, 1914, the minister of internal affairs, I. L. Goremykin, spoke in the State Council, urging the body to accept the bill as it stood and insisting that present guarantees would protect both state interests in the region and the prerogatives of local Russians. His efforts were to no avail; the bill was voted on and rejected at the same meeting.[78]

Faced with a stubborn State Council and fearing unrest in Poland, the government was prepared to override the legislature on this occasion, as it had before. On June 5, 1914, minister of internal affairs Goremykin was instructed by an imperial order (*vysochaishii reskript*) to reintroduce the Polish city bill to the Duma "immediately." Five days later Goremykin was instructed to publish the first reskript, possibly to placate the Poles but probably also to make clear to the State Council the emperor's displeasure with

its position. Goremykin, as is well known, was no Stolypin, and no immediate action was taken.[79] When, only days later on June 28 (June 15 old
style), Gavrilo Princip shot Archduke Franz Ferdinand in Sarajevo the Russian government was faced with a crisis that preempted any further consideration of city government in Poland.

St. Petersburg's attention was not distracted for long from the Polish
question, however. The desire to retain the loyalty of the Poles made it imperative for the Russian government to offer some sort of city government
plan to the region. A law giving the cities of the Polish Kingdom elective
governments was promulgated under article 87 in the spring of 1915. But
once again, the Russian government offered far too little and much too late.
The law promulgated in March 1915 was practically identical to the Duma-
approved project; that is, it retained stringent restrictions on Polish language use, and it was based on national curiae. The reaction to this half
measure, which, for Warsaw, would not even go into effect until January 1,
1916, was uniformly negative.[80]

The sad history of attempts to extend elective city government to Russian Poland graphically illustrates the imperial government's clumsiness in
dealing with national minorities. Unwilling to assume a strictly Russian-
national stance but at the same time unable to resist the pressures of Russian chauvinism, both within and outside the bureaucracy, the Russian
Empire was condemned to a kind of national purgatory, detested by the
Poles and Jews, despised by the liberal Kadets, despaired of by the true-
Russians. Here, as on so many other occasions, the Russian government
ventured little and lost everything.

Nine

The Dubious Triumph of Russian Nationalism

Formation of the Kholm Province

The unattractive thing about chauvinism is not
so much the aversion to other nations
but the love of one's own.

—Karl Kraus

❖   Perhaps no other issue more inflamed Polish and Russian nationalism during the last decade of Romanov rule than the "Kholm question." This diminutive, inconsequential strip of land, completely lacking in military, economic, or cultural importance, became the focal point of Polish and Russian national passions, adopted by both sides as an integral part of the Polish or the Russian heartland. Zealous nationalists of a historical bent traced Kholmshchina/Chełmszczyzna's pedigree (alternately purely Polish or utterly Russian) back to the times of Volodymyr, when the area's residents were probably still worshiping pagan idols.[1] The discourse used by Russians and Poles alike in defending their claims to the area may serve as cautionary examples of the multifarious uses to which history can be applied. Patriots similarly drew on ethnographic arguments to bolster their case, conveniently ignoring irritating discrepancies and (more important) ambiguities in their data. In short, the Kholm controversy strikingly laid bare the "national daltonism" that dominated the era; it also illustrated the Russian government's seeming inability to harness nationalist forces to its own advantage.

The arguments and counter-arguments surrounding the Kholm issue show the difficulty of separating religion from nationality in the western borderlands of the Russian Empire. In essence, the effort to put together a new Kholm Province was based almost entirely on anti-Polish and anti-Catholic arguments. It is interesting that the Jewish population of the region—which comprised a very significant percentage of the urban population, including that of the proposed province's capital—is nearly altogether absent from these discussions.[2] The sizable local Jewish population had no place in the controversy; the creation of the Kholm Province, it would seem, corroborated once again Pushkin's words: "Eto spor slavin mezhdu soboiu, / Domashnii, staryi spor, uzh vzveshennyi sud'boiu, / Vopros, kotorogo ne razreshite vy" (This is a dispute of Slavs among themselves, / a private, old dispute, already weighed out by fate, / A question that will not be solved by you).[3] From the start this measure was defined as a "family argument" exclusively between Poles and Russians, aiming to counteract Polish influence and to shield "Russians" from Catholicizing *polskość*.[4] Thus defined, any mention of the Jewish or Ukrainian inhabitants of the region could simply be shrugged aside as being beside the point.

To complicate matters, moreover, many of the "Russians" whom this project ostensibly aimed to protect had adopted Catholicism and, in many cases, even called themselves Poles. Thus the Russian nationalists found themselves forced to admit that Catholics were not necessarily Poles and that many "Poles" would realize their "true" nationality and return to the mother (Orthodox) church, if only given the chance.[5] This kind of mystical nationalism remains impervious to ethnographic or sociological data. And the Russian nationalists held no monopoly on this kind of national mythologizing: Polish writers put forth passionate nationalist pamphlets that certainly equal their Russian counterparts in passion, one-sidedness, and outraged national pride. Even more than a nationalist attack on one ethnic and religious group (which it, of course, was), the Kholm question must be seen as the collision of two national myths, and the strength of both may be gauged by the fury of the controversy.[6]

Efforts to create a separate province out of the lands west of the Bug River, settled in large part by Ukrainians, date from 1863. This territory had been included in the Kingdom of Poland by the Congress of Vienna, which clearly cared little about ethnographic boundaries. Then, as later, the eastern border of the Congress Kingdom followed the Bug River, an obvious geographical boundary (which today forms the boundary between the Republic of Poland and Ukraine). After the administrative reforms in the Kingdom of Poland during the 1860s, Kholmshchina and Podlasie constituted the eastern edges of Siedlce and Lublin Provinces. The local population consisted of three main national groups: a Polish Catholic landowning (noble) class; Jewish town dwellers, artisans, and traders; and Uniate peasants of Ukrainian stock. (The Uniate factor was to be of great importance.)

After the 1863 uprising, as in the western territory, the Russian government took great pains to weaken Polish influence in all ways possible, and the creation of a "Russian" province out of these territories was proposed as one possible measure to this end. In July 1865, during deliberations on the administrative future of Poland, Prince Cherkasskii put forth a project for a separate Kholm Province, cut off from the Polish Kingdom, "with the aim of countering the polonization of the local Russian population." Cherkasskii's colleagues N. A. Miliutin and Friedrich Berg rejected this project as inconsistent with general administrative aims, particularly as the proposed province would have been quite small, of irregular shape, and would have entailed increased administrative costs with no appreciable increase of efficiency or security.[7]

A decade later came the second major effort to combat Polish influence in Kholmshchina: the abolition of the Uniate church there, or, to use the official phrase, the "reunification" *(vozsoedinenie)* of the Uniate church with the Orthodox.[8] The Uniate church, dating from the Union of Brest (1596), had long been a thorn in the side of the Russian government; nearly a century earlier Tsar Paul I had denounced the Uniates as "Ni miaso, ni ryba" (Neither fish nor fowl)."[9] In 1839 the Uniates of the Northwest Provinces had been ushered (not to say driven) back into the fold of Orthodoxy, and in 1875 came the turn of the Uniates living in the Kholm and Podlasie areas.[10]

The 1875 "reunion" of Uniates and the Orthodox church may serve as a textbook example of how not to solve religious differences. After 1866, in the wake of repressions following the failed 1863 uprising, St. Petersburg took measures to remove from the Uniate churches all ceremonies and objects that could be seen as Catholic and Polish, such as church organs and Polish prayers and hymns. These "purification" measures gave rise to rumors among Uniates in the Kholm-Podlasie area that their church was about to be suppressed altogether on orders from St. Petersburg. The decatholicizing measures and the fear of a complete takeover by the Orthodox church authorities caused disturbances in many areas. These disturbances, in turn, gave impetus to the Siedlce governor S. Gromeka (the villain of the piece) to act boldly and brutally by sending out troops to crush the "uprisings" and, with the connivance of the Holy Synod, to formally abolish the local Uniate church.[11]

The "union" was formally attained on May 13, 1875, and was accompanied by a good deal of unrest and bloody "administrative measures." To quote a later official source, "The Uniate Church [Unia] was abolished all at once, with noise, the din of church bells, administrative commands, instructions, and the like [bez promezhutnykh stepenei, s shumom, trezvonom, rasporiazheniiami, prikazaniiami i t.p.] as if the effecting of a mass religious revolution [perevorot] were but a simple administrative matter."[12] At the time, however, local officials reported that the conversions went "voluntarily, consciously and completely tranquilly" and spoke of the "success" of the operation.[13]

Along with religious reform came proposals for parallel administrative changes. In 1875 the governor general of Warsaw, P. Kotzebue, proposed to St. Petersburg the formation of a Kholm Province, but once again the plan was turned down by the central authorities, namely Alexander II himself and the Komitet po delam Tsarstva Pol'skogo (Committee on the Affairs of the Polish Kingdom). Thus, from the point of view of Russian nationalists, the government followed the "successful" conversions with a fall back into its usual somnolent lack of firm policy, thereby allowing the former Uniates to continue and strengthen their links with the Polish-dominated Catholic church. One source stated that although, after 1875, the minister of internal affairs N. P. Ignatiev wished to "give the Uniate question in the Vistula lands a direction favorable to the Orthodox church and the Russian nationality," he was prevented from doing so by opposition on the part of Warsaw governor general Albedinskii.[14]

As even Russian nationalists and arch-Orthodox writers admitted by the turn of the century, the reunification was rushed through with the help of police and "administrative" measures and lacked almost entirely any spiritual component.[15] Indeed, the process by which both local and central government lurched toward unification reveals the Russian government's lack of serious planning vis-à-vis the Uniates and other "dissenting" subjects, and the power that an ambitious local figure (Siedlce governor Gromeka) could arrogate to himself.

It did not take long at all for the negative effects of the hasty and brutal abolition of the Uniate church to show up. Many thousands of former Uniates refused to be absorbed into the Orthodox congregations. The problem of the "persisters" (uporstvuiushchie; Polish: uporni) had been born. These staunch Uniates continued to worship according to the old rites, usually without their own priests, and to shun the Orthodox clergy in every way possible. Baptisms and funerals were consecrated in secret or not at all. Whenever possible, the persisting Uniates traveled to the Austrian Empire to solemnify their marriages, so much so that the expression "Cracow marriages" became a standard phrase for such unions. Faced with this kind of stubborn resistance, soon even Russian nationalists and Orthodox patriots came to admit that the rapid, headlong destruction of the Uniate church had been a mistake.[16]

Although the problem of persisters cannot be developed in any great detail here, some mention must be made of these underground Uniates, for they made up the bulk of converts to Catholicism in the area after the decree on religious freedom of April 17, 1905. A poignant—and partisan—description of the plight of these peasants caught between their official Orthodox status and their deeply felt connection with the no longer existing Uniate church may be found in W. Reymont's Z ziemi chełmskiej.[17] In this short and impassioned account, we read of Uniate (persister) children being forcibly christened by Orthodox priests; of hasty burials in the dead of night to thwart lurking "Muskovite" (moskalewski) authorities; and of secret Uniate congregations held deep in the forests amid fearful rumors of planned raids by the Russian authorities. The author described how the persisters' disbelief and fear changed to relief and rejoicing when they were informed that, after April 17, 1905, one could openly and officially leave the Orthodox church. (It is important to note in this context that, because the

Uniate church had been completely dismantled in the Russian Empire, the persisters had no choice upon leaving the Orthodox church but to embrace the Roman Catholic faith.)

On the other side of the religious equation, the Orthodox authorities accused Catholic clergy of encouraging the persisting Uniates and of illegally using the Uniate issue to spread Catholic propaganda.[18] Nor did this accusation lack all foundation. From the 1880s Jesuit missionaries secretly and illegally administered to the spiritual needs of the Kholm persisters.[19] Furthermore, a society called Towarzystwo Opieki nad Unitami (Polish Society for the Protection of Uniates) existed and, in printed brochures and in secret meetings, encouraged Uniates to resist the Russian and Orthodox authorities and to remain true to their Uniate faith. The proximity of a large Uniate population with well-organized Catholic and Uniate priests, across the frontier in Galicia, greatly facilitated the spread of pro-Uniate (hence anti-Orthodox) propaganda.[20]

In the decades after 1875, the imperial government expended a great deal of effort and expense in the Kholm area, aiming to strengthen the position of the Orthodox church and the Russian cause there. The number of schools built in the eastern parts of Lublin and Siedlce Provinces, where the former Uniates were concentrated, far exceeded that of schools in the purely Polish western areas of these provinces.[21] Similarly, a large contingent of Orthodox priests administered the religious needs of the former Uniates, and the material support for these priests far exceeded that of their brethren in the interior of Russia. To quote the governor of Siedlce Province:

> The church, school, and local authorities unceasingly see to the strengthening in the population of the holy fundaments of devotion to and love of the Russian mother tongue and to the Orthodox church, gradually preparing the younger generation of the formerly Uniate population to full communion [*obshchenie*] with her [that is, the Orthodox church].[22]

There is a peculiar ambiguity in these words. On one hand, the efforts of church and state usher the younger generation of former Uniates into full communion with the Orthodox church. On the other hand, when one considers that nearly thirty years had passed since 1875, the admission that local authorities still needed to expend serious energies in this direction is an indirect acknowledgment that many former Uniates continued to consider themselves separate from, and possibly hostile to, the Russian-Orthodox authorities.

Returning to the prehistory of the Kholm Province, the year 1891 witnessed a new and significant development. The Orthodox bishop of Warsaw, Leontii, petitioned St. Petersburg for the introduction of the Julian calendar to the Kholm region. The procurator of the Holy Synod, K. Pobedonostsev, took this suggestion up and expanded the request for calendar reform into a new project for the creation of a Kholm Province. But Pobedonostsev's 1890 plan met with strong opposition from the governor general of Warsaw, I. Gurko, as well as with apathy and suspicion in St. Petersburg. So it came to naught.[23] Recalling Gurko's sinister reputation as an arch-russifier and oppressor of Polish nationality, it is instructive to note that in this case he opposed this anti-Polish measure. To be sure, his opposition was based not on respect for Polish rights but on mundane administrative arguments.

After Nicholas II's ascension to the throne, several plans for creating a Kholm Province followed one another in rapid succession. In 1895 and 1896 Warsaw governor general P. Shuvalov had plans for the new province drawn up to protect the "longtime resident Russian population" in Kholmshchina. When Shuvalov left his position in Warsaw after barely two years, his project was bequeathed (as it were) to his successor, Prince A. Imeretinskii. At first Imeretinskii seemed cautiously in favor of the project, but after careful consideration he came to oppose the plan. He argued that the creation of a new province would complicate military matters without increasing administrative efficiency and, most important, that the reform would not be an effective measure for defending local Russians from becoming catholicized and polonized.[24]

Two years later, at a special Kholm commission in Warsaw, the governor of Lublin, V. F. Tkhorzhevskii, proposed a "great Kholm province" that would include over a million inhabitants. Once again this plan was opposed by the governor general. When Imeretinskii left his post in Warsaw in November 1899, Tkhorzhevskii hastened to renew his efforts for the new province. His annual report for 1900 pointedly urged that "the only way to preserve Orthodoxy and the Russian nationality among the former Greek Uniates is the separation [*vydelenie*] of Transbug Rus' from the Polish Kingdom through the formation of a new Kholm province." Once again Tkhorzhevskii's ambition was stymied by his superior in Warsaw; governor general Chertkov strongly opposed the proposal.[25]

Nonetheless, Tkhorzhevskii's suggestion was taken seriously enough to cause a special conference *(Osoboe Soveshchanie)* to be formed in St. Petersburg for discussion of the matter. This conference was chaired by Pobedonostsev, and members included governor general Chertkov and the ministers of finance (S. Witte), of the interior (D. Sipiagin), of war (A. Kuropatkin), and of justice (N. Muraviev). In March 1902 this committee met and considered the advantages and drawbacks of the proposed new province. Pobedonostsev strongly supported creating the new province, as is evident from his previous (1890) plan. The other members of the committee were less committed, pointing out that only 38 percent of the population in the new province would be Orthodox and questioning the efficacy of a change in administrative boundaries in order to strengthen the Russian cause *(russkoe delo)* in the area.[26] In the end Pobedonostsev was obliged to back down and accept the "unanimous" decision of the committee:

> The formation of a Kholm Province without applying to the local population serious measures of russification would not achieve the desired goal.

And since the application of such measures in the present situation is found to be impossible, the formation of a separate province out of the Russian Transbug territory cannot take place at this time.[27]

Sipiagin defeated Pobedonostsev by a clever tactic: the minister of internal affairs declared himself in favor of protecting the Russian population of the Kholm area from Polonism but then argued that "in the present situation" this would require severe measures beyond the government's powers. Despite several plans and projects and a seemingly universal belief among Russian officials that the Russian element in the area deserved some sort of protection against Polonism, the Kholm Province remained before 1905 but a dream of polonophobic Russians.

It should not be thought that pressure for measures against Poles in Kholmshchina emanated exclusively from official circles. On the contrary, the government—especially in St. Petersburg, but also in Warsaw—tended to distance itself from the issue. The real pressure for change came from such Russian Nationalist publications as *Novoe vremia* and *Moskovskie vedomosti,* and from local "Russian patriots" (for the most part government officials) who dedicated their lives to "the Orthodox cause on the borderlands." Especially after 1905, Nationalist periodicals such as *Mirnyi trud* and *Okrainy Rossii* agitated for government support for true-Russians against Poles and Catholics in the region. Such agitation had a long history, with two names looming above all others as ideological fathers of the Kholm Province concept: P. N. Batiushkov and E. M. Kryzhanovskii.

❖ Batiushkov's works on the history of the area are serious scholarly tomes whose official connection is readily apparent—and not only from the remark on the title page, "s Vysochaishogo soizvoleniia izdano pri Ministerstve vnutrennikh del" (with the most high permission published in the Ministry of Internal Affairs).[28] Despite their bias, however, Batiushkov's works do provide much information about the region's history, particularly from a religious (read: Orthodox) point of view. For Batiushkov, the history of "Western Russia" is the history of the struggle between the forces of good (Orthodoxy) and evil (Polono-Jesuit Catholicism). Curiously absent are the Jews who made up, after all, a significant percentage of the local population (between 15 and 17 percent).[29] There was no place for non-Christians in this epic struggle for the "true cross": the historical stage was occupied fully by the Orthodox Russians and the Catholic Poles. And the end of the history was also clear for Batiushkov:

The persevering, unswerving introduction of Russian principles into the public, societal life of this region sooner or later must convince the most implacable aliens and non-Orthodox [*inorodtsy i inovertsy*] of the impossibility in the future of national [*plemennoi*] and religious exclusivity and political separatism.[30]

In other words, Poles in the Western Provinces should realize the hopelessness of retaining their national and religious traditions, should convert to Orthodoxy and become Russians. Whereas Batiushkov would have surely protested against such a bald interpretation of his words, this does in fact seem to be the ultimate goal he sought. Whereas Russian nationalists (whether bureaucrats or "private citizens") consistently denied that they sought the denationalization of any group, their words—particularly when they waxed eloquent about long-range plans and ultimate dreams—seem to belie such protests.

E. M. Kryzhanovskii's works reached similar conclusions about the "fate of Western Russia."[31] Kryzhanovskii spent most of his official career in the Kingdom of Poland, and his works reflect the tenor of a provincial Russian *chinovnik* ("bureaucrat"), zealously dedicated to the spread of the Russian cause in the borderlands. Kryzhanovskii served from 1865 to 1871 as the supervisor *(nachal'nik)* of the educational directory in Siedlce Province, then as the director of the first men's *Gymnasium* in Warsaw until 1883. In that year he was promoted to serve on the educational committee of the Holy Synod.[32] An American scholar, Robert Byrnes, calls Kryzhanovskii "a mentor on the Uniates" to Pobedonostsev and "a specialist on religious groups in the Western Provinces and in the Government General of Warsaw." Kryzhanovskii's voluminous works also tell the story of an epic contest of wills between the sophisticated, treacherous Poles-Catholics-Jesuits and the open-hearted, guileless Orthodox flocks. Kryzhanovskii did not even attempt to deny that the Catholic priests were richer, more zealous, even more hard-working and better trained than their Orthodox counterparts. Instead, he transformed the Orthodox simplicity and guilelessness into a virtue that he contrasted with the Jesuitic sophistry of the haughty Lechites. Kryzhanovskii's writings on the Uniate church in Podlasie and Kholmshchina repeated the themes of crafty Papists and beguiled Orthodox peasants. Clearly troubled by the ambiguous position of the Uniate church between Catholicism and Orthodoxy, Kryzhanovskii heaved a sigh of relief when the Uniate "problem" was "solved." Of the events of 1875 he wrote, "a great matter was decided, the Gordian knot was cut through," and he warned against the negative descriptions of the unification of 1875 that one could find in the "pseudo-liberal press."[33]

Batiushkov and Kryzhanovskii present us with a "type"—the relatively minor but ambitious provincial chinovnik, wishing to make a name for himself by zeal, and probably at the same time firmly convinced in the justice of his cause. The Lublin governor V. F. Tkhorzhevskii, with his pleas for a separate Kholm Province, and his colleague in Siedlce and Kholm some years later, A. N. Volzhin, might also fit into this category. Higher up the bureaucratic ladder, however, both in Warsaw and in St. Petersburg, such diligence and national zeal met with indifference and even irritation. At least until 1905, the MVD expressed no desire to take on any anti-Polish crusades in the West, maintaining as its motto "let sleeping dogs lie." Only the Synod, and especially Ober-Prokuror Konstantin Pobedonostsev,

seemed interested in further attempts at repressing Polono-Catholic influences; but even this interest faded when confronted by the general indifference and unwillingness of the other ministries to support such measures.
Such was the situation before 1905.

The Decree on Religious Toleration

The inadequacies of the "reunion" of Uniates and Orthodox had the effect that thirty years later—when Nicholas II issued the April 17, 1905, decree granting his subjects religious freedom, including the right to abandon
Orthodoxy for another faith—tens of thousands of Kholm "Orthodox" immediately converted to Catholicism. The decree on religious toleration
caught the Orthodox church in the Kholm region almost completely by surprise. The then bishop of Kholm recalled the following in his memoirs:

> The thunderstorm [*groza*, that is, the social tensions and threat of upheaval
> caused by defeats in the Japanese war] slowly approached even us. The
> storm exploded over Kholmshchina in the spring of 1905. The decree of re-
> ligious freedom! It was published on the 17th of April, on the first day of
> Easter. A beautiful idea under the conditions of the national [*narodnyi*] life
> of our region led to a desperate struggle of Catholicism with Orthodoxy.
> Neither the Archbishop of Warsaw nor I was warned about the decree, and
> it came as a complete surprise. Later it turned out that Polish Catholic cir-
> cles had found out in advance and had deliberately prepared their attack.[34]

Even before the April 17 decree, Evlogii had been in communication with
the Holy Synod on the subject of policy toward the former Uniates. Not
two weeks before the decree was published, Evlogii had telegraphed to
Pobedonostsev, warning of disastrous consequences if full religious freedom were granted. After the granting of religious freedom, as thousands of
"Orthodox" peasants converted to Catholicism, Evlogii's letters took on
apocalyptic tones, as when he declared in a telegram to Pobedonostsev
dated May 2, 1905, "The Orthodox Russian cause is perishing." Probably
the shock of these mass conversions and the concern over his own position
as religious head of a rapidly diminishing body of faithful gave rise to
Evlogii's crusade for a separate, Russian, and Orthodox Kholm Province.[35]

Evlogii's feelings of helplessness and frustration found vivid expression
in a letter he wrote to Pobedonostsev only weeks after the promulgation of
the decree of religious freedom. Complaining bitterly that the decree, especially because of the failure to warn local Orthodox authorities of its coming, severely discredited the Orthodox clergy in the Kholm area, Evlogii
continued,

> the very credit of our priests has been undermined. For thirty years they
> repeated to the people [*narod*] that the Kholm-Podlasie country will always
> be Orthodox and Russian, and now the people see, on the contrary, the
> complete, willful takeover [*polnoe, svoevol'noe khoziaistnichan'e*] in the coun-

try of the enemies of the Orthodox Russian cause. . . . It is inexpressibly painful to live through this rapid collapse [*krushenie*] of the Orthodox, Russian cause.[36]

Evlogii's letters and memoirs exhibit a rather typical phenomenon that one might uncharitably call the "Russian national inferiority complex." Russian nationalists of this era seemed convinced that Poles (and Jews) were somehow better provided with information, funds, and skills than the "rooted Russian population." Despite the statement in his memoirs that the April 17 decree took him by surprise, Evlogii obviously knew something was in the air; witness his telegram of April 6, 1905. Furthermore, it was general knowledge that in January the Committee of Ministers had discussed the implementation of paragraph 6 (on religious freedom) of the decree of December 12, 1904. On the whole, the tenor of Evlogii's description of the situation in 1905 consistently reflects the contemporary view presented in Russian nationalist accounts: the imperial government, officially the defender of the Orthodox faith, did nothing to prepare its own pastors in border areas for the consequences that were clearly foreseeable once legal conversion from Orthodoxy became possible.[37]

Even at this point, in the wake of mass conversions, Russian political authorities in Poland maintained a considerably more sanguine view of the situation. In response to the many complaints (including Evlogii's) about Catholic excesses, the governor general of Warsaw, Konstantin K. Maksimovich, pointed out in a letter to Pobedonostsev that the bulk of these complaints lacked substantiation or represented exaggerated versions of minor incidents. Explaining the protests from Orthodox folk in the area as a function of their "feeling of grief" *(skorbnoe chuvstvo)* at the spectacle of mass conversions to Catholicism, Maksimovich sympathized with the petitioners but pointed out that during discussions of the consequences of religious freedom in the Committee of Ministers, mass conversions of 100,000–150,000 former Uniates had been expected.[38]

Exactly how many conversions took place in the Kholm region and under what conditions will probably never be known. That there occurred a mass wave of conversions to Catholicism, however, remains beyond doubt.[39] Nearly all of the converts, it seems clear, were former Uniates who had never really accepted Orthodoxy, despite their official "conversion." Several years later in the State Council discussions of the Kholm project, the remark was made that "Those who went over to Catholicism after the promulgation of the [April 17, 1905] decree had never been true Orthodox [*istinnymi pravoslavnymi*]." As far as numbers are concerned, estimates ranged up to 200,000 converts, but a more sober examination offered rather less spectacular figures.[40] From 1905 to 1907, the number of Catholics in Siedlce and Lublin Provinces rose by 127,892, and the number of Orthodox fell by 114,111. Even this relatively modest number meant that nearly a third of the "Orthodox" in the region had converted.[41]

The reasons and motives behind these conversions became the subject of endless controversy and mutual recrimination, with the arguments again tending to divide along national lines. The Poles and Russian liberals argued that the converts had never really accepted Orthodoxy, hence the conversions only brought into the open what had once been kept secret. While this explanation is largely valid, the activities of Catholic missionaries in the area cannot entirely be discounted.[42]

Many Russians, on the other hand, saw a Catholic conspiracy at work and complained that such large numbers of conversions could not possibly have been effected in so short a time without advance planning by the local Catholic clergy, in cahoots with local Polish landowners. Bishop Evlogii and, indeed, the entire right and nationalist camp shared this view.[43] And it would have been difficult for them to argue otherwise. To admit a mass, popular flight from Orthodoxy would have completely negated the logic for a Kholm Province "to protect Orthodoxy." The ideology of Russian nationalism required a Polish conspiracy to justify its own "administrative methods" against the Catholics.

The Kholm controversy found its Orthodox champion in the figure of Archbishop Evlogii of Kholm and Lublin. Born in 1868, a priest's son from Tula Province, he had rapidly advanced within the hierarchy of the Orthodox church and in 1897, not even thirty years of age, had been named rector of the Kholm seminary.[44] When named to this position, Evlogii later recalled, he did not even know where Kholm was located and was obliged to look the town up in an atlas. In Kholm, Evlogii dedicated himself to the Russian and Orthodox cause and was named bishop of Kholm at the end of 1902. When the Kholm bishopric was separated from the Warsaw diocese and elevated to the status of archbishopric on June 16, 1905, Evlogii became Kholm's first archbishop. Evlogii's popularity among the Orthodox locals may be gauged by the fact that in 1908 the Russian population of Kholm petitioned to create a scholarship in his name at the Kholmskoe Mariinskoe Zhenskoe Uchilishche. Evlogii was also elected to the Second and Third Dumas by the Orthodox population of Lublin and Siedlce Provinces, that is, for the most part, the future Kholm Province.[45]

In his memoirs, Evlogii complained that the local "Russian" population showed an irritating tendency to call themselves Poles and to speak Polish. This confusion on the part of the local population as to their true nationality awoke in Evlogii a strong missionary zeal to encourage the development of Russian national feeling in the region:

> By means of a return to [their] native language and to forgotten Russian folklore, [I set out to] attempt to revive the dormant [*zaglokhshee*] feeling among the people [*narod*] of the Russian element. By this method, neither external nor violent, but rather a free and cultural influence on the national soul [*narodnaia dusha*], I saw for the moment the only means that could arouse in my flock Russian national self-consciousness.

Evlogii's metaphysical concept of a "true" nationality that had to be coaxed out of the ignorant peasants also typified Russian nationalists of the time:

I saw national feeling, gradually bestirred it; it may be that I did wrong, it may be, I overdid it [*peregibal*], but what was to be done in the face of national amnesia [*narodnaia bezpamiatnost'*], when they forgot about their Russian roots and naively answered the question, "where do you live?" with "in Poland"?[46]

Some argued at the time that Evlogii's nationalism was fueled to a great extent by his burning ambition. Such motives are impossible to prove and moreover inconsequential. However sincere in his beliefs, Evlogii's view held that a given individual did have a nationality as an objective and unchanging part of his person. This outlook prevailed, to a greater or lesser degree, throughout the political spectrum. The idea that a person's nationality may change, or that a "Pole" could emerge from "Russian" forefathers, or vice versa, seemed a preposterous proposition at the time. Practically the only exception to this rule can be found among such atypical antinationalist individuals as Jan Baudouin de Courtenay.[47]

Battling Statistics

The notion that individuals bear within themselves a "real nationality" bedeviled the Kholm controversy from beginning to end. Obviously, this kind of argument could be used to prove that the Kholm population in toto was "really" Polish or "really" Russian, although it was never taken quite that far. But the ambiguous national status of the numerous recent converts and the lack of a concrete and generally accepted definition of "Pole" and "Russian" enabled partisans of either side to demonstrate a Russian or Polish majority in many areas of the province, firmly based on "serious" statistical results. Before we plunge into the most crucial period of the debate (1906–1912), let us consider some of the various statistics offered at the time.

First of all, one must be aware of the source of the statistical data. Nearly everyone used official statistics, at least to some extent, and usually with "corrections."[48] These official data were (to say the least) suspect. As the Polish Duma deputy Lubomir Dymsza pointed out, the governor of Siedlce Province, A. N. Volzhin, in two different years, 1907 and 1909, gave wildly differing numbers on the percentage of Poles in one district of his province. In 1907 Poles made up 53 percent of the population of Konstantinov district, whereas two years later their percentage ostensibly shrank to 22.4 percent.[49] Since no zemstvo statisticians were at work in these districts, one had to depend on data provided by the local Russian administration.

Perhaps we are being unfair to Governor Volzhin in imputing, with Dymsza, a dishonest motive to his varying statistics. After all, there was no objective measure of who was to be considered a Pole (*litso pol'skogo proiskhozhdeniia*) and who a Russian.[50] Two decisive characteristics were used freely, each side using the one most advantageous to its own aims. One could either equate religion with nationality, a common enough practice for this time and place, or one could seek an ethnolinguistic basis for

Table 9. Orthodox and "Russian" Population of Lublin and Siedlce Provinces

	Orthodox	Russian	Belorussian	Ukrainian
Lublin	248,061	47,912	525	196,476
Siedlce	120,811	19,613	226	107,785

Source: *Pervaia vseobshchaia perepis' naseleniia Rossiiskoi Imperii. Obshchii svod* (St. Petersburg, 1905), vol. 1, p. 256; ibid., vol. 2, p. 38 ("Rodnoi iazyk": "Veliko-russkii, Malorusskii, Belorusskii").

nationality. For obvious reasons, the Poles tended to select the religious measure. As Dymsza wrote, "The concepts of nationality and confession in the Bug region are indistinguishable. . . . [A]t the present moment only the presence of this factor [that is, religion] can be [considered] decisive." The Russians, on the other hand, chose the linguistic: Frantsev gives both religious and linguistic statistics but lends greater significance to the latter. For example, he points out that in most cases the converts to Catholicism "continue to speak Russian" and should thus be considered Russians. Since two differing standards were used, both explicitly and implicitly, it is no wonder that Polish and Russian nationalists could find no common ground for argument, much less for compromise.[51]

The Kholm guberniia was to be formed from the eastern regions of Siedlce and Lublin Provinces. Specifically, eleven districts *(uezdy)* were to be included, in whole or in part: Konstantinskii, Belskii, Radzinskii, and Vlodavskii in Siedlce Province; Liubartovskii, Kholmskii, Krasnostavskii, Zamostskii, Grubeshovskii, Tomashovskii, and Belgoraiskii in Lublin Province. In the 1897 census, figures were given on Orthodox and Russian-speaking populations in Siedlce and Lublin Provinces (see table 9). It is interesting to note that the total of the three groups of Russian speakers (244,913 for Lublin, 127,624 for Siedlce Province) is almost exactly equal to the number of Orthodox (248,061 and 120,811 respectively). Apparently the widely held belief that religion determined nationality did hold true—at least in these statistics and at that time.[52] Looking at these figures, we must keep in mind that they reflect the entire provinces, not just those eastern districts that were later to form the Kholm Province.

The target group for the future Kholm project is found in the 304,261 Little Russians who inhabited the two provinces. Whereas the Great Russian population consisted mostly of officials and soldiers, the Ukrainians were natives of the region and lived almost exclusively in the eastern districts of the two provinces. It was these individuals who had been semi-forcibly converted from the Uniate church to Orthodoxy just a generation earlier, and it was estimated that nearly two-thirds of these Orthodox Little Russians were Orthodox on paper only. This was the group that converted en masse to Catholicism in 1905 and 1906.

Table 10A. Orthodox Population in Siedlce Province

District	Warsaw Stat. Committee	Parish Records
Konstantinskii	13.7%	11.2%
Bel'skii	39.7	26.7
Radzinskii	4.6	4.0
Vlodavskii	44.7	22.0

Table 10B. Orthodox Population in Lublin Province

District	Warsaw Stat. Committee	Parish Records
Liubartovskii	1.8%	1.7%
Kholmskii	39.8	32.1
Krasnostavskii	6.8	5.9
Zamostskii	10.9	9.5
Grubeshovskii	54.9	47.6
Tomashovskii	43.6	38.2
Belgoraiskii	30.4	25.9

Source: Adam Zakrzewski, *Materialy k voprosu ob obrazovanii kholmskoi gubernii,* vol. 1, p. 27.
Note: Figures are in percentages. These percentages refer only to those parts of the districts that were to be included in the new province; the specific *gminy* are listed in ibid.

When the Kholm project began to be seriously considered a decade later, these figures needed to be significantly revised. Statistics on Orthodox population in the region (shown in table 10) were compiled by a Polish source. Another Polish commentator, Lubomir Dymsza, offers alternative figures (shown in table 11) in his immensely detailed *Kholmskii vopros.*[53]

What do all these numbers tell us? Most obviously, they attest to the almost complete lack of agreement on precisely which religion and nationality predominated in any given area. Also relevant is the fact that the gatherers of statistics consistently ignored the Jewish population, at least when presenting major data. This contest was between Poles and Russians; "others" played no role in the controversy. (To complicate the matter further, one would also have to take into account the German settlers of the area.) Still, one should note that even the Russian statistics indicate a larger percentage of Catholics than Orthodox in nearly every district, hence Frantsev's efforts to base his argument on "ethnographic" (that is, linguistic)

Table 11. Religious Groups, Percentage of Total Population

District	Spravka (1909)[a]		Frantsev (1908)[b]	
	Orthodox	Catholic	Orthodox	Catholic
Konstantins.	18.57%	68.90%	14.06%	62.1%
Bel'skii	36.08	41.36	27.43	41.1
Radzinskii	16.86	81.68	10.70	75.5
Vlodavskii	46.5	33.45	39.60	10.7
Total Siedlce Prov.[e]	35.13	47.39	28.00	46.3
Liubartovs.	17.34	61.15	14.7	62.4
Kholmskii	41.21	32.00	28.1	24.3
Krasnostavs.	35.27	61.15	26.1	65.9
Zamostskii	16.38	72.73	11.2	68.6
Grubeshovs.	53.35	29.14	41.93	27.0
Tomashovs.	46.0	41.16	38.0	37.3
Belgoraiskii	34.24	56.15	28.8	54.7
Total Lublin Prov.	39.37	44.27	30.4	40.94

rather than religious characteristics. Clearly, from the Polish point of view there existed no basis whatsoever for the claims that the new province's purpose was to protect the Orthodox population. If this were truly the case, they argued, why did Catholics outnumber Orthodox in practically every district of the new province?

The Russians had an answer ready—or, rather, two answers. First, their figures showed a larger percentage of Orthodox in the area, and second, they argued that many of the Catholics claimed by Poles as their own should have been included among the "Russians," both for ethnographic reasons and on account of their recent (perhaps not sincerely felt) conversion.[54] Many of the conversions of April and May 1905 had occurred under extraordinary circumstances, and given the chance, the Russians felt, many of these "Catholics" would find their way back into the Orthodox fold. Thus the Russian nationalist group emphasized the ethnographic element over the religious—Why should a Catholic, after all, not be as good a Russian as an Orthodox?—a rather unusual argument in the annals of Russian nationalism.[55]

Professor Frantsev of Warsaw University provided the most widely used statistics for the Russian nationalist camp. Frantsev admitted the frequent difficulty in establishing whether a given individual was, in fact, a Pole or a *Maloross*, but then proceeded to ignore this difficulty throughout

Table 11—*Continued*

District	Dziewulski (1907)[c]		Wiercieński (1906)[d]	
	Orthodox	Catholic	Orthodox	Catholic
Konstantins.	12.1%	75.4%	——	——
Bel'skii	25.8	50.8	——	——
Radzinskii	10.5	88.1	——	——
Vlodavskii	41.0	38.6	——	——
Total Siedlce Prov.	27.4	55.0	——	——
Liubartovs.	14.9	59.7	13.9%	59.3%
Kholmskii	35.4	37.7	32.1	36.8
Krasnostavs.	28.2	69.0	28.4	68.9
Zamostskii	11.4	78.7	13.0	68.1
Grubeshovs.	49.2	35.3	47.6	36.4
Tomashovs.	40.3	46.5	40.7	47.2
Belgoraiskii	29.5	60.8	13.0	68.1
Total Lublin Prov.	33.6	50.5	33.7	48.7

Source: Dymsza, *Kholmskii vopros*, chart appended to book.

Notes: [a] *Spravka k Zakonoproektu Ministra Vn. Del o vydelenii iz sostava gubernii Tsarstva Pol'skogo vostochnykh chastei Liublinskoi i Sedletskoi gubernii s obrazovaniem iz nikh osoboi Kholmskoi gubernii* (St. Petersburg, 1909).

[b] V. A. Frantsev, *Karty russkogo i pravoslavnogo naseleniia Kholmskoi Rusi s statisticheskimi tablitsami k nim* (Warsaw, 1909).

[c] Stefan Dziewulski, *Statistika naseleniia Liublinskoi i Sedletskoi gub. po povodu proekta obrazovaniia Kholmskoi gubernii* (Warsaw, 1909).

[d] Vertsinskii, *Raspredelenie naseleniia Liublinskoi gubernii k l ianvaria 1906 g. po veroispovedaniiam* (Warsaw, 1908). Both works are quoted in Dymsza, *Kholmskii vopros*.

[e] The totals for both Siedlce and Lublin Provinces reflect only those areas slated for incorporation into the proposed Kholm *guberniia*.

his study: "The mixture of Polish with one's own native Russian is so common a phenomenon here that sometimes a girl, having begun a song in Little Russian, without even noticing it herself, ends the song in Polish or vice versa." Frantsev also ignored city populations, saying, "the language of village [*sela i derevni*] dwellers has primary and even exclusive significance over that of urban residents, where the population is made up of a Polono-Russian-Jewish mixture." Frantsev continues: "Only the composition of the peasant population, for ages residing on the soil of their fathers and grandfathers, determines the character of a country in the ethnographic respect. This is why on our map we do not specially note either the religious or the

Table 12. Total Population by Religion

	Catholic	Orthodox	Jewish	Other
Siedlce Prov.				
Konstantins.	25,909	7,705	5,696	——
Bel'skii	36,940	25,998	24,504	417
Radzinskii	12,919	3,522	662	332
Vlodavskii	33,857	45,359	15,303	4,860
Lublin Prov.				
Liubartovs.	431	1,678	——	——
Kholmskii	42,204	60,533	16,646	22,134
Krasnostavs.	4,300	6,171	——	——
Zamostskii	36,255	10,198	8,292	——
Grubeshovs.	38,714	67,838	25,014	693
Tomashovs.	37,608	44,887	13,293	——
Belgoraiskii	41,540	30,997	5,000	——
Total Kholm Prov.	310,677	304,886	114,410	28,436

Source: Dmitrii N. Chikhachev, *K obrazovaniiu kholmskoi gubernii: Doklad Gosudarstvennoi Dume* (St. Petersburg, 1912), pp. 7–9.

ethnographic character of cities, towns and [suburban] settlements." Thus Frantsev takes native language as the deciding factor and restricts himself to the rural population.[56]

One peculiarity of Frantsev's work is the lack of a comprehensive table setting down the numbers of "Russian" (that is, Ukrainian) and Polish speakers throughout the area. Instead, Frantsev offered the reader detailed charts of every rural settlement in the region with remarks as to which language was spoken by the "rooted population" at the present time. One learns, for example, that in the village of Teresin, Voislavitsy *gmina*, Kholm district, out of a total population of 724, in 69 households Polish was spoken and in only two "Russian" was used.[57] The confusing and uncorrelated data presented by Frantsev could hardly add clarity to the controversy over the ethnic identity of Kholmshchina's residents.

Finally, we have the statistics offered by the Duma Commission on the formation of the Kholm Province (see table 12). Even official sources admitted that the Orthodox population of Kholm Province would be smaller than the Catholic, though not by much.[58] Again we must remember that Chikhachev and his allies considered many of the 310,885 Catholics in the new province to be "Russians," ripe for national (and perhaps religious) awakening. This attitude comes through clearly in the Duma debates.

❖   Before turning to the Duma discussions, it would not be amiss to fill in some of the key events between the mass conversions and the introduction of the MVD project *(predstavlenie)* to the Duma on April 24, 1909. Just weeks after the April 17, 1905, edict, Evlogii had led a group of his parishioners to St. Petersburg to petition the tsar for protection against aggressive Polish and Catholic propaganda, by approving the formation of a separate Kholm Province.[59] Nicholas received the delegation and promised protection. His personal interest in the Kholm question probably played a not inconsequential role in the issue's further development.[60] At the same time, Evlogii and his allies in Kholm kept up a steady stream of telegrams and petitions signed by local "Russians," begging for protection against polonizing forces and specifying that this protection should best take the form of a new province detached from the jurisdiction of the Warsaw governor general.[61]

Already in early 1906 the MVD was hard at work on a plan for detaching Kholmshchina from the Kingdom of Poland and forming a new province out of it. In April of that year the issue was discussed in the Council of Ministers. As was so often the case in imperial Russia, the decision reached here was to postpone any decision. The Council of Ministers, making reference to the complexity of the issue and the impending introduction of self-government in Poland, recognized the desirability of detaching Kholm from the Polish Kingdom, but felt that the exact details of this project should be further developed in the MVD.[62]

Thus the project was returned to the ministry. A special conference on the issue met at the end of 1906.[63] The conference members presented their conclusions to the Council of Ministers early the following year. Here Stolypin, noting the urgency of this reform, proposed that the Kholm Province be created by means of article 87. The council, however, opted for a more cautious path and, while expressing its sympathy with the project, concluded that it would be more prudent not to resort to emergency measures and recommended instead that the project be presented to the legislative bodies.[64] Finally in early 1909 the MVD once again placed a Kholm project before the Council of Ministers.[65] This time the council, while offering several minor amendments, generally approved the project, which was then forwarded to the Duma some two months later. The project, however, had changed significantly between 1906 and 1909, with nearly all of these changes aimed at the strengthening of the "Russian" and Orthodox element in the area and to the detriment of the Polish and Catholic.

The Kholm bill, introduced in tandem with the municipal government project for Poland, dominated many Duma sessions from 1909 to 1912. It was introduced by the minister of internal affairs on April 24, 1909 (no.

1363), and was finally passed by the Duma plenum on June 23, 1912.[66] The debates were rather evenly divided between members of the Koło such as Dymsza and Russian Nationalists and Rightists such as Bishop Evlogii and Chikhachev.[67]

Early in the discussions on the Kholm project, minister of internal affairs Makarov gave a speech in the Duma, encouraging the Duma members to pass the measure without undue delay. The project, Makarov mentioned, had attracted enormous attention both in Russia and abroad, and a great deal of the polemics on the Kholm question were simply "agitation" that the "modest compass [skromnyi ob"em]" of the bill did not justify. In fact, the minister emphasized, in this project the government was not seeking "discord and persecution" but aimed only to give the local Russian population the opportunity to "develop and strengthen national self-consciousness and the related feeling of attachment to the Russian state idea." In the conclusion to his speech, Makarov tried to balance the Russian state idea with assurances to the non-Russian peoples in the empire:

> It is up to you, gentlemen of the Duma, to prove that Poland is but one of the constituent parts of a single Russia [edinaia Rossiia], of that Russia, which is solicitous of the prosperity of all of her peoples, but which at the same time firmly recalls that her might and state idea [gosudarstvennost'] were created by the harmonious work and strivings, over many centuries, of the Russian people.[68]

The Polish representatives in the Duma were not convinced by Makarov's eloquence. Along with the Kadets, they spoke against the project as being an unnecessary and foolish administrative measure, as well as catastrophic for Polish-Russian relations. However, they were overruled by the combined Octobrist, nationalist, and rightist groups in the Duma.[69] In the end, the project passed easily, and borders of the proposed province were revised to include more territory, much of which was inhabited mainly by Catholics.[70]

In the State Council, the Kholm debate assumed much less passionate forms. But even here, in the sedate upper chamber of the Russian legislature, some members accused the bill's supporters of rushing it through without proper discussion.[71] Arguments in the State Council centered mainly on the efficacy of the project to protect Russian and Orthodox interests and the advisability of introducing new, restrictive laws on the Polish population of the province. Many members pleaded for a more careful, lengthy examination of the issue, which would have delayed action on the project until the next session, but their efforts were to no avail. On June 14, 1912, at one of the final meetings of the State Council's seventh session, the Kholm project was approved.[72]

While Poles and liberals battled Rightists and Russian Nationalists in the Duma, it was recognized within the Interior Department that the bill might well tarry some time in the legislature. A year after the MVD project had been presented to the Duma, assistant minister of the interior S. E. Kryzhanovskii wrote to the secretary of the Council of Ministers, N. Plehve, that, because of the "disputes and obstruction" encountered by the bill, it would be at least two years before it could be expected to pass. Meanwhile, Kryzhanovskii continued, the government should form an interministerial commission to discuss measures necessary for the establishment of the new province. Less than a week later the Council of Ministers, in a "special journal" that echoed many of Kryzhanovskii's points, set up precisely such a commission.[73] It is significant that, even before the Kholm project had received legislative sanction, the government had already established a body to consider specific measures to be applied in the as yet nonexistent Kholm Province. This commission worked steadily until 1914, and its conclusions were instrumental in giving concrete shape to measures to "strengthen the Russian character" of the new province.[74]

At the same time, a public debate raged on the subject. The lines were clearly drawn: Poles and Russian liberals lined up against nearly everyone else, from the Octobrists to the right. By the beginning of 1912, relations between Kadets and Poles had become severely strained by Polish anti-Semitism in connection with the Polish urban self-government bill. The issue became further complicated by the Ukrainian element, a side of the argument that had been almost totally ignored by the official and nationalist camp.[75]

Compared with the western zemstvo or Polish city government bills, the Kholm bill found little difficulty in passing the Duma and, more important, the State Council. This may be explained by the efforts of the government to downplay the project as a minor retracing of administrative boundaries. Furthermore, the controversial Stolypin had been removed from the scene before the Kholm bill came up for a vote. Another factor may have been the shock felt by many of the conservative Russians serving in the State Council over the mass conversions from Orthodoxy after the decree of religious toleration. Whatever the reasons, on April 26, 1912, the bill easily passed the Duma, by 156 to 108. The bill was forwarded to the State Council on May 4 and passed that body with almost lightning speed. Just over a month later the bill was approved. It was signed by the tsar on June 23, 1912. The Kholm Province had become a reality, or, to quote *Okrainy Rossii*, "At last it has dissipated, that narcotic administered by the Poles over Russia, as if the Poles could be lords and masters over the Russian people."[76]

Long before the Kholm bill was passed, the MVD had already been hard at work drawing up the specific measures to be applied in the new province. After 1912 these measures were rapidly put into effect. For example, a special commission labored long at devising new Russian names for the provinces' villages and towns. It was similarly proposed that funding for Russian schools, public lectures, and the periodical press be increased, while penalties for illegal Polish schools be sharpened significantly. Domestic correspondence sent from post offices in the new province was required to have addresses written in Russian, even in the case of letters bound for Warsaw or other localities of the Vistula country. (Because of the difficulties in enforcing this rule it was specified that the regulation applied only to letters presented at post offices, and not to those deposited in mailboxes.)[77] The Gregorian calendar was to be retained for the present time in the new province, but the commission recommended radical measures to end the economic dependency of "Russian" peasants on Polish landlords. Furthermore, the commission expressed concern that Ukrainophile elements not be allowed to secure employment in the province's schools.[78] In short, everything possible was done to further the interests of Russians and the Orthodox. Throughout the controversy, the large Jewish population of the area was nearly completely ignored. The Poles and Catholics found themselves reduced to a barely tolerated group.

It took a few months to set up the provincial government in the new capital, but the special attention of the minister of internal affairs, N. A. Maklakov, enabled the official "opening" (otkrytie) of the Kholm Province to take place on September 1, 1913, before the buildings to house the new provincial officials had even been erected.[79] The post of governor of the new province was filled by Aleksandr Nikolaevich Volzhin, the previous governor of the now defunct Siedlce Province. Volzhin's was a clear case of the possible congruency between career advancement and nationalist ideology.

As Chikhachev and Governor Volzhin had made clear, the formation of the Kholm Province was to be only the first step toward the "reconversion" of the local "Russians" back to their true nationality and faith. After the formation of the province, many further measures were planned, from universal education to rural and city self-government, to cheap credit for peasants, and even the depolonization of the Catholic church in the province. To take just one example, Volzhin immediately instructed the local police to forbid signs in Polish.[80] Even before the official "opening" of the province, Volzhin issued a long list of regulations (Obiazatel'nye postanovleniia) forbidding the singing of "revolutionary hymns" such as "Boże coś Polskę" and "Jeszcze Polska nie zginęła" and warning that any agitation "in any form or area" (v kakoi by to ni bylo forme i oblasti) against the Russian language would not be tolerated.[81] Truly, the future appeared bleak for Poles and Catholics of the new province.

Unfortunately for the ambitious plans of Russian nationalists and Orthodox patriots, the Kholm Province was to remain under Russian control barely three years, and—when the dust had settled after the cataclysm of World War I, revolution, and the war between Poland and Russia— Kholmshchina, now officially Chełmszczyzna, found itself firmly in Polish hands. Henceforth, the Kholm question was to plague not the Russian but the Polish government.[82]

Conclusion

❖   At the beginning of the twentieth century, the Russian Empire was faced with enormous—and, in the end, insurmountable—obstacles to its continued existence. Political, economic, and social issues were complicated in this vast state by the multinational character of its population. As the Russian Empire lurched forward toward "modernity" (that is, toward industrialization, literacy, urbanization, social mobility, and a more open and powerful public sphere), the national issue gained steadily in strength and, in the end, helped bring the empire down. But we must not indulge in post facto chiding of the defunct empire, particularly after the recent demise of a far stronger, far more modern, and considerably more repressive Soviet Union. More important, and more interesting from the historical point of view, is the question, Did the Russian Empire have any chance of survival?

This quandary has been endlessly debated in the literature, mainly in reference to the social question, particularly regarding the working class and the peasantry and their support—or active resistance—to the Romanov state.[1] Here let us consider the issue from the viewpoint of nationality, based on the data we have presented thus far. It appears clear that, in the last decades of the empire's existence, nationalist sentiments (both Russian and "other") were gaining strength, and on the whole attitudes within the government itself were shifting to a more activist pro-Russian stance, symbolized by Peter Stolypin. When we move from such a general statement to specific trends and policies, however, the picture becomes considerably more murky and contradictory. Stolypin's activism in the "defense of Russian state interests" did not win him the confidence of the tsar nor that of the Russian public. If we admit, then, that the Russian Empire was becoming more "national-Russian" as it entered the twentieth century (and particularly after 1905), we must also concede that this process was by no means a universal one. Although it does seem plausible—considering government actions after 1905—to foresee an increase in "protective" measures for the Russian nationality (read: worsening cultural, economic, and social possibilities for non-Russians), it is impossible to predict with any confidence the direction that this kind of russifying policy might have taken had World War I and revolution not intervened and cut short the empire's existence.

Between 1855 and 1914, the Russian Empire was faced with an economic imperative that rapidly translated into a political program. If the empire was to remain a European power, it would have to industrialize, modernize its transportation system, rebuild its armed forces along western European lines, and in effect mobilize its entire population to protect its great power status. The Great Reforms of the 1860s and 1870s attempted to create the preconditions for such "modernization," which would transform the rigid ancien régime state and society of Russia into more fluid, literate, and mobile "modern" entities.[2] The weaknesses of the reforms themselves lie beyond the scope of this study. But quite aside from any weaknesses in actual institutions of post-reform Russia, the very theory behind the reforms—to open up, if cautiously, the Russian state to Russian society—required a major rethinking of the terms "Russian" and "Russia." Before the Russian Empire could become a "normal" European state with one army, one administrative system, and one legal code, enormous inroads against "local privilege" would have to be made. Such incursions would inevitably, particularly in the empire's borderlands, take on the trappings of russification.

Similarly, reforming local government and opening it up to local society led inexorably to national conflicts. Opening up the public sphere necessarily meant allowing the use of non-Russian languages in the press, on the stage, in schools. And yet, on the whole, official Russia refused to accept this simple fact: while never ceasing to deny that they aimed at destroying local cultures, they nonetheless unceasingly demanded a hegemonic role for the Russian language, the Orthodox church, and Russian institutions. Perhaps in an earlier, less nationalistic age these demands could have been met. By the twentieth century, however, non-Russian nationalisms were too strong and too well developed to allow themselves to be relegated to the private, "non-official" sphere.

It was the tragedy of official Russia (and, it must be said, of much of the Russian public) that it could never really accept Russia as a multinational empire. We have seen in the controversy between Count S. Witte and I. Goremykin over the western zemstvo that both officials insisted that Russia—unlike Turkey—had the ability to assimilate culturally "backward" peoples. But even in the case of highly cultured nations such as the Poles, the fear of rebellion always acted to stymie significant concessions. It is instructive to recall that Russian officialdom, without fail, insisted that the majority of the state's population (some two-thirds of the total) was "Russian." Furthermore, the bulk of the non-Russians lived far from the capitals and could thus be more easily dismissed, or simply forgotten, by Russian officials. Unlike the situation in the Habsburg Empire, the cultural and political "specific gravity" of the non-Russians in the Romanov Empire never reached a point that would force the reigning house—or the government's loyal servants—to reconsider their own national/state identity. To the end the Rossiiskaia Imperiia behaved as if it were simply russkaia.[3]

Could the empire and the Russians have behaved differently? Given the nature of the Russian state and the tsarist government, combined with the enormous pressures coming to bear on Russia, it is perhaps unreasonable to expect a more rational nationality policy. In many ways the Russian state remained in a pre-nationalist mode. As is well known, neither Nicholas II's mother nor wife was Russian by origin. The ruling class in St. Petersburg continued to be dominated, even after 1905, by the scions of nobility who, although Russian by culture, almost certainly defined themselves primarily as aristocrats, and only then as "Russian."[4] (One can also not ignore the presence of Polish and Baltic German magnates in the State Council and other influential bodies.) Nicholas II's legitimacy as a ruler derived from historical precedents (and ultimately from God); it was by no means dependent on the approval of the Russian "nation." Whereas Nicholas appears to have cherished a belief in a spiritual link between himself and the Russian narod (read: peasantry), he continued to rely on traditional elites as the actual agents of state power. Indeed, Nicholas's very concept of the Russian "people" as an undifferentiated mass of loyal Orthodox peasants hardly corresponded to the realities of the Russian Empire in the early twentieth century. With the establishment of an elected legislature, even a weak one like the Duma, the concept of the government's responsibility to the people (or nation) did become increasingly important, but, until 1914, this concept remained a demand of liberal Russia, not any constituent part of the Russian political system.

Remaining in many respects pre-national, the Russian imperial government most assuredly harbored various stereotypes regarding national groups. The exclusion of Jews from most official posts can be explained as a combination of religious, social, and ethnic prejudices. The figure of the arrogant, mutinous Pole, a nearly universal stereotype in official circles, did not prevent many Poles from entering government service, except—an important exception—in those provinces with significant Polish populations, the western territory and the Vistula lands. Whereas the national factor was gaining steadily in importance throughout this period, social factors for official Russia continued to be at least as important as nationality, even in 1914. To put the same idea another way, even in 1914 the society of the Russian state (not necessarily "Russian society") remained the society of an ancien régime state, organized horizontally according to social estate (and, increasingly, according to class) more than vertically according to nationality.

The previous remarks have focused primarily on official Russia and the imperial government. But government perceptions also reflected trends and conditions existing in Russian educated society, which, whether reactionary or socialist, tended to underestimate the power and importance of the national question. In this respect, for all the apparent dissimilarities between reactionary and socialist perceptions, they resembled those of official Russia very closely. Social democrats, while proclaiming the need for national freedoms in a future free Russia, nonetheless failed to allow such autonomy within their own party (particularly in the Bolshevik case). Liberals foresaw an end to the national question coming simultaneously with the end of legal restrictions on non-Russians, but they refused to countenance the possibility that, in fact, non-Russian national movements could and did pose a danger to the integrity of the Russian state. Conservative nationalists, meanwhile, grudgingly admitted the possibility that non-Russians could retain their cultures and languages at home, but they doggedly insisted that all public and official utterances in the Russian Empire had to be made in the Russian language and that all government institutions, even at the local level, had to conduct business in that language. The extreme intolerance of certain factions of official Russia toward the use of non-Russian languages in public institutions came out blatantly in the controversy over the project to introduce elected city governments in the Polish provinces. Or, at the very least, the bitter and uncompromising debates on this project revealed the convenient possibility for the chauvinist right to make political capital out of the national issue. It was a precedent that boded evil for the future of the empire.

We cannot help but condemn the blindness (or, at least, "daltonism") of the Russian government and public regarding the national problem, but we should also not indulge in ahistorical hindsight. For the government and most of the Russian public, the majority of the empire's population (if only barely) consisted of "Russians." The assimilation of peasant Belorussians and Ukrainians seemed to many (including national liberals like Petr Struve) to be only a matter of time. In a similar fashion (at least from a superficial point of view), one could point to significant successes in the assimilation of Russian Jews: consider, for example, the case of Vladimir Zhabotinskii, Iulii Gessen, and others like them, who were important contributors to Russian press polemics on the national question.

The Poles, however, could not be "assimilated"—even the most ardent Polonophobes admitted as much. It was perhaps not unreasonable, however, to assume that Russia's Polish community might reconcile itself to Russian rule in the long run, retaining their language in local schools and institutions, but also learning and using the "reigning language." As for the dozens, even hundreds, of smaller ethnic groups living in the empire, particularly in its Asian borderlands, the ability of "superior Russian culture" to assimilate, at least to some degree, these smaller peoples might well have seemed within the realm of possibility. We should keep in mind that this was the age of European imperialism, and for the most part Russians shared an unabashed belief in the superiority of their own culture over that of Asian peoples, even after the shock of defeat in 1905 at the hands of the Japanese.[5]

These attitudes are exemplified in the three case studies we have seen in this work. When considering the introduction of elective zemstva to the Western Provinces, the government found itself trapped by its own fears of a Polish takeover and by the machinations of its political allies in the Duma (particularly the Nationalist Party) to create zemstva tailored to their own benefit, which (not by chance) meant harsh restrictions on local Polish landowners. The desire of the government to open up rural administration to local elements, even in this modest way, collided with the distrust of official Russia toward the Polish landowning elite and with misgivings about the "reliability" of the peasant element. Age-old national fears combined with modern political machinations and produced, in the end, a complete impasse that could only be broken by the use of extra-parliamentary methods, that is, article 87. The western zemstvo project taught Stolypin and the Russian government the bitter lesson that their nationalist "allies" might be pursuing interests not entirely congruent to those of the imperial government.

A similar situation developed when the government attempted to extend elective municipal governments to the ten Polish provinces. Once again, the economic imperative of broadening public participation in local government clashed with national antagonisms and also with legislative politics. The government's plan to limit Jewish participation in Polish municipal bodies called forth the anger of Russian liberals, which rapidly developed into a major crisis when Polish representatives in the Duma refused to protest these restrictions. The explosion of Polish-Jewish hatred in these years, culminating in the boycott campaign of 1912, was a direct result of the city government controversy in the Duma. Meanwhile, the government continued to press for passage of the project in the legislature, only to find its plans torpedoed, not by the Poles or the Russian liberals but by conservatives in the State Council whose pretensions for the hegemony of the Russian language exceeded even those of the imperial government. Once again, the prospect of more efficient administration through greater public participation, desired by the government, was blocked by reactionary, true-Russian elements.

The creation of the Kholm Province represents the only unabashed victory of militant Russian nationalism among the three projects we have considered. From the official viewpoint, however, the new province aimed not to repress any nationality but to preserve and protect "Russian" and Orthodox elements in the area. The choice, as expressed by the proponents of the project, was not one of national freedom versus government repression but rather between militant Polonism and government protection. The success of the project may be ascribed to several factors. For one, it presented the government with a relatively cheap and easy way to assure continued Russian nationalist support. Also, the stereotyped image of persecuted "Russian" peasants being forced into Catholicism by militant Poles was a notion that was amply familiar to patriotic Russians and a popular banner for the government to take up. At the same time, one should not underestimate the importance of personality in this affair: without the energetic and ambitious Bishop Evlogii and his ally within the MVD, S. E. Kryzhanovskii, it seems unlikely that a Kholm Province would have been created. The creation of the Kholm Province allowed the imperial government to present itself as an active force in protecting Russian and Orthodox rights in the post-1905 period.

The ultimate question underlying any discussion of late imperial Russia's national policy (or, indeed, any policy of that ill-fated empire) consists of two parts: What were the choices available? and, Did the empire have a chance? The quick answers are "few" and "probably not," respectively. Russia's treatment of minority nationalities in the imperial period was in many respects repugnant, and most likely counterproductive. Still, when we consider the policies of contemporary European states, Russian policy seems at times even liberal. Both Prussia and Hungary were on the whole even more restrictive than Russia toward their national minorities, and the relative liberality of Austria and the Ottoman Empire can be explained more in terms of state weakness than by recourse to any enlightened policy.[6] To be sure, Russian "nationality policy" (to use a quite anachronistic term) from the mid-nineteenth century steadily took on a more Russian-nationality hue, and after 1905, the demagogic use of national antagonisms to garner political support was a constant temptation not only for the government itself but more importantly for the conservative political groupings upon which official Russia found itself obliged to depend.

Russian nationality policy was based, more than anything else, on the political imperative to keep together a sprawling, ethnically and religiously diverse empire. Democratic principles and the right for national self-determination played no part in the empire's calculations. The Russian government unfailingly and repeatedly disavowed any policy of explicit denationalization, but official Russia's very conception of nationality and the relation between nation and state produced a significant and openly admitted bias toward the Russian nation and the Orthodox religion. From the perspective of the late twentieth century it seems obvious that a policy of greater local autonomy, legal equality, and a lessening of political centralism would have been far preferable to restrictions and bureaucratic control. The dangers of a more liberal nationality policy for the integrity of the Russian Empire were, however, very real indeed. Furthermore, the difficulties of reconciling state and national interests in this region during the twentieth century should alert us to the almost impossible difficulties involved.

During the past decade, we have observed—with astonishment, joy mixed with fear, and increasing concern—the collapse of one of the most powerful political entities on earth, the Soviet Union, and its replacement by a number of independent sovereign states. In its seventy years of history, Soviet nationality policy attempted to solve the national problem by allowing the free development of nationalities (in principle), while attempting to create a "supranational" loyalty to socialism and the Soviet state. This attempt ended in utter failure. Thus today the "national question" in the lands of the former Russian Empire remains nearly as open as a century ago. We can only hope that the present leaders of these states, unlike those of the Russian and Soviet Empires, will be guided not by ethnic stereotypes and historical fears but by a spirit of reconciliation between nations and the knowledge that dissimilar national groups can coexist peacefully within one state. May the example of late imperial Russia serve as a cautionary example.

Notes

Note on Calendar

Unlike most of Europe, the Russian Empire never accepted the Gregorian calendar, first introduced in 1582 by Pope Gregory XIII. The Russians continued to follow the Julian calendar, which ran twelve days behind the Gregorian in the nineteenth century and thirteen days behind in the twentieth. Poles, being Catholics, accepted the Gregorian calendar early on and continued to use that calendar even in the period covered by this volume. In general, all dates here follow the Russian, that is the Julian, calendar ("old style"). The only exception is for references to Polish periodicals, which after 1906 were dated exclusively according to the Gregorian calendar ("new style"). When two dates are given (as in the case of Polish periodicals up to 1906), the first is the old style, the second the new.

Chapter 1: Nation, State, and Nationalism

1. For an excellent recent study of the ruling elite of the imperial period during the reign of Nicholas II, see Dominic Lieven, *Russia's Rulers under the Old Regime* (New Haven, 1989).

2. For the term *lavirovanie*, see A. Ia. Avrekh, *Tsarizm i tret'eiiun'skaia sistema* (Moscow, 1966), p. 21. Here, as so often, Avrekh is quoting Lenin, in this instance on the meaning of the term "bonapartism." I shall use the term "nationality policy" (in quotes) to refer to the totality of policies toward non-Russian nationalities in the Empire.

3. A good example of this tendency is the brilliant work by Reinhard Bendix, which, nonetheless, can hardly be applied outside Western Europe: *Nation Building and Citizenship* (New York, 1964).

4. On the frailty of "unitary French culture," even at the end of the nineteenth century, see Eugen Weber, *Peasants into Frenchmen: The Modernization of Rural France, 1870–1914* (Stanford, 1976). It must be admitted, however, that French elites, generally speaking, accepted the hegemony of Parisian culture and did not present a separatist threat—unlike the situation in the Russian Empire.

5. Here I am paraphrasing Ernest Gellner paraphrasing Weber. E. Gellner, *Nations and Nationalism* (Ithaca, N.Y., 1983), p. 3. For Max Weber on the nation/state dilemma, see H. H. Gerth and C. Wright Mills, eds., *From Max Weber: Essays in Sociology* (New York, 1958), pp. 171–79.

6. An admirable compendium of various theories of state is Martin Carnoy, *The State and Political Theory* (Princeton, 1984). On the nation/state nexus, see John Breuilly, *Nationalism and the State* (Chicago, 1982), and Hugh Seton-Watson, *Nations and States: An Enquiry into the Origins of Nations and the Politics of Nationalism* (London, 1977).

7. Or do they? It would be wrong to ignore the ambiguities and strains existing in present-day multilingual states such as Belgium, Canada, Switzerland, or even Finland. Yet, on the whole, one may justifiably speak (for the time being, at least) of a Belgian, Finnish (either *finsk* or *suomalainen*), or Swiss nation.

8. For some theoretical considerations of the term and concept of "nation," see Louis L. Snyder, *The Meaning of Nationalism* (New Brunswick, N.J., 1954), esp. "The Tyranny of Words" and "The Concept of the Nation," pp. 3–55. A more recent theoretical discussion is Walker Connor, "A Nation Is a Nation, Is a State, Is an Ethnic Group, Is a . . . ," *Ethnic and Racial Studies* 1, no. 4 (1974), pp. 377–400.

9. Gellner, *Nations and Nationalism*, pp. 53, 55.

10. Benedict Anderson, *Imagined Communities: Reflections on the Origin and Spread of Nationalism* (London, 1983), p. 15; Peter Alter, *Nationalismus* (Frankfurt, 1985), p. 16.

11. "Uchrezhdennaia b. Varshavskim General-Gubernatorom, General-Ad"iutantom Chertkovym 10 Noiabria 1904 goda Instruktsiia Komissaram po krest'ianskim delam o poriadke vydachi udostoverenii krest'ianam i meshchanam-pol'nikam na poluchenie ssud iz Krest'ianskogo Banka," quoted in *Spravka o predpolozhennykh meropriiatiiakh v otnoshenii Kholmskoi gubernii* (St. Petersburg, 1912), p. xxix. (Throughout the text, unless otherwise noted, all translations from the original foreign language are my own.)

12. In official parlance, almost always "persons of Russian descent" *(litsa russkogo proizkhozhdeniia),* making nationality dependent not on what one is but on one's origins. I doubt that this distinction was at all conscious to most Russian bureaucrats. That the imperial government wished to get away from the religious element in nationality determination is obvious throughout the Kholm controversy (because many of the "Russians" ostensibly in need of protection from Poles were of Catholic faith) and may also be observed within the Ministry of Internal Affairs in the 1909 discussions on introducing zemstva to the Western Provinces. See, for example, "Doklad nachal'nika VII Otdeleniia Departamenta Obshchikh Del Statskogo Sovetnika Strol'mana komissiiam Soveta po delam mestnogo khoziaistva, po voprosu o tom, kogo sleduet schitat' 'litsami pol'skogo proiskhozhdeniia'," in RGIA, f. 1278, op. 2, 1910, d. 1171, ll. 101–2.

13. The case is made by a Polish specialist that, in the absence of a state around which the nation could develop in Eastern and Central Europe, language often assumed a central role in national movements. This argument would apply to Czechs and Lithuanians, for example, but not to Russians or even Poles. Józef Chlebowczyk, *Procesy narodotwórcze we wschodniej Europie środkowej w dobie kapitalizmu, od schyłku XVIII do początków XX w.* (Warsaw, 1975), pp. 21–22.

14. In Russian, a distinction is made between the two aspects of Jewishness by the words *evrei* (Jew, but not necessarily a religious Jew) and *iudei* (specifically a man of the Jewish faith).

15. The first line of Gellner's book makes this clear: "Nationalism is primarily a political principle, which holds that the political and the national unit should be congruent." Gellner, *Nations and Nationalism*, p. 1.

16. Ibid., p. 24.

17. Ibid., p. 34.

18. It should also be remembered that in 1914 plans were in place to introduce universal elementary education in the Russian Empire. To quote one specialist, "Only the compounding of war, revolution, and civil war postponed the joint commitment [of both "society" and the government] to universal compulsory elementary education." Patrick L. Alston, *Education and the State in Tsarist Russia* (Stanford, 1969), p. 248.

19. Gellner, *Nations and Nationalism*, p. 18.

20. It would be wrong to take an overly cynical attitude toward this phe-

nomenon; however, it would be equally misleading to deny that, for example, a Russian schoolmaster in Ukraine might oppose Ukrainian nationalism in part because of the negative effects it could have on his own career there. On the sociology of nationalist groups in several small European countries in general, see Miroslav Hroch, *Social Preconditions of National Revival in Europe: A Comparative Analysis of the Social Composition of Patriotic Groups among the Smaller European Nations*, trans. Ben Fowkes (Cambridge, U.K., 1985); see also Paul R. Magocsi, *National Cultures and University Chairs* (Toronto, 1980).

21. Anderson, *Imagined Communities*, p. 46: "What, in a positive sense, made the new [national] communities imaginable was a half-fortuitous, but explosive, interaction between a system of production and productive relations (capitalism), a technology of communications (print), and the fatality of human linguistic diversity."

22. Ibid., pp. 15, 31, 82 (citing Seton-Watson, *Nations and States*, p. 148), 82–83.

23. Hans Rogger, "Nationalism and the State: A Russian Dilemma," *Comparative Studies in Society and History* 4, no. 3 (April 1962), pp. 253–64 (253). Indeed, the third element of the Uvarovian trinity, *narodnost'* (which Anderson and Seton-Watson incorrectly give as *natsional'nost'*) bears little resemblance to nationalism in a modern, political sense. The term refuses to be tied down to any precise definition and includes such elements as devotion to the Tsar and the Orthodox church and a vague romantic belief in the mission of the Russian people. The term *narodnost'* appears to be a calque of the equally vague and romantic German *Volkstümlichkeit*. Neither term suggests the kind of political program implied in modern nationalism: that is, for every nation there must be a state, and each state must contain only one nation. For a more complete discussion of this "most obscure, puzzling, and debatable member of the official trinity," see Nicholas V. Riasanovsky, *Nicholas I and Official Nationality in Russia, 1825–1855* (Berkeley, 1959), pp. 124–67. Even at this time, Riasanovsky points out, "the two views of 'nationality,' which we may call 'the dynastic' and 'the nationalistic,' were in essential contradiction to each other" (p. 124).

24. Liah Greenfeld, *Nationalism: Five Roads to Modernity* (Cambridge, Mass., 1992), pp. 260–61.

25. This is not to deny the efforts, under Alexander III and later, to limit the hegemony of German culture in the Baltic region. On the situation of the Germans in the Russian Empire in general, see Andreas Kappeler et al., eds., *Die Deutschen im Russischen Reich* (Cologne, 1987).

26. This latter expectation, shared by nearly all Europeans of the period, could cause difficulties among non-Christian and non-European peoples. One may note (to take a trivial instance) the economic and administrative difficulties entailed by the traditional Jewish observance of Saturday as a day of rest in a state where the governing powers looked upon any kind of business activity on Sundays as near sacrilege.

27. Polish historians, for example, tend to use the term *rusyfikacja* in an undifferentiated and derogatory sense. See, for example, the monumental and informative dissertation by Paweł Piotr Wieczorkiewicz, "Polityka rosyjska wobec Królestwa Polskiego w latach, 1909–1914" (Ph.D. diss., University of Warsaw, 1976). Similarly, in a recent work by a historian of Lithuanian extraction, the imperial government is described as "bent on a policy of russification." Leonas Sabaliunas, *Lithuanian Social Democracy in Perspective, 1893–1914* (Durham, N.C., 1990), p. 7.

28. Edward C. Thaden, ed., *Russification in the Baltic Provinces and Finland, 1855–1914* (Princeton, 1981), pp. 15–108. On the Russian bureaucracy and the Jews, see I. M. Aronson, "Russian Bureaucratic Attitudes towards Jews, 1881–1894"

(Ph.D. diss., Northwestern University, 1973), and Aronson's other articles listed in the bibliography. Hans Rogger's important articles, which call into question the long-accepted thesis that pogroms were instigated by the tsarist government, are collected in *Jewish Policies and Right-Wing Politics in Imperial Russia* (Berkeley, 1986).

29. Sidney Harcave, ed. and trans., *The Memoirs of Count Witte* (Armonk, N.Y., 1990), p. 200 (the original statement may be found in S. Iu. Witte, *Vospominaniia* [Moscow, 1960], vol. 1, p. 417, the key phrase being *vneshnepravoslavnoe napravlenie*); A. P. Vladimirov, "O polozhenii Pravoslaviia v severo-zapadnom krae," *Russkoe obozrenie* 4, no. 20 (March 1893), pp. 187–88. A similar complaint, aimed specifically against the governor of Kovno Province, may be found in a denunciatory letter dated January 30, 1896, to minister of internal affairs I. L. Goremykin, in RGIA, f. 1626, op. 1, 1896, d. 201.

30. The case against Wilno university as an intellectual center for the uprising of 1830 is much better substantiated than similar accusations against the Szkoła Główna ("Main School," the nucleus of today's University of Warsaw) for 1863. More important than historical facts, however, are the Russian government's interpretations at the time. For an arch-conservative view from a Polish aristocrat who blamed Russian repressions on the Poles themselves, see Graf Ignacy Korwin-Milewski, *Golos pol'skogo dvorianina o vybore chlena gosudarstvennogo soveta v Vil'ne* (St. Petersburg, n.d. [ca. 1910]).

31. For a detailed exposition of this attitude, given by a "Little Russian" *(maloross)* and inhabitant of Ukraine, see S. N. Shchegolev, *Ukrainskoe dvizhenie kak sovremennyi etap iuzhnorusskogo separatizma* (Kiev, 1912).

32. Law of 1906 quoted in Marc Szeftel, *The Russian Constitution of April 23, 1906: Political Institutions of the Duma Monarchy* (Brussels, 1976), p. 84. For the original law, see *Polnoe Sobranie Zakonov Rossiiskoi Imperii (PSZ)*, 3d series, vol. 26, ot. 1, no. 27805 (April 23, 1906), pp. 456–61. Andreas Kappeler, "Historische Voraussetzungen des Nationalitätenproblems im russischen Vielvölkerreich," *Geschichte und Gesellschaft* 8, no. 2 (1982), pp. 159–83 (163).

33. Ibid., p. 174. See, for example, the arguments presented within the Ministry of Internal Affairs on the polonization of Belorussian peasants included in RGIA, f. 821, op. 128, 1912, d. 697, and 1914, d. 1216. The latter file includes the minutes of a conference held in 1914 that was dedicated to combating this process of polonization.

34. See, for example, Manfred Hagen, "Russification via 'Democratization'? Civil Service in the Baltic after 1906," *Journal of Baltic Studies* 9, no. 1 (spring 1978), pp. 56–65.

35. To be sure, recent research has shown that imperial bureaucrats were hardly the Gogolian characters sometimes portrayed. For a defense of the imperial *gubernator*, see Richard G. Robbins, *The Tsar's Viceroys: Russian Provincial Governors in the Last Years of the Empire* (Ithaca, N.Y., 1987). For a contemporary inside view, see E. N. Berendts, *O proshlom i nastoiashchem russkoi administratsii: Zapiska sostavlennaia v dekabre 1903 goda* (St. Petersburg, 1913).

36. Secret statutes *(polozheniia)* of February 26, 1865, and June 14, 1867 (not included in *PSZ*). See B. G. Ol'shamovskii, *Prava po zemlevladeniiu v zapadnom krae* (St. Petersburg, 1899). Even after 1905, Poles were allowed to purchase land in the Western Provinces only from other Poles *(ukaz* of May 1, 1905). For a compendium of anti-Polish restrictions in effect in the Russian Empire at the turn of the century, see Count Anton Tyszkiewicz [Graf Leliva, psued.], *Russko-pol'skie otnosheniia: Ocherk* (Leipzig, 1895).

37. Witte, *Vospominaniia*, vol. 2, p. 210. It needs to be stressed that Witte did

not in any way contemplate genocide. When he made this statement, the very idea of intentional extermination of entire peoples would have seemed utterly fantastic. In our own times, unfortunately, the conceptual and technical possibility of genocide has been amply and repeatedly demonstrated.

38. A similar phenomenon is described in Edward Said, *Orientalism* (New York, 1979). In my view, Said's main weakness is his insistence that, as a phenomenon of cultural misunderstanding, "orientalism" is unique.

39. For nearly all of the cities of this region, at least two or three names exist: Wilno/Vilne/Vil'na/Vilnius or Kiev/Kiiv/Kijów, to name only two of the most famous. Since this is primarily a study of Russian government politics, I shall use the Russian forms for cities in the western territories (Kiev, Vil'na), and the Polish names for those located in the Kingdom of Poland (Lublin, Siedlce) unless an English name (Warsaw) exists. This convention should in no way be interpreted as an acceptance of Russian claims in the region, but merely as a convenience.

40. For the case of Finland, see C. Leonard Lundin, "Finland," in Thaden, ed., *Russification in the Baltic Provinces and Finland*. For a general theory of the development of Russian government to 1905, see George Yaney, *The Systemization of Russian Government: Social Evolution in the Domestic Administration of Imperial Russia, 1711–1905* (Urbana, 1973).

Chapter 2: Non-Russians in Russian Public Discourse

1. Frederic Jameson, *The Prison-House of Language: A Critical Account of Structuralism and Russian Formalism* (Princeton, 1972).

2. An excellent collection of essays on this important segment of imperial Russian society has recently appeared: E. W. Clowes, S. Kassow, J. West, eds., *Between Tsar and People: Educated Society and the Quest for Public Identity in Late Imperial Russia* (Princeton, 1991).

3. On the beginnings of the split between rulers and "society," see Nicholas V. Riasanovsky, *A Parting of Ways: Government and the Educated Public in Russia, 1801–1855* (Oxford, 1976).

4. On the politicalization of the Russian right during 1905, see the important new book, Don C. Rawson, *Russian Rightists and the Revolution of 1905* (Cambridge, 1995).

5. This is, of course, greatly simplified, almost to the point of parody. For a more detailed discussion of Marx and nationality, see Solomon Bloom, *The World of Nations: A Study of the National Implications of the Work of Karl Marx* (New York, 1941; reprint, New York, 1967); Richard Pipes, *The Formation of the Soviet Union* (Cambridge, Mass., 1964), pp. 21–49; and Roman Szporluk, *Communism and Nationalism: Karl Marx versus Friedrich List* (Oxford, 1988). For a detailed account of Russian socialism and the national question, see Walker Connor, *The National Question in Marxist-Leninist Theory and Strategy* (Princeton, 1984), esp. pp. 5–42. For a contemporary view, see M. B. Ratner, "Natsional'nyi vopros v svete sotsialisticheskogo mirovozzreniia," *Russkoe bogatstvo*, no. 2 (February 1908), pp. 25–63.

6. Gellner, *Nations and Nationalism*, p. 129.

7. For a recent study of the changing attitudes within the Jewish Bund of the relative importance of the national, political, and economic struggles, see Yoav Peled, *Class and Ethnicity in the Pale: The Political Economy of Jewish Workers' Nationalism in Late Imperial Russia* (London, 1989).

8. In the Russian Empire, Polish and Jewish socialists by necessity did the

most thinking about reconciling socialism and nationalism. See, for example, the essays collected in Kazimierz Kelles-Krauz, *Naród i historia: Wybór pism* (Warsaw, 1989); Julian Marchlewski, *Antysemityzm a robotnicy* (Cracow, 1913); and the works of Ber Borochov (Borokhov), for example, *Klassovye momenty natsional'nogo kharaktera* (Odessa, 1906).

9. V. I. Lenin, "Kriticheskie zametki po natsional'nomu voprosu," in *Sobranie Sochinenii* (Moscow, 1961), vol. 24, pp. 113–150 (esp. 117–18). This article was written in late 1913 and originally published in *Prosveshchenie*, nos. 10–12 (November–December 1913).

10. The bible on the relation between social democracy and nationality was Bauer's *Die Nationalitätenfrage und die Sozialdemokratie* (1907) in *Werkausgabe* (Vienna, 1975), vol. 1, pp. 49–622. On the Austro-Marxist position on nationality, in more general terms, especially prior to 1907, see Hans Mommsen, *Die Sozialdemokratie und die Nationalitätenfrage im habsburgischen Vielvölkerstaat* (Vienna, 1963). Lenin heaped scorn on the defenders of "national culture" (that is, the Bundists) in his essays collected under the title "Kriticheskie zametki po natsional'nomu voprosu," in *Polnoe sobranie sochinenii* (Moscow, 1961), vol. 24, pp. 113–50. An English translation of this and many other articles on the Jewish and national questions may be found in Hyman Lumer, ed., *Lenin on the Jewish Question* (New York, 1974). The Lithuanian Social Democrats (LSDP) also reacted negatively to the Russian SD party's "centralizing aspirations." Michał Romer, *Litwa: Studium o odrodzeniu narodu litewskiego* (Lwów, 1908), p. 282.

11. The literature on Marxism and nationality is enormous. Most pertinent for our purposes are E. Anisimova, *Razrabotka V. I. Leninym marksistskoi teorii i programmy po national'nym voprosam* (Moscow, 1958); V. I. Lenin, *The Right of Nations to Self-Determination: Selected Writings* (New York, 1951); and I. V. Stalin, *Marksizm i national'nyi vopros* (1913; reprint, Moscow, 1939). See also T. Iu. Burmistrova and V. S. Gushakova, *Natsional'nyi vopros v programmakh i taktike politicheskikh partii v Rossii, 1905–1917 gg.* (Moscow, 1976). Since I am limiting myself to Russian views here, I am unable to go into the fascinating Polish situation, where, in the immediate prewar period, there were three major socialist groups: PPS-right, PPS-moderates, and SDKPiL—not even to mention the Jewish socialist groups active in the Kingdom of Poland. On the socialist/national nexus in Poland, see Ulrich Haustein, *Sozialismus und nationale Frage in Polen* (Cologne, 1969).

12. *Gosudarstvennaia Duma: Stenograficheskie otchety* (henceforth *GDSO*) 4, s. 1, ch. 2, zased. 51 (May 20, 1913), cols. 1778–92.

13. Ibid., cols. 1786–87.

14. Ibid., cols. 1779, 1790.

15. Ibid., col. 1785 (the last line is, of course, biblical).

16. Ibid., cols. 1787–88.

17. On Russian liberalism and the Kadet party, see Charles Timberlake, ed., *Essays on Russian Liberalism* (Columbia, Mo., 1972), and Victor Leontovitsch, *Geschichte des Liberalismus in Rußland*, 2d ed. (Frankfurt-am-Main, 1974). For the Kadets' stance on non-Russian nationalities, see the Constitutional Democratic party platform, especially points 1, 2, 11, 12, 25, and 26 in V. Ivanovich, *Rossiiskie partii, soiuzy i ligi* (St. Petersburg, 1906), pp. 14–16.

18. For the Polish complaints, see, for example, Tytus Filipowicz, *Polska i autonomia* (Warsaw, 1908), pp. 14–15, 23–24. Filipowicz stressed that Poles would achieve autonomy not through the Duma but only by a thoroughgoing reform of the Russian state. Quotation is from Paul Miliukov, *Political Memoirs, 1905–1917*, ed.

Arthur P. Mendel (Ann Arbor, Mich., 1967), pp. 213–14. The Russian Jews' disillusionment with the failure of Russian liberalism to deliver on its promises is expressed in the pamphlet by David I. Zaslavskii and S. Ivanovich, *Kadety i evrei* (Petrograd, 1916). To the end, however, Russian Jews (particularly those of assimilationist views) supported the Kadets in large numbers.

19. M. Slavinskii, "Natsional'naia struktura Rossii i Velikorossy," in A. I. Kastelianskii, ed., *Formy natsional'nogo dvizheniia v sovremennykh gosudarstvakh: Avstro-Vengriia, Rossiia, Germaniia* (St. Petersburg, 1910), pp. 277–303 (291).

20. Ibid., pp. 296, 292 (296).

21. M. Slavinskii, "Russkaia intelligentsiia i natsional'nyi vopros," in K. Arsen'ev et al., *Intelligentsiia v Rossii: Sbornik statei* (St. Petersburg, 1910), p. 234.

22. *GDSO* 3, s. 3, ch. 4, zased. 104 (May 8, 1910), cols. 873–90 (Rodichev). Rodichev characterized the bill as only externally concerned with self-government whereas its "lining" *(podkladka)* was hatred of the Poles (col. 874). Zemstva were organs of rural self-government, introduced in most provinces of European Russia in the 1860s. For more detail, see chapter 7.

23. Ibid., col. 887; *GDSO* 3, s. 2, ch. 4, zased. 123 (May 30, 1909), col. 2796.

24. *GDSO* 3, s. 3, ch. 4, zased. 105 (May 10, 1910), col. 994.

25. On this intriguing figure, see the detailed biography in two volumes by Richard Pipes, *Struve: Liberal on the Left, 1870–1905* (Cambridge, Mass., 1970), and *Struve: Liberal on the Right, 1905–1944* (Cambridge, Mass., 1980).

26. It is perhaps not without interest to note that "Russian Federation" is a translation of *Rossiiskaia Federatsiia*. The problem of nomenclature remains very pertinent, as article 1, paragraph 2, of the constitution of the Russian Federation (1993) shows.

27. P. Struve, "Intelligentsiia i natsional'noe litso," in *Po vekham: Sbornik statei ob intelligentsii i 'natsional'nom litse'* (Moscow, 1909), pp. 34, 36. This collection contains various replies to Struve's article, including one by P. Miliukov, "Natsionalizm protiv natsionalizma," pp. 37–41.

28. The Ukrainian school bill was introduced in the Duma on March 29, 1908 (*GDSO* 3, s. 1, ch. 2, zased. 44, col. 1337). The text of the proposed bill, with a lengthy defense of the use of Ukrainian in primary education, may be found in "O iazyke prepodavaniia v nachal'nykh shkolakh mestnostei s malorusskim naseleniem," *GDSO, Prilozhenie,* s. 1, tom 1, no. 238, pp. 1230–40. See the account in V. V. Sadovskii, "Ukrainskii vopros v tret'ei Dume," *Ukrainskaia zhizn',* no. 5 (May 1912), pp. 17–27; and RGIA, f. 1276, op. 4, 1908, d. 701, for minister of education Shvarts's arguments against the Duma bill.

29. To quote Richard Pipes, "The Ukraine was always Struve's blind spot" (p. 675). On Struve and the Ukrainians in general, see R. Pipes, "Peter Struve and Ukrainian Nationalism," *Harvard Ukrainian Studies* 3–4 (1979–1980), pp. 675–83.

30. P. Struve, "Chto zhe takoe Rossiia," *Russkaia mysl'* (January 1911), p. 184.

31. Bogdan Kistiakovskii, writing under the name of Ukrainets, "K voprosu o samostoiatel'noi ukrainskoi kul'ture: Pis'mo k redaktsii," *Russkaia mysl'* (May 1911), pp. 131–46. Bogdan Kistiakovskii was Ukrainian by birth but Russian by culture. See Susan Eva Heuman, "Bogdan Kistiakovskii and the Problem of Human Rights in the Russian Empire, 1899–1917" (Ph.D. diss., Columbia University, 1977). Kistiakovskii's Russian counterpart in this controversy was F. E. Korsh, "K sporu ob ukrainskoi kul'ture," *Ukrainskaia zhizn'* (February 1912), pp. 32–47.

32. P. Struve, "Obshcherusskaia kul'tura i ukrainskii partikuliarizm (otvet Ukraintsu)" *Russkaia mysl'* (January 1912), pp. 65–86.

33. Kistiakovskii, "K voprosu o samostoiatel'noi ukrainskoi kul'ture," esp. pp. 133–41. Kistiakovskii stated that progressive Russians did not support the "cultural needs" *(kul'turnye potrebnosti)* of the Ukrainian people, such as primary education in Ukrainian (p. 135). One of the few exceptions to this rule, according to Kistiakovskii, was Professor Korsh (p. 136). Rodichev quoted in Sadovskii, "Ukrainskii vopros v tret'ei Dume," *Ukrainskaia zhizn'* (May 1912), p. 20. An interesting collection of essays, exhibiting various shades of (mainly liberal) opinion on the national question is *Po vekham: Sbornik statei ob intelligentsii i 'natsional'nom litse'*.

34. For such a denunciation, see A. Ia. Avrekh, *Stolypin i tret'ia Duma* (Moscow, 1968), pp. 30–43. Avrekh goes so far as to state that Kadet attitudes on the nationality question did not differ significantly from Octobrist or even nationalist views.

35. See, for example, Slavinskii, "Russkaia intelligentsiia i natsional'nyi vopros," p. 229: "The history of the past forty years of Austria's existence gives evidence of the many-sided strength that nationalities are capable of developing when rights to national self-determination are guaranteed to a certain extent."

36. The case for exclusion is stated in M. M. Artsybashev, *Griadushchaia gibel' Rossii* (St. Petersburg, 1908), pp. 59–117. The more moderate rightists advocated a choice: either conversion or leaving Russia. On the controversy that arose over Artsybashev's proposal, see Wieczorkiewicz, "Polityka rosyjska," pp. 154–57.

37. K. N. Leont'ev, *Natsional'naia politika, kak orudie vsemirnoi revoliutsii* (Moscow, 1889).

38. The term "true-Russian" *(istinno-russkii)* denoted not only Russian ethnicity but (perhaps more important) a conservative monarchist political orientation. So easily did "national" characteristics become political.

39. A. N. Kuropatkin, *Rossiia dlia russkikh: Zadachi russkoi armii*, 3 vols. (St. Petersburg, 1910). General Kuropatkin, after military disasters on the fields of Manchuria, returned to Russia to militate for the cause of the Russian nation.

40. Ibid., vol. 3, passim. (pp. 258–59, 61; original emphasis).

41. Ibid., pp. 61–62, 346 (346).

42. In official bureaucratic parlance, the term *inorodets* had a specific meaning, referring mainly to the Jews and to nomadic ethnic groups in Siberia. In general nationalist speech, however, any non-Russian (even Catholic Poles) could be included under this rubric. For a recent discussion of this term, see John Klier, "The Concept of 'Jewish Emancipation' in a Russian Context," in Olga Crisp and Linda Edmondson, eds., *Civil Rights in Imperial Russia* (Oxford, 1989), pp. 132–33. For a contemporary view, see *Entsiklopedicheskii slovar' Brokgauz-Efron* (St. Petersburg, 1894), vol. 13:1, pp. 224–25, entry "inorodtsy."

43. Kuropatkin, *Rossiia dlia russkikh*, vol. 3, p. 239.

44. Ibid., pp. 72–73.

45. "Tol'ko material dlia rasporiazhenii i meropriiatii vysshei i nizshei administratsii." L. Slonimskii, "Natsional'naia programma A. N. Kuropatkina," *Vestnik Evropy*, no. 12 (December 1910), p. 313.

46. A. P. Vladimirov, *Istoriia raspoliacheniia zapadno-russkogo kostela* (Moscow, 1896), p. 120.

47. "Osobenno Pol'ka opasna dlia Rossii." Vladimirov, *Istoriia*, p. 46.

48. V. I. Gurko [V. R., pseud.], *Ocherki Privislian'ia* (Moscow, 1897), p. 21.

49. RGIA, f. 1284, op. 190, 1899, d. 84B, l. 27v.

50. Vladimirov, *Istoriia*, pp. 45, 48.

51. *Okrainy Rossii*, no. 3 (January 20, 1907), p. 38, in response to Count Tyszkiewicz's appeal in *Rech'* on December 28, 1906.

52. The Uniate church was "united" with Orthodoxy in 1839 (Northwest Provinces) and 1875 (Kholm area). On these events, see "O vozsoedinenii uniatov s pravoslavnoiu tserkov'iu v Rossiiskoi Imperii," *Khristianskoe chtenie*, no. 4 (1839), pp. 351–423; M. O. Koialovich, *Istoriia vozsoedineniia zapadnorusskikh uniatov starykh vremen* (St. Petersburg, 1873); and Luigi Glinka, *Diocesi ucraino-cattolica di Cholm (liquidazione ed incorporazione alla Chiesa russo-ortodossa)* (Rome, 1975). The ex-Uniates often did not accept Orthodoxy, despite their official conversion, which thereby caused serious difficulties for local religious and civil administrators. For more on this topic, see chapter 9 on the formation of the Kholm Province.

53. M. O. Koialovich, *Istoriia russkogo samosoznaniia po istoricheskim pamiatnikam i nauchnym sochineniiam* (St. Petersburg, 1893). The issue of Russian identity is of enormous interest but deserves its own monograph. My admittedly oversimplified comments are based in part on the following works: P. N. Podligailov, *Natsional'nye zadachi Rossii i mery k ikh osuchchestvleniiu* (St. Petersburg, 1888); Baron M. F. Taube [M. Vashutin, pseud.], *K vozrozhdeniiu slaviano-russkogo samosoznaniia: Sbornik* (Petrograd [*sic*], 1911); M. Borodkin, *Natsional'nost' v nauke (Molodomu pokoleniiu)* (St. Petersburg, 1912); Viktor Stroganov, *Russkii natsionalizm, ego sushchnost', istoriia i zadachi* (St. Petersburg, 1912); P. I. Kovalevskii, *Osnovy russkogo natsionalizma* (St. Petersburg, 1912); V. G. Sakhnovskii, *O Russkoi narodnosti: Natsional'nyi lik Rossii* (Moscow, 1914–1915).

54. Norman Cohn, *Warrant for Genocide: The Myth of Jewish World-Conspiracy and the Protocols of the Elders of Zion* (Chico, Calif., 1981). One attempt—highly interesting but flawed—to plumb the sexual depths of anti-Semitism is Klaus Theweleit, *Männerphantasien*, 2 vols. (Frankfurt-am-Main, 1977–1978). Theweleit is concerned, however, only with Weimar Germany and his argumentation is rather too fanciful to provide any kind of concrete theoretical model. Still, Theweleit's emphasis on the subconscious and sexual origins of anti-Semitic behavior bears more detailed study. For some typical views, see D. V. Tutkevich, *Chto takoe evrei?* (Kiev, 1906), or A. P. Liprandi, *Evreistvo i anti-Semitizm* (Khar'kov, 1914).

55. Ia. Demchenka, *Evreiskoe ravnopravie ili russkoe poraboshchenie? Issledovanie tainykh evreiskikh planov i programm, napravlennykh k oslableniiu i razrusheniiu korennogo naseleniia i poraboshcheniiu ego evreistvu* (Kiev, 1907), pp. 167–68. Demchenka's proposed solutions to the Jewish question (amounting to an absolute apartheid of Jews in Russia) are set down on pp. 170–71.

56. Demchenka's work (ibid.) is one of the first detailed expositions on the Protocols of the Elders of Zion. Similar historico-conspirational views are found in G. Butmi, *Vragi roda chelovecheskogo*, 4th ed. (St. Petersburg, 1907) and in A. S. Shmakov, *Evreiskii vopros na stsene vsemirnoi istorii* (Moscow, 1912). A. P. Liprandi, *Ravnopravie i evreiskii vopros* (Khar'kov, 1911), pp. 1–5 (2).

57. Liprandi, *Ravnopravie i evreiskii vopros*, pp. 16–23. The parallel here with contemporary Polish economic anti-Semitism is only too obvious. See, for example, Jan Jeleński, *Nie bić żydów, ale im się nie dawać* (Warsaw, 1906).

58. Liprandi, *Ravnopravie i evreiskii vopros*, pp. 62, 68–78, 92–95.

59. Heinz-Dietrich Löwe, *Anti-Semitismus und reaktionäre Utopie* (Hamburg, 1978). Most notably, G. Butmi, author of the anti-Semitic classic *Vragi roda chelovecheskogo* (Enemies of the human race), also penned a work denouncing the gold standard, *Zolotaia valiuta* (St. Petersburg, n.d.).

60. On the Russian right in general, see V. Levitskii, "Pravye partii," in A. Potresov, L. Martov, and P. Maslov, eds., *Obshchestvennoe dvizhenie v Rossii v nachale XX-go veka* (St. Petersburg, 1914), vol. 3, bk. 5, pp. 345–469; John W. Bohon,

"Reactionary Politics in Russia, 1905–1909" (Ph.D. diss., University of North Carolina, 1967); and Hans Rogger, "Russia," in H. Rogger and Eugen Weber, eds., *The European Right: A Historical Profile* (Berkeley, 1965).

61. *Sbornik kluba russkikh natsionalistov* 1 (Kiev, 1909), p. 5.

62. Ukrainian nationalists, but not, it must be stressed, the masses whom we would term Ukrainian (Russian nationalists would call them Little Russians). This conceptual and terminological split is crucial for understanding how Russian nationalists were able to denounce Ukrainian political leaders while still including Ukrainian peasants among "our own."

63. *Natsionalisty v 3-ei Gosudarstvennoi Dume* (St. Petersburg, 1912), p. 7.

64. *GDSO* 3, s. 2, ch. 4, zased. 123 (May 30, 1909), cols. 2767–68.

65. *Natsionalisty v 3-ei Gosudarstvennoi Dume*, p. 8.

66. A. V. Bogdanovich, *Tri poslednikh samoderzhavtsa* (Moscow, 1990), pp. 151–52 (entry for February 25, 1892). On Meshcherskii, his life, and his influence at court, see W. E. Mosse, "Imperial Favourite: V. P. Meshchersky and the *Grazhdanin*," *Slavonic and East European Review* 59, no. 4 (October 1981), pp. 529–47; and Petr A. Zaionchkovskii, *Rossiiskoe samoderzhavie v kontse XIX stoletiia* (Moscow, 1970), pp. 74–81. Zaionchkovskii characterizes Meshcherskii as a man about whom "nobody had anything good to say" (p. 74) and his views as "the quintessence of reaction" (p. 79).

67. V. P. Meshcherskii, *Moi vospominaniia* (St. Petersburg, 1897), vol. 1, p. 267 (on Murav'ev, the Polish uprising, and Valuev in general, see pp. 279–81, 418–21).

68. Quotation is from ibid. (St. Petersburg, 1912), vol. 3, p. 152. On Katkov, see ibid. (St. Petersburg, 1898), vol. 2, pp. 84–87; on Ignat'ev, see ibid., vol. 3, p. 48.

69. Meshcherskii's characterization of Suvorin as a socialist was noted by A. Bogdanovich in a diary entry dated March 6, 1892. Bogdanovich, *Tri poslednikh samoderzhtsa,* p. 155.

70. Precisely this sentiment, emphasizing the lack of a unifying Russian national feeling among the peasantry, is echoed in the statement in 1915 of army chief of staff General N. N. Yanushkevich: "a Tambovets is ready to stand to the death for Tambov Province, but the war in Poland seems strange and unnecessary." Quoted in D. Lieven, *Nicholas II: Tsar of All the Russias* (London, 1993), p. 206. To complicate the matter further, one may point out that the general's surname may perhaps more correctly be spelled Januszkiewicz.

71. "O patriotizme," *Grazhdanin* 28, no. 44 (June 13, 1899), p. 4.

72. Ibid., p. 5.

73. For another example of this attitude, see "Chem my nezdorovy," *Grazhdanin* 30, no. 54 (July 19, 1901), pp. 2–6.

74. A. Babetskii, "Okrainyi vopros," cited in *Grazhdanin* 34, no. 76 (September 25, 1905), pp. 2–4 (4). See, for example, "Dnevniki," *Grazhdanin* 26, no. 21 (March 16, 1897), pp. 21–22; and *Grazhdanin* 26, no. 65 (August 21, 1897), pp. 14–15, praising the Polish "reconciliator" Erazm Piltz.

75. See, for example, the articles in *Grazhdanin,* no. 17 (1910) and no. 33 (1911) on the western zemstvo, and no. 4 (1912) against the formation of the Kholm Province.

76. A recent broad treatment of this issue is Eli Weinerman, "Racism, Racial Prejudice, and Jews in Late Imperial Russia," *Ethnic and Racial Studies* 17, no. 3 (July 1994), pp. 442–95.

77. I. Turgenev, *Zapiski okhotnika* (Berlin, 1920), p. 430.

78. Quotation is from RGIA, f. 821, op. 9, 1881, d. 126, ll. 34–35. For a view of

the causes of the 1881 pogroms quite opposing that expressed in the Russian official document, see Omeljan Pritsak, "The Pogroms of 1881," *Harvard Ukrainian Studies* 9 (1987), pp. 8–43.

79. See, for example, Jeffrey Brooks, *When Russia Learned to Read: Literacy and Popular Literature, 1861–1917* (Princeton, 1985), pp. 214–45; and Louise McReynolds, *The News under Russia's Old Regime: The Development of a Mass-Circulation Press* (Princeton, 1991).

80. S. N. Bulgakov, "Geroizm i podvizhnichestvo," in *Vekhi: Sbornik statei o russkoi intelligentsii*, 5th ed. (Moscow, 1910), p. 61. For a criticism of the views expressed on the national issue in *Vekhi*, see M. Ratner, "Natsional'noe litso i national'nyi vopros," in *"Vekhi" kak znamenie vremeni: Sbornik statei* (Moscow, 1910), pp. 321–52.

Chapter 3: Official Russia and Non-Russians

1. Lieven, *Russia's Rulers under the Old Regime*.

2. For more on Sviatopolk-Mirskii's "clan," which traced its roots back to 1620, see *Entsiklopedicheskii slovar' Brokgauz-Efron* (St. Petersburg, 1900), vol. 57, p. 273, entry "Sviatopolk-Mirskie"; and P. N. Petrov, *Istoriia rodov russkogo dvorianstva* (St. Petersburg, 1885), pp. 249–50. Prince P. Sviatopolk-Mirskii was also the father of the famous literary critic Prince D. S. Mirsky.

3. V. N. Kokovtsov, *Out of My Past: The Memoirs of Count Kokovtsov*, ed. H. H. Fisher, trans. Laura Matveev (Stanford, 1935).

4. S. E. Kryzhanovskii, *Vospominaniia* (Berlin, n.d. [ca. 1938]), esp. pp. 94 and 152–53.

5. S. D. Urusov, *Memoirs of a Russian Governor*, trans. and ed. Herman Rosenthal (London, 1908).

6. Witte, *Vospominaniia*, esp. vol. 1, pp. 40, 52, 88, 180. For Witte's view of Stolypin and the Jewish question, see ibid., pp. 492–93.

7. For a short description of the family and the career of Iosif V. Gurko, see *Entsiklopedicheskii slovar' Brokgauz-Efron*, vol. 18, pp. 913–14.

8. Gurko, *Ocherki Privislian'ia*, pp. 16–17. In a letter printed in *Russkoe Slovo* (December 8, 1911), V. Gurko admitted his authorship of *Ocherki Privislian'ia* and wrote that his father, Warsaw governor general I. Gurko, had opposed administrative russification. RGIA, f. 821, op. 10, 1910, d. 220, l. 35.

9. The *Ocherki Privislian'ia*, as the title attests, is concerned only with the Vistula region and not with the western territory. However, Gurko's comments on the Poles seem applicable to the *szlachta* of Minsk and Volhynia Provinces as much as to Poles in Kalisz and Warsaw.

10. Gurko, *Ocherki Privislian'ia*, pp. 22–28 (20).

11. Ibid., pp. 44, 296. "Russia not only never oppressed [*ugnetala*] the Polish people, as a whole, but, on the contrary, devoted and does not cease to devote all its energies to their further economic and intellectual development" (p. 296).

12. Ibid., pp. 75–81 (79). The term *serwituty* refers to the complicated system of rights that regulated peasants' use of landlords' pasture and forests. Polish historians have suggested that in the peasant liberation of 1863 in the Kingdom of Poland, the Russian government intentionally did not abolish serwituty because it aimed to exacerbate relations between former lord and former serf. By 1894, however, these rights were almost universally denounced by governors as a source of serious friction between peasants and noble landlords and as an obstacle to improving agricultural methods.

13. Ibid., pp. 99, 225–26, 107, and 113. Gurko saw the Germans as a positive counterweight to Jewish domination in the area (ibid., pp. 131–37).

14. Ibid., pp. 29, 14–16 (29). Furthermore, Gurko complained, the Russian administration in Poland was itself becoming polonized. Referring to the period of the early 1880s, under Warsaw governor general P. Al'bedinskii, he wrote, "Among many representatives of local administration there was expressed a noticeable Polonophilism [*zametnoe polonofil'stvo*]" (p. 15).

15. At times even Gurko admitted that in many respects the behavior of Russian *chinovniki* in Poland left much to be desired. He remarked that because of poor pay and the antagonism of the local population, for example, it was very difficult to obtain even minimally adequate personnel, especially at the lower levels of the bureaucracy (ibid., p. 354). The need for a strong and clearly defined policy in the Polish Kingdom is particularly emphasized in the conclusion (ibid., pp. 358–77).

16. This comes out most clearly in Gurko's treatment of *Kraj*. After describing *Kraj*'s stated desire for Poles to live in peace within the Russian state and as loyal Russian citizens (while retaining Polish culture and language), he continued, "However, this organ, too, is not known for its sincerity." He based this opinion on *Kraj*'s stated principle that Poles were generally not enemies of the Russian state (ibid., pp. 231–32). If even the mild-mannered *Kraj* could not be regarded as a potential ally, there was truly little chance for reconciliation between Russians and Poles.

17. The report may be found in RGIA, f. 1284, op. 190, 1899–1914, d. 84B, ll. 3–47, the spravka in ll. 136–241.

18. Ibid., l. 3.

19. Ibid., ll. 4–5.

20. Ibid., ll. 8v–10v. Whereas the word *szlachta* in Polish means simply "nobility" or "gentry," in Russian it took on the connotation of impoverished noble class, a kind of Polish *hidalguería*.

21. Ibid., ll. 11–14.

22. Ibid., l. 13.

23. Ibid., ll. 14v, 17–18. In speaking of the two "leading" Christian denominations, Mirskii uses the adjective *gospodstvuiushchii*, which in general use (in laws and official documents, for example) is restricted to the Orthodox faith.

24. Ibid., ll. 38v, 39.

25. Ibid., ll. 40–41, 41–45.

26. Ibid., l. 47v.

27. RGIA, f. 1263, op. 2, 1899, st. 253–332, d. 5385, ll. 588–609.

28. RGIA, *Chital'nyi Zal*, op. 1, 54 (Mogilev, 1910), p. 17; RGIA, f. 1284, op. 194, 1911, d. 56 (governor generalship of Kiev, 1910), l. 2v.

29. RGIA, f. 821, op. 150, 1910, d. 150. See also ibid., op. 128, 1914, d. 1215.

30. RGIA, f. 821, op. 125, 1884, d. 312, ll. 9–61.

31. RGIA, f. 1284, op. 194, 1908, d. 66 (Vil'na, 1907), l. 6; RGIA, *Chital'nyi Zal*, op. 1., d. 71 (Podolia, 1898), ll. 85–86.

32. RGIA, f. 1284, op. 223, 1898, d. 11 lit.B.P., l. 15.

33. RGIA, f. 1284, op. 194, 1904, d. 52 (Vil'na, 1903), ll. 2, 3, 8, 14v (2).

34. Note, for example, the exclamation of the Warsaw Oberpolitseimeister in his report for 1905: "The fanatical attitude of Polish society and hostility to Russians has taken on dimensions never before reached," in RGIA, f. 1263, op. 4, d. 49, l. 55.

35. RGIA, *Chital'nyi Zal*, op. 1, d. 36 (Kalisz, 1894), p. 7; ibid., d. 40 (Kielce, 1894), p. 7 (a marginal note—probably by K. P. Pobedonostsev—reads, "I hope that these are not just words!"); ibid., d. 84 (Siedlce, 1899), p. 8.

36. RGIA, f. 1284, op. 194, 1913, d. 93 (Lublin, 1912), l. 3.

37. RGIA, *Chital'nyi Zal*, op. 1, d. 54 (Mogilev, 1894), p. 8.

38. RGIA, f. 1282, op. 3, d. 267 (governor generalship of Kiev, 1898–1900), ll. 2–4.

39. RGIA, *Chital'nyi Zal*, op. 1, d. 17 (Volhynia, 1894), pp. 4–5; ibid., d. 53A (Minsk, 1902), p. 5, and RGIA, f. 1284, op. 194, 1903, d. 90 (Podolia, 1902), l. 5v; ibid., 1912, d. 38 (Mogilev, 1911), l. 5v.

40. Possible exceptions to this rule are the celebrated reports submitted by Warsaw governor general Alexander Imeretinskii in 1897, 1898, and 1899. Whereas Imeretinskii did express some confidence in the possibility of Russo-Polish conciliation *(ugoda)* in the 1897 report, two years later he noted that the influence of ugoda in Polish society had dropped considerably. The reports for 1898 and 1899 are found in RGIA, f. 1282, op. 3, d. 230; reports for 1897 in RGIA, f. 1263, op. 2, d. 5326. The Polish Socialist party published the 1897 report in Polish translation, with a suitably antagonistic foreword, as *Tajnie dokumenty rządu rosyjskiego w sprawach polskich* (London, 1898).

41. RGIA, *Chital'nyi Zal*, op. 1. d. 22 (Grodno, 1907), ll. 93v–94; RGIA, f. 1284, op. 194, 1907, d. 87, l. 4v.

42. For a more general treatment of Russian officialdom and Jews in this period, see Irvin M. Aronson, "Russian Bureaucratic Attitudes towards Jews" and "The Attitudes of Russian Officials in the 1880s toward Jewish Assimilation and Emigration," *Slavic Review* 34, no. 1 (1975), pp. 1–18.

43. RGIA, *Chital'nyi Zal*, op. 1, d. 22 (Grodno, 1910), l. 103v; RGIA, f. 1284, op. 223, 1898, d. 11 lit.B.P. (Podolia, 1897), l. 11.

44. RGIA, f. 1282, op. 3, d. 167, l. 9.

45. For Jewish use of land, see (all in RGIA), f. 1263, op. 2, zh.st. 398, d. 5447 (Mogilev, 1899), ll. 186, 203–4; f. 1284, op. 194, 1903, d. 90 (Podolia, 1902), l. 5v; *Chital'nyi Zal*, op. 1., d. 40 (Kielce, 1911), pp. 3–5. For Jewish participation in urban commerce, see f. 1282, op. 3, d. 443 (Suwałki, 1899), l. 3; f. 1284, op. 194, 1911, d. 98 (Siedlce, 1910), l. 3v; *Chital'nyi Zal*, op. 1, d. 71 (Podolia, 1896), l. 73.

46. RGIA, f. 1263, op. 2, st. 253–332, f. 5385, 1898, ll. 585–86.

47. RGIA, f. 1282, op. 3, 1898, d. 230, l. 66.

48. Ibid., op. 194, 1902, d. 159 (Vitebsk, 1901), l. 12; RGIA, f. 1284, op. 223, 1898 lit.B.P. (Suwałki, 1897), d. 18, l. 2v.

49. Such complaints were repeated almost annually. See, for example, RGIA, f. 1282, op. 3., d. 302 (Siedlce, 1898), l. 25v.

50. For self-mutilation, see RGIA, f. 1284, op. 194, 1911, d. 33 (Łomża, 1910), l. 5. It needs to be pointed out that many Jews "avoiding" military service had in fact left the empire long before. On the general issue of Jewish fitness for military service—a burning issue at the time—see *Evrei i voina* (St. Petersburg, 1912).

51. RGIA, f. 1284, op. 223, 1895, d. 160 (Vitebsk, 1894), l. 9v–10. For political provocation, see RGIA, f. 1284, op. 194, 1907, d. 31 (Vil'na, 1906), l. 2v; ibid., 1905, d. 82 (Mogilev, 1904), l. 2; and ibid., 1908, d. 54 (Vitebsk, 1907), l. 6v.

52. Ibid., 1907, d. 38 (Radom, 1906), l. 6; ibid., 1906, d. 40 (Łomża, 1904–1905), l. 18v.

53. RGIA, f. 1282, op. 3, d. 545 (Mogilev, 1901), l. 79.

54. RGIA, f. 1263, op. 2., st. 253–332, d. 5385, l. 586. Zionism was, however, quickly perceived as a threat by Russian officialdom. See the circular from the MVD Department of Police dated June 24, 1903, in RGIA, f. 1284, op. 190, 1903, d. 101. For details, see Symcha Lew, *Perokim yidishe geshikhte* (Brooklyn, 1941).

55. RGIA, f. 1282, op. 3, 1900, d. 355, l. 8.

56. Sivers's report can be found in RGIA, f. 1282, op. 2, 1876, d. 84, l. 25v. Ibid., op. 3, d. 545 (Kovno, 1900–1901), l. 164. For other governors' reports, see RGIA, f. 1284, op. 194, 1904, d. 92 (Mogilev, 1903), l. 5; ibid., 1913, d. 42 (Volhynia, 1912), l. 6v.

57. RGIA, f. 1282, op. 2, d. 334, ll. 187–208 (letter dated November 25, 1861). Ibid., d. 64, ll. 1–14 (memorandum dated October 6, 1860).

58. RGIA, f. 1284, op. 194, 1902, d. 159 (Vitebsk, 1901), l. 8v; RGIA, *Chital'nyi Zal*, op. 1, d. 17 (Volhynia, 1895), p. 8; RGIA, f. 1282, op. 3, 1899, d. 250 (Vil'na, 1898), l. 34v; RGIA, f. 1284, op. 224, 1905, d. 56, ll. 1–2 (letter dated November 24, 1905).

59. One governor even saw in the Jews of his province a "counterweight" for Russian culture against the Poles. RGIA, *Chital'nyi Zal*, op. 1, d. 53A (Minsk, 1898), p. 7.

60. This complex and fascinating question—no less troublesome for Russian intellectuals than for the government—has barely been touched upon in the literature. See, for example, I. M. Aronson, "The Prospects for the Emancipation of Russian Jewry during the 1880s," *Slavonic and East European Review* 55, no. 3 (1977), pp. 348–69.

61. RGIA, f. 1276, op. 1, 1905, d. 106, l. 419v.

62. RGIA, *Chital'nyi Zal*, op. 1, d. 84 (Siedlce, 1909), p. 6; RGIA, f. 1263, op. 4, d. 49 (Podolia, 1905), l. 535v.

63. RGIA, f. 1276, op. 4, 1908, d. 701, ll. 14, 19.

64. For a police report on the Ukrainian movement in 1914, see GARF, f. 102, Osobyi otdel, op. 244–1914, d. 231. For the closing of Prosvita, see GARF, f. 579, op. 1, 1915, d. 1898. "Zapiska ob ukrainskom dvizhenii za 1914–1916," RGIA, Pechatnaia Zapiska, no. 262.

65. RGIA, f. 1284, op. 190, 1899, d. 84A, ll. 88–90. This letter is dated August 20, 1906.

66. RGIA, f. 1284, op. 194, 1908, d. 66 (Vil'na, 1907), ll. 9–10. For other reports, see ibid., 1911, d. 34 (Vitebsk, 1910), l. 13; ibid., d. 72 (Vil'na, 1910), ll. 7–8; and RGIA, *Chital'nyi Zal*, op. 1, d. 53A (Minsk, 1913), pp. 4–6.

67. RGIA, f. 1284, op. 194, 1911, d. 72 (Vil'na, 1910), l. 23v.

68. Ibid., ll. 7–8.

69. RGIA, f. 821, op. 128, 1912, d. 697; ibid., 1914, d. 1216; ibid., op. 150, 1912, d. 167.

70. The relative percentages of nationalities within the Russian Empire, according to the 1897 census (quoted in Kastelianskii, *Formy natsional'nogo dvizheniia*, p. 280) are as follows: Russians *(Velikorossy)* 43.30, Ukrainians *(Malorossy)* 17.41, Poles 6.17, Belorussians 4.57, Jews 3.94, Germans 1.40, Lithuanians 1.29, and Latvians 1.12 percent (all other groups under 1 percent). Kastelianskii also points out that the figures for Russians are "undoubtedly" somewhat high—thus the figures for "Ukrainians, Jews, Poles, Armenians, and others" should be adjusted upward.

71. RGIA, f. 1284, op. 194, 1904, d. 52 (Vil'na, 1903), l. 3.

72. For example, the governor of Suwałki Province in 1902, in RGIA, f. 1284, op. 194, 1903, d. 85, l. 5. The arch-conservative governor general of Vil'na, V. Trotskii, continued to oppose any change in this prohibition, but by the 1890s, his was a minority opinion. RGIA, f. 1282, op. 3, d. 355 (report for 1899), l. 45.

73. RGIA, f. 1284, op. 194, 1907, d. 49 (Suwałki, 1906), l. 5; ibid., 1908, d. 66 (Vil'na, 1907), l. 6v.

74. On the cultural and national conflict between Lithuanians and Poles, see ibid., 1911, d. 72 (Vil'na, 1910), ll. 16–20; ibid., 1909, d. 45 (Suwałki, 1908), l. 4v; RGIA, f. 1282, op. 3, d. 376 (Kovno, 1899), ll. 23–24.

Chapter 4: West of Russia

1. For an extremely useful compendium of the legal restrictions based on nationality, religion, and gender in the Russian Empire after 1905, see *Ogranichitel'nye*

uzakoneniia i osobye zakonopolozheniia izdannye po soobrazheniiam natsional'nogo ili veroispovednogo svoistva libo obuslovlivaemym razlichiem polov (St. Petersburg, 1906–1907). Part 2 of this work deals exclusively with legal restrictions on Jews.

2. For one example of the consequences for one nationality of restrictions on another, see John Klier, "Russification and the Polish Revolt of 1863: Bad for the Jews?" *Polin* 1 (1986), pp. 91–106.

3. *Imennoi Ukaz* of December 10, 1865; *PSZ*, 2d ser., 40, no. 42759, pp. 326–27. At least, this was one criticism of the restrictive laws. For two opposing accounts of the effects of land policy in the Western Provinces, see Ol'shamovskii, *Prava po zemlevladeniiu v Zapadnom krae*, esp. pp. 29–92; and A. P. Vladimirov, "O russkom zemlevladenii v severo-zapadnom krae," *Russkoe obozrenie* (July 1894), pp. 217–41; (August 1894), pp. 748–67; (September 1894), pp. 171–92.

4. Many Poles considered this a deliberate government policy, an opinion for which I find no evidence. For this argument, see S. Stempowski, *Pamiętniki, 1870–1914* (Wrocław, 1953), pp. 222–23. Stempowski, no anti-Semite, speaks of an artificial concentration in Poland of Jewish paupers from Russia.

5. "Zapiska o nekotorykh voprosakh po ustroistvu Severo-Zapadnogo kraia," in S. D. Sheremetev, ed., *Iz bumag Grafa M. N. Murav'eva* (St. Petersburg, 1898), p. 37. While Murav'ev is referring specifically to the Northwest Provinces here, his comments reflect a general attitude toward the entire western region.

6. Petr A. Stolypin, *Gosudarstvennaia deiatel'nost' predsedatelia Soveta ministrov Stats-sekretaria Petra Arkad'evicha Stolypina* (St. Petersburg, 1911), vol. 1, p. 23. Stolypin delivered this famous speech on October 15, 1909, before assembled dignitaries and societal leaders who had been called together to consider projects for introducing rural and municipal self-government in the Kingdom of Poland.

7. See, for example, the correspondence between the Warsaw governor general and local governors in AGAD, GGW 2723 (1906–1907). The organization Polska Macierz Szkolna was closed by order of the Warsaw governor general on December 1/14, 1907 (see note at beginning of endnote section concerning the two calendars). Herman Rappaport, ed., *Reakcja Stołypinowska w Królestwie Polskim, 1907–1910* (Warsaw, 1974), document 193, pp. 164–65.

8. My account is, of course, a simplification of the contradictory attitudes of Russian government figures toward the Jews. For more detail, see Aronson, "Attitudes of Russian Officials in the 1880s," pp. 1–18; Löwe, *Anti-Semitismus und reaktionäre Utopie*, esp. pp. 99–117; and the essays collected in Rogger, *Jewish Policies and Right-Wing Politics*. The General Jewish Labor Union in Lithuania, Poland, and Russia—founded in 1897—was usually known as the Bund ("Union" in Yiddish). The predominance of Jews and especially of Jewish youth in the revolutionary movements in the Western Provinces was a constant theme in governors' annual reports. For a few examples, see RGIA, f. 1282, op. 3, 1901, d. 455 (Vil'na, 1900), l. 11; RGIA, f. 1284, op. 194, 1906, d. 45 (Vitebsk, 1905), l. 6; RGIA, f. 1284, op. 194, 1907, d. 46 (Mogilev, 1906), l. 2.

9. On the Polish/Lithuanian nexus, see the following annual reports (listed by guberniia): RGIA, f. 1282, op. 3, 1900, d. 376 (Kovno, 1899); RGIA, f. 1284, op. 194, 1908, d. 51 (Suwałki, 1907). On the concern about German colonists, see, for example, A. A. Velitsyn, *Nemtsy v Rossii (Ocherki istoricheskogo razvitiia i nastoiashchogo polozheniia nemetskikh kolonii na iuge i vostoke Rossii)* (St. Petersburg, 1893). Velitsyn was concerned with all German settlers in Russia, both in the three Southwest (Ukrainian) Provinces and on the Volga, but he does not mention the Baltic German nobility. Concern about German settlers found expression in governors' reports

especially after 1905. For example, in his report for 1910, the governor general of Kiev pointed to increasing numbers of German colonists in the Southwest and stated that new restrictive laws on such settlers should be promulgated. RGIA, f. 1284, op. 194, 1911, d. 56, ll. 5–7.

10. For an overview of this period in Polish history, see Stefan Kieniewicz, *Historia Polski, 1795–1918* (Warsaw, 1970), pp. 13–147. On the 1830 uprising, see Robert F. Leslie, *Polish Politics and the Revolution of 1830* (London, 1956).

11. The institution of the governor general also existed in the Baltic Provinces and the Caucasus. For a general overview of administration in the non-Russian areas of the Empire during this period, see N. P. Eroshkin, *Istoriia gosudarstvennykh uchrezhdenii dorevoliutsionnoi Rossii,* 2d ed. (Moscow, 1968), pp. 252–57, 293–94.

12. Here I am using the official terminology, as cited in A. Ia. Avrekh, "Vopros o zapadnom zemstve i bankrotstvo Stolypina," *Istoricheskie zapiski* 70 (1961), p. 65. In common parlance, the "northwest region" most often referred to the six Lithuanian and Belorussian provinces together, and the "southwest region" to the three provinces of the Kiev governor general.

13. On the legal side of governors' and governor generals' rights and prerogatives, see Korkunov, *Russkoe gosudarstvennoe pravo,* vol. 2, pp. 311–12; and RGIA, f. 1284, op. 190, 1899, d. 84B, ll. 190–241. In this document *(spravka)* the Committee of Ministers attempted to bring together existing laws and regulations regarding the prerogatives of governor generals ("O General-Gubernatorskoi Vlasti") in response to the report of the Vil'na governor general of 1902–1903.

14. "Ob uprazdnenii Vilenskogo, Kovenskogo, i Grodnenskogo General-gubernatorstva," March 2, 1911, in RGIA, f. 1278, op. 2, 1911, d. 1621, ll. 3–18. It was also proposed at this time to abolish the governor generalship of Kiev; RGIA, f. 1278, op. 2, 1908, d. 2337. Even the position of the Warsaw governor general, according to Polish sources, was slated to be abolished in order to bind the former Kingdom of Poland yet more tightly to the Russian Empire. Stanisław Bukowiecki, writing under the name of Drogoslav, *Rosya w Polsce* (Warsaw, 1914), pp. 29–30. Bukowiecki stated that the Russian nationalists, not the government, were pressing in 1912 for the abolition of the governor generalship of Warsaw. This is corroborated in RGIA, f. 1278, op. 2, 1912, d. 2457. For the Vil'na general governorship, *PSZ,* 3d ser., 32, no. 37665.

15. Edward Czyński, *Etnograficzno-statystyczny zarys liczebności i rozsiedlenia ludności polskiej* (Warsaw, 1909), p. 73. The exact figure given is 4,680,000 (over 18 percent of the total population of the region).

16. A recent historian mentions, in rather extreme terms, "Indeed, the Lithuanians were apt to view the Jews as masters of their economy." Leonas Sabaliunas, *Lithuanian Social Democracy in Perspective, 1893–1914* (Durham, N.C., 1990), p. 3. On the rightists in the Western Provinces, particularly in Kiev, Minsk, and Volhynia, see Don C. Rawson, *Russian Rightists and the Revolution of 1905* (Cambridge, U.K., 1995), pp. 91–106.

17. For two different views of the position and role of Poles "na Litwie," see Wanda Dobaczewska, *Wilno i Wileńszczyzna w latach, 1863–1914: Dzieje ruchów społecznych i politycznych* (Wilno, 1938), and Ignacy Korwin-Milewski, *K chemu dolzhno stremit'sia litovskoe dvorianstvo* (St. Petersburg, n.d. [ca. 1912]).

18. To be sure, Mickiewicz's generation differed greatly in its national outlook from that of Roman Dmowski, Zygmunt Balicki, and other Polish nationalist ideologues of the early twentieth century. One may compare the "integral nationalism" of Balicki and Dmowski with the "enlightened" nationalism of Kościuszko and oth-

ers, so well described in Andrzej Walicki, *The Enlightenment and the Birth of Modern Nationhood: Polish Political Thought from Noble Republicanism to Tadeusz Kościuszko* (Notre Dame, Ind., 1989). Still, many Poles at the turn of the century, and later, considered *Litwa* their homeland; one thinks, for example, of Czesław Miłosz, Józef Piłsudski, and Tadeusz Borowski.

19. One encounters in the archives many lists of specific positions that could not be held by Poles or Catholics in certain areas, such as the West, the Kholm/Podlasie area, and the Kingdom of Poland. See, for example, RGIA, f. 1276, op. 1, 1905, d. 106, ll. 157–58 (positions in the schools of the Western Provinces); RGIA, f. 1276, op. 1, 1905, d. 105, ll. 316–24 (positions in the Kingdom of Poland); RGIA, f. 1284, op. 190, 1886, d. 420, ll. 9v–11v (positions in the Kholm area).

20. In what follows I am drawing particularly from the following sources: pertinent entries in the Brokgauz-Efron encyclopedia for the individual provinces; A. P. Subbotin, *V cherte evreiskoi osedlosti* (St. Petersburg, 1888–1890); Vladimirov, "O russkom zemlevladenii v severo-zapadnom krae."

21. RGIA, *Chital'nyi Zal,* op. 1, d. 71 (Podolia, 1896), l. 65v.

22. On the predominance of Jews in the commerce of the Northwest, see Subbotin, *V cherte evreiskoi osedlosti,* esp. vol. 1, pp. 10–11 (Minsk), 66–67 (Vil'na), and 116–17 (Kovno); vol. 2, pp. 15–16 (Grodno). Subbotin is on the whole sympathetic to the Jews and speaks against the institution of the Pale. For a list of the types and numbers of Jewish artisans in the cities of Grodno, Lublin, and Zhitomir, see G. B. Sliozberg, *Obsledovanie polozheniia evreev* (St. Petersburg, 1907), pp. 106–10. This report was prepared and presented to the minister of internal affairs I. Goremykin in 1898 but was published nine years later. As the author points out in the preface, "Since then the situation has deteriorated even further."

23. See, for example, the deliberations within the MVD regarding the advisability of introducing zemstva to the Northwest (Lithuanian) Provinces. RGIA, f. 1278, op. 2, 1910, d. 1171, esp. ll. 89–99, 103–4.

24. F. Meier, *Nesostoiatel'nost' zakona o cherte osedlosti evreev* (Vil'na, 1910), pp. 13–14.

25. Władysław Studnicki, *Zarys statystyczno-ekonomiczny ziem północnowschodnich z XXXVII tablicami statystycznemi* (Wilno, 1922), pp. 93, 94. The exact figures (rubles per capita of industrial production) per province were as follows: Grodno 22.2, Vil'na 14.9, Kovno 9.2, Minsk 7.1, Mogilev 6.1, and Vitebsk 6.0. Note that industry was more prevalent in the western regions, especially in the city of Białystok (Belostok) at the far western edge of Grodno Province. The description of Białystok is from Subbotin, *V cherte evreiskoi osedlosti,* pp. 38–65. Subbotin (p. 38) pointed out, however, that even Białystok did not give the impression of a major industrial town because of the predominance of small factories.

26. I. S. Bliokh, *Budushchaia voina* (St. Petersburg, 1898), vol. 7 *(Prilozhenie),* table 126: "Protsent evreiskikh fabrik i zavodov" *(Prilozhenie* k str. 191, toma 4). The exact percentages by province were Kovno 48.5, Vil'na 40.0, Vitebsk 16.7, Mogilev 28.8, Grodno 49.1, and Minsk 39.2 percent.

27. This is more true in the Northwest than in the Southwest Provinces. On the Jewish *shtetl,* see Elizabeth Herzog and Mark Zborowski, *Life Is with People: The Jewish Little-Town of Eastern Europe* (New York, 1962).

28. The figure of the isolated, russifying, intolerant teacher comes up in various sources. The governor general of Vil'na, Prince P. D. Sviatopolk-Mirskii, complained that teachers often went out of their way to offend the sensibilities of Polish and Catholic children and in general behaved as if the insurrection of 1863 had just

occurred. RGIA, f. 1284, op. 190, 1899, d. 84B, ll. 22–24. The governor of Płock Province voiced a similar criticism in his annual report for 1901. RGIA, *Chital'nyi zal,* op. 1, d. 70A (Plotsk, 1901), p. 5.

29. RGIA, *Chital'nyi zal,* op. 1, d. 53A (Minsk, 1894), p. 8. On the fascinating story of Jewish workers in this region, see Ezra Mendelsohn, *Class Struggle in the Pale* (Cambridge, U.K., 1970), and Henry J. Tobias, *The Jewish Bund in Russia: From Its Origins to 1905* (Stanford, 1972).

30. On the connection between nationality and employment, see Studnicki, "Konstrukcja zawodowa i społeczna grup narodowościowych w kraju," *Zarys,* pp. 50–69. The survival of the stereotype of the Polish gentleman *(Pan)* in Belorussia is described by Ernest Gellner, "Ethnicity and Faith in Eastern Europe," *Daedalus* 119, no. 1 (winter 1990), pp. 279–80.

31. For general information on the Southwest, see P. N. Batiushkov, *Podoliia* (St. Petersburg, 1891), and *Volyn': Istoricheskie sud'by Iugo-zapadnogo kraia* (St. Petersburg, 1888); S. M. Karetnikov, *Volynskaia guberniia: Geograficheskii-istoricheskii ocherk gubernii i opisanie uezdov* (Kremenets, 1910); A. Lichkov, "Iugo-zapadnyi krai po dannym perepisi 1897 g.," *Kievskaia starina* 90 (September 1905), pp. 317–66; and Robert Edelman, *Proletarian Peasants: The Revolution of 1905 in Russia's Southwest* (Ithaca, N.Y., 1987), pp. 133–68.

32. Edelman, *Proletarian Peasants,* p. 55: "The immensity of the southwest's sugar plantations cannot be over stressed. The four Kiev estates of Mar'ia Brannitskaia covered almost 97,000 *desiatiny* [over 250,000 acres]."

33. In official statistics, Ukrainians, Belorussians, and Russians are often lumped together under the general rubric "Russian." The figures from the 1897 census ("Russian" percentage of total population by province): Kiev 82.9, Volhynia 73.4, and Podolia 77.7 percent. *Ezhegodnik Rossii* 1 (St. Petersburg, 1904), p. 87.

34. The precise percentages by province are Kiev 41.1, Volhynia 45.7, and Podolia 53.0 percent. Figures from J. Bartoszewicz, *Na Rusi: Polski stań posiadania* (Kiev, 1912), p. 51. It must be admitted that Bartoszewicz is at pains to stress the strength of the Polish element in the Southwest, but similar figures may be found even in official statistics. See also Eugeniusz Starczewski, *Życie polskie na Ukrainie* (Kiev, 1907).

35. This is the case on several of the (model) estates described in F. L. Liubanskii, *Opisanie imenii podol'skoi gubernii* (Vinnitsa, 1908).

36. Edelman, "Sugar Beets, Workers, and Refineries," *Proletarian Peasants,* pp. 50–61 (also pp. 47, 61–71).

37. Witold Kula, *Historia gospodarcza Polski w dobie popowstaniowej, 1864–1918* (Warsaw, 1947), p. 60; A. Kahan, "Notes on Jewish Entrepreneurship in Tsarist Russia," in G. Guroff and F. Carstensen, eds., *Entrepreneurship in Imperial Russia and the Soviet Union* (Princeton, 1983), p. 115. On the sugar industry in Ukraine in general, see Witold Walewski, "Cukrownictwo na Ukraine," in *Pamiętnik kijowski* (London, 1959), vol. 2, pp. 167–94. P. Struve, "Obshcherusskaia kul'tura i ukrainskii partikuliarizm," *Russkaia mysl'* (January 1912), p. 72.

38. The area of competency of the governor generals of Warsaw was more circumscribed than during the Paskevich era. Still, the governor general retained a good deal of personal political prerogative. Krzysztof Groniowski and Jerzy Skowronek, *Historia Polski, 1795–1914,* 3d ed. (Warsaw, 1987), pp. 179–80.

39. For the record, before 1912 (when the Kholm Province was formed and Siedlce Province dissolved) the ten provinces were Warsaw, Siedlce/Sedlets, Lublin/Liublin, Piotrków/Petrokov, Łomża/Lomzha, Suwałki/Suvalk, Radom,

Kielce/Kelets, Kalisz/Kalish, and Płock/Plotsk. For the sake of simplicity, I shall refer to the provinces using the Polish form of its capital city. On the administration of the Kingdom of Poland in general, see Leon Wasilewski, *Administracja rosyjska w Królestwie Polskim* (Vienna, 1915).

40. A. Zakrzewski, *Pol'sha: Statistichesko-etnograficheskii ocherk* (Kiev, 1916), p. 13. The percentage would be yet higher without the heavily Lithuanian Suwałki Province.

41. Here I use the term "bureaucratic" (following Russian usage of the period) to contrast with *obshchestvennyi* ("of society," of the "better" people).

42. On the structure of the *gmina*, see H. Konic, *Samorząd gminy w Królestwie Polskim w porównaniu z innemi krajami europejskimi* (Warsaw, 1906) or, for a short course, Bolesław Koskowski, "Ustrój administracyjny," in Zygmunt Gloger et al., eds., *Królestwo Polskie* (Warsaw, 1905), pp. 179–80. The inadequacies of the gmina is one major topic in W. Spasowicz and E. Piltz, eds., *Ocherednye voprosy v Tsarstve Pol'skom: Etiudy i issledovaniia* (St. Petersburg, 1902), esp. "Gminnoe upravlenie," pp. 31–48,

43. According to Kieniewicz, in 1914 Warsaw was the eighth largest city in Europe after London, Paris, Berlin, Vienna, the two Russian capitals, and Budapest. Stefan Kieniewicz, *Warszawa w latach, 1795–1914* (Warsaw, 1976), p. 185. For a concise account of the structure of municipal government in the Kingdom of Poland at this time, see Adolf Suligowski, "Gorodskoe upravlenie v guberniiakh Tsarstva Pol'skogo," *Vestnik Evropy*, no. 3 (March 1902), pp. 675–98.

44. Such a case is mentioned in a letter to the editor of the St. Petersburg daily *Rus'*. An editor of a Warsaw daily wrote *Rus'* in 1904 that he had been forbidden by the Warsaw censors to reprint an article from *Rus'* entitled "Brat'iam—Poliakam" (To our Polish brothers), *Pol'skii vopros v gazete "Rus'"*, vol. 1 (St. Petersburg, 1905), p. 118. This letter was printed in *Rus'* on November 10, 1904.

45. *Kraj* appeared weekly (for a time biweekly) from 1882 to 1909 and was edited for most of that time by Erazm Piltz. This journal has been described as liberal (especially in its earlier years) and criticized as being overly friendly and deferential to the Russians and especially to the Russian government. Jerzy Moszczyński, *Fiziologia szowinizmu polskiego na tle rosyjsko-polskich stosunków* (Cracow, 1897), pp. 42, 67–109.

46. *Ezhegodnik Rossii* 11 (St. Petersburg, 1915), pp. 33–50. The high population percentages in the provinces of Warsaw and Piotrków reflect the predominant position of the cities of Warsaw and Łódź in these two provinces. Figures from *Pervaia vseobshchaia perepis', Obshchii svod*, vol. 1, p. 267, and Czyński, *Etnograficzno-statystyczny zarys*, p. 91.

47. On Polish industry at this time, see Rosa Luxemburg, *Die industrielle Entwicklung Polens* (Berlin, 1898); Stanisław Koszutski, *Nasz przemysł wielki na początku XX wieku: Obraz statystyczno-ekonomiczny* (Warsaw, 1905); Irena Pietrzak-Pawlowska, ed., *Wielkomiejski rozwój Warszawy do 1918 r.* (Warsaw, 1973); and Maria Nietyksza, *Rozwój miast i aglomeracji miejsko-przemysłowych w Królestwie Polskim, 1865–1914* (Warsaw, 1986).

48. For a literary portrayal of the industry of Łódź, juxtaposed to more traditional Polish rural life, see the classic novel by Władysław Reymont, *Ziemia obiecana*, first published in 1899 (translated into English as *The Promised Land*). Reymont described the crushing inhumanity of the industrial juggernaut in naturalistic terms.

49. K. Krynicki, *Rys geografii Królestwa Polskiego* (Warsaw, 1907), p. 92. Krynicki does not give a precise date for these statistics but cites Witold Załęski, *Królestwo Polskie pod względem statystycznym* (Warsaw, 1901), part 2. On the agricultural situation

in the Kingdom of Poland at this time, see S. Koszutski, "Rolnictwo," *Rozwój eko-nomiczny Królestwa Polskiego w ostatnim trzydziestoleciu, 1870–1900* (Warsaw, 1905), pp. 331–53. See also Spasowicz and Piltz, *Ocherednye voprosy*, pp. 105–24, 139–84; and Witold Załęski, *Z statystyki porównawczej Królestwa Polskiego: Ludność i rolnictwo* (Warsaw, 1908).

50. On the difficulties the government faced in reconciling its desire to protect "Russians" and its reluctance to violate its own legal principles after 1905, see T. Weeks, "Defending Our Own: Government and the Russian Minority in the King-dom of Poland, 1905–1914," *Russian Review* 54 (October 1995), pp. 539–51.

51. *Ezhegodnik Rossii* 7 (1910), p. 66.

52. This figure (14.97 percent), from Zakrzewski, *Pol'sha*, p. 12, reflects the population on January 1, 1913. Most sources agree that Jews made up approxi-mately 14 percent of the population of the Congress Kingdom before 1914.

53. As usual, the situation was considerably more complex, both de facto and de jure. For most purposes, Jews enjoyed civil equality in Russian Poland. On this is-sue, see Artur Eisenbach, *Kwestia równouprawnienia Żydów w Królestwie Polskim* (War-saw, 1972), and Michael Jerry Ochs, "St. Petersburg and the Jews of Russian Poland, 1862–1905" (Ph.D. diss., Harvard University, 1986), esp. chap. 3, "The Fate of Jewish Equality after 1862." On the legal situation of Jews in Russian Poland in general throughout this period, see Jacob Kirszrot, *Prawa Żydów w Królestwie Polskim* (War-saw, 1917). However, there did occur cases in which Jews were "deported" illegally from rural regions of Poland by overzealous local officials. Jews were not allowed to purchase peasant land (law of June 11, 1891); and in his 1898 report the "liberal" gov-ernor general of Warsaw, Prince Imeretinskii, asked that the Jews in Russian Poland be forbidden even to rent peasant houses, arguing, "It would appear that the goal of our government in this country should consist not in protecting the rights of the Jews, . . . but in protecting that estate [*soslovie*] which up to now has been the most loyal to the government [that is, the peasants]." To this remark Nicholas II com-mented, "Razumeetsia" (Of course). RGIA, f. 1282, op. 3, d. 230, ll. 65–66.

54. Erich Zechlin, *Die Bevölkerungs- und Grundbesitzverteilung im Zartum Polen* (Berlin, 1916), p. 27.

55. Bohdan Wasiutyński, *Ludność żydowska w Królestwie Polskim* (Warsaw, 1911), pp. 50–67. Wasiutyński points out that these are figures gathered by the local administration and must be used with caution. However, it seems unlikely that Russian officials would knowingly over-report the numbers of Jews living in cities.

56. For more detailed statistics on the breakdown of these three "Russian" groups, see *Pervaia vseobshchaia perepis' naseleniia Rossiiskoi Imperii: Obshchii svod* (St. Petersburg, 1905), vol. 2, chart 13a *(rodnoi iazyk)*, pp. 20–23. See also my sections on Ukrainians and Belorussians in chapter 6.

57. Any conscious effort to skew the figures would, of course, be in favor of Russians to the detriment of Poles and Ukrainians. For example, one finds a letter dated September 16, 1896, from the governor general of Warsaw to the Lublin gov-ernor, with instructions on how the census figures are to be gathered. These instruc-tions aimed to prevent "people of Russian descent who do not recognize themselves as such" from claiming themselves to be Polish in the census. Henryk Wiercieński, *Ziemia chełmska i Podlasie* (Warsaw, n.d.), pp. 48–50. Criticisms of the 1897 census came from members of several nationalities. For a few examples, see Lichkov, "Iugo-zapadnyi krai po dannym perepisi 1897 g.," esp. pp. 327–29; V. P. Koshevoi, "Mechty pol'skikh natsionalistov i deistvitel'nost'," *Ukrainskaia zhizn'* (November 1913), pp. 20–21; Edward Maliszewski, *Polacy i polskość na Litwie i Rusi* (Warsaw,

1914), p. 5. For a detailed study of the 1897 census from a national point of view, see H. Bauer, A. Kappeler, and B. Roth, eds., *Die Nationalitäten des russischen Reiches in der Volkszählung von 1897*, 2 vols. (Stuttgart, 1991).

58. Alternative figures are found in Stolypin's project, "Ob otsrochke vyborov chlenov Gosudarstvennogo Soveta ot zemlevladel'tsev gubernii Vilenskoi, Vitebskoi, Volynskoi, Grodnenskoi, Kievskoi, Kovenskoi, Minskoi, Mogilevskoi, Podol'skoi," in RGIA, f. 1278, op. 2, 1909, d. 885, l. 51. Here only the percentages of Russian and Polish landholding were taken into account, which may explain some of the differences from the *Kraj* figures. Polish/Russian percentages of private land owned by province were as follows: Kovno 75/25, Vil'na 73/27, Grodno 69/31, Minsk 28/72, Vitebsk 16/84l, Mogilev 20/80, Volhynia 24/76, Podolia 35/65, Kiev 29/71 percent.

59. Daniel Beauvois, in *La Bataille de la terre en Ukraine, 1863–1914: Les Polonais et les conflits socio-ethniques* (Lille, 1993), comes to similar conclusions—despite a significantly different view of general Russian policy—about the strength of Polish landholding in the Southwest.

60. RGIA, f. 1278, op. 2, 1910, d. 1171, ll. 149–52.

61. In 1897, the percentages of urban population in the nine provinces of the western territory were as follows: Vil'na 12.4, Vitebsk 14.5, Volhynia 7.8, Grodno 15.9, Mogilev 8.7, Kiev 12.9, Kovno 9.3, Minsk 10.5, and Podolia 7.3 percent. Computed from figures found in N. A. Troinitskii, ed., *Obshchii svod po Imperii rezul'tatov razrabotki dannykh pervoi vseobshchoi perepisi naseleniia Rossiiskoi Imperii* (St. Petersburg, 1905), vol. 1, pp. 2–5 (total population and total urban population).

62. For example, Professor V. A. Frantsev ignores the urban population of the Kholm area in his work *Karty russkogo i pravoslavnogo naseleniia Kholmskoi Rusi* (Warsaw, 1909), see esp. p. xv: "for us the primary and I daresay even exclusive significance belongs to data on the language of rural residents [*zhiteli sela, derevni*] and not urban dwellers [*zhiteli gorodov, mestechek ili posadov*] where the population has always and from olden times [*vsegda i izdavna*] been made up of mixed Polish-Russo-Jewish elements." A Ukrainian publicist describing the national makeup of the western region excluded the urban population in a similar manner, because "in all countries [cities] are becoming more and more international" (a debatable point for such cities as Zhitomir, Kamenets-Podolsk, and Berdichev). Koshevoi, "Mechty pol'skikh natsionalistov i deistvitel'nost'," p. 20.

63. As usual, this statement simplifies the situation. Jews were not forced to sell rural lands they had owned previous to the 1882 decree. Jews could also often obtain temporary exceptions in order to reside in rural areas, especially for the purpose of setting up or running factories there. Governors were also frequently heard complaining of the Jews' ability to circumvent the laws.

64. The "Polozhenie zapadnogo komiteta" of May 22, 1864, for all practical purposes closed government employment in the western territory to Poles. Tyszkiewicz, *Russko-pol'skie otnosheniia*, pp. 40–42. This restrictive law was followed by others in subsequent years. Many Poles did serve in the tsarist bureaucracy and army outside the Kingdom of Poland and the Western Provinces, but even there, according to one eminent jurist, "in our administrative practice there has arisen in recent times an almost total exclusion of Jews from entering government service and a limitation on Catholics [for the most part Poles] to a certain percentage of total civil servants." Korkunov, *Russkoe gosudarstvennoe pravo*, vol. 1, p. 386.

65. The northwest region (particularly in Troki/Trakai, Vil'na Province) was also the home of the Karaites (or Karaims), a Jewish sect that rejected the Talmud

and thus was not subject, as Jews, to restrictions by the tsarist government. Space considerations preclude closer discussion of this small but fascinating group, but see, for example, Ananiasz Zajączkowski, *Karaims in Poland: History, Language, Folklore, Science* (Warsaw, 1961).

66. Leon Trotsky, *My Life* (New York, 1930), p. 32: "The German settlers constituted a group apart. There were some really rich men among them. They stood more firmly on their feet than the others." Indeed, it was because of the efficiency of these German settlers that they were often seen as a threat to the more backward local peasants. RGIA, *Chital'nyi Zal*, op. 1, d. 17 (Volhynia, 1908), p. 2.

67. RGIA, *Chital'nyi Zal*, op. 1, d. 22 (Grodno, 1901), ll. 77–78. Actually, the law of March 14, 1887, forbade foreigners from purchasing or renting rural land in all the Western Provinces except Mogilev. Ol'shamovskii, *Prava po zemlevladeniiu*, pp. 61–62. Especially after 1905 measures were taken to stem the flow of foreign settlers into the Southwest and Bessarabia. For these projects, see RGIA, f. 1278, op. 2, 1910, d. 1213, and 1911, d. 1619. Still, the effectiveness of these laws may be questioned. To cite just one example, in 1909 and 1910 the governor general of Kiev complained of increasing numbers of foreign, especially German, settlers in the Southwest. RGIA, f. 1284, op. 194, 1911, d. 56, ll. 5–7.

68. Dietmar Neutatz, *Die "deutsche Frage" im Schwarzmeergebiet und in Wolhynien: Politik, Wirtschaft, Mentalitäten, und Alltag im Spannungsfeld von Nationalismus und Modernisierung, 1856–1914* (Stuttgart, 1993). The argument of this enormously detailed and valuable study is impossible to sum up in a few sentences. A. P. Liprandi [A. Volynets, pseud.], *Kak ostanovit' mirnoe zavoevanie nashikh okrain? Nemetskii vopros, sushchnost i znachenie ego v iugo-zapadnoi Rossii* (Kiev, 1890).

69. On the original logic behind inviting in the Czechs, see RGIA, f. 821, op. 125, 1882, d. 3315. On the Volhynian Czechs, a fascinating document is Evfimii Kryzhanovskii, "Chekhi na Volyni" in *Sobranie sochinenii* (Kiev, 1890), vol. 3, pp. 805–981. In 1886 the MVD sent Kryzhanovskii to the Volhynia to study the Czech settlements there. The essay cited above is the product of that investigation. For the original report, see RGIA, f. 821, op. 125, 1882, d. 3315, ll. 160–89.

70. Leon Wasilewski, *Litwa i jej ludy* (Warsaw, 1907), p. 13. The census of 1897 shows the largest numbers of "Muslims" *(magometany)* in the western territory in the provinces of Vil'na (4,375), Volhynia (4,877), Grodno (3,781), and Minsk (4,619).

71. F. K. Dobianskii, *O litovskikh tatarakh* (Vil'na, 1906), pp. 12–16, 19 (19).

72. Official reports highly favorable to the Lithuanian Tatars and pointing out their loyalty to the Russian government in 1863 may be found in RGIA, f. 1284, op. 189, 1865, d. 4, ll. 72–82.

Chapter 5: East Meets West

1. Obviously my overview presents a simplified picture. For examples of the kind of history I have in mind, see P. I. Kovalevskii, *Istoriia Rossii s natsional'noi tochki zreniia* (St. Petersburg, 1912), or the many works of A. Ilovaiskii—for example, *Kratkie ocherki russkoi istorii: Kurs starshogo vozrasta* (Moscow, 1912). Specifically on the effects of Polish culture on this region, see the polemical Fedor Elenev, *Pol'skaia tsivilizatsiia i eia vliianie na zapadnuiu Rus'* (St. Petersburg, 1863).

2. The extensive works of P. N. Batiushkov are exemplary for this line of historico-nationalist argumentation. See especially his *Volyn'*. A similar study for the Northwest is V. Ratch, *Svedeniia o pol'skom miatezhe 1863 goda v Severo-zapadnoi Rossii*

(Vil'na, 1867), vol. 1, *Severo-zapadnaia Rossiia do padeniia Rechi Pospolitoi.*

3. On Polish nationalist perceptions of this issue, see Brian A. Porter, "Who Is a Pole and Where Is Poland? Territory and Nation in the Rhetoric of Polish National Democracy," *Slavic Review* 51, no. 4 (winter 1992), pp. 639–53.

4. Perhaps the outraged attitudes of nationalist Russians and Russian officialdom toward expressions of Ukrainian national feeling can be explained by the Ukrainians' rejection of this simple dichotomy, that is, rejecting both Russian and Polish and advocating their own cultural and political values. From the conservative Russian point of view, the Ukrainian nationalists were violating the most basic rules of the game.

5. On the Russian Empire's "Polish problem" under Nicholas I, see James T. Flynn, "Uvarov and the 'Western Provinces': A Study of Russia's Polish Problem," *Slavonic and East European Review* 64, no. 2 (1986), pp. 212–36.

6. On Wielopolski and his career, there are two sympathetic accounts published not long after the marquis's death: Henryk Lisicki, *Aleksander Wielopolski, 1803–1877,* 4 vols. (Cracow, 1878–1879), based on Wielopolski's personal archives and written with the approval of the Wielopolski family; and W. Spasowicz, *Markiz Aleksandr Velepol'ski, ego zhizn' i politika,* in *Sochineniia* (St. Petersburg, 1902), vol. 10, pp. 1–346. It comes as no surprise that Spasowicz, one of the leaders of *ugoda,* would feel sympathy for the conservative reformer Wielopolski. For more recent treatments, see Adam M. Skałkowski, *Aleksander Wielopolski w świetle archiwów rodzinnych (1803–1877),* 3 vols. (Poznań, 1947), and Zbigniew Stankiewicz, *Dzieje wielkości i upadku Aleksandra Wielopolskiego* (Wrocław, 1967).

7. The death of Nicholas I in 1855 was followed one year later by the death in Warsaw of the hated Marshall Ivan Paskevich, the suppressor of the Polish uprising of 1831 and the Hungarian revolution of 1848–1849 and viceroy in Warsaw from 1831 to his death. "It seemed logical in the light of Russia's general position that with the death of Paskevich in 1856 a milder system of government should be introduced in the Kingdom and Lithuania." Robert F. Leslie, *Reform and Insurrection in Russian Poland, 1856–1865* (London, 1963), p. 47.

8. The Russian in Warsaw was A. A. Sidorov, *Russkie i russkaia zhizn' v Varshave (1815–1895): Istoricheskii ocherk* (Warsaw, 1899–1900), vol. 3, p. 132. Wielopolski was not the only conservative reformer prominent on the Polish scene in the years before 1863. He was opposed by the popular Andrzej Zamoyski, who headed the conservative Towarzystwo Rolnicze (Agricultural Society) until its dissolution by Wielopolski in 1861. On Zamoyski, see Stefan Kieniewicz, *Między ugodą i rewolucją (Andrzej Zamoyski w latach 1861–1862)* (Warsaw, 1961).

9. For more detail on the situation of peasants in the Kingdom of Poland and the terms of the peasant reform, see Krzysztof Groniowski, *Uwłaszczenie chłopów w Polsce* (Warsaw, 1976), esp. pp. 22–30, 116–52. For the main lines along which Wielopolski planned his reforms, see Lisicki, *Aleksander Wielopolski,* vol. 2, pp. 24–30 (Polish text) and pp. 31–37 (French text). In this document, a letter from Wielopolski to Alexander II dated February 11, 1861, Wielopolski praises Alexander for the hope that his reign has brought to Poles: "Le règne de V.M. a été salué avec espérance par tous Vos sujets polonais, comme inaugurant une époque de grâce, de confiance et de conciliation" (The reign of Your Majesty has been greeted with hope by all your Polish subjects, as inaugurating an era of grace, confidence, and conciliation [p. 31]). The letter also bewails the situation in the Polish Kingdom since the abrogation of the 1815 Constitution: "L'inéxécution de la loi fondamentale de 1815 nous enlève toutes nos garanties; les droits, les interêts du pays s'en alarment" (The abrogation

of the fundamental law of 1815 has taken away all our guarantees; the rights, the interests of the country are thereby outraged [p. 35]). And it begs for reform of censorship, of the legal and educational systems, and an end to legal restrictions placed on Polish Jews. It is indicative of Wielopolski's conservatism that he does not mention the peasant question. On the Wielopolski reforms and the Jews, see also Jacob Shatzky, *Geshikhte fun yidn in varshe* (New York, 1953), vol. 3, pp. 11–12.

10. Quoted in Leslie, *Reform and Insurrection in Russian Poland,* p. 48. On Alexander's attitude toward political change in Poland, see Stefan Kieniewicz, *Powstanie styczniowe* (Warsaw, 1972), pp. 15–18.

11. K. Poznański, *Reforma szkolna w Królestwie Polskim w 1862 r.* (Wrocław, 1968). Edward C. Thaden, *Russia's Western Borderlands, 1710–1870* (Princeton, 1984), pp. 157–58.

12. For the Russian side of the story, see Sidorov, *Russkie i russkaia zhizn',* vol. 3, pp. 125–38. For a general account of this turbulent period, see Leslie, *Reform and Insurrection in Russian Poland,* esp. pp. 89–153.

13. Kieniewicz, *Powstanie styczniowe,* pp. 203–5 (205).

14. On the spiral of events leading to the outbreak of the insurrection in January 1863, see Stankiewicz, *Dzieje wielkości,* pp. 115–20, and Kieniewicz, *Powstanie styczniowe,* pp. 60–205. Kieniewicz's massive work remains the point of departure for any serious study of the uprising.

15. The 1863 insurrection in the *kresy* (to use the Polish term for the Western Provinces) has been inadequately studied. But, besides Kieniewicz, see Józef Olechnowicz, "Polska myśl patriotyczna i postępowa na ziemiach ukrainnych w latach 1835–1863," *Pamiętnik kijowski* (London, 1963), vol. 2, pp. 1–48; and A. F. Smirnov, *Vosstanie 1863 goda v Litve i Belorussii* (Moscow, 1963).

16. The literature on Poles and Jews between 1861 and 1863 is enormous. See, for example, Ia. Shchatskin, "K istorii uchastiia evreev v pol'skom vozstanii 1863 g.," *Evreiskaia starina* 1 (1915), pp. 29–37; Majer Balaban, "Żydzi w powstaniu 1863 r. (Próba bibliografii rozumowanej)," *Przegląd historyczny* 34 (1937), pp. 564–99; N. M. Gelber, *Die Juden und der polnische Aufstand 1863* (Vienna, 1923); and two works by Jacob Shatzky, "Yidn in dem poylishn oyfshtand fun 1863," *YIVO historishn shriftn* 1 (Warsaw, 1929), pp. 423–68, and *Geshikhte fun yidn in varshe,* vol. 2, pp. 209–57.

17. On "pacification" under Murav'ev after 1863, see "Otchet grafa M. N. Murav'eva po upravleniiu Severo-zapadnym kraem s 1 maia 1863 g. po 17 aprelia 1865 g.," in RGIA, f. 1622, op. 1, d. 719, and the very detailed N. Tsylov, ed., *Sbornik rasporiazhenii grafa Mikhaila Nikolaevicha Murav'eva po usmireniiu pol'skogo miatezha v Severo-zapadnykh guberniiakh 1863–1864* (Vil'na, 1866).

18. RGIA, f. 1622, op. 1, d. 719, l. 4.

19. Murav'ev speaks of the "terrorism" of the Polish "revolutionaries" in a report on his actions as Vil'na governor general, 1863–1865 (ibid., l. 3). One anecdotal indication of the support for Murav'ev in St. Petersburg is found in a poem by Fedor Tiutchev written at the time of Murav'ev's death in 1866, which reads, "Na grobovoi ego pokrov / My, vmesto vsekh venkov, kladem slova prostye: / Nemnogo bylo by y nego vragov, / Kogda by ne tvoi, Rossiia!" (On his shroud / Instead of all laurels we will place the simple words: / Few would his enemies have been, / Had they not been yours, too, O Russia!). Even more shocking, the radical poet Nikolai Nekrasov wrote an ode praising Murav'ev. See Kornei Chukovskii, *The Poet and the Hangman (Nekrasov and Muravyov)* (Ann Arbor, 1977). On a more prosaic level, see the articles collected in Ivan Aksakov, *Pol'skii vopros i zapadno-russkoe delo, Sochineniia,* vol. 3 (St. Petersburg, 1900), esp. "Po povodu uvol'neniia general-gubernatora Murav'eva," pp. 272–78.

20. *Voennaia entsyklopediia* (Moscow/St. Petersburg, 1914), vol. 16, p. 477. The only biography of Murav'ev ends, unfortunately, many years before 1863: D. A. Kropotov, *Zhizn' gr. M. N. Murav'eva* (St. Petersburg, 1874). For a laudatory account of his activities, see *Podvig Murav'eva: Nastol'naia kniga praviteliam i pravitel'stvam* (St. Petersburg, 1898).

21. RGIA, f. 1622, op. 1, d. 719, ll. 7–8.

22. Murav'ev mentioned this issue only in passing: in "Vvesti prepodavanie zhmudskoi gramoti russkimi bukvami vo vsekh shkolakh Samogitii." RGIA, f. 1284, op. 190, 1899, d. 84A, l. 11. In other words, the Lithuanian language should be taught in "Russian" schools but should be printed and written using Russian Cyrillic characters.

23. A. N. Mosolov, *Vilenskie ocherki, 1863–1865 gg. (Murav'evskoe vremia)* (St. Petersburg, 1898), p. 144–45.

24. Many of the details of this process may be found in the Russian State Historical Archive (RGIA) in St. Petersburg. See, for example, "Komitet po delam Tsarstva Pol'skogo," RGIA, f. 1270, and "Katolicheskoe ispovedanie v Rossii i v Tsarstve Pol'skom," RGIA, f. 821, op. 3. For a general account of these repressive measures, see Tyszkiewicz, *Russko-pol'skie otnosheniia*, and T. Weeks, "Defining Us and Them: Poles and Russians in the 'Western Provinces,' 1863–1914," *Slavic Review* 53, no. 1 (spring 1994), pp. 26–40.

25. On the Poles in the western territory and their history, see Daniel Beauvois, *Polacy na Ukrainie, 1831–1863: Szlachta polska na Wołyniu, Podolu, i Kijowszczyźnie* (Paris, 1987) and the essays collected in Daniel Beauvois, ed., *Les Confins de l'ancienne Pologne: Ukraine, Lithuanie, Biélorussie, XVIe–XXe siècles* (Lille, 1988). On the period after 1863 in the three Southwest ("Ukrainian") Provinces, Beauvois continues the story in *La Bataille de la terre en Ukraine*.

26. Piotr Wandycz, *The Lands of Partitioned Poland, 1795–1918* (Seattle, 1974), p. 242 (the figures date from 1867). According to one official source, in 1861 Poles made up 90 percent of landowners *(pomeshchiki)* and owned 83 percent of all serfs in the three Southwest Provinces. Otchet General-Gubernatora Kievskogo [M. I. Dragomirov] za 1898–1900, RGIA, f. 1282, op. 3, 1898, d. 267, l. 3.

27. *PSZ*, 3d ser., vol. 40 (1865), no. 42759, pp. 326–27. A compendium of the measures designed to restrict Polish landowning and to encourage Russian immigration in the Northwest Provinces is in *Sbornik pravitel'stvennykh rasporiazhenii po vodvoreniiu russkikh zemlevladel'tsev v Severo-zapadnom krae*, 2d ed. (Vil'na, 1886). For the deliberations leading up to these restrictions, see RGIA, f. 1282, op. 2, 1864, d. 367.

28. See the detailed account of the *ukaz* of May 1, 1905, in *Kraj*, no. 18 (May 6/19, 1905), supplement, pp. 1–6. The actual text of this law is in *Sobranie uzakonenii i rasporiazhenii Pravitel'stva*, 1 ot., no. 91 (May 3, 1905), stat'ia 574, pp. 793–96; and "Ob otmene nekotorykh ogranichitel'nykh postanovlenii, deistvuiushchikh v deviati Zapadnykh guberniiakh, i o poriadke vypolneniia punkta sed'mogo Imennogo Ukaza 12 Dekabria 1904 goda v otnoshenii sikh gubernii," *PSZ*, 3d ser., 25 (1905), no. 26162, pp. 285–87.

29. And to Baltic Germans who, for the purposes of the law, were included among the "persons of Russian descent." This was explained by reference to the Baltic Germans' loyalty and their role as "excellent executors of the government's directives [*prevoskhodnye ispol'niteli prednachertanii pravitel'stva*]." RGIA, f. 1284, op. 190, 1900, d. 85, l. 5v. By 1900, however, the Russian government had begun to question the wisdom of this earlier policy, as may be seen in ibid.

30. According to *Kraj*, of privately owned lands in the provinces in 1905, the following percentages were in the hands of Poles: Kovno 75, Vil'na 73, Grodno 54,

Minsk 50, Vitebsk 41, Volhynia 48, Mogilev 33, and Podolia 49 percent. No figures were given for Polish landowning in Kiev Province, but it was stated that Russians owned 59 percent of the manorial land there. Since in this article *Kraj* attempts to minimize the extent of Polish influence in the West, I do not think the figures are exaggerated, at least not intentionally.

31. On the strengthening of Russian institutions in the area, particularly educational institutions, see a report written by an enthusiastic participant in these actions, I. P. Kornilov, *Russkoe delo v Severo-zapadnom krae: Materialy dlia istorii vilenskogo uchebnogo okruga preimushchestvenno v murav'evskuiu epokhu* (St. Petersburg, 1908).

32. Quotation from Wandycz, *Partitioned Poland*, p. 240. Hipolit Korwin-Milewski, *Siedemdziesiąt lat wspomnień, 1855–1925* (Poznań, 1930), pp. 48–69, 79–80.

33. For a report on this journey, presumably written by N. Miliutin himself, see "Poezdka po nekotorym mestnostiam Tsarstva Pol'skogo v oktiabre 1863 goda," in Petr Bartenev, ed., *Deviatnadtsatyi vek. Istoricheskii sbornik* (Moscow, 1872), pp. 282–311. On the reforms in the Kingdom of Poland and on N. Miliutin, the driving force behind them, see P. K. Shchebalskii, *Nikolai Alekseevich Miliutin i reformy v Tsarstve Pol'skom* (Moscow, 1882).

34. For the details of the liberation of the peasants in Russian Poland, see Stefan Kieniewicz, *The Emancipation of the Polish Peasantry* (Chicago, 1969), and Stanley J. Zyzniewski, "Russian Policy in the Congress Kingdom of Poland, 1863–1881" (Ph.D. diss., Harvard University, 1956), pp. 55–107.

35. To be sure, by the end of the century it had become evident that the Polish peasants might not, after all, be so loyal and trustworthy. See governor general Imeretinskii's famous annual report of 1897, *Tajne dokumenty rządu rosyjskiego w sprawach polskich*, 2d ed. (London, 1899), pp. 23–25. Imeretinskii warns that "the peasantry here [in Poland] does not feel an inner, spiritual connection with the government" (p. 24, Au. trans.). The original document may be found in RGIA, f. 1282, op. 3, d. 230, ll. 25–46. Still, most governors of Polish provinces continued to emphasize the loyalty of the Polish peasant masses, even after 1905. In the aftermath of the disturbances of 1905–1906, the Kielce governor could still write, "In nearly all districts the peasant estate remained devoted to the government." RGIA, f. 1284, op. 194, 1907, d. 33, l. 2v (1906 annual report for Kielce Province).

36. *Vzgliady N. A. Miliutina na uchebnoe delo v Tsarstve Pol'skom* (St. Petersburg, 1897) and Zyzniewski, "Russian Policy," pp. 110–14. On Miliutin's role in reforming Russian Poland after 1863, see [N. I. Miliutin], *Issledovaniia v Tsarstve Pol'skom (po vysochaishemu poveleniiu)*, 4 vols. (St. Petersburg, n.d. [ca. 1865]), esp. vol. 2, *Predpolozheniia i materialy po ustroistvu uchebnoi chasti* (1864). On tsarist education policy in Russian Poland and the changes introduced after 1863, see Edmund Staszyński, *Polityka oświatowa caratu w Królestwie Polskim od powstania styczniowego do I. wojny światowej* (Warsaw, 1968).

37. Zyzniewski, "Russian Policy," p. 189. The figures from the 1897 census show an average of 305 in 1,000 people literate in the Kingdom of Poland, the highest literacy being in Warsaw Province (391 in 1,000) and the lowest in Kielce Province (227 in 1,000). *Ezhegodnik Rossii* (1914), p. 95. For a contemporary description of the effects of tsarist education policy in Russian Poland, see A. Suligowski, *Miasto analfabetów* (Cracow, 1905). On the introduction of Russian to the courts and administration of the Polish Kingdom, see Nikolai Reinke, *Ocherk zakonodatel'stva Tsarstva Pol'skogo (1807–1881 gg.)* (St. Petersburg, 1902), pp. 166–72.

38. Kieniewicz, *Warszawa*, p. 236. Zyzniewski makes the point that the original policy of Cherkasskii and Miliutin after 1864 did not aim to forbid the use of

Polish in education. Stanley J. Zyzniewski, "Miljutin and the Polish Question," *Harvard Slavic Studies* 4 (1957), pp. 242–43.

39. RGIA, f. 821, op. 150, 1852, d. 361, l. 34v and passim. For the discussions in St. Petersburg surrounding the 1862 reform and on the conditions of Jews in the Kingdom of Poland in general before that date, see RGIA, f. 1269, op. 1, dd. 5A, 5B; also Artur Eisenbach, *The Emancipation of the Jews in Poland, 1780–1870* (Oxford, 1991).

40. The vagaries of Russian policy toward the Jews of the Polish Kingdom and attempts to further restrict Jewish rights there is a story well told in Ochs, "St. Petersburg and the Jews." See also RGIA, f. 821, op. 9, 1869, d. 82, and 1872, d. 99.

41. The quotation is from Wandycz, *Partitioned Poland*, p. 201. To take two voices from opposite ends of the Russian political spectrum: Vladimir Solov'ev, *Natsional'nyi vopros v Rossii*, in his *Sobranie Sochinenii* (St. Petersburg, n.d. [ca. 1911]), vol. 5, p. 36, wrote that the freeing of Polish peasants after 1863 "liberated Poland from that cruel antagonism between masters and serfs [*mezhdu panstvom i khlopami*] which gnawed away at the root of living forces in Poland and would eventually have led the Polish nationality to a final catastrophe [*konechnaia gibel'*]"; and V. V. Esipov, *Privislinskii krai* (Warsaw, 1912), p. 2, wrote that, "thanks to the great reforms of such Russian statesmen as Miliutin, Cherkasskii and others, this region has made colossal progress in the area of economic and cultural growth." For an opposing, Polish view, see H. Tennenbaum, "Rynki rosyjskie," in *Z Rosją czy przeciw Rosji?* (Warsaw, 1916), pp. 73–85.

42. Apologists for Russian policy in Poland also compared development there with the economic stagnation in Galicia, an example constantly cited by Russian nationalists. For one such argument, see G. Simonenko, *Tsarstvo Pol'skoe sravnitel'no s Poznan'iu i Galitsiei: Publichnaia lektsiia* (Warsaw, 1878).

43. For the shelving of the zemstvo reform, see "O primenenii Polozheniia o zemskom uchrezhdenii 12 iiunia 1890 g. k guberniiam Vitebskoi, Volynskoi, Kievskoi, Minskoi, Mogilevskoi, i Podol'skoi," in RGIA, f. 1278, op. 2, 1910, d. 1171, l. 3. Although the Russian legal reforms were implemented in the Kingdom of Poland in 1875, the Code Napoleon remained the basis of Polish law throughout this period. On legal reform in Russian Poland, see the pamphlet by Adolf Suligowski, *O reformie sądowej w Królestwie Polskiem* (Warsaw, 1875).

44. To be sure, de facto the Kingdom remained an administrative unit, even if it was called not Tsarstvo Pol'skoe but Privislinskii krai or Varshavskoe General-Gubernatorstvo. Even at the end of our period, Leon Wasilewski could point to a dozen institutions peculiar to the Kingdom. Wasilewski, *Administracja rosyjska w Królestwie Polskiem*, p. 9.

45. Quoted in M. P. Dragomanov, *Politicheskie sochineniia*, ed. I. M. Grevs and B. A. Kistiakovskii, vol. 1 (Moscow, 1908), p. xlviii. On the restrictions placed on the Ukrainian language after 1863, see Imperatorskaia Akademiia Nauk, *Ob otmene stesnenii malorusskogo pechatnogo slova* (St. Petersburg, 1910), esp. pp. 16–22; Oleksander Lotots'kyi, *Storinky minuloho* (Warsaw, 1933), vol. 2, pp. 365–66; and Anthony M. Ivancevich, "The Ukrainian National Movement and Russification" (Ph.D. diss., Northwestern University, 1976), pp. 417–723.

46. On this early period in the Lithuanian national movement, see A. Pogodin, "Litovskoe natsional'noe vozrozhdenie v kontse XIX veke," *Russkaia mysl'* 30, no. 1 (January 1909), pp. 127–51.

47. For the "Orthodox" story, see E. M. Kryzhanovskii, "Volnenie uniatov na Podlias'e" and "Kniaz' V. A. Cherkasskii i kholmskie greko-uniaty," in *Sobranie sochinenii*, vol. 2, pp. 5–280; and A. Dem'ianovich, "Stremlenie uniatov byvshei

kholmskoi eparkhii k vozsoedineniiu s pravoslavnoiu Tserkov'iu s 1837–1875 gg.," *Kholmsko-varshavskii eparkhial'nyi vestnik* 2 (1878). A contemporary Polish account is Józef Bojarski, *Czasy Nerona w XIX w., czyli ostatnie chwile unii* (Lvov, 1878).

48. On Mosolov and his career, see Lieven, *Russia's Rulers:* "In M. N. Murav'yov, his first chief in the civil service, Alexander Mosolov found something of an alternative father-figure" (p. 89).

49. This tendency was admitted and denounced by the MVD when in 1905 it reviewed restrictions on Poles in the Western Provinces. RGIA, f. 1276, op. 1, 1905, d. 106, p. 5v.

50. For Berg as viceroy, see *Russkii biograficheskii slovar'* (St. Petersburg, 1900), vol. 2, p. 727. See also N. Berg, *Zapiski o pol'skikh zagovorakh i vosstaniiakh* (Moscow, 1873). For Kotzebue as viceroy, see S. Krzemiński, *Dwadzieścia pięć lat Rosji w Polsce, 1863–1888* (Lvov, 1892).

51. See, for example, Franco Venturi, *Roots of Revolution: A History of the Populist and Socialist Movements in Nineteenth-Century Russia* (Chicago, 1983); and Abbot Gleason, *Young Russia* (Chicago, 1980).

52. On this period, see P. A. Zaionchkovskii, *Krizis samoderzhaviia na rubezhe 1870–1880–kh godov* (Moscow, 1964). On Panslavism, see Michael B. Petrovich, *The Emergence of Russian Panslavism, 1856–1870* (New York, 1958). A Polish view is given in Mieczysław Tanty, *Panslawizm, carat, Polacy: Zjazd słowiański w Moskwie 1867 roku* (Warsaw, 1970).

53. Gurko, *Ocherki Privislian'ia*, pp. 7–8.

54. For the pogroms of 1881, see Irvin M. Aronson, *Troubled Waters: The Origins of the 1881 Anti-Jewish Pogroms in Russia* (Pittsburgh, 1990). For the text of the law, see *PSZ*, 3d ser., vol. 2 (May 3, 1882), no. 854, p. 181.

55. P. I. Kovalevskii, *Aleksandr III: Tsar'-Natsionalist* (St. Petersburg, 1912). On russification, see Thaden et al., *Russification in the Baltic Provinces and Finland*. On political reaction under Alexander, see Heide Whelan, *Alexander III and the State Council: Bureaucracy and Counter-Reform in Late Imperial Russia* (New Brunswick, N.J., 1982). For a general survey of the period, see Hans Rogger, *Russia in the Age of Modernization and Revolution, 1881–1917* (London, 1983).

56. Norman Naimark, *The History of the "Proletariat": The Emergence of Marxism in the Kingdom of Poland, 1870–1887* (Boulder, 1979). The quotation is from *Voennaia entsiklopediia* (Moscow, 1912), vol. 8, p. 544. For a most unflattering portrait of both Gurko ("Hurko" in Polish) and Apukhtin, see Baronowa X.Y.Z. "List II: Rosjanie w Warszawie," *Towarzystwo Warszawskie: Listy do przyjaciółki*, 2d ed. (Cracow, 1888), vol. 1, pp. 124–208.

57. Alkar [Aleksander Kraushar], *Czasy szkolne za Apuchtina. Kartka z pamiętnika (1879–1897)* (Warsaw, 1915). The quotation is from V. Smorodinov, "Popechitel' Varshavskogo uchebnogo okruga Aleksandr L'vovich Apukhtin (Iz vospominanii pedagoga)," *Russkaia starina* 43, no. 4 (April 1912), p. 83. A similarly laudatory tone is taken in I. Skvortsov, *Russkaia shkola v Privislin'e s 1879 po 1897 gg.* (Warsaw, 1897).

58. Petr Varta [E. Piltz], *Povorotnyi moment v russko-pol'skikh otnosheniiakh: Tri stat'i Petra Varty* (St. Petersburg, 1897).

59. Abraham Ascher, *The Revolution of 1905*, 2 vols. (Stanford, 1988–1992).

60. Andreas Kappeler, *Rußland als Vielvölkerreich: Entstehung, Geschichte, Zerfall* (Munich, 1992), esp. "Die Revolution von 1905 als Völkerfrühling," pp. 268–77.

61. A thought-provoking discussion of these years and the difficulties faced by the imperial government is found in Lieven, *Nicholas II*, chap. 7, "Constitutional

Monarch? 1907–1914," pp. 161–203. See also Manfred Hagen, *Die Entfaltung politischer Öffentlichkeit in Rußland, 1906–1914* (Wiesbaden, 1982).

62. This not only was the view of *ugoda* but was also shared to a great extent by Roman Dmowski, most obviously after 1905 in *Germaniia, Rossiia, i pol'skii vopros* (St. Petersburg, 1909), but already at the turn of the century in *Myśli nowoczesnego Polaka* (Lvov, 1904).

63. In any case, the socialists—whether PPS, SDKPiL, or the Bund—were more interested in present conditions and the future than in historical musings. For the opinions of one Polish socialist on the uprising, see Józef Piłsudski, *Rok 1863* (Warsaw, 1989).

64. In his memoirs, *Na rubezhe dvukh stoletii: Vospominaniia, 1881–1914* (Prague, 1929), p. 110, the Kadet statesman A. A. Kizevetter wrote that the Russian nationalist policies under Alexander III were not so much a thought-out system as an "unconscious mood [*bezotchetnoe nastroenie*]." This observation could be extended, I think, to much of Russian "nationality policy" until 1914.

65. As Witte (who should have known) admitted, "under the present system . . . law is one thing and administrative organs are another." Witte, *Vospominaniia*, vol. 2, p. 367. Although Witte was referring to the specifics of the Stolypin land reform, the gap between policy and reality at the local level was a constant theme in Russian society and government at the time.

66. Evidence of this may be found in the huge number of files kept by the *Okhrana* on various Polish and Jewish political groups in the Polish Kingdom during this period. Many of these files are preserved at the Archiwum Głównie Akt Dawnych (AGAD) in Warsaw and especially at the Gosudarstvennyi Arkhiv Rossiiskoi Federatsii (GARF) in Moscow.

67. This point is made in Semen M. Dubnov, *Evrei v Rossii v tsarstvovanie Nikolaia II (1894–1914)* (Petrograd, 1922), and L. Wasilewski, *Rosya "konstytucyjna" wobec Polaków* (Cracow, 1913).

Chapter 6: National Awakenings

1. "Introduction," in A. Kappeler, ed., *The Formation of National Elites* (New York, 1992), pp. 1–10; also pp. 277–326.

2. M. Hroch, *Die Vorkämpfer der nationalen Bewegungen bei den kleinen Völkern Europas* (Prague, 1968), p. 23. An expanded translation by Ben Fowkes has been published as *Social Preconditions of National Revival in Europe*. Hroch's approach to the relationship between nation and nationalism is precisely the opposite of Gellner's: "We consider the origin of the modern nation as the fundamental reality and nationalism as a phenomenon derived from the existence of that nation" (p. 3).

3. See, for example, J. Chlebowczyk, *O prawie do bytu małych i młodych narodów: Kwestia narodowa i procesy narodotwórcze we wschodniej Europie środkowej w dobie kapitalizmu (od schyłku XVIII do począ tków XX w.)* (Warsaw, 1983), p. 18. An English translation of an earlier version of this book is available: *On Small and Young Nations of Europe: Nation-Forming Processes in Ethnic Borderlands in East-Central Europe* (Wrocław, 1980).

4. On the Polish exception, see Andrzej Walicki, *The Enlightenment and the Birth of Modern Nationhood: Polish Political Thought from Noble Republicanism to Tadeusz Kościuszko* (Notre Dame, 1989).

5. Andrzej Walicki, *Philosophy and Romantic Nationalism* (Oxford, 1982), p. 337.

6. It may be objected that this description is unfair to the positivists who were

certainly passionately concerned with the betterment (and not just economic enrichment) of their native land. Perhaps one could better describe the positivists, following Kieniewicz, as "sober enthusiasts." Stefan Kieniewicz, *Dramat trzezwych entuzjastów: O ludziach pracy organicznej* (Warsaw, 1964).

7. A British historian describes the periodical in the following terms: "[*Przegląd Tygodniowy*] rejected the *szlachta* tradition and the outlook of romanticism and the stuffy clericalism of the Galician conservatives. Instead emphasis was laid upon the humdrum virtues of thrift and industry. All classes were invited to unite in the common effort to increase the wealth of Poland." R. F. Leslie, ed., *The History of Poland since 1863* (Cambridge, U.K., 1980), p. 47. Władysław Pobóg-Malinowski, *Najnowsza historia polityczna Polski, 1864–1945* (Paris, 1953), vol. 1, pp. 26–27. For a general study of the Warsaw positivists, see Stanislaus A. Blejwas, *Realism in Polish Politics* (New Haven, Conn., 1984). For criticisms from the conservative camp of the positivists as "tools of capitalists," see Andrzej Jaszczuk, *Spór pozytywistów z konserwatystami o przyszłość Polski, 1870–1903* (Warsaw, 1986), pp. 84–105.

8. In general, *ugoda* is portrayed as the conservative opponent to "liberal" positivism. However, both ugoda and positivism were one in their opposition to nationalist "adventures" and, as such, were condemned in the late years of the century by nationalist activists of (for example) the National Democratic party. Especially after 1880 the views of certain "conciliators" (especially of the *Kraj* group) and the views of certain positivists often came to resemble each other closely. Ugoda in Russian Poland must be seen as a variant of the conservative philosophy of Triple Loyalty, which found proponents throughout the Polish lands during the second half of the nineteenth century. According to an American historian this trend "produced some results in Austria where the loyalty of Polish conservatives to the Habsburgs was appreciated and needed. It was bound to degenerate into servility under Prussia and Russia." Wandycz, *Partitioned Poland*, p. 193.

9. A recent study describes Aleksander Wielopolski as the "first *ugodowiec*." Andrzej Szwarc, *Od Wielopolskiego do Stronnictwa polityki realnej: Zwolennicy ugody z Rosja, ich poglądy i próby działalności politycznej, 1864–1905* (Warsaw, 1990), p. 31. The quotation is from Wilhelm Feldman, *Geschichte der politischen Ideen in Polen seit dessen Teilungen, 1795–1914* (Munich, 1917; reprint Osnabrück, 1964), pp. 283–84. On this important figure and his position between the Polish and Jewish nationalities, see Ezra Mendelsohn, "Jewish Assimilation in Lvov: The Case of Wilhelm Feldman," *Slavic Review* 28, no. 4 (December 1969), pp. 577–90.

10. For a critical—but fair—description of the early history of *Kraj* and its founders by a contemporary, see Feldman, *Geschichte der politischen Ideen*, pp. 280–85. See also Zenon Kmiecik, *"Kraj" za czasów redaktorstwa Erazma Piltza* (Warsaw, 1969). Both Piltz and Spasowicz rejected the label *ugoda* as sounding overly passive. Szwarc, *Od Wielopolskiego*, p. 15. For the credo of this revitalized ugoda, see the works of Erazm Piltz, published under various pseudonyms: Petr Varta, *Povorotnyi moment v russko-pol'skikh otnosheniiakh* (St. Petersburg, 1897); Skriptor, *Nasze stronnictwa skrajne* (Cracow, 1903); Piotr Warta, *Z chwili obecnej* (St. Petersburg, 1907); and Tensam, *W chwili ciężkej i trudnej* (Warsaw, 1912).

11. In an unpublished manuscript dated "Warsaw in May 1895," Erazm Piltz wrote, "a new ruler in a state with unlimited power—this is simultaneously a new era." Biblioteka Narodowa, Warsaw, Papiery E. Piltza, IV 8355, k. 3. In this document, written in Russian, Piltz described the anti-Polish policies that had been followed during the reign of Alexander III and argued that a new, more liberal and conciliatory policy would benefit both the Russian state and its Polish subjects alike.

12. On the Realist party (Stronnictwo Polityki Realnej), see *Stronnictwo Polityki Realnej i jego myśli przewodnie* (Warsaw, 1906).

13. On the early socialist movement, see A. Pogodin, *Glavnye techeniia pol'skoi politicheskoi mysli, 1863–1907 gg.* (St. Petersburg, 1907), pp. 141–279; and Naimark, *History of the "Proletariat."*

14. A. L. Apukhtin, curator of the Warsaw educational district (1879–1897), and I. V. Gurko, governor general of Warsaw (1883–1894), were seen by contemporary Polish society as embodiments of the russifying anti-Polish tendencies in the Polish Kingdom. Apukhtin was particularly hated for his russification of Polish schools, as is shown by the following inscription on a medallion, parodying prizes for faithful service that were presented to loyal bureaucrats at the end of their careers: "Vechnaia anafema ego imeni, vechnyi pozor ego postydnoi deiatel'nosti v Tsarstve Pol'skom 1879–1897" (Eternal anathema unto him, eternal infamy for his shameful activities in the Kingdom of Poland). RGIA, f. 1574, op. 2, d. 50.

15. The quotation is from Pogodin, *Glavnye techeniia pol'skoi politicheskoi mysli,* pp. 115–32. By linking positivists and *ugodowcy* in this manner, I do not mean to equate the two movements. However, at the end of the nineteenth century in Russian Poland, both ugodowcy and positivists favored a more or less conservative acquiescence to the currently existing powers, whereas both socialists and nationalists (especially before 1905) aimed at the radical reordering of society and political power.

16. For example, *Kraj* was published until 1909, and both Piltz and Święto-chowski survived the Romanov Empire by many years. An excellent source for tracing the development of moderate positivism is Bolesław Prus, *Kroniki*, 20 vols. (Warsaw, 1953–1970). The *Kroniki* collected here were originally published during the period 1874–1909.

17. On the period from 1905 to 1907 in the Kingdom of Poland and the Western Provinces, see Kieniewicz, *Historia Polski,* pp. 433–55; Leslie, ed., *History of Poland,* pp. 76–92; and Ascher, *Revolution of 1905,* vol. 1, pp. 134–35, 288–89, and passim.

18. R. Dmowski, *Polityka polska i odbudowanie państwa* (Warsaw, 1926), pp. 39–51. On the topic of the National Democrats, despite the work's political bias, see S. Kalabiński, *Antynarodowa polityka Endecji w rewolucji, 1905–1907* (Warsaw, 1955). For the reaction of the moderates, see, for example, Piotr Plitz, *Z chwili obecnej.* The question of Polish autonomy is examined at length in Glenn Alfred Janus, "The Polish Kolo, the Russian Duma, and the Question of Polish Autonomy" (Ph.D. diss., Ohio State University, 1971); see also "Samorząd i autonomja w programach politycznych," *Kraj,* no. 48 (December 2/15, 1905), pp. 17–18.

19. On the original electoral law and the First Duma, see "Ordynacja wyborcza dla Królestwa," *Kraj,* no. 41 (October 15/28, 1905), pp. 3–5; and "Duma Państwowa," *Kraj,* no. 17 (May 11/April 28, 1906), supplement, pp. 17–21. For short biographies of the representatives from the Polish and Western Provinces, see M. M. Boiovich, ed., *Chleny Gosudarstvennoi Dumy (portrety i biografi)* (Moscow, 1906), pp. 413–48. For the Third Duma, see M. M. Boiovich, ed., *Chleny Gosudarstvennoi Dumy: Tret'i sozyv, 1907–1912* (Moscow, 1910), pp. 404–17.

20. Wasilewski, *Rosya "konstytucyjna" wobec Polaków.*

21. For Dmowski, see in particular his *Germaniia, Rossiia, i pol'skii vopros.* Unfortunately very little work has been done on the Polish liberals. See, for example, the works by Tadeusz Stegner listed in the bibliography.

22. This topic will be considered in more detail later in chapter 8. See, for example, Paweł Korzec, "Anti-Semitism in Poland as an Intellectual, Social, and Political Movement," in Joshua Fishman, ed., *Studies on Polish Jewry* (New York, 1974), pp. 12–104.

23. For an excellent overview of Russia's Jewish community in the nineteenth century, combining socioeconomic and political history, see Israel Sosis, *Di geshikhte fun di yidishe gezelshaftlekhe shtremungen in rusland in 19 y"h* (Minsk, 1929). On the political and national movements among Jews, see Symcha Lew, *Perokim yidishe geshikhte: Sotsiale un natsionale bavegungen bay yidn in poyln un rusland fun 1897 biz 1914* (Brooklyn, 1941). An important recent study of Russian Jewry between acculturation and "separatism" is John D. Klier, *Imperial Russia's Jewish Question, 1855–1881* (Cambridge, U.K., 1995).

24. On the process leading up to the granting of civil equality, see Eisenbach, *Kwestia równouprawnienia Żydów*. A useful summary of the reform may be found in N. M. Gelber, "Zur Geschichte der jüdischen Frage in Polen (Die polnische Judenreform unter Kaiser Alexander II und Marquis Wielopolski)," *Zeitschrift für osteuropäische Geschichte* 4 (1913–1914), pp. 483–513. On the use of Polish, see RGIA, f. 821, op. 8, 1869, d. 546. On the use of Polish in Warsaw synagogues and the authorities' attitudes toward Polish-Jewish relations, see Shatzky, *Geshikhte fun yidn in varshe*, vol. 3, esp. pp. 158–63. On the important and complex issue of assimilation, see Alina Cała, *Asymilacja Żydów w Królestwie Polskim, 1864–1897* (Warsaw, 1989).

25. The position that Jews were usurping the place of a "native Polish" middle class may be found in Dmowski, *Myśli nowoczesnego Polaka*. For an account of the Polish anti-Semitic movement during these years, by a Pole who was deeply revolted by nationalist excesses and xenophobia of any kind, see Jan Baudouin de Courtenay, *W sprawie "antysemityzmu postępowego"* (Cracow, 1911), and *W kwestji żydowskiej* (Warsaw, 1913).

26. On the Litwaks, see the many articles in *Myśl niepodległa* during this period (esp. 1909–1913), and "W sprawie tak zwanych litwaków," *Przegląd narodowy* 2, no. 11 (November 1909), pp. 630–38. The anti-Litwak view is also given in Ignacy Grabowski, *Niewdzięczni goście: W sprawie żydowskiej* (Warsaw, 1912), and Julian Unszlicht [W. Sedecki, pseud.], *Socjal-litwactwo w Polsce: Z teorii i praktyki "Socjaldemokracji Królestwa Polskiego i Litwy"* (Cracow, 1911). Of course, most Litwaks spoke Yiddish as their first language, but many Jews in the northwest territory learned Russian (considered a language of enlightenment). Subbotin, visiting Vil'na in the late 1880s, noted that "nearly all the Jews try to speak Russian" (*V cherte evreiskoi osedlosti*, vol. 1, p. 58). At a somewhat later date, Jewish workers in the region, it is said, would add Russian phrases such as "tak chto" and "takim obrazom" (both roughly "so," or "thus") to their Yiddish speech to give an air of refinement. Mendelsohn, *Class Struggle*, p. 38.

27. This topic deserves its own book. Meanwhile, see Frank Golczewski, *Polnisch-Jüdische Beziehungen, 1881–1922: Eine Studie zur Geschichte des Anti-Semitismus in Osteuropa* (Wiesbaden, 1981).

28. For restrictions, see RGIA, f. 821, op. 9, 1869, d. 82, and 1872, d. 99. The latter file was published as "Po Tsarstvu Pol'skomu," in F. Berg, ed., *Materialy kommisii po ustroistvu byta evreev* (St. Petersburg, 1874), vol. 2. For the general position of the Kommissiia po ustroistvu byta evreev po Tsarstvu Pol'skomu, see Ochs, "St. Petersburg and the Jews," pp. 65–72. Gurko's advice to Alexander III (AGAD, GGW 1773, pp. 2, 7) is quoted in Ochs, "St. Petersburg and the Jews," p. 85.

29. P. I., *Evrei v Privislianskom krae* (St. Petersburg, 1892). The book's subtitle is *Kharakteristika ikh deiatel'nosti sredi khristianskogo naseleniia etogo kraia* ("a characterization of their activity among the Christian population of the country").

30. Ochs wrote, "Plehve's maneuvers in 1891–1892 constituted the last serious

initiative undertaken by the government against Jewish equality in Poland." Ochs, "St. Petersburg and the Jews," p. 116. In general, see ibid., pp. 114–16, 81–82.

31. For a concise overview of the political history of Russian Jewry under Alexander III and Nicholas II, see Salo Baron, *The Russian Jew under Tsars and Soviets* (New York, 1964), pp. 51–75. Hans Rogger has largely laid to rest the old presumption that the tsarist government consciously set out to foment pogroms: H. Rogger, "The Jewish Policy of Late Tsarism: A Reappraisal," in *Jewish Policies and Right-Wing Politics*, pp. 25–39, and the other articles in this excellent collection. However, at the local level, there is much evidence that local police and gendarmes did not go out of their way to protect Jews from *pogromshchiki*. See, for example, *Pogromy v Rossii (po ofitsial'nym dannym)* (Berlin, n.d. [ca. 1907]), and Iu. Lavrinovich, *Kto ustroil pogromy v Rossii* (Berlin, 1908). On the Christmas 1881 pogrom in Warsaw, see Golczewski, *Polnisch-Jüdische Beziehungen*, pp. 41–51. A recent important contribution to research on pogroms in Russia is John D. Klier and Shlomo Lambroza, eds., *Pogroms: Anti-Jewish Violence in Modern Russian History* (Cambridge, U.K., 1992).

32. The heyday of the Haskalah as a movement belongs to the first part of the nineteenth century, but as we can see from many sources, including the autobiography of Sholom Aleichem, the ideals of the Haskalah survived into the reign of Alexander II and beyond. On the Haskalah, see Jacob Raisin, *The Haskalah Movement in Russia* (Philadelphia, 1913), and Israel Zinberg, *A History of Jewish Literature*, trans. and ed. Bernard Martin (Cincinnati, 1978), vol. 11, *The Haskalah Movement in Russia*, and vol. 12, *Haskalah at Its Zenith*.

33. On the pogrom wave of the early 1880s, see Aronson, *Troubled Waters*. Primary materials may be found in S. M. Dubnov and G. Ia. Krasnyi-Admoni, eds., *Materialy dlia istorii antievreiskikh pogromov v Rossii* (Petrograd, 1923), vol. 2, *Vosmidesiatye gody (15 aprelia 1881 g.–29 fevralia 1882 g.)*, ed. G. Ia. Krasnyi-Admoni. See also S. Dubnov, "Anti-evreiskoe dvizhenie v Rossii v 1881 i 1882 gg.," *Evreiskaia starina* 1 (1909), pp. 88–110, 265–76. For the text of the law, see *PSZ*, 3d ser., 2 (1882), no. 834, p. 181. The quoted portion of the first article reads, in Russian, "v vide vremennoi mery i do obshchego peresmotra, v ustanovlennom poriadke, zakonov o evreiakh."

34. On the 1891 expulsion of Jews from Moscow, see Louis Greenberg, *The Jews in Russia* (New Haven, Conn., 1951), vol. 2, pp. 41–45. When the Polish-Jewish conflict took on threatening proportions after 1905, contemporaries often dated the Litwak problem from the Moscow exodus.

35. On Jewish life see, for example, Lucy Dawidowicz, *The Golden Tradition: Jewish Life and Thought in Eastern Europe* (New York, 1967); and, specifically on the culture of the *shtetl*, Herzog and Zborowski, *Life Is with People*. I. G. Orshanskii, *Russkoe zakonodatel'stvo o evreiakh* (St. Petersburg, 1877), esp. p. 336. Regarding the consequences—material, political, and spiritual—of the 1881–1882 pogroms on Russian Jewry, see David Berger, ed., *The Legacy of Jewish Migration: 1881 and Its Impact* (New York, 1983). See also Stephen M. Berk, *Year of Crisis, Year of Hope: Russian Jewry and the Pogroms of 1881–1882* (Westport, Conn., 1985).

36. The memorandum (in Polish) is reprinted in Artur Eisenbach, *Z dziejów ludności żydowskiej w Polsce w XVIII i XIX wieku: Studia i szkice* (Warsaw, 1983), pp. 262–302. On Natanson and Bloch, see Shatzky, *Geshikhte fun yidn in varshe*, vol. 3, pp. 72–74, 80–88. The study is I. S. Bliokh, *Sravnenie material'nogo byta i nravstvennogo sostoianiia v cherte osedlosti evreev i vne eia* (St. Petersburg, 1891).

37. The issue of assimilation deserves far more space than can be devoted to it here. See, for example, the excellent collection of essays by J. Frankel and S. J.

Zipperstein, eds., *Assimilation and Community: The Jews in Nineteenth-Century Europe* (Cambridge, 1992), and Bela Vago, ed., *Jewish Assimilation in Modern Times* (Boulder, 1981). Also P. S. Marek, *Ocherki po istorii prosveshcheniia evreev v Rossii: "Dva vospitaniia"* (Moscow, 1909). Marek's work contrasts the traditional religious education of Jews and chronicles the triumphs of modern, secular education among Jews in Russia from the 1840s to 1870s.

38. *Izraelita* was published in the Polish language in Warsaw from 1866 to 1912. It was generally regarded as the organ of the "Poles of Mosaic confession" *(Polacy wyznania mojżeszowego)*. M. Fuks, *Prasa żydowska w Warszawie, 1823–1939* (Warsaw, 1979), pp. 85–102. *Voskhod* first appeared in 1881 and was specifically aimed at a semi-assimilated, "enlightened" public. Nearly any Russian Jew in 1881 who would subscribe to a sophisticated journal written in Russian would ipso facto fall into this group. On Ahad Ha'am, see Steven Zipperstein, *Elusive Prophet: Ahad Ha'am and the Origins of Zionism* (Berkeley, 1993).

39. Alexander Orbach, *New Voices of Russian Jewry: A Study of the Russian-Jewish Press of Odessa in the Era of the Great Reforms, 1860–1917* (Leiden, 1980). On the Yiddish press in Russia, see Judel Mark, "Yiddish Literature in Russia," in Jacob Frumkin et al., eds., *Russian Jewry, 1860–1917* (New York, 1966), pp. 352–55; and *Fun noentn ovar*, vol. 2, *Yidishe prese in varshe* (New York, 1956). On the literature of this period, see Zinberg, *A History of Jewish Literature*, vol. 12, and Dan Miron, *The Traveller Disguised: A Study in the Rise of Modern Yiddish Fiction in the Nineteenth Century* (New York, 1973).

40. A biography of Judah Leib Gordon, a major figure and key Hebrew poet, is provided by Michael Stanislawski, *For Whom Do I Toil? Judah Leib Gordon and the Crisis of Russian Jewry* (Oxford, 1988). The best study of Russian Jewish politics at this time is Jonathan Frankel, *Prophecy and Politics: Socialism, Nationalism, and the Russian Jews, 1862–1917* (Cambridge, U.K., 1981). On the Bund, see Tobias, *The Jewish Bund in Russia*, and Koppel S. Pinson, "Arkady Kremer, Vladimir Medem, and the Ideology of the Jewish 'Bund'," *Jewish Social Studies* 7 (1945), pp. 233–64. For one contemporary's angry denunciation of Zionism, see I. Bikerman, "O sionizme i po povodu sionizma," *Russkoe bogatstvo*, no. 7 (July 1902), pp. 27–69.

41. See, for example, David Vital, *The Origins of Zionism* (Oxford, 1975): "The lasting consequence of the events of 1881–4 was . . . to destroy for all except an insignificant minority any real hope that Russia would move, however slowly, towards more liberal rule and towards the legal emancipation of the Jews in particular" (p. 59). On Smolenskin, Lilienblum, Pinsker, and Ha'Am, see Shlomo Avineri, *The Making of Modern Zionism* (New York, 1981), pp. 56–82, 112–24. On the eight legal Jewish parties, see S. Dubnov, "Evrei," in Kastelianskii, *Formy natsional'nogo dvizheniia*, pp. 399–423 (esp. pp. 412–19).

42. The Suwałki Province belonged to the Kingdom of Poland or, to speak officially, to the general governorship of Warsaw, even though ethnographically there is no break between the Lithuanians on the different sides of the border—just one more example to show that administrative boundaries of the Russian Empire were oblivious to "national" or ethnographic criteria.

43. In Vil'na Province, Lithuanians made up 17.6 percent of the total population; in Kovno, 66.0 percent. *Pervaia vseobshchaia perepis' naseleniia Rossiiskoi Imperii: Obshchii svod*, vol. 2, pp. 20–21. In computing these percentages, I have combined native speakers of *litovskii* and *zhmudskii*. For an early historical and ethnographic description, see A. Gil'ferding, "Litva i zhmud'," in *Sobranie sochinenii* (St. Petersburg, 1868), vol. 2, pp. 363–85. The Polish commentator is Wasilewski, *Litwa*, p. 10. See also Manfred Hellman, *Grundzüge der Geschichte Litauens* (Darmstadt, 1966);

Constantine B. Jurgela, *The History of the Lithuanian Nation* (New York, 1948); and Jerzy Ochmański, *Historia Litwy* (Wrocław, 1967).

44. See, for example, the Kovno governor's annual report for 1899, in which he pleads for an abolition of this law. RGIA, f. 1282, op. 3, d. 376, ll. 21–24. An account sympathetic to the Lithuanians is found in Jan Baudouin de Courtenay, *Kwestia alfabetu litewskiego w państwie rosyjskim i jej rozwiązanie* (Cracow, 1904).

45. Wasilewski, *Litwa*, pp. 40–51 (47, 50).

46. The various hardships suffered by Lithuanians at the hands of the Russian authorities are recounted in letters to the editor of *Rus'* in early 1905: among other things, Lithuanian peasants were not allowed to purchase more than sixty desiatins of land, and Lithuanians of other social classes were forbidden to purchase land at all. *Pol'skii vopros v gazete "Rus'"*, pp. 392–402. However, these restrictions were not aimed at Lithuanians per se, but at Catholics.

47. See, for example, Hipolit Korwin-Milewski, *Observations sur le conflit des langues polonaise et lithuanienne dans le diocèse de Wilna* (Paris, 1913). One interesting source on the Polish-Lithuanian dispute may be found in two books made up of contemporary newspaper articles: *Kwestya litewska w prasie polskiej* (Warsaw, 1905) and *Ze stosunków litewsko-polskich. Głosy Litwinów. Audeatur et altera pars* (Warsaw, 1907). The second collection was published specifically as a rebuttal to the first. A thorough and very fair account of the Lithuanian national movement may be found in Romer, *Litwa*. See also Józef A. Herbaczewski, *Głos bolu (Sprawa odrodzenia narodowego Litwy w związku ze spraw wyzwolenia narodowego Polski* (Cracow, 1912), and Jonas Puzinas, *Vorgeschichtsforschung und Nationalbewegung in Litauen* (Kaunas, 1935).

48. Petitions from Lithuanians to the tsarist authorities may be found in RGIA, f. 821, op. 128, 1911, d. 36. On Polish-Lithuanian relations, see P. Łossowski, *Po tej i tamtej stronie Niemna: Stosunki polsko-litewskie, 1883–1939* (Warsaw, 1985). A contemporary Polish pamphlet, hostile to the Lithuanians, is S. Sękta [L. Czarkowski], *Ostrzeżenie: W kwestii litewskiej słów kilka* (Wilno, 1907). On the events leading up to the establishment in 1918 of the Lithuanian Republic, see Alfred E. Senn, *The Emergence of Modern Lithuania* (New York, 1959), pp. 1–27.

49. M. Grushevskii, *Ocherk istorii ukrainskogo naroda*, 2d ed. (St. Petersburg, 1906), p. 416. George S. Luckyj, *Young Ukraine: the Brotherhood of Saints Cyril and Methodius in Kiev, 1845–1847* (Ottawa, 1991).

50. Only in 1905 was it permitted to publish the Bible in Ukrainian. See "Po reskriptu Prezidenta Akademii Nauk, o razreshenii dopushcheniia v Rossiiu perevoda Sv. Chetveroevangeliia na malorusskom iazyke ispolnennogo v 1862 g. F. S. Morachevskim," in RGIA, f. 797, op. 75–1905, II otd., stol 3, d. 9, and "Po otnosheniiu Upravliaiushchogo Delami Komiteta Ministrov po voprosu ob otmene ogranichenitel'nykh mer po izdaniiu Sviatogo Pisaniia na malorusskom iazyke," in ibid., d. 114. On the Ems Decree (the name derives from the place of its signing, the German spa Bad Ems), see E. Borschak, "Ukraine in the Russian Empire in the Nineteenth and Twentieth Centuries (1800–1917)," in *Ukraine: A Concise Encyclopaedia* (Toronto, 1963), vol. 1, p. 684. On this period, see also Orest Subtelny, *Ukraine: A History* (Toronto, 1988), pp. 279–84.

51. Ukrainians made up the following percentages of the total population of these provinces: Volhynia 70.1, Grodno 22.6, Kiev 79.2, and Podolia 80.9 percent. Computed from figures found in *Pervaia vseobshchaia perepis', Obshchii svod*, vol 2, p. 20. On the complex intercourse between nationalities in the region's main city, Kiev, see Michael F. Hamm, *Kiev: A Portrait, 1800–1917* (Princeton, 1993).

52. The best single example of this mind-set is Shchegolev, *Ukrainskoe dvizhenie*. Shchegolev's book is no mere polemic; it combines a broad knowledge of the

subject with a complete inability to concede the existence of a Ukrainian language and nation separate from the Russian. Shchegolev himself was a *maloross* (to use his own term) but also a loyal Russian subject, having served for many years as a government censor in Kiev.

53. One Pole who came close to this position, and who is distinguished, as it were, for his rabid attacks on the Ukrainians, was Franciszek Rawita Gawroński. See, for example, his *Kwestia ruska wobec Austryi i Rosyi* (Cracow, 1913). It is indicative of strained relations between Poles and Ukrainians in the Habsburg lands that the Kastelianskii collection contains not separate essays on Ukrainians and Poles in Austria-Hungary but a duo of essays—one by a Pole (L. Wasilewski) and one by a Ukrainian (M. Hrushevs'kyi)—under the combined title, "Polish-Ukrainian Strife." Kastelianskii, *Formy natsional'nogo dvizheniia*, pp. 129–77.

54. On the Ukrainian movement in Russia, especially during the reign of Nicholas II, see Volodymyr Doroshenko, *Ukrainstvo v Rossii: Noviishi chasy* (Vienna, 1916). See also M. Grushevskii (Hrushevs'kyi), "Universitetskii vopros," in *K pol'sko-ukrainskim otnosheniiam Galitsii* (Kiev, 1905), pp. 24–54. On the general importance of university professorships for developing national consciousness, see Magocsi, *National Cultures and University Chairs*.

55. The percentage figures are given, by guberniia, in the 1897 census for literacy in the Southwest: Volhynia 17.2, Kiev 18.1, and Podolia 15.5 percent. One reason for the low level of literacy in the Ukrainian Provinces, it was often pointed out, was that children were taught in Russian, not in their native tongue.

56. On the development of Ukrainian national consciousness, see Bohdan Krawchenko, *Social Change and National Consciousness in Twentieth-Century Ukraine* (New York, 1985), which in chapter 1 details the situation of the Ukrainian people in the first years of the twentieth century. To quote Krawchenko, "On the eve of the First World War and the Revolution, Ukrainians were a people who had not yet developed a crystallised national consciousness and whose emergence to the stature of nationhood seemed like a distant goal" (p. 3). For contemporary accounts on the state of the Ukrainian nation and national movement, see *Ukrainskii vopros*, 3d ed. (Moscow, 1917); and F. K. Volkov, M. S. Hrushevs'kyi, et al., eds., *Ukrainskii narod v ego proshlom i nastoiashchem*, 2 vols. (St. Petersburg, 1914–1916).

57. It is possible that my conclusion reflects the mainly Russian and Polish sources used, and that more national feeling was present than I have noticed. Certainly Ukrainian national leaders, including Hrushevs'kyi, took great interest in the project. See, for example, M. Hrushevs'kyi, *Za ukrains'kyi maslak / V spravy Kholmshchyny* (Kiev, 1907). It is remarkable that Hrushevs'kyi was himself a native of Kholm.

58. N. I. Kostomarov, "Dve Russkie natsional'nosti: Pis'ma k redaktoru," *Osnova* (St. Petersburg) pt. 2 (March 1861), pp. 33–80. On the early stages of the Ukrainian national movement, see P. A. Zaionchkovskii, *Kirillo-Mefodievskoe obshchestvo* (Moscow, 1959), and Georges Luciani, ed. and trans., *Le Livre de la genèse du peuple ukrainien* (Paris, 1956). A general account of tsarist policy vis-à-vis the Ukrainians from the time of Catherine II to 1876 is found in Ivancevich, "The Ukrainian National Movement and Russification."

59. Among the most pertinent of M. P. Dragomanov's works for the present study are "Evrei i poliaki v iugo-zapadnom krae: Po novym materialam dlia iugo-zapadnogo kraia," *Vestnik Evropy* 10 (July 1875), pp. 133–79, and *Velikorusskii internatsional i Pol'sko-Ukrainskii vopros* (Kazan', 1906). See also Dragomanov, *Politicheskie sochineniia*, vol. 1. Leon Wasilewski, *Moje wspomnienia ukraińskie* (Warsaw, 1932), pp.

9–10. Wasilewski, though a Pole by nationality, was very sympathetic to the Ukrainian movement. See, for example, his work *Ukraina i sprawa ukraińska* (Cracow-New York, 1911).

60. See Olga Andriewsky, "The Politics of National Identity: The Ukrainian Question in Russia, 1904–1912" (Ph.D. diss., Harvard University, 1991); and Thomas M. Prymak, *Mykhailo Hrushevsky: The Politics of National Culture* (Toronto, 1987).

61. For Ukrainian parties after 1905, see A. Kappeler, "The Ukrainians of the Russian Empire, 1860–1914," in *Formation of National Elites*, pp. 105–32; and Kerstin S. Jobst, "Die ukrainische Nationalbewegung bis 1917," in Frank Golczewski, ed., *Geschichte der Ukraine* (Göttingen, 1993), pp. 156–71. On the 1905 revolution and its effects on non-Russians, see Michael H. Voskobiynyk, "The Nationalities Question in Russia in 1905–1907: A Study in the Origin of Modern Nationalism, with Special Reference to the Ukrainians" (Ph.D. diss., University of Pennsylvania, 1972).

62. In the *Sbornik kluba russkikh natsionalistov* (Kiev, 1909–1913), one finds denunciations of attempts to introduce Ukrainian as a language of instruction (vol. 1 [1909], pp. 10–11, 31–32). One of the leaders of the club (and later a leader of the nationalist fraction in the Duma), A. I. Savenko, called the Ukrainian movement "a phenomenon that is to the same degree harmful and groundless [*bezpochvennyi*]" (vol. 2 [1910], p. 56).

63. This is admitted even by Belorussian-minded historians. See, for example, Nicholas P. Vakar, *Belorussia: The Making of a Nation* (Cambridge, Mass., 1956), and F. Turuk, *Belorusskoe dvizhenie: Ocherk istorii natsional'nogo i revoliutsionnogo dvizheniia Belorussov* (Moscow, 1921). Turuk's account is considerably weakened by his desire to emphasize the Belorussian national movement's socialist strain.

64. That is, the Northwest Provinces except Kovno. In 1897 Belorussians made up the following percentages of the population in these provinces: Vil'na 56.05, Vitebsk 52.9, Grodno 44.0, Minsk 76.0, and Mogilev 82.4 percent (computed from *Pervaia vseobshchaia perepis', Obshchii svod*, vol. 2, p. 20). The total number of Belorussians in the empire was 5,885,547—as compared to 22,380,551 Ukrainians. Ibid., vol. 2, p. 2, table 13. On the situation in Galicia and Lviv from a Ukrainian point of view, see Hrushevs'kyi, *K pol'sko-ukrainskim otnosheniiam Galitsii*. A rather extreme Polish rebuttal to Hrushevs'kyi may be found in Gawroński, *Kwestia ruska wobec Austryi i Rosyi*.

65. Czeslaw Milosz, *Native Realm: A Search for Self-Definition* (Garden City, N.Y., 1968), p. 58.

66. In the five provinces where Belorussians made up a significant part of the total population, the following percentages of Belorussians also belonged to the Catholic church (by province): Vil'na 58.5, Vitebsk 10.4, Grodno 30.3, Minsk 9.1, and Mogilev 2.0 percent. These figures are computed from data from *Pervaia vseobshchaia perepis'*, tables 13 *(Rodnoi iazyk)* and 14 *(Veroispovedanie + Rodnoi iazyk)*, vol. 4, *tetrad'* 3 (Vil'na); vol. 5 (Vitebsk); vol. 11 (Grodno); vol. 22 (Minsk); and vol. 23 (Mogilev). Note that the percentage of Catholic Belorussians decreases as one moves from west to east.

67. Vakar, *Belorussia*, p. 75. At that time, A. P. Vladimirov was one of the most vociferous partisans of depolonizing the Catholic church in the Northwest, as is evident in his work *Istoriia raspoliacheniia zapadno-russkogo kostela*. In this work Vladimirov complains bitterly about the opposition he encountered from local Russian officials, who apparently were unwilling to confuse the issue by introducing Russian (Belorussian) into the Catholic churches (for sermons, and so on). Letters from Belorussian Catholics complaining of discrimination were reprinted in *Pol'skii vopros v gazete "Rus'"* (Moscow, 1905), pp. 223–25, 285–86.

68. Anton Novina, "Belorussy," in Kastelianskii, *Formy natsional'nogo*

dvizheniia, pp. 383–95. An informative, if biased, account is found in "Formirovanie belorusskoi natsii," *Istoriia BSSR,* 2d ed. (Minsk, 1961), pp. 410–31.

69. On the restrictions on Polish landowning, see Ol'shamovskii, *Prava po zemlevladeniiu.* For the texts of the laws in question (many of which were not published in the *Polnoe sobranie zakonov*), see *Sbornik uzakonenii i rasporiazhenii po zemlevladeniiu v Zapadnykh guberniiakh* (Kiev, 1885). On the nationalists, see Robert Edelman, *Gentry Politics on the Eve of the Russian Revolution: The Nationalist Party, 1907–1917* (New Brunswick, N.J., 1980).

70. Here, of course, Great Russian is meant. These figures are for native tongue *(rodnoi iazyk).* See *Pervaia vseobshchaia perepis': Obshchii svod,* vol. 2, p. 20 (for the Western Provinces) and p. 38 (for the Polish Kingdom). The relatively large percentage of Russians in Vitebsk Province reflected the existence there of Old Believer communities. According to figures gathered by the MVD around the turn of the century, an average of only 17 percent of Orthodox middle and large landowners in the nine Western Provinces actually lived on their estates, whereas 31 percent of the Catholic landowners did so. Especially extreme was the situation in the Northwest where, in Vil'na and Kovno Provinces respectively, only 9.0 and 4.9 percent of Orthodox and 43.8 and 43.9 percent of Catholic landowners resided on their property. RGIA, f. 1149, op. 13, 1901, d. 183, ll. 421–22.

71. Boiovich, *Chleny Gosudarstennoi Dumy: Tret'i sozyv,* pp. 16–28, 40–52, 73–79, 117–37, 164–79, 236–48. Just to give one example, Duma member I. I. Balakleev from Podolia Province was also the chairman of the Balta branch of the Union of Russian People. Ibid., p. 237. See also Don C. Rawson, *Russian Rightists and the Revolution of 1905* (Cambridge, U.K., 1995), esp. pp. 91–106.

72. *Pervaia vseobshchaia perepis': Obshchii svod,* vol. 1, p. 252. The category is "Staroobriadtsy i otkloniaiushchiesia ot Pravoslaviia." The exact numbers for these three provinces were Vil'na 25,673, Vitebsk 83,022, and Kovno 32,940. On the Old Believers in the lands of the former Polish Rzeczpospolita, see Eugeniusz Iwaniec, *Z dziejów staroobrzędowców na ziemiach polskich, XVII–XX ww.* (Warsaw, 1977). The Suwałki governor in his 1907 report stressed the loyalty of the Old Believer communities resident in the area since the sixteenth century. This loyalty was shown during the upheavals *(smuta)* of 1905–1906 by the Old Believers' willingness to aid the government authorities in putting down rebellious non-Russians *(podavlenie volnuiushchikh inorodtsev).* RGIA, f. 1284, op. 194, 1908, d. 51, l. 8.

73. Studnicki, *Zarys statystyczno-ekonomiczny,* pp. 20–22.

74. Wasilewski, *Administracja rosyjska w Królestwie Polskim,* p. 7. For a general discussion of the conditions of bureaucratic service in the Polish Kingdom, see Stefan Godlewski, "Prawo do służby rządowej i przywileje służbowe," *Kraj* 24, no. 13 (April 1/14, 1905), pp. 3–6. The statute setting down the privileges may be found in *PSZ,* 3d ser., 6, no. 3817 (June 13, 1886), pp. 347–57.

75. The figures for the Lublin governor's salary are from *Spisok grazhdanskim chinam pervykh trekh klassov (ispravlen po 15-e Oktiabria 1896 goda)* (St. Petersburg, 1896), pp. 549–50. The quotation is from Andrzej Niemojewski, in Josef Melnik, ed., *Russen über Rußland: Ein Sammelwerk* (Frankfurt-am-Main, 1906), p. 590. Niemojewski, a free thinker and anticlerical publicist, was editor of the biweekly *Myśl niepodległa.*

It must be admitted, however, that by the late nineteenth century the real wages of Russian officials of the Ministry of Internal Affairs had shrunk considerably. Salaries were still paid according to the budget *(shtat)* of 1866. In 1898, Warsaw governor general Prince Aleksandr Imeretinskii pointed out that governors in the Russian interior were paid 10,000 rubles per annum whereas those of the Polish Kingdom received only 7,000. RGIA, f. 1282, op. 3, d. 282, l. 69v. This situation was also mentioned by several governors of Polish Provinces both before and after 1905, for example, in the annual reports from Płock (1896), Łomża (1901), and Lublin (1909) Provinces. Indeed, efforts were afoot to abolish the privileges altogether as both expensive and outdated. See "O peresmotre Polozheniia o preimushchestvakh sluzhby v otdal. Mestakh, Zapadnom krae i Tsarstve Pol'skom," in RGIA, f. 1276, op. 4, 1908, d. 35.

76. On the institution of maioraty in general, see "Ob izmeneniiakh maioratnykh: Obshchie osnovaniia," in RGIA, f. 1284, op. 190, 1885, d. 81AB. The absentee landlord illegally leasing lands to Jews is a stock figure in the writings of Russian nationalists (though hardly their invention). See, for example Vladimir Istomin, "O Russkom zemlevladenii v guberniiakh Privislinskogo kraia," *Moskovskie Vedomosti,* nos. 274–77 (November 11–15, 1906), and *Sovremennoe polozhenie russkogo voprosa v Privislinskom krae* (Moscow, 1906).

77. *Vsepoddaneishii otchet o proizvedennoi v 1910 godu po Vysochaishemu poveleniiu Senatorom Neidgartom revizii pravitel'stvennykh i obshchestvennykh ustanovlenii Privislinskogo kraia i Varshavskogo voennogo okruga* (St. Petersburg, n.d.), pp. 108–16. About the leasers of maiorat land it is noted, "According to data from 1908, out of 530 leasers of maiorat estates only 7 were Orthodox, [while there were] 421 Catholics, and 50 Jews" (p. 109). Excerpts from this report, with an interesting introduction and commentary, were published by Włodzimierz Dzwonowski under the title *Raport Neidgarta o rewisji senatorskiej w Królestwie Polskim* (Warsaw, 1916). For more on the institution of maioraty, see Anatol Radliński, *Rosyjskie majoraty w Królestwie Polskim* (Warsaw, 1918).

78. According to the 1897 census, 49,997 Russians lived in the city of Warsaw. However, it should be pointed out that the ratio between the sexes in this group was something on the order of 3:1 in favor of the males. This can be explained by the large numbers of military personnel in the area and by young civil servants, who would start their careers in Poland. For lists of every Russian in Warsaw eligible to vote in the Third Duma, see AGAD, GGW 9012.

79. To be sure, Poles in Warsaw often did their best to keep aloof from the Russian "occupiers." N. Kareev mentions this when describing his experiences as a young Russian professor at the University of Warsaw in the early 1880s. Kareev generally sympathized with the Poles. N. Kareev, *Polonica: Sbornik statei po pol'skim delam, 1881–1905* (St. Petersburg, 1905), esp. p. 209. Accounts of conflicts between Russians in Warsaw and local Poles also made their way into the archives. See, for example, "O stolknovenii lits russkogo proizkhozhdeniia s mestnymi urozhentsami," in AGAD, GGW 2212, and "O iavleniiakh i proisshestviiakh kharakterizuiushchikh pol'sko-russkie otnosheniia," in AGAD, GGW 2213.

80. In the Neidgart inspection *(reviziia)* of 1910 *(Vsepoddaneishii otchet o proizvedennoi v 1910 . . .)*, it was mentioned that money was appropriated for a Russian theater in 1903 but that seven years later the theater had still not been built (p. 59). In 1910, the Russkoe obshchestvo v Varshave (Russian Society in Warsaw) gathered several hundred signatures on a petition in favor of construction of a Russian theater and cultural center *(narodnyi dom).* AGAD, GGW 2606, ll. 11–24. The exact cost of the Orthodox cathedral was 3,195,094 rubles and 31 kopecks. RGIA, f. 1278, op. 2, 1911, d. 1628, l. 5. The MVD paid nearly 2.5 million rubles of this sum (l. 8v). The cathedral on Saxon Square was completed in 1912. Local Orthodox clergymen continued to complain, nonetheless, about the lack of Orthodox fervor among their compatriots living in Warsaw.

81. See, for example, Alekseev's speeches in the Duma on February 25, 1909 (*GSDO* 3, 2, ch. 2, zased. 60, cols. 2382–83) and on March 3, 1909 (zased. 67, cols. 2952–55). On Alekseev, formerly a teacher of Latin in Warsaw, see AGAD, GGW 9012 (esp. l. 106v), and Boiovich, *Chleny Gosudarstennoi Dumy: Treti sozyv*, p. 404.

82. At the same time, the entire non-Orthodox population of Lublin Province (numbering over 1.5 million) was also represented in the Duma by one delegate. On the complicated story that exemplifies the Russian government's ambiguous position on the definition of Russian nationality, see Weeks, "Defending Our Own."

83. It should go without saying that these words reflect not the reality of the situation but the exaggerated fears of Poles in the region.

84. One must remember that the empire's official representatives always insisted that the Union of Russian People was not, on the whole, guilty of fomenting pogroms and that such disturbances were to be blamed on individual excesses.

Chapter 7: Rural Administration and Nationality

1. Regarding the weaknesses of the zemstva, two literary references come immediately to mind: Chekhov's "Muzhiki" (Peasants), where the protagonists see their misery as the fault of zemstvo taxes and, from a somewhat earlier period, Levin's weariness after a zemstvo meeting in *Anna Karenina*. For an indication of the firm link between Russian progressive society and the zemstvo, see M. Dragomanov, *Liberalizm i zemstvo v Rossii* (Geneva, 1889).

2. In what follows I have depended heavily on two works: the classic Boris Veselovskii, *Istoriia zemstva*, 4 vols. (St. Petersburg, 1911), esp. vols. 3 and 4, and a more recent collection of essays, Terence Emmons and Wayne S. Vucinich, eds., *The Zemstvo in Russia: An Experiment in Local Self-Government* (Cambridge, U.K., 1982). Specifics of the original zemstvo reform and the later 1890 zemstvo law may be found in Kermit E. McKenzie, "Zemstvo Organization and Role within the Administrative Structure," in Emmons and Vucinich, *Zemstvo in Russia*, pp. 31–78. See also Veselovskii, *Istoriia zemstva*, vol. 3 (1864), pp. 1–47, and vol. 4 (1890), pp. 315–68. A general overview of zemstvo-related legislation may be found in N. N. Avinov, "Glavnye cherty iz istorii zakonodatel'stva o zemskikh uchrezhdeniiakh," in B. B. Veselovskii and Z. G. Frenkel', eds., *Iubileinyi zemskii sbornik, 1864–1914* (St. Petersburg, 1914), pp. 1–34.

3. RGIA, f. 1287, op. 10, 1901, d. 887, l. 50.

4. The emperor's mistrust of the Poles found its parallel in Russian society as a whole in the immediate aftermath of 1863. See, for example, V. A. Tvardovskaia, *Ideologiia poreformennogo samoderzhaviia (M. N. Katkov i ego izdaniia)* (Moscow, 1978).

5. The text of the original zemstvo law is in *PSZ*, 2d ser., 39, no. 40457 (January 1, 1864). McKenzie, "Zemstvo Organization," p. 31. See also Veselovskii, *Istoriia zemstva*, vol. 3, pp. 34–40.

6. McKenzie, "Zemstvo Organization," p. 45. On zemstvo-bureaucracy relations, see Thomas Fallows, "The Zemstvo and the Bureaucracy, 1890–1904," in Emmons and Vucinich, *Zemstvo in Russia*, pp. 177–242. Fallows points out that the traditional dichotomy of evil bureaucracy and virtuous zemstvo (to be encountered again later) masks a more complicated reality.

7. On the development of Russian attitudes toward self-government in the nineteenth century, see S. Frederick Starr, *Decentralization and Self-Government in Russia, 1830–1870* (Princeton, 1972) and especially on the zemstvo (pp. 241–347).

Francis William Wcislo examines the "structural contradictions" between local self-government and the centralist Russian state, as well as the bureaucratic *mentalité* on this issue, in his *Reforming Rural Russia: State, Local Society, and National Politics, 1855–1914* (Princeton, 1990).

8. Roberta Manning, "The Zemstvo and Politics, 1864–1914," in Emmons and Vucinich, *Zemstvo in Russia,* pp. 133–75 (133). Clearly, the liberal view contained a contradiction at its very core: how could the zemstvo both be above politics and yet be the first step toward more democratic government? This issue is far too complex to deal with here, but two key elements of this contradictory view must be noted. The liberals on one hand wished to downplay the political nature of the zemstvo for tactical reasons, while on the other hand they were themselves not entirely conscious of the political nature of much zemstvo work.

9. *Pervaia vseobshchaia perepis': Obshchii svod,* vol. 2, p. 20.

10. See, for example, Graf Mikhail Nikolaevich Murav'ev, "Zapiski o miatezhe v Severozapadnoi Rossii v 1863–1865 gg.," *Russkaia Starina* 13 (November 1882), pp. 387–432, 13 (December 1882), pp. 623–46, 14 (January 1883), pp. 131–66, 14 (February 1883), pp. 291–304, and 14 (March 1883), pp. 615–30; *Prilozhenie* (April 1883), pp. 193–230, and (May 1883), pp. 459–63.

11. *Vestnik Evropy* 31, no. 9 (September 1896), p. 336. The request was incorporated into the State Council *mnenie* of April 22, 1896. See *PSZ,* 3d ser., vol 16 (1896), otd. 1, no. 12804, pp. 308–311 (esp. article 20, p. 311).

12. *Vestnik Evropy* 31, no. 9 (September 1896), pp. 336, 337.

13. See, for example, the following articles, chosen from among many others: "W kwestji ziemstw," *Kraj,* no. 47 (November 21/December 3, 1896), p. 11; "Etnografja ziemstw," *Kraj,* no. 8 (February 21/March 5, 1897), pp. 4–5; "Własność ziemska w prowincjach zachodnich," *Kraj,* no. 30 (July 23/August 4, 1899), pp. 9–10; Bohdan K., "Prowincje Zachodnie i samorząd ziemski," *Kraj,* no. 39 (September 24/October 6, 1899), pp. 3–5; "Reforma ziemska w gub. zachodnich," *Kraj,* no. 15 (April 13/26, 1901), pp. 9–10; "Projekt ustawy ziemskiej dla guberni zachodnich," *Kraj,* no. 48 (November 30/December 13, 1901), pp. 18–19.

14. The complete printed text of the "Vsepoddaneishii otchet o sostoianii Mogilevskoi gubernii za 1893 g." is in RGIA, *Chital'nyi zal,* op. 1, d. 54. Excerpts from this report regarding the zemstvo (from which all quotations are taken) are in RGIA, f. 1287, op. 10, 1906, d. 887, l. 6.

15. Letter of minister of internal affairs P. Durnovo to the Committee of Ministers, June 5, 1895, no. 95, in RGIA, f. 1287, op. 10, d. 887, l. 7.

16. Ibid., l. 22. The entire text of the 1894 report for Kiev Province may be found in RGIA, f. 1284, op. 223, 1895, d. 789.

17. RGIA, f. 1284, op. 223, 1895, d. 789, ll. 9, 10.

18. "Luchshaia shkola russkogo grazhdanskogo vospitaniia," in RGIA, *Chital'nyi zal,* op. 1, d. 17 (Volhynia, 1894), pp. 4, 5.

19. For the specific comments (many of them positive) of governors and official commissions on the introduction of zemstva in non-zemstvo provinces, including the western territory, Baltic region, and Caucasus, see "Vopros o vvedenie zemskikh uchrezhdenii v nezemskie gubernii," *Russkoe bogatstvo* 18, no. 7 (July 1897), sec. 2, pp. 166–76.

20. For the MVD officials' doubts, see, for example, the MVD Department of Police rebuttal of the Kiev governor's opinion that Poles no longer presented a political danger in that province (letter of November 27, 1896, no. 10260, in RGIA, f. 1287, op. 10, 1901, d. 887, ll. 134–35). For the meetings, see "Zhurnal obrazovannogo

pod predsedatel'stvom Tovarishcha MVD DDS kn. A. D. Obolenskogo soveshchaniia gg. gubernatorov zapadnogo kraia po voprosu o preobrazovanii zemskogo ustroistva zapadnykh gubernii," in "Zakliucheniia mestnykh [. . .] nachalstv po voprosu o preobrazovanii zemskogo ustroistva" (RGIA, Pechatnaia zapiska, no. 222/1, doc. 1, pp. 187–224).

21. Sukhodol'skii cited in RGIA, Pechatnaia zapiska, no. 222/1, doc. 1, p. 190. As late as 1908, according to official figures gathered specifically for the western zemstvo project, only 6 percent of the population of Kovno Province was Orthodox and only 7 percent Russian. The next smallest percentages were in neighboring Vil'na Province, 28 and 61 percent respectively. RGIA, f. 1278, op. 2, 1909, d. 885, l. 51.

22. "Zhurnal . . . ," RGIA, Pechatnaia zapiska, no. 222/1, doc. 1, p. 191.

23. Ibid., pp. 192, 193.

24. Ibid., pp. 194–95. The governors of Kiev, Volhynia, and Kovno Provinces voted for the full zemstvo; the governors of Mogilev, Podolia, Vitebsk, Grodno, and Vil'na Provinces wanted only provincial zemstva with restrictions. The other sessions considered such issues as voting procedure (or whether to allow elections at all), national restrictions on zemstvo delegates (the Podolia governor wanted them to be exclusively Russian), and the issue of allowing Orthodox clergy to participate in the new zemstva.

25. *Vestnik Evropy* (December 1898), p. 760. Land captains were introduced in Vitebsk, Minsk, and Mogilev gubernii by the law of July 12, 1900 (*PSZ*, 3d ser., vol. 20, no. 18854, pp. 762–64). See "Proekt vvedeniia zemskikh nachal'nikov v Iugo-zapadnom i Zapadnom krae," *Russkoe bogatstvo* 21, no. 5 (May 1900), pp. 181–85. Governors of the Western Provinces universally welcomed the introduction of the land captain law in the West as a measure that brought more efficient administration to the region.

26. For the text of the 1898 Goremykin project, along with comments from the other ministers, see RGIA, f. 1287, op. 44, 1898, d. 656. An extensive explanatory appendix to the project may be found in "Prilozhenie k predstavleniiu Ministra Vnutrennikh Del v Gosudarstvennyi Sovet" ot 189—g. za No. —" (the date and number were left blank, a common practice among projects of laws still under deliberation), in RGIA, Pechatnaia zapiska, no. 222/1, doc. 1.

27. *Vestnik Evropy* (December 1898), pp. 760–61. For the major differences between the Goremykin project and the 1890 zemstvo law, see RGIA, f. 1288, op. 4, 1909, d. 37A, l. 7.

28. Ibid., pp. 767, 771–72, 772.

29. "Ob"iasneniia ministra finansov na zapisku ministra vnutrennikh del o politicheskom znachenii zemskikh uchrezhdenii" (S. Witte [14.XII.1898], Biblioteka RGIA, Pechatnaia zapiska no. 219). The text was published abroad by P. Struve as Sergei Iu. Witte, *Samoderzhavie i zemstvo: Konfidentsial'naia zapiska Ministra finansov Stats-Sekretaria S. Iu. Vitte (1899 g.), S predisloviem i primechaniiami R. N. S.* [Petr B. Struve] (Stuttgart, 1901). After the 1905 revolution an edition of this work was published within Russia with an extremely interesting introduction, under the title *Zapiska b. ministra finansov stats-sekretaria Gr. S. Iu. Vitte* (St. Petersburg, 1908).

30. Goremykin's memorandum is in RGIA, f. 1626, op. 1, 1899, d. 247; Witte is cited from *Zapiska b. ministra finansov*, p. 16. These arguments are found in Goremykin's memorandum, RGIA, f. 1626, op. 1, 1899, d. 247, ll. 2, 4v, 5, 10, 18v. As the Witte-Goremykin exchange was dominated by the finance minister, I place more emphasis on Witte's argumentation.

31. Witte quotes N. Miliutin's description of the zemstvo as the "embryo of representative government" *(zarodysh predstavitel'nogo pravleniia)* and speaks of the "constitutional tendency" of the zemstvo. Toward the end of his work, Witte further comments, "In a constitutional state, zemstva may be an excellent means of administration." *Zapiska b. ministra finansov*, pp. 67, 92, 197.

32. Ibid., pp. 48–49. Leroy-Beaulieu devotes a chapter of his classic *L'Empire des Tsars et les Russes* to the subject of Russian centralism. Anatole Leroy-Beaulieu, *The Empire of the Tsars and the Russians*, trans. by Zenaide A. Ragozin (New York, 1894), vol. 1, pp. 58–68.

33. Goremykin spoke of "self-government in the form of the *aul, ulus, aimak* and *khoton* [*samoupravlenie v vide aulov, ulusov, aimakov, khotonov*]" in Russia. Quoted in Witte, *Zapiska b. ministra finansov*, p. 62. It is interesting to note that Witte's statement here about the Russian state's ability to assimilate foreign populations would seem to contradict the repeated denials by tsarist officials of a policy of russification. The seeming contradiction here may be explained (at least in part) by the fact that Witte had here Asian, not European, peoples in mind. Needless to say, the general European imperialist attitude of superiority toward non-Europeans was not alien to Russians. See N. Riasanovsky, "Asia through Russian Eyes," in Wayne S. Vucinich, *Russia and Asia: Essays on the Influence of Russia on the Asian Peoples* (Stanford, 1972), pp. 3–29.

34. "Polnaia neprimenimost' ikh k Zapadnomu kraiu," in Witte, *Zapiska b. ministra finansov*, p. 3. Goremykin's presentation in RGIA, f. 1626, op. 1, 1899, d. 247, ll. 36–37, is cited in Witte's rebuttal *Zapiska b. ministra finansov*, pp. 178, 278. On Witte's system and its significance in the late Russian Empire, see Theodore von Laue, *Sergei Witte and the Industrialization of Russia* (New York, 1974). The importance of interministerial rivalry is stressed by Yaney, *Systemization of Russian Government*.

35. Witte, *Zapiska b. ministra finansov*, p. 179. Witte also quotes Gradovskii's warning about the unsuitability of self-government in nationally mixed regions: "In areas that lack national uniformity, self-government is incapable of giving satisfactory results" (*Zapiska b. ministra finansov*, p. 181). See A. D. Gradovskii, *Istoriia mestnogo upravleniia v Rossii* (St. Petersburg, 1868), p. cxvii: "Esli mestnye organizmy dolzhny udovletvoriat' trebovaniiam *gosudarstvennogo* edinstva, to v bol'shei eshche stepeni oni dolzhny byt' proisvedeniem *natsional'nogo edinstva*" (If local organisms are expected to satisfy the demands of *state* unity, then to an even greater degree they must be the product of *national unity*). K. Pobedonostsev, *Otzyv* (December 20, 1898), no. 252, in RGIA, f. 1149, op. 13, 1901, d. 183, ll. 324v–325, cited in Witte, *Zapiska b. ministra finansov*, p. 181. Incidentally, Pobedonostsev generally agreed with Witte's views on the zemstvo as expressed in his book but thought that Witte failed to draw the correct conclusion (that is, that zemstva throughout Russia should be dismantled). RGIA, f. 1622, op. 1, d. 355, ll. 1–2.

36. Witte, *Samoderzhavie i zemstvo* (1901), p. xxii.

37. Both quotes from Witte, *Zapiska b. ministra finansov*, p. i. Witte's political "flexibility" was denounced as simple opportunism, especially in 1905. See, for example, Wcislo, *Reforming Rural Russia*, pp. 166–94, and Andrew M. Verner, *The Crisis of Russian Autocracy: Nicholas II and the 1905 Revolution* (Princeton, 1990), esp. pp. 221–321. Verner (p. 275) quotes a remark Nicholas II made about Witte: "I never saw such a chameleon or a man who changed his convictions as he does."

38. RGIA, f. 1626, op. 1, 1899, d. 247, esp. ll. 20–23. Goremykin held that the 1890 zemstvo (counter)reform was a step in the right direction toward making the zemstvo part of the overall administration.

39. Ibid., ll. 5v, 11v, 18v.

40. The law is in *PSZ*, 3d ser., vol. 23, pp. 334–35, no. 22757, and was also published as a pamphlet, *Polozhenie ob upravlenii zemskim khoziaistvom v guberniiakh Vilenskoi, Vitebskoi, Volynskoi, Grodnenskoi, Kievskoi, Kovenskoi, Minskoi, Mogilevskoi, i Podol'skoi* (St. Petersburg, 1903).

41. Sipiagin's exact words were "in view of the particular local conditions of our borderlands, the granting to them of institutions based on the elective principle would be premature." *Zhurnal Komiteta Ministrov*, February 13, 1901, in RGIA, f. 1287, op. 10, 1901, d. 887, ll. 321v–322.

42. The MVD official was Nikitin, who raised this objection within the MVD conference *(soveshchanie)* formed to discuss this reform, April and May 1901. RGIA, f. 1287, op. 10, 1901, d. 888, l. 5. The reform had originally been slated for thirteen provinces: the nine Western Provinces plus Arkhangel'sk, Astrakhan, Orenburg, and Stavropol'. In a letter of September 17, 1902, Plehve pointed to the contrasting situations in the Western Provinces and the four others and proposed limiting the scope of the reform to the West. Letter in RGIA, f. 1287, op. 10, 1901, d. 887, ll. 62–63.

43. RGIA, Pechatnaia zapiska, no. 222/1, doc. 2, ll. 10–17, 18–22. This group included, among others, Plehve, Witte, Goremykin, and Durnovo.

44. Plehve also agreed that the lack of district bodies represented a step backward from the 1890 law but countered that such bodies could not be introduced "for practical reasons" and because they would both complicate the project and increase costs. Ibid., ll. 96–98.

45. To list only the most important moments in the process, in 1898 Goremykin placed two separate zemstvo bills before the State Council, one for the nine Western Provinces, the other for Astrakhan, Orenburg, and Stavropol'. In 1901 D. S. Sipiagin introduced a new project for the twelve provinces just mentioned, plus Arkhangel'sk. On this project, see "Vnutrennee obozrenie," *Vestnik Evropy* (May–June 1901). The final law of April 2, 1903, closely followed the Sipiagin project but concerned only the nine Western Provinces. For details, see *Vestnik Evropy*, no. 6 (June 1903), pp. 731–40; "Ustawa o zarządzie gospodarki ziemskiej," *Kraj*, no. 19 (May 9/22, 1903), special supplement; and V. D. Kuz'min-Karavaev, *Upravlenie zemskim khoziaistvom v deviati zapadnykh guberniiakh* (St. Petersburg, 1904).

46. V. D. Kuz'min-Karavaev, *Proekt zemskogo upravleniia v 13-ti nezemskikh guberniiakh* (St. Petersburg, 1902), p. 50. Kuz'min-Karavaev was criticizing the 1901 project, but this project was essentially identical to the 1903 law.

47. Bohdan Kutylowski, "Nowe institucje," *Kraj* 22, no. 51 (December 19, 1903/January 1, 1904), p. 7; W. Spasowicz, *Zametki o proekte zemskogo upravleniia dlia 13 nezemskikh gubernii* (St. Petersburg, 1902), pp. 7, 45–47. Spasowicz's comment about the Russian state interests (p. 45) is especially interesting: "The Russian state idea [*gosudarstvennost'*] can consist only in the assimilation of parts of the state, in fastening them together into one whole, subordinating them to one state type. This process of unification is hindered by exclusive laws [such as that proposed for the Western zemstvo]."

48. Veselovskii, *Istoriia zemstva*, vol. 3, p. 515. In fact, the war and revolution did not take attention entirely away from the problems of zemstvo reform in the West. See "Novyi tip zemskikh uchrezhdenii," *Vestnik Evropy* 39, no. 4 (April 1904), pp. 788–92.

49. "Imennoi vysochaishii ukaz Pravitel'stvuiushchemu senatu" (December 12, 1904), printed in *Grazhdanin*, no. 100 (December 16, 1904), pp. 2–3. See also *PSZ*, 3d ser., vol. 24, otd. 1, no. 25495, pp. 1196–98. The deliberations of the Committee of

Ministers regarding implementation of point 7 of this decree in the western territory are in RGIA, Pechatnaia Zapiska, no. 279.

50. The unpopularity of the margarine zemstva is documented in various sources, including the MVD *predstavlenie* to the Duma on the western zemstvo project dated January 20, 1910. RGIA, f. 1278, op. 2, 1910, d. 1171, ll. 7–9. Another negative report may be found in the Volhynia governor's report of 1905, in which he stated that these new bodies were extremely unpopular because they significantly raised local taxes (the *zemskoe oblozhenie*) without noticeably improving services. RGIA, f. 1284, op. 194, 1906, d. 47, l. 4. For a sympathetic history of the margarine zemstva, see "Kratkii obzor deiatel'nosti zemskikh upravlenii v 6 zapadnykh guberniiakh s momenta vvedeniia polozheniia 2-go Aprelia 1903 g.," in RGIA, f. 1288, op. 4, 1909, d. 38, ch. 3, ll. 61–82.

51. For some of the considerations that went into the new western zemstvo project, see RGIA, Pechatnaia Zapiska, no. 279, and RGIA, f. 1276, op. 1, 1905, d. 106, esp. ll. 51–52.

52. MVD, Glavnoe upravlenie po delam mestnogo khoziaistva (November 22, 1906, no. 206), V Sovet Ministrov, "O vvedenii Polozheniia o zemskikh uchrezhdeniiakh 12 iiunia 1890 g. v guberniiakh Vilenskoi, Vitebskoi, Volynskoi, Grodnenskoi, Kievskoi, Kovenskoi, Minskoi, Mogilevskoi, i Podol'skoi." RGIA, f. 1276, op. 2, 1906, d. 60, ll. 2–25 (15–16). The request to put through this reform by article 87 is found on l. 10.

53. Two Polish criticisms—one from Genrik Ippolitovich Sventsitskii [Święcicki?], the other from the well-known Lithuanian landowner and State Council member Hipolit Korwin-Milewski—may be found in ibid., ll. 27–31. For the Council of Ministers, see letter of November 30, 1906, to S. N. Gerbel', head of the MVD Department of Local Economy in ibid., l. 34.

54. Furthermore, as has been pointed out many times, the impetus to present the Duma with the western zemstvo project came from the desire on the part of Stolypin and the nationalists to change the State Council electoral procedures in the Western Provinces. Without zemstva, the Western Provinces elected exclusively Poles to the State Council. With "Russian" zemstva, it was thought, these elected State Council members would be Russians. See Edward Chmielewski, *The Polish Question in the Russian State Duma* (Knoxville, Tenn., 1970), pp. 84–86. Specifically on changing the electoral procedures in the Western Provinces, see RGIA, f. 1288, op. 2, 1909, d. 885.

55. For a quite detailed discussion of the 1909 project as it concerns the six Northwest Provinces, see Józef Folejewski, *O samorządzie ziemskim na Litwie i Białej Rusi* (Vil'na, 1911).

56. It is interesting that the project included all nine provinces until late 1909. Only then did the MVD Sovet po delam mestnogo khoziaistva (Council on Local Economy) point out the difficulties stemming from the inclusion of the Northwest Provinces in the reform. On November 5, 1909, shortly after this recommendation was made, the proposal to exclude the three Lithuanian Provinces received the approval of an MVD conference *(soveshchanie)* headed by Peter Stolypin. Thus, just over two months before the authoritative western zemstvo project was presented to the Duma, the MVD moved to exclude the Polish-dominated Vil'na, Kovno, and Grodno Provinces from the bill. RGIA, f. 1288, op. 4, 1909, d. 38, ch. 3, ll. 259–67, and 1906, d. 89B, ll. 118–20.

57. For the development of the western zemstvo project within the MVD, see RGIA, f. 1288, op. 4, 1909, dd. 37A, 38, ch. 1–4, and d. 39, ch. 1–3; RGIA, f. 1288, op.

2, 1909, d. 24; and especially RGIA, f. 1278, op. 2, 1910, d. 1171; RGIA, f. 1276, op. 5, 1909, d. 73. See also V. Shul'gin, *Vybornoe zemstvo v iugo-zapadnom krae* (Kiev, 1909).

58. This is most apparent in Avrekh, "Vopros o zapadnom zemstve," pp. 61–112, and Edward Chmielewski, "Stolypin's Last Crisis," *California Slavic Studies* 3 (1964), pp. 95–126.

59. Mary S. Conroy, "Stolypin's Attitude toward Local Self-Government," *Slavonic and East European Review* 46 (July 1968), pp. 446–61. Another treatment of Stolypin's plans for reform of local self-government may be found in Alexander V. Zenkovsky, *Stolypin: Russia's Last Great Reformer,* trans. Margaret Patoski (Princeton, N.J., 1986). Zenkovsky's book was originally published under the title *Pravda o Stolypine* (New York, 1956) and portrays a Stolypin keenly interested in transforming Russia into a liberal Western democracy, a view I do not find supported by other documents. On Stolypin's early life and career, see A. Izgoev, *P. A. Stolypin: Ocherk zhizni i deiatel'nosti* (Moscow, 1912), pp. 6–8.

60. P. A. Stolypin, *P. A. Stolypin, 1862–1911* (Paris, n.d. [ca. 1927]), pp. 68–80; Vladimir Maevskii, *Borets za blago Rossii: K stoletiiu so dnia rozhdeniia* (Madrid, 1962), pp. 8–9. See also Mary S. Conroy, *Peter Arkad'evich Stolypin: Practical Politics in Late Tsarist Russia* (Boulder, 1976), pp. 4–10. According to the *Adres-Kalendar'* listings, Stolypin served as Marshal of the Nobility in Kovno Province from 1900 to 1902. In 1899 he held the same position in Kovno district.

61. "Perepiska N. A. Romanova i P. A. Stolypina," *Krasnyi Arkhiv* (1924), pp. 102–28. Nicholas was scarcely open to arguments in favor of his Jewish subjects; thus Stolypin's insistence on this point, much to the tsar's irritation, is arguably an indication of the premier's genuine interest in improving the legal status of Russian Jewry.

62. Speech to Duma on May 7, 1910, reprinted in *Gosudarstvennaia deiatel'nost' predsedatelia soveta ministrov stats-sekretaria P. A. Stolypina* (St. Petersburg, 1911), vol. 1, pp. 114, 122 (114). Henceforth referred to as *GDStolypin.*

63. Ibid., vol. 2, p. 161.

64. Stolypin's speech in Duma on November 16, 1907, reprinted in P. A. Stolypin, *Rechi v gosudarstvennoi Dume, 1906–1911* (St. Petersburg, n.d.), pp. 121–22. The reference to first-class citizens is a retort to the Polish Duma deputy Roman Dmowski, who charged the government with treating Poles as second-class citizens (*grazhdane vtorogo razriada*). For some criticisms of the western zemstvo bill by conservative Poles, see RGIA, f. 1288, op. 4, 1909, d. 39, ch. 1, ll. 1–18, 53–55.

65. On the Nationalist party, see Edelman, *Gentry Politics.* The attitude of the Kiev Russian nationalists toward the western zemstvo project is expressed in *Sbornik kluba russkikh natsionalistov,* vol. 2 (Kiev, 1910), pp. 164–93. One V. K. Tychinin, Duma deputy from Grodno guberniia, warned that the introduction of zemstva in his area would amount to "giving this Russian country up to be devoured by Poles [*otdat' russkii krai na s"edenie poliakam*]" (*Sbornik kluba russkikh natsionalistov,* vol. 2, p. 191).

66. One finds in the files of the MVD, and specifically in the files concerning the western zemstvo project, many telegrams, protests, and petitions from Russian nationalist organizations. See, for example, a telegram from the Soiuz Russkogo Naroda (Vil'na Union of Russian People) to Stolypin, praising the decision not to extend elective zemstva to the three Northwest Provinces, and a letter from Kiev Russian Nationalists Club asking for measures to protect the interests of the Russian nationality in the cities of Western Russia. RGIA, f. 1288, op. 1, 1909, d. 38, ch. 3, ll. 321–22 and ll. 358–59.

67. On the western zemstvo bill in the Duma, see Avrekh, "Vopros o zapad-

nom zemstve," pp. 61–112; Mirosław Wierzchowski, *Sprawy Polskie w III i IV Dumie Państwowej* (Warsaw, 1966), pp. 144–56; Chmielewski, *Polish Question*, pp. 82–110; and Wieczorkiewicz, "Polityka rosyjska," pp. 291–478. Various aspects of Stolypin's relations with the Third Duma are discussed in Geoffrey A. Hosking, *The Russian Constitutional Experiment: Government and Duma, 1907–1914* (Cambridge, U.K., 1973), pp. 44–45. For Chikhachev's report on behalf of the committee within the Duma Commission on Local Self-Government, see *GDSO* 3, 3d sess., *Prilozhenie*, vol. 2, no. 330.

68. See, for example, the speech of Duma member from Vil'na Province, Montvill, in *GDSO* 3, s. 3, ch. 4, zased. 103 (May 7, 1910), cols. 762–74.

69. See the speech of Uvarov from Saratov Province, in ibid., cols. 797–804. It is clear that the State Council elections played some role at least in the timing of the western zemstvo bill. See Chmielewski, *Polish Question*, pp. 84–86. On the issue of State Council elections in the western territory, see RGIA, f. 1278, op. 2, 1909, d. 885, and f. 1327, op. 2, 1913, d. 253.

70. *GDSO* 3, s. 3, ch. 4, zased. 103 (May 7, 1910), cols. 810–24 (823–24). Sventsitskii also noted that under the MVD project, the number of Poles in the new zemstva would be even less than that of Poles serving (by appointment) in the margarine zemstva.

71. Ladomirskii cited in *GDSO* 3, s. 3, ch. 4, zased. 104 (May 8, 1910), cols. 869–73; Shul'gin cited in ibid., zased. 105 (May 10, 1910), col. 960 (Shul'gin represented Volhynia in the Duma); Bishop Evlogii cited in ibid., cols. 1223–26.

72. *GDSO* 3, s. 3, vol. 4, zased. 125, cols. 2979–81. For the complete text of the bill as passed by the Duma, see ibid., cols. 3061–86. Some nationalists worried that the western zemstvo law would turn out to be overly favorable to the Poles. See the various articles in *Okrainy Rossii*, nos. 11, 13, 14, 15, 19, 20 (1911).

73. On the discussions of the zemstvo bill in the Duma and State Council and the disagreements between these two bodies, see RGIA, f. 1288, op. 4, 1909, d. 39, ch. 1, ll. 19–40; RGIA, f. 1148, op. 12, 1911, d. 312; and RGIA, f. 1288, op. 2, 1909, d. 23. It is interesting that arch-conservatives such as Witte (as he was seen at the time) adamantly rejected national curiae. A good deal of this opposition may be explained by personal enmity between Witte and Stolypin, as well as by Witte's ambition to return to a more active role in the government by ousting Stolypin. However, many other conservatives in the State Council supported Witte against the national curiae. See *GSSO*, s. 6, zased. 18 (January 28, 1911), cols. 752–818, and Stolypin's retort at the next session (February 1, 1911), cols. 866–80. Prince Meshcherskii also despised the Nationalists (and Stolypin) and opposed national curiae. See the article "Mysli russkogo zemlevladel'tsa v Zapadnom Krae o proekte zemskoi reformy," *Grazhdanin*, no. 6 (February 13, 1911), pp. 6–7; and Meshcherskii's criticisms of the rightist deputy V. V. Shul'gin, in *Grazhdanin*, no. 17 (May 16, 1910), pp. 14–17.

74. For Witte's arguments, see especially *GSSO*, s. 6, zased. 18 (January 28, 1911), cols. 808–18.

75. The final vote against the project was something of a landslide, with 23 votes for and 134 against. Ibid., zased. 27 (March 11, 1911), col. 1362. For more detail on the western zemstvo bill in the State Council, see RGIA, f. 1148, op. 12, 1911, d. 312. On Stolypin's reaction to the defeat of the western zemstvo bill in the State Council, see Avrekh, "Vopros o zapadnom zemstve," pp. 105–6, and Chmielewski, "Stolypin's Last Crisis." Avrekh points out (p. 107) that the law promulgated by Stolypin on March 14, 1911 (*PSZ*, 3d ser., 31, no. 34903) was identical to the project passed by the Duma earlier (on May 29, 1910).

76. See, for example, the deliberations of the Council on Local Economy in

RGIA, f. 1278, op. 2, 1910, d. 1171, ll. 89–99, 103. Kiev, Podolia, Volhynia were the Southwest or "Ukrainian" Provinces; Minsk, Vitebsk, and Mogilev the "Belorussian" Provinces. The "Lithuanian" Provinces (the adjective is used geographically, not in a national sense) were Kovno, Grodno, and Vil'na.

77. The first designation was used as the determining factor, for example, in several districts of Vitebsk Province ("v Dvinskom, Liutsinskom i Rezhitskom uezdakh, Vitebskoi gubernii"). See article 2, paragraph 10 of the law. The second designation, "Non-Poles," made up the first curia, for example, in Minsk Province and most of the districts of Kiev and Volhynia Provinces. For details, see article 2, paragraph 21 of the law.

78. RGIA, f. 1278, op. 2, 1910, d. 1171, l. 19v. For the executive boards, see article 2, paragraph 22 of the law. Here, too, specific mention is made of the Dvinskii, Liutsinskii, and Rezhitskii districts of Vitebsk guberniia, where the majority of the boards was to be made up of *litsa russkogo proiskhozhdeniia*. For the Jews, see article 2, paragraph 4.

79. This is pointed out again in a contemporary discussion of the bill. Maksim Kovalevskii, "Zemstvo v shesti guberniiakh Zapadnogo kraia," *Vestnik Evropy* 46, no. 3 (March 1911), p. 257. For Vitebsk, see Prilozhenie 1 k st. 3, otd. 3 (*PSZ*, 3d ser., vol. 31, ot. 2, pp. 82–83), quoted in *GDStolypin*, vol. 2, p. 113. For the arithmetic mean, see RGIA, f. 1278, op. 2, 1910, d. 1171, l. 15v.

80. For the Fundamental Laws (*osnovnye zakony*) of the Russian Empire, see N. P. Balkanov and V. E. Gertsenberg, eds., *Svod zakonov Rossiiskoi Imperii: Izdanie neofitsial'noe* (St. Petersburg, 1912), vol. 1, pp. 1–17 (article 87 is on p. 6, chapter 9). For a thorough discussion of the legal fundaments of the Russian state from 1906, see Szeftel, *The Russian Constitution of April 23, 1906.*

81. "Pospeshnoe vvedenie zapadnogo zemstva," *Vestnik Evropy* 46, no. 8 (August 1911), p. 355. On the actual introduction of the western zemstva, see RGIA, f. 1288, op. 2, 1911, d. 36, and op. 4, 1911, d. 46. The latter file contains newspaper articles regarding the fledgling zemstva in the West.

82. RGIA, f. 1288, op. 2, 1911, d. 9, l. 125, and d. 36, l. 140 (copy of "*sekretnoe pis'mo*" of Kiev governor general to governors of Podolia, Kiev, and Volhynia, April 27, 1911). Ibid., op. 4, 1909, d. 39, ch. 2, l. 220 (letter from Volhynia governor to governor general Trepov, April 22, 1911). According to the latter report, the Volhynia Poles had decided not to boycott and not to push their own candidates but to support sympathetic Russians. Ibid., op. 4, 1909, d. 39, ch. 2, l. 478.

83. For more details, see "Bor'ba natsionalistov s chekhami," *Vestnik Evropy* 46, no. 8 (August 1911), pp. 358–61, 369–72.

84. "Lozungi 'natsionalistov' pered vyborami v zapadnoe zemstvo—'Russkie komitety' i pravoslavnye pastyri," *Russkoe bogatstvo*, no. 8 (August 1911), pp. 119–43. In certain districts among smallholders (*melkie vladel'tsy*), it is reported (ibid., p. 139) that the electoral participation rate was well under 10 percent (39 out of 1,046; 16 out of 1,876; 19 out of 1,170; 59 out of 867). RGIA, f. 1288, op. 4, 1909, d. 39, ch. 1, l. 236.

85. Conservative Poles serving on the Council on Local Economy argued in 1913 that the failure to introduce zemstva in the three Northwest Provinces exhibited an ungrounded mistrust for the Polish landowners there and caused not only economic damage to local Poles but had more important negative effects for the entire region and indeed for the Russian state. RGIA, Pechatnaia Zapiska, no. 222/1, doc. 4, pp. 35–38. On the efforts to bring margarine zemstvo to the Northwest, see RGIA, Pechatnaia Zapiska, no. 222/1, doc. 4, in RGIA, f. 1288, op. 4, 1909, d. 39, ch. 1 and 2.

86. *Zemskoe delo*, nos. 15–16 (August 5, 1911), p. 1101. For a similar description of the new zemstvo in Mogilev Province, see ibid., no. 20 (October 20, 1911), pp. 1388–91. On the achievements of the western zemstva up to 1914, see Vladimir Trutovskii, *Sovremennoe zemstvo*, edited and with a foreword by B. B. Veselovskii (Petrograd, 1915), pp. 166–78. Unfortunately, Trutovskii's work was badly mangled by the censors, leaving many pages nearly blank (or even entirely blank, as on pp. 196–97).

Chapter 8: Poles, Russians, and Jews in Conflict

1. On May 29, 1910, minister of internal affairs Stolypin presented the Duma Komissiia po Mestnomu Samoupravleniiu (Commission for Local Self-Government) with the MVD's project to introduce elective city government in the Kingdom of Poland. The Duma plenum did not begin to discuss the measure until November 23, 1911. *GDSO* 3, s. 5, 1, zased. 28, cols. 2429–526.

2. The municipal reform statute was the last of the Great Reforms, except for the military reform of 1874. For the original law, see *PSZ*, 2d ser., 45, otd. 1, no. 48498 (June 16/28, 1870), pp. 821–39. See also W. Bruce Lincoln, *The Great Reforms: Autocracy, Bureaucracy, and the Politics of Change in Imperial Russia* (DeKalb, Ill., 1990), pp. 134–43, 187. It is interesting to note that the text of the counter-reforming law was longer than the original statute itself. *PSZ*, 3d ser., 12, no. 8708 (June 11, 1892), pp. 430–56.

3. Michael F. Hamm, "Introduction," in M. Hamm, ed., *The City in Late Imperial Russia* (Bloomington, Ind., 1986), p. 5. For a detailed discussion of municipal government in Russia prior to and during this period, see Walter Hanchett, "Tsarist Statutory Regulation of Municipal Government in the Nineteenth Century," in M. Hamm, ed., *The City in Russian History* (Lexington, Ky., 1976), pp. 91–114.

4. *PSZ*, 2d ser., 45, otd. 1, no. 48498 (June 16/28, 1870), p. 821. It is also interesting that the date is given here also in its Gregorian form. This was usually done only for laws concerning regions that used this calendar (that is, Poland, Finland, and the Baltic Provinces).

5. RGIA, f. 1278, op. 2, 1910, d. 1171, l. 66. On the city government in Kiev, see Michael F. Hamm, "Continuity and Change in Late Imperial Kiev," in Hamm, *City in Russian History*, pp. 99–102; L. Podhorodecki, *Dzieje Kijowa* (Warsaw, 1982), p. 182; and Hamm, *Kiev*, esp. pp. 36–40.

6. The municipal statute was put into law for the Kingdom of Poland using paragraph 87 (like the western zemstvo) on March 17, 1915, but was never actually introduced because of the German occupation of Warsaw and the Polish Kingdom. For the text of the law, see *Sobranie uzakonenii i rasporiazhenii pravitel'stva*, no. 91, otd. 1, stat'ia 762 (March 22, 1915), pp. 1131–46.

7. The inadequacies of the 1870 and 1892 statutes were pointed out very clearly in the article on the subject in *Entsiklopedicheskii slovar' Brokgauz-Efron* (St. Petersburg, 1893), entry "Gorod," vol. 17, pp. 326–31. The author of this section, K. Arsen'ev, saw the greatest weaknesses of the municipal statutes in three areas: the narrow electorate, which completely excluded members of the "free professions" who rented apartments; restrictions on Jews; and the exaggerated amount of administrative/bureaucratic tutelage over city government.

8. On the city government in Warsaw specifically, see Kieniewicz, *Warszawa*, pp. 179–95. A general description of city government in Poland is given by Adolf Suligowski, "Gorodskoe upravlenie v guberniiakh Tsarstva Pol'skogo," *Vestnik Evropy* 37, no. 6 (June 1902), pp. 675–97. For greater detail, see Adolf Suligowski,

Zapiska o sisteme gorodskogo upravleniia v guberniiakh Tsarstva Pol'skogo (St. Petersburg, 1905).

9. Kieniewicz, *Powstanie styczniowe* (Warsaw, 1972), pp. 182–83. On the city government elections in 1861, see pp. 191–97.

10. A. Suligowski, *Istoricheskaia zapiska ob upravlenii gorodami v Tsarstve Pol'skom* (Warsaw, 1906), p. 3. Suligowski notes that the counter-reform of city government was but part of the general reform of the administration of Russian Poland undertaken in the years after the 1863 uprising. For more detail on these reforms, see RGIA, Pechatnaia Zapiska, no. 2473.

11. For F. Berg, see RGIA, f. 1276, op. 5, 1909, d. 44, l. 127v. For MVD study, see RGIA, Pechatnaia Zapiska, no. 2479, doc. 1, ll. 58–59. This document is undated but speaks of the peasant reform in Poland as having taken place fourteen years earlier; hence it must be dated around 1878. For correspondence between Al'bedinskii and Ignat'ev, see AGAD, GGW 1767, kk. 1–2. The two letters are dated June 9 and June 28, 1881.

12. Suligowski, "Gorodskoe upravlenie," p. 697.

13. Corrsin has this to say about Starynkevich: "[He] (president, 1875–92) was the city president best and most kindly remembered by Polish historians (indeed, he was the only Russian official for whom they consistently had kind words)." Stephen D. Corrsin, "Warsaw: Poles and Jews in a Conquered City," in Hamm, *City in Late Imperial Russia,* p. 135. Despite his name, Starynkevich was not of Polish descent and was born in Taganrog on the Sea of Azov. On this important figure, see Anna Słoniowa, *Sokrates Starynkiewicz* (Warsaw, 1981). One indication of Starynkevich's popularity is the presence to this day of a square in downtown Warsaw that bears his name.

14. *Słowo,* quoted in *Kraj,* no. 44 (November 2/14, 1895), p. 19.

15. I use the word "conservative" with some reluctance. In the political context of the first decade of Nicholas II's reign, the *ugodowcy* grouped around *Kraj* favored many liberal measures such as the zemstvo and city reforms and advocated, in their timid way, a greater opening of society. However, they were fundamentally conservative in their belief in the overwhelming power of the Russian state and their desire for modest reforms issuing from a benevolent emperor. A detailed study is provided by Kmiecik, *"Kraj" za czasów redaktorstwa Erazma Piltza.* Piltz, *Kraj,* and ugoda were so inextricably entwined that the history of the journal and the man becomes at the same time a history of the movement.

16. It must be pointed out that this positive assessment of city government activities in the Western Provinces was generally not shared by local officials. See, for example, the complaints in the following governors' reports: RGIA, f. 1284, op. 194, 1902, d. 159 (Vitebsk, 1901), ll. 5–6; RGIA, *Chital'nyi Zal,* op. 1, d. 54 (Mogilev, 1896), pp. 8–9; RGIA, *Chital'nyi Zal,* op. 1, d. 71 (Podolia, 1902), l. 116.

17. Quoted in *Kraj,* no. 44 (November 2/14, 1895), p. 19.

18. Regarding the *Varshavskii Dnevnik,* see "O subsidii redaktsii gazety 'Varshavskii Dnevnik'," in AGAD, GGW 6355, 1911. See also the short history of the paper by its longtime editor, V. Esipov, *"Varshavskii dnevnik" za 50 let* (Warsaw, 1914); and Zenon Kmiecik, *Prasa warszawska, 1886–1904* (Wrocław, 1989), p. 22.

19. Comment to the Warsaw oberpolitseimeister's annual report for 1897, in RGIA, f. 1284, op. 223, 1898, d. 60–lit.B.P., l. 6v.

20. *Moskovskie Vedomosti,* no. 190 (July 13, 1897). "O samorząd," *Kraj,* no. 46 (November 16/28, 1895), p. 17.

21. For more arguments for reform, see "O Warszawie," *Kraj* 17, no. 29 (July

17/29, 1898), pp. 7–8; and "Zarząd miejski w Królestwie Polskiem," *Kraj* 18, no. 35 (August 27/September 8, 1899), pp. 12–13. The latter article—drawing on a study published in two articles in *Peterburgskie Vedomosti* by M. I. Kornilowicz from Radom—examined in some detail the finances of municipal governments in the Kingdom of Poland and pointed out the negative effects of the present system of administration.

22. This Russian attitude comes out most clearly, perhaps, in the works of V. V. Esipov, editor of *Varshavskii Dnevnik* after 1908. See, for example, his *Avtonomiia Pol'shi, s tochki zreniia finansovykh, ekonomicheskikh i drugikh interesov Rossii* (Warsaw, 1907), *Varshava i Lodz', ikh proshloe i nastoiashchee* (Warsaw, 1907), and *Ocherk zhizni i byta Privislinskogo kraia* (Warsaw, 1909).

23. This tendency manifests itself in the monumental two-volume work by Stefan Dziewulski and Henryk Radziszewski, *Warszawa* (Warsaw, 1913–1915), especially volume 2, *Gospodarstwo Miejskie*, which provides a detailed summary of the development of municipal administration in Warsaw before going on to specific areas in which the municipality was involved (for example, lighting, transport, water supply, roads, commerce, public health, slaughterhouses, policing, schools, and others). See also Adolf Suligowski's works collected in four volumes, *Pisma* (Warsaw, 1916), esp. vol. 1, *Potrzeba samorządu*, and vol. 2, *Kwestje miejskie*.

24. Another indication that "society" in the Kingdom of Poland was troubled by the issue of administrative reform, particularly in urban areas, may be found in the collection of essays put together by *Kraj* editors E. Piltz and W. Spasowicz [E. Pil'ts and V. Spasovich], *Ocherednye voprosy v Tsarstve Pol'skom: Etiudy i issledovaniia* (St. Petersburg, 1902), especially the essay "Gorodskoe khoziaistvo v guberniiakh Tsarstva Pol'skogo," on pp. 1–30. An anti-Polish, Russian nationalist retort to this work and this article is given in "Privislianets," in Dmitrii Tutkevich and A. N. Druzhinin, eds., *Rossiia i eia zapadnye okrainy: Otvet na "Ocherednye voprosy v Tsarstve Pol'skom"* (Kiev, 1903).

25. *PSZ*, 3d ser., 24, otd. 1, no. 25495 (December 12, 1904), pp. 1196–98. The ukaz was printed in Russian in *Grazhdanin*, no. 100 (December 16, 1904), pp. 2–3 and in Polish in *Kraj* 23, no. 51 (December 18/31, 1904), pp. 3–4.

26. See the enthusiastic article greeting the December 12, 1904, decree, "Nowe fundamenty," *Kraj* 24, nos. 1/2 (January 14/27, 1905), pp. 3–4. *Kraj* also printed a review of Polish press reactions to the ukaz in "Prasa Polska o Reformach," *Kraj* 23, no. 52 (December 24, 1904/January 6, 1905), pp. 6–7, and called on its readers to send in examples of present restrictions and suggestions for reform, in *Kraj* 23, no. 53 (December 31, 1904/January 13, 1905), p. 3.

27. "W komitecie ministrów," *Kraj* 24, no. 14 (April 8/21, 1905), p. 16. The meetings of the Committee of Ministers occurred on April 5–6, old style. For the rather conservative findings of the committee, see RGIA, f. 1276, op. 1, 1905, d. 105, ll. 294–95.

28. I use the adjective "Polish" geographically. Contemporary Poles (and not only they), however, tended to conflate geography and nationality in this instance.

29. "Z Królestwa Polskiego: przyszły samorząd," *Kraj*, no. 19 (May 13/26, 1905), pp. 11–12.

30. On 1905 in Russian Poland, see Robert Blobaum, *Rewolucja: Russian Poland, 1904–1907* (Ithaca, N.Y., 1995), and Halina Kiepurska, *Warszawa w rewolucji, 1905–1907* (Warsaw, 1974). For a detailed account of the Polish parties' behavior in the period from 1904 to 1907, see Pogodin, *Glavnye techeniia*, pp. 449–616 and (specifically on autonomy projects) 638–62.

31. On the delegation from the Warsaw Stock Exchange, see Pogodin, *Glavnye techeniia*, p. 543. For two Polish petitions to Sviatopolk-Mirskii, both dating from late (October and November) 1904, see GARF, f. 1729, op. 1, 1904, d. 152 (L. Krasinskii) and d. 154 (W. Spasowicz). See also the petitions printed by the MVD in the pamphlet "Zapiski, kasaiushchie pol'skogo voprosa," in RGIA, Pechatnaia Zapiska, no. 2934.

32. "Osobyi zhurnal Komiteta Ministrov 5 i 6 Aprelia i 3 Maia 1905 g. po delu o poriadke vypolneniia punkta sed'mogo Imennogo Vysochaishogo Ukaza 12 Dekabria 1904 g. v otnoshenii gubernii Tsarstva Pol'skogo." RGIA, f. 1276, op. 1, 1905, d. 105, ll. 283–301. Here I follow the accounts in Henryk Radziszewski, *Warszawa*, vol. 2, *Gospodarstwo Miejskie*, pp. 28–34; and Adolf Suligowski, "Motywy do projektu ustawy miejskiej dla miast Królestwa Polskiego" (originally published in 1906) in *Pisma* (Warsaw, 1915), vol. 1, pp. 91–113, and "Losy tego projektu," in *Pisma*, vol. 1, pp. 193–211. See also the unpublished manuscript by Erazm Piltz kept at the Biblioteka Narodowa in Warsaw (IV.8360, microfilm 62408), "Sprawa samorządu w Królestwie Polskim."

33. Adolf Suligowski later recounted his meeting in February 1906 with the assistant governor general of Warsaw, Senator Podgorodnikov, and emphasized the great difference of opinion then existing between the Russian administration and Polish society on the subject of self-government. Suligowski, *Pisma*, vol. 1, pp. 121–25.

34. Ibid., pp. 93, 98–99.

35. The texts of both projects, with a short introduction, are in Adolf Suligowski, *Projekty ustaw samorządu miejskiego w Królestwie Polskiem* (Warsaw, 1906). The printers' proofs of this book, apparently corrected by Suligowski himself, are located at the Biblioteka Narodowa in Warsaw.

36. Radziszewski, *Warszawa*, p. 31, and Suligowski, *Projekty ustaw*, pp. 11–12.

37. It was not necessarily preferable from a Polish national viewpoint, to be sure. Even Radziszewski (himself no anti-Semite) complained that this project could have led to a Jewish majority in the Warsaw city council. Even the literacy requirement would not have helped here, Radziszewski pointed out, because "the dark Jewish mass [*tłum*] in general has a higher literacy rate (even in Polish) than the gray mass of the Polish population." Radziszewski, *Warszawa*, p. 34. Radziszewski evidently considered a Jewish majority in the Warsaw city council to be unacceptable.

38. For Skalon's letter to Stolypin, see RGIA, f. 1288, op. 4, 1906, d. 73, ch. 1, ll. 28–30 (28v, 29v). Skalon's adamant opposition to allowing Polish in local self-government in 1906 contrasts with his opinion five years later, when he supported the government's Polish city reform bill. For Skalon's second project, see RGIA, f. 1276, op. 5, 1905, d. 44, l. 405. The Skalon project was dated October 7, 1906 (no. 19150). Skalon wished to keep Suligowski—whom he described as a "man proud to the point of pettiness [*chelovek do melochnosti samoliubivyi*]"—out of any government committees on the future city government law in the Polish Kingdom. RGIA, f. 1288, op. 4, 1906, d. 73, ch. 1, l. 12.

39. "Protokoly osobogo soveshchaniia dlia rassmotreniia proektov polozheniia o zemskikh uchrezhdeniiakh v guberniiakh Tsarstva Pol'skogo i gorodovogo polozheniia dlia gorodov tekh-zhe gubernii," in RGIA, f. 1288, op. 4, 1906, d. 73, ch. 1, ll. 232–333. For Suligowski, see ibid., l. 268. Zhurnal no. 3, October 31, 1906. For Zaremba, see ibid., l. 268v.

40. Suligowski, *Pisma*, vol. 1, p. 196.

41. The protocols of the discussions in both of these commissions can be

found in RGIA, f. 1276, op. 5, 1909, d. 44, ll. 177–254. On the language question, see ibid., ll. 182–85, 231–34; on the Jewish issue, see ibid., ll. 187, 224, 239–40. Suligowski, *Pisma*, vol. 1, p. 199.

42. For April, see Avrekh, *Stolypin i tret'ia Duma*, p. 93; also "Osobyi Zhurnal Soveta Ministrov 6 i 27 Aprelia 1910 g." RGIA, f. 1276, op. 5, 1909, d. 44, ll. 280–82. For July, see Radziszewski, *Warszawa*, p. 35. The text of the MVD project sent to the Duma (dated May 29, 1910) is in RGIA, f. 1276, op. 5, 1909, d. 44, ll. 442–74.

43. For a discussion of the government project, see Radziszewski, *Warszawa*, pp. 34–38. The project is discussed in greater detail in Adolf Suligowski, *Projekt przyszłego samorządu miejskiego* (Warsaw, 1911), in which the complete text of the government project may be found on pp. 35–89. It may also be found in RGIA, f. 821, op. 10, 1910, d. 50, ll. 1–67.

44. *Pravitel'stvennyi vestnik*, no. 252 (November 26, 1909), p. 4. The following statistics are from Suligowski, *Projekt ustawy*, p. 41. It is interesting to note that, according to the terms of the law, in the city of Chełm (population 17,555 with 5,061 "Russians," 7,814 Jews, and 4,680 "others") the "Russians" and Poles would have eighteen seats each on the city council, whereas the Jews, who formed the plurality of the population, would have only four.

45. Suligowski, *Projekt przyszłego samorządu*, article 29, pp. 42–43. A note to this article (p. 42) specifically defines Jews as "those born into Judaism." The MVD project *(predstavlenie)* states that admitting Jews into city government on an equal footing with Christians would constitute a "partial solution to the general question on the legal standing of Jews in the Empire [*chastichnym razresheniem obshchogo voprosa o pravovom polozhenii evreev v Imperii*]," and as such could not be allowed. RGIA, f. 1276, op. 5, 1909, d. 44, l. 448.

46. Suligowsky, *Projekt przyszłego samorządu*, p. 7. The renters clause was necessary to allow the many Russian officials, temporarily resident in Warsaw, to vote. For figures on the number of voters in several Polish cities, see RGIA, f. 821, op. 10, 1910, d. 50, ll. 54–67. Here are just a few examples: in Warsaw 22,662 out of a population of 782,641 would have the vote; in Kalisz 2,148 out of 48,964; in Łódź 12,003 out of 408,442; in Siedlce 2,032 out of 30,472; in Suwałki 1,113 out of 25,051. A similar reform had long been urged by governors in the Western Provinces who complained of the low intellectual and "moral" level of the townsmen *(meshchane)* dominating the city governments in these provinces.

47. Suligowski, *Projekt przyszłego samorządu*, p. 16. See section 2 of the project on pp. 38–40, and articles 83–88 on pp. 58–59, for relations between governor and city government. The outrage felt by Polish society at the State Council's exclusion of the use of Polish from the city government project is also mentioned in governors' and police reports from Poland. See, for example, RGIA, f. 1284, op. 194, 1913, d. 87 (Warsaw Province, 1912), l. 5v; APW, T. 24, sygn. 261 (1913), k. 15; AGAD, PomGGW 1224 (1913), k. 46.

48. "Doklad komissii po gorodskim delam po zakonoproektu o preobrazovanii upravleniia gorodov v guberniiakh Tsarstva Pol'skogo," *GDSO* 3, s. 4, Prilozhenie, tom 3, no. 217 (178 pages). Quoted in Radziszewski, *Warszawa*, pp. 38–40.

49. *GDSO* 3, s. 5, ch. 1, zased. 28 (November 23, 1911), cols. 2429–44 (2436, 2440).

50. Ibid., cols. 2448–51.

51. For Bulat, see ibid., cols. 2471–81. It is interesting that Bulat did not think Yiddish should be used in the city governments, on the grounds that Jews knew Lithuanian and Polish, but almost no Poles or Lithuanians knew Yiddish (col. 2480).

For Shchepkin, see ibid., cols. 2459–71 (2460, 2462). For Fridman, see ibid., cols. 2504–7.

52. Ibid., zased. 32 (November 28, 1911), cols. 2758–64. For some of the amendments to the commission's project, see ibid., cols. 2789–824.

53. Radziszewski, *Warszawa,* p. 42. Radziszewski wrote these words in February 1913, when the city government bill was moving between the Duma and the State Council. On the Polish city government bill in the Duma and State Council, see Avrekh, *Stolypin i tret'ia Duma,* pp. 92–108; Wierzchowski, *Sprawy Polski* (Warsaw, 1966), pp. 196–202; Chmielewski, *Polish Question,* pp. 138–60; and Wieczorkiewicz, "Polityka rosyjska," pp. 683–845.

54. See Ochs, "St. Petersburg and the Jews," and Jacob Kirszrot, *Prawa Żydów.* Indeed, the Kadets were essentially alone among the Russian political parties in supporting the Poles. For the right (including, for the most part, Octobrists), Polonophobia was an article of faith; and to the left of the Kadets, the socialists either were uninterested in supporting Polish national pretensions or were actively hostile to the Koło as a bourgeois conservative group. All members of the Koło, incidentally, were affiliated to a greater or lesser extent with the National Democrat party.

55. Jaroński's speech was given on November 23, 1911. *GDSO* 3, s. 5, ch. 1, zased. 28, cols. 2499–500. It must be noted, however, that this speech was also controversial within the Koło: both L. Dymsza and A. Parczewski opposed it, and W. Grabski expressed his disapproval of restrictions on Jews. Wieczorkiewicz, "Polityka rosyjska," p. 713. Considering that the entire Koło in the Third Duma consisted of only ten members (*GDSO,* Tret'i sozyv, sessiia 3 [St. Petersburg, 1910], p. 16), the dissention of three members must be considered significant. However, when faced with attacks from without, the Koło closed ranks and did not reveal its internal disagreements on this question.

56. See *Ezhegodnik gazety Rech',* pp. 319–30 (1913, events of 1912); pp. 256–57 (1914, events of 1913). In the 1914 volume, the commentator I. Clemens referred to the National Democrats (*endeks*) as "black hundreds, reaction" (p. 256), mainly because of the ND-led anti-Jewish boycott. The Russian Rightists (*pravye*) and Nationalists were apparently not struck by the similarity of the Koło's position in this instance with their own general attitude: after all, the Russians also demanded rights and privileges exclusively for their own nationality.

57. For the Harusewicz (Garusevich) speech, see *GDSO* 4, s. 1, ch. 3, zased. 75 (June 12, 1913), cols. 2067–71.

58. It has been suggested (both at the time and later) that the Kholm bill and the municipal project for Poland were sent to the Duma at the same time as a sort of quid pro quo: one bill for the Russian nationalists, the other for the Poles. See Wierzchowski, *Sprawy Polski,* pp. 197–98; Avrekh, *Stolypin i tret'ia Duma,* p. 96; Eugeniusz Starczewski, *Sprawa polska,* 2d ed. (Warsaw, 1913), p. 222. On the other hand, an internal MVD memo (*spravka*) of 1913 suggested that the Polish city government bill was compensation for restrictions on Poles in the western zemstvo. RGIA, f. 1276, op. 5, 1909, d. 44, l. 408v.

59. I. Moszczeńska, "Samorząd i kwestja żydowska," *Myśl Niepodległa* 5, no. 153 (November 1910), pp. 1600–1605. For "Jewish domination," see Wierzchowski, *Sprawy Polski,* pp. 198–99. For the ND position on liberals, Jews, and city government, see R. Dmowski, "Liberalna Rosja i Polacy," *Gazeta Warszawska,* nos. 315, 316, 318, 320 (1910); R. Dmowski, "Polityka polska, kadeci i sprawa żydowska," *Gazeta Warszawska* (November 27, 1910). The ugoda/realist view is expressed in "Kurie w samorządzie," *Słowo,* no. 369 (August 17, 1910), which called curiae an outdated

system and favored proportional representation. Roman Dmowski lambasted the realist posture on this issue as an inability to decide "between love and duty, between love for the Jews and duty toward the country [*kraj*]." *Upadek myśli konserwatywnej w Polsce* (Warsaw, 1914), p. 140.

60. I. Kirilov, "Ocherk sovremennogo sostoianiia Privislinskogo kraia i neobkhodimykh v nem meropriiatii," dated April 4, 1905, in RGIA, f. 1284, op. 190, 1901, d. 90A, l. 74.

61. The contemporary literature of Polish anti-Semitism is enormous, though the secondary literature remains spotty. For some idea of the more extreme variety of Polish anti-Semitism, see I. Grabowski, *Polacy, Żydzi, Rosjanie* (Warsaw, 1915), or Jan Jeleński, *Nie bić żydów, ale im się nie dawać!* (Warsaw, 1906). Jeleński may be called the founder of modern Polish anti-Semitism. Dmowski and most of the National Democrats were less rabid but fundamentally no less antagonistic to Jews (see *Przegląd narodowy* or *Gazeta warszawska* for this period). Even progressives such as Aleksander Świętochowski and Andrzej Niemojewski joined the anti-Semites; on this phenomenon, see Baudouin de Courtenay, *W sprawie "antysemityzmu postępowego."* On the Litwaks, see Unszlicht, *Socjal-litwactwo w Polsce,* and "W sprawie tak zwanych litwaków," *Przegląd narodowy* 2, no. 11 (November 1909), pp. 630–38. For a general overview, see Wilhelm Feldman, *Dzieje polskiej myśli politycznej, 1863–1914,* 2d ed. (Warsaw, 1933), pp. 366–71.

62. S. Corrsin, "Political and Social Change in Warsaw from the January 1863 Insurrection to the First World War: Polish Politics and the Jewish Question" (Ph.D. diss., University of Michigan, 1981), pp. 143–44. Corrsin states that no evidence has been found to support this view. Indeed, the local authorities (at least at the higher levels) seem to have taken measures to prevent any violence between Poles and Jews. See, for example, RGIA, f. 821, op. 128, 1913, d. 989; RGIA, f. 1327, op. 2, 1912, d. 241, l. 27 (about the Polish-Jewish conflict during the Fourth Duma election in Warsaw); AGAD, GGW 1893 (1903–1904), k. 160v (about efforts to prevent clashes in the wake of disturbing rumors after the Kishinev pogrom).

63. I. Berlin, "Nationalism: Past Neglect and Present Power," in *Against the Current: Essays in the History of Ideas* (London, 1979), p. 346.

64. See, for example, the essays collected in Vladimir Zhabotinskii, *Fel'etony* (St. Petersburg, 1913). In his 1910 essay "Poliaki i evrei" (pp. 143–45), Zhabotinskii advised the Poles to accept the existence in Poland of "two nations," Poles and Jews. The angry reactions to this suggestion in the Warsaw press are found in *Poliaki i Evrei—Sbornik Statei: Materialy o pol'sko-evreiskom spore po povodu zakonoproekta o gorodskom samoupravlenii v Pol'she* (Odessa, n.d. [ca. 1912]), pp. 19–29.

Although certain Bund and Zionist activists may indeed have come to the Kingdom of Poland from the Russian interior, the most important factor was the increasing unwillingness of Jews, whether from Warsaw or Berdichev, to relinquish their Jewish identity and consider themselves "Poles of the Mosaic faith." See *Poliaki i Evrei,* pp. 20–23. Polish National Democrats rejected assimilation in most cases, regarding the Jews of Poland (to quote ND leader Roman Dmowski) as a "foreign body" guided by a "hostile ethic" (ibid., pp. 50–51).

65. Ezra Mendelsohn, *Zionism in Poland: The Formative Years, 1915–1926* (New Haven, Conn., 1981), p. 20. To be sure, many highly visible members of the Warsaw bourgeoisie were Jewish or of Jewish origin (the distinction was not always clear). See, for example, Ryszard Kołodziejczyk, *Burżuazja polska w XIX i XX wieku: Szkice historyczne* (Warsaw, 1979), and *Jan Bloch, 1836–1902: Szkic do portretu "króla polskich kolei"* (Warsaw, 1983).

66. The Russian representative was, in both the Third and Fourth Dumas, the notorious Polonophobe S. N. Alekseev. On this figure, formerly a teacher of Latin at a Warsaw gymnasium, see AGAD, GGW 9012, k. 106v. It should be kept in mind that total suffrage in Warsaw was limited to 80,000 people, or well under 10 percent of the city's population.

67. Wieczorkiewicz, "Polityka rosyjska," p. 732. It should be noted that Wieczorkiewicz generally favors the Poles over the Jews and, after 1912, accuses Russian liberals and the Kadets of bad faith in their championing of the Jewish cause against the Poles (see esp. p. 817, n. 237).

68. Kucharzewski had stated publicly that "I am a supporter of the principle of Jewish equal rights." Quoted in Stephen D. Corrsin, *Warsaw before the First World War*, p. 95. For more detail on the 1912 Duma election in Warsaw, see pp. 89–104. For a defense of Kucharzewski from a progressive (and anti-ND) point of view, see Leo Belmont, "Dlaczego przepadł p. Kucharzewski," in Leo Belmont and Jerzy Huzarski, *Zwycięstwo Romana Dmowskiego* (Warsaw, n.d. [ca. 1913]), pp. 40–81. On the Fourth Duma elections in Warsaw, see also AGAD, PomGGW 1138, 1149.

69. On the 1912 election in Warsaw, see Corrsin, "Political and Social Change in Warsaw," pp. 273–322. The Jewish point of view may be found in I. A. Kleinman, *Mezhdu molotom i nakoval'nei: Pol'sko-evreiskii krizis* (St. Petersburg, 1910), and in Kleinman's innumerable articles in *Novyi voskhod* during this period. Kleinman reports on the 1912 elections in "Pered vyborami v Pol'she," *Novyi voskhod*, no. 22 (May 31, 1912), pp. 4–5; no. 23 (June 7, 1912), pp. 9–11; no. 33 (August 16, 1912), pp. 5–7; and "Posle vyborov: Pis'ma iz Varshavy i Lodzi," *Novyi voskhod*, no. 45 (November 15, 1912), pp. 7–10. Łódź actually sent a Jewish delegate, Dr. Mejer Bomasz, to the Fourth Duma.

70. The boycott also disquieted Russian authorities in the area. See Skalon's letter dated May 20, 1913, to minister of internal affairs Maklakov, in RGIA, f. 821, op. 128, 1913, d. 989, ll. 17–20. For more on the government's perceptions of the boycott, see the Warsaw city report for 1912 in RGIA, f. 1284, op. 194, 1913, d. 89, l. 4; "O boikote poliakami evreev v Privislinskom krae," in GARF, f. 102, 4 d-vo, 1912, d. 310; "Pamiatnaia Zapiska pomoshchika varshavskogo general-gubernatora Utgofa o nastroenii v Tsarstve Pol'skom," in APW, T. 24, sygn. 261 (1913); also AGAD, PomGGW 1212; GARF, f. 579, op. 1, 1912, d. 1977.

71. Chmielewski, *Polish Question*, p. 145.

72. On the differences between the Duma and the State Council, see the internal MVD memorandum of November 10, 1913, in RGIA, f. 1276, op. 5, 1909, d. 44, ll. 414–18. This document saw the two main issues as being language and the extent of government supervision (*nadzor*).

73. *GSSO*, sess. 9 (1913–1914), *Prilozhenie*, p. 301. Gurko received his mandate to the State Council from the Tver' provincial zemstvo (ibid., p. 295). Ibid., pp. 341–47. Radziszewski, *Warszawa*, p. 42. Radziszewski continues: "on the other hand, one may certainly grant a worse system of self-government." The bill was first introduced to the State Council plenum on December 4, 1912, but was sent back to committee as insufficiently prepared. See *GSSO*, s. 8, zased. 5 (December 4, 1912), cols. 149–59. The bill was returned to the plenum some five months later. *GSSO*, s. 8, zased. 27 (April 3, 1913), cols. 1373–413. See also Avrekh, *Stolypin i tret'ia Duma*, p. 104.

74. Among the changes was the removal of the offending phrase *Tsarstvo Pol'skoe* (Kingdom of Poland) from the bill's name and replacement with the names of the nine Polish gubernii (with the formation of the Kholm Province in 1912 Siedlce Province disappeared, leaving only nine provinces in the Vistula country).

See *GSSO*, s. 8, zased. 29 (April 5, 1913), cols. 1507–50. The bill was passed during the same meeting. Strictly speaking, the State Council did not reject the bill but merely handed it back to the Duma–State Council special commission. The effect, however, was the same. *GSSO*, s. 9, zased. 6 (November 29, 1913), col. 197.

75. Avrekh, *Stolypin i tret'ia Duma*, p. 107; RGIA, f. 1276, op. 5, 1909, d. 44, l. 494.

76. RGIA, f. 1276, op. 5, 1909, d. 44, ll. 341–47. For the main objections expressed in the State Council regarding the use of Polish in the city governments, see *GSSO*, s. 8, cols. 1404–13.

77. RGIA, f. 1276, op. 5, 1909, d. 44, ll. 478–91.

78. *GSSO*, s. 9, zased. 40 (May 12, 1914), col. 2131. Specifically, the State Council rejected the Duma version of "point 4, article 31, section 23" on the language question by 87 votes to 71. Goremykin's remarks (cols. 2081–82) were addressed specifically to this issue.

79. RGIA, f. 1276, op. 5, 1909, d. 44, l. 495. When Goremykin was called to the premiership in January 1914, he reportedly compared himself with an "old fur coat, pulled out of the mothballs [*staraia shuba, vynuta iz naftalina*]." S. S. Ol'denburg, *Tsarstvovanie Imperatora Nikolaia II* (Washington, 1981), p. 492.

80. On discussions concerning the future of Poland after the war, see D. N. Chikhachev, *K voprosu o budushchem ustroistve Pol'shi* (Petrograd, 1917); also RGIA, f. 1162, op. 4, 1915, d. 57, and f. 1276, op. 10, 1914, dd. 71–73. The law was published in *Sobranie uzakonenii i rasporiazhenii pravitel'stva*, no. 91, ot. 1 (March 22, 1915), article 762; it bears the date March 17, 1915. For the negative reaction, see "Pogrzębanie samorządu," *Przegląd narodowy* 7, no. 5 (May 1914), pp. 533–36. The law is discussed in rather sober (but not approving) terms in a review in *Gorodskoe delo* 5, no. 4 (April 1915), pp. 338–41, which ends with the sentence, "True self-government remains in the future [*eshche vperedi*] both for the Kingdom of Poland and the Russian Empire."

Chapter 9: The Dubious Triumph of Russian Nationalism

1. Henceforth I shall use the Russian form of the city's and region's names, Kholm and Kholmshchina. I do this merely out of expediency and because this is primarily a study of Russian governmental policy and national psychology. The city of Kholm and the surrounding region had practically no Great Russian residents, though the form "Kholm" would also correspond to Ukrainian usage. The city now lies in the Republic of Poland and is known as Chełm. The Yiddish form of the city name resembles the Polish. In Yiddish folklore (perhaps not incidentally), Khelmers are renowned fools, like the German Schildbürger.

2. According to one official source, in 1910 there resided in Kholm 7,809 Jews (44.5%); 4,808 "Russians"/Orthodox (27.4%); 4,667 Poles/Catholics (26.6%); 253 Germans/Protestants (1.4%); and 18 Moslems/Tatars (0.1%), *Goroda Rossii v 1910 g.* (St. Petersburg, 1914), p. 792. (Note the exact correlation between nationality and religious affiliation in this instance.)

3. The lines are from Pushkin's furious "Klevetnikam Rossii" (To the slanderers of Russia), written in 1831 during the Polish uprising.

4. The term *polskość* refers to the essence of Polishness. On this concept and its importance, see E. Starczewski, "Czym jest polskość," in *Nasze sprawy* (Kiev, 1916). It is interesting that there is no corresponding Russian term. When Russian nationalists or the imperial bureaucracy spoke of "Russians" in the Kholm area, they had in mind the mainly peasant Ukrainian population.

5. However, there was no clear agreement on the question of who was to be

considered a Russian. See, for example, the discussions of the definition of "Russian" for service privileges *(sluzhebnye l'goty)* in the West, in RGIA, f. 1284, op. 190, 1900, d. 85. For a somewhat later definition of "Pole," see the report *(doklad)* by one K. A. Strol'man, given to the MVD commissions of the Council on Local Economy in 1909, in RGIA, f. 1278, op. 2, 1910, d. 1171, ll. 101–2. Strol'man speaks against using "Catholic" as synonymous with "Polish," but in practice this was nearly always done. For a somewhat earlier discussion of the issue "who is a Pole" *(chto takoe litso pol'skogo proiskhozhdeniia)*, see Graf Leliva, *Russko-pol'skie otnosheniia*, pp. 5–14.

6. For some examples of Russian and Polish polemics on the Kholm question, see *Istoricheskaia zapiska o kholmskoi Rusi i gorode Kholme, o sud'bakh Unii v kholmskom krae i sovremennom polozhenii v nem uniatskogo voprosa*, printed by the Holy Synod (St. Petersburg, 1902); *K voprosu o vydelenii Kholmskoi Rusi*, printed by the Galitsko-Russkoe Blagotvoritel'noe Obshchestvo v S. Peterburge (St. Petersburg, 1906); *Czterdzieści lat prześladowania Unii na Podlasiu* (Cracow, 1909); Aleksander Janowski, *Chełmszczyzna* (Warsaw/Lublin, 1918). Janowski's work adorns its title page with a crown of thorns, which should give the reader an indication of the quality of the argumentation within.

7. Szymon Askenazy, "Gubernia Chełmska," *Biblioteka Warszawska* 1, no. 1 (January 1909), p. 217. On this period in general, see Zyzniewski, "Russian Policy." Zyzniewski published the conclusions of his dissertation in the article "Miljutin and the Polish Question," pp. 237–48. See also the introduction to Arthur K. Steinberg, "The Kholm Question in the Russian Duma Period, 1906–1912: Opinion and Action" (Ph.D. diss., Kent State University, 1972). On Cherkasskii's efforts vis-à-vis the Uniates of the Kholm area, see "Kniaz' Cherkasskii i kholmskie greko-uniaty," *Kholmsko-Varshavskii eparkhial'nyi vestnik* 2, nos. 9–12, 16–18, 19 (1878).

8. The literature on the elimination of the Uniate church in the Kholm-Pobuzh'e area is large, and rarely without serious bias. For the period leading up to 1875, see the essays included in E. M. Kryzhanovskii, *Russkoe Zabuzh'e: Kholmshchina i Podliash'e*, (St. Petersburg, 1911); and A. Dem'ianovich, "Stremlenie uniatov b. Kholmskoi eparkhii k vozsoedineniiu s pravoslavnoiu Tserkov'iu s 1837 do 1875 gg.," *Kholmsko-Varshavskii eparkhial'nyi vestnik* 2, nos. 4, 5, 6, 8, 21, 23 (1878). For a Polish Catholic view (written by the Suffragan Bishop of Poznan), see Edward Likowski, *Dzieje Kościoła Unickiego na Litwie i Rusi w XVIII i XIX wieku uważane głównie ze względu na przyczyny jego upadku*, 2d ed. (Warsaw, 1906), esp. vol. 2, pp. 139–260. More recent works include Roman Grabowski, "Likwidacja Kościoła Grekokatolickiego w Królestwie Polskim, 1864–1875," *Studenckie zeszyty naukowe Uniwersytetu Jagiellońskiego* 5 (Cracow, 1985), pp. 69–101, and Ievhen Pasternak, *Narys istorii Kholmshchyny i Pidliashshia: Novishi chasy* (Winnipeg, 1968), esp. pp. 68–76, 81–100.

9. Quoted in Batiushkov, *Volyn'*, p. 246. On the Synod and Union of Brest, see Oskar Halecki, *From Florence to Brest, 1439–1596* (Hamden, Conn., 1968), "The Origins of the Union of Brest," pp. 199–286, and "The Union of Brest," pp. 287–419. An interesting recent collection on the origins and history of the Union of Brest and the Uniates is Ryszard Łużny, Franciszek Ziejka, and Andrzej Kępiński, eds., *Unia brzeska: Geneza, dzieje, i konsekwencje w kulturze narodów słowiańskich* (Cracow, 1994).

10. On the Uniate church in the west (especially northwest) of Russia, see M. O. Koialovich, *Litovskaia tserkovnaia Uniia*, 2 vols. (St. Petersburg, 1859–1861), and *Istoriia vozsoedineniia zapadnorusskikh uniatov starykh vremen;* and I. Filevich, *Vopros o vozsoedinenii zapadno-russkikh uniatov v ego noveishei postanovke* (Warsaw, 1891).

11. On the events leading up to the "reunion" of 1875, see Grabowski, "Lik-

widacja Kościoła Grekokatolickiego." A contemporary, quite detailed account is "Prześladowanie Unii na Podlasiu," *Przegląd polski* 10, no. 10 (Cracow, April 1875), pp. 47–81.

12. *Istoricheskaia zapiska o kholmskoi Rusi i gorode Kholme, o sud'bakh Unii v kholmskom krae i sovremennom polozhenii v nem uniatskogo voprosa* (St. Petersburg, 1902), pp. 34–46 (45). This pamphlet was published "by order of the *Ober-Prokuror* of the Holy Synod." On this episode, see T. Weeks, "The 'End' of the Uniate Church in the Russian Empire: The *Vozsoedinenie* of 1875," *Jahrbücher für Geschichte Osteuropas*, vol.44, no.1 (1996).

13. These quotations are taken from the annual report for 1875 of the governor of Lublin Province, in RGIA, f. 1270, op. 1, 1875, d. 1526, l. 153. The Siedlce governor—who is generally mentioned as the true instigator of the "reunion"—did not mention the Uniates at all in his report for that year (ibid., ll. 632–35).

14. Askenazy, "Gubernia Chełmska," p. 218. The quotation is from S. M. Karetnikov, *Kholmskaia guberniia: Geografichesko-istoricheskii ocherk* (Lubny, 1913), p. 199.

15. For the government views on the eve of "reunification," see the March 12, 1875, report by minister of internal affairs L. Makov, "O polozhenii Uniatskogo dela v Liublinskoi i Sedletskoi gubernii," in RGIA, f. 821, op. 4, 1875, d. 1607, ll. 1–37. This report (esp. l. 29v) stresses that Uniates should not be forced into Orthodoxy. Further discussion of the Uniate issue in the Committee for the Polish Kingdom is found in RGIA, f. 1270, op. 1, 1875, d. 1110.

16. For example, the MVD report to the Council of Ministers on the Kholm project (January 7, 1907) stated that the quick and superficial police measures that brought the Uniates into the Orthodox church tended to have a superficial effect and "did not penetrate into the popular consciousness [*ne pronikla v narodnoe soznanie*]." RGIA, f. 1276, op. 2, 1906, d. 35, l. 106. An official account reported, "The Uniate question not only did not disappear [after 1875] but on the contrary gained particular interest and emphasis in light of the Russian tasks in the region." *Istoricheskaia zapiska o kholmskoi Rusi*, p. 47.

17. W. Reymont, *Z ziemi chełmskiej: Wyrażenia i notatki* (Warsaw, 1911), originally published in *Tygodnik Illustrowany*. This book was published in Russian as *Iz Kholmskogo Kraia* (St. Petersburg, 1910), translated by the well-known Slavicist and Polonophile Aleksandr L. Pogodin. The book's bias is obviously for the Uniate peasant and against the Orthodox church and Russian authorities, which are portrayed as brutal, intolerant, and inhumane. A facsimile edition of Reymont's work has recently been published (Warsaw: Wydawnictwo Archidiecezji Warszawskiej, 1990) with an informative afterword on the Uniates in the Polish Kingdom by Hanna Dylągowa.

18. See, for example, RGIA, f. 797, op. 73–1903, 2 otd., stol 3, d. 158, in which the bishop of the Orthodox Kholm-Warsaw Diocese (Kholmsko-Varshavskaia Eparkhiia) complained of Catholic propaganda being spread among former Uniates. Even after 1905, the spreading of religious propaganda with the aim to convert Orthodox Christians to other confessions remained proscribed.

19. Jan Urban, *Wśród Unitów na Podlasiu: Pamiętniki wycieczek misyjnych* (Cracow, 1923). Urban, a Jesuit, was himself engaged in missionary work in the Podlasie region in 1902–1903.

20. On the Towarzystwo Opieki nad Unitami, see Wieczorkiewicz, "Polityka rosyjska," p. 552. Regarding this organization's activities after 1905, see "Dar Chełmski" (APAN, Papiery S. Kozickiego, sygn. 30, t. 7). The facility of spreading Catholic propaganda from Galicia to the Kholm area was stressed in A. Obolenskii's

report (ca. 1898) on the "Uniate question" in the Kholm area (WAPL, Lublin, Kanc. gubernatora lubelskiego: 1897, 3/2 t, kk. 60–66). For an example of the Catholic-Uniate propaganda, see the flyers entitled "Bracia Unici" (Brethren Uniates) and "Bracia Rodacy" (Brethren Countrymen) in RGIA, f. 797, op. 75–1905, 2 otd., stol 3, d. 161, ll. 19–20.

21. See, for example, the Lublin governor's annual report for 1905, in which he states that the Poles of western Lublin Province are at least equally in need of the russifying influence of government schools as the former Uniates in the Kholm area. RGIA, f. 1284, op. 194, 1906, d. 85, l. 8.

22. RGIA, *Chital'nyi Zal*, op. 1, d. 84, 1903, p. 7. On the relative numbers and income of Orthodox and Catholic clergy in the Kholm area, see Henryk Wiercieński, "Świątynie i duchowieństwo dwóch głównych wyznań chrześcijańskich," in his *W sprawie wydzielenia Chełmszczyzny* (Warsaw, 1910), pp. 49–64. Wiercieński (p. 51) claims that 2,090 rubles were spent on each Orthodox priest *(pop)* in 1905, whereas Catholic priests had to content themselves on the average with a scant 207 rubles. On the efforts to strengthen Orthodoxy in the area, see "O merakh k uprocheniiu pravoslaviia i podderzhaniia russkoi narodnosti v srede uniatov Privislinskogo kraia," in RGIA, f. 1284, op. 190, 1886, d. 420. Note the conflation of "Orthodox" and "Russian" in this file's title.

23. Askenazy, "Gubernia Chełmska," pp. 218–20. The existence of two calendars caused many problems, it was pointed out, for Catholic and Orthodox holidays were celebrated on different days. For example, Catholic Christmas would generally precede the Orthodox holiday by one or more weeks and the Catholic festivities would often attract the Orthodox. The difficulties were especially acute in mixed marriages, and the tendency, according to this source, was to neglect the Orthodox holidays in favor of the Catholic. "Neudobstva ot dvukh kalendarei," *Kholmsko-Varshavskii eparkhial'nyi vestnik* 14, no. 5 (March 1/13, 1890), pp. 71–72.

24. RGIA, f. 797, op. 68, 1 otd., stol 1, d. 4, ll. 4–12 (1897), ll. 41–65 (1899). In his second letter, Imeretinskii (l. 60) emphasized that "at the present time the higher local authorities are taking all possible measures to protect the Russian nationality [*narodnost'*] from being catholicized and polonized and the formation of a Kholm Province can not provide any new directives [*ukazaniia*] to this matter."

25. AGAD, PomGGW 1a (1898). Tkhorzhevskii's proposals and the Warsaw governor general's responses are in the Lublin archive, WAPL. Kanc. gubernatora lubelskiego, 1897: 3t, cz. 1. Tkhorzhevskii's annual report for 1900 is quoted in Askenazy, "Gubernia Chełmska," p. 222. The *otchet* may be found in RGIA, f. 797, op. 68, 1 otd., stol 1, d. 4, ll. 80–84.

26. On Pobedonostsev's interest in the Uniate question, see RGIA, f. 1574, op. 2, 1881, d. 61. Criticisms of the proposal may be found in "Zhurnal vysochaishe utverzhdennogo v 14–yi den' marta 1902 g. osobogo Soveshchaniia po voprosu ob obrazovanii kholmskoi gubernii. 26–go marta 1902 goda," published by S. Askenazy under the title *Sprawa gubernii chełmskiej* (Cracow, 1907), pp. 16–18.

27. Quoted in Askenazy, "Gubernia Chełmska," p. 226. The complete conclusions of the commission are in Askenazy, ed., *Sprawa gubernii chełmskiej*, pp. 43–46. This conclusion closely echoed Imeretinskii's argument of three years earlier that forming the new province could only be successful if combined with severe anti-Polish measures as in the Western Provinces. RGIA, f. 797, op. 68, 1 otd., stol 1, d. 4, l. 59.

28. I repeat, these are not crude works of propaganda, though their pro-Orthodox, pro-Russian bias is evident. Batiushkov's works most pertinent here are *Podoliia, Volyn'*, and most especially *Kholmskaia Rus': Istoricheskie sud'by russkogo*

Zabuzh'ia (St. Petersburg, 1887). In the work on Podolia, Batiushkov is described as active in "church-building activities [*tserkovno-stroitel'naia deiatel'nost'*]" in that province in 1863. By 1871, he was a member of the council *(sovet)* of the Ministry of Education, having achieved the third-highest rank *(tainyi sovetnik)* in 1866, most likely because of his work in Podolia. *Spisok grazhdanskim chinam pervykh trekh klassov*, p. 264.

29. The Jews are not entirely absent from Batiushkov's accounts, but very nearly so. In his works, their role in the history of the region was almost entirely passive, becoming significant only when Jews were portrayed as being in league with the Poles.

30. Batiushkov, *Podoliia*, p. 264.

31. It is not entirely beside the point to note that Krzyżanowski is a typically Polish surname. For example, Mme. Bogdanovich spoke of Evfimii's son, Sergei Efimovich (one of the architects of the ultimately successful Kholm project), as a "Pole-Anarchist." Bogdanovich, *Tri poslednikh samoderzhavtsa*, p. 351 (entry for May 26, 1905).

32. I. Filevich, Foreword to Kryzhanovskii, *Russkoe Zabuzh'e*, pp. xxxviii–xliv. A detailed account of Kryzhanovskii's life and career, with bibliography, may be found in the foreword to his collected works, by E. M. Kryzhanovskii, *Sobranie sochinenii*, vol. 1, pp. iii–xlix. The life and career of Kryzhanovskii *père* are also featured in I. Sidorskii, "Efim Mikhailovich Kryzhanovskii v 1865–1888 gg.," *Russkaia starina* 66 (March 1890), pp. 717–26.

33. Robert F. Byrnes, *Pobedonostsev: His Life and Thought* (Bloomington, Ind., 1968), p. 193; Evfimii M. Kryzhanovskii, *Sobranie sochinenii*, 3 vols. (Kiev, 1890); Kryzhanovskii, *Russkoe Zabuzh'e*, p. 428.

34. Evlogii (Mitropolit), *Put' moei zhizni: Vospominaniia Mitropolita Evlogiia*, T. Manukhina, ed. (Paris, 1947), p. 150. Evlogii later became Metropolitan of the Russian Orthodox church in Western Europe. For more on this important figure, see Paweł Piotr Wieczorkiewicz, "Biskup Eulogiusz i oderwanie Chełmszczyzny od Królestwa Polskiego," in *Historia XIX i XX wieku: Studia i szkice. Prace ofiarowane Henrykowi Jabłońskiemu w siedemdziesiątą rocznicę urodziń* (Wrocław, 1979), pp. 86–98; and the obituary by P. B. Anderson, "Metropolitan Eulogius," *Slavonic and East European Review* 47 (1947), p. 562.

35. Evlogii's telegram to Pobedonostsev, dated April 6, 1905, on the solution of the Uniate question *(reshenie uniatskogo voprosa)* may be found in RGIA, f. 797, op. 75–1905, 2 otd., stol 3, d. 161, l. 1. Among other things, in this telegram Evlogii stressed that granting complete religious freedom would mean the loss of a hundred thousand former Uniates for the Russian people. Evlogii's second telegram to Pobedonostsev, May 2, 1905, may be found in RGIA, f. 821, op. 10, 1905, d. 1064, l. 21.

36. RGIA, f. 797, op. 75–1905, 2 otd., stol 3, d. 161, l. 22.

37. The conclusions of the Committee of Ministers deliberations were published in "Osobyi zhurnal Komiteta Ministrov 25go Ianvaria 1905 g. o poriadke vypolneniia punkta 6 Im. Vys. Ukaza 12 Dekabria 1904 g." RGIA, f. 797, op. 75–1905, 2 otd., stol 3, d. 97, ll. 2–4. This file also contains copies of circulars sent out to governors regarding the implementation of these decisions. For one contemporary Russian nationalist reaction to the decree of religious freedom and its effect in the Kholm/Podlasie area, see "Iz Podliash'ia," *Okrainy Rossii*, no. 25 (August 20, 1906), pp. 422–23, and "Vopros o sud'be Kholmskoi Rusi," ibid., no. 41 (December 10, 1906), pp. 687–89.

38. RGIA, f. 797, op. 75–1905, 2 otd., stol 3, d. 161, ll. 76–79. The letter is dated June 7, 1905, za no. 722. Maksimovich ended his letter by emphasizing that Catholic

propaganda and proselytizing could not be allowed and that special measures should be taken to strengthen the Orthodox church in these areas.

39. According to *Tserkovnye vedomosti* (March 6, 1910), there were 119,728 conversions from Orthodoxy to Catholicism in the Kholm diocese. John S. Curtiss, *Church and State in Russia: The Last Years of the Empire, 1900–1917* (New York, 1940), p. 228. After the shock of 1905, the government gathered many statistics on apostates from Orthodoxy *(otpavshie ot pravoslaviia)*. See, for example, "Statistika otpavshikh," in RGIA, f. 821, op. 10, 1905, d. 287, and similar compilations may be found in dd. 263, 270, 285, 288, 290. Since these figures came from governors' reports, however, their accuracy may be questioned.

40. RGIA, f. 1278, op. 2, 1909, d. 883, l. 1201. In his report to the Duma regarding the Kholm project, D. N. Chikhachev stated that according to official statistics some 120,000 Orthodox converted, whereas unofficially figures of up to 180,000 were mooted. Chikhachev, *K obrazovaniiu Kholmskoi gubernii* (St. Petersburg, 1912), p. 92.

41. Stefan Dziewulski, "Statystyka ludności guberni lubelskiej i siedleckiej wobec projektu utworzenia gubernii chełmskiej," *Ekonomista* (Warsaw, 1909), pp. 157–93. These figures include natural growth and reduction due to births and deaths. One should also keep in mind that in 1897, according to official figures, the total Orthodox population of both provinces (and not just their eastern districts) amounted to only 368,872 (*Pervaia vseobshchaia perepis' naseleniia, Obshchii svod*, vol. 1, p. 256). Although this number may have increased somewhat in the ensuing eight years, even Dziewulski's figures indicate a conversion of nearly a third of the local Orthodox population.

42. For the Polish view, published in the Kadet organ, see Graf V. Tyshkevich, "Kholmskaia Rus' i poliaki," *Rech'*, no. 253 (December 28, 1906), p. 2; I. A. K[uchinskii], "K voprosu ob otdelenii Kholmskoi Rusi," *Rech'*, no. 289 (December 7, 1907), p. 5. For a more nationalist view, see Henryk Wiercieński, "Czy potrzebną była propaganda katolicka?" and "Czy propaganda była możliwą?" in his *W sprawie wydzielenia Chełmszczyzny*, pp. 113–21. Wiercieński concluded that propaganda was neither necessary nor possible.

For the role of the Catholic missionaries, see, for example, Wieczorkiewicz, "Polityka rosyjska," p. 493, where he states that the conversions in 1905 were much aided by the activities of the Liga Narodowa and the Towarzystwo Opieki nad Unitami, led by Aleksander Zawadzki, also known as Ojciec (Father) Prokop. Wieczorkiewicz's statement is corroborated by testimony given in 1920 by participants in pro-Uniate (and anti–Kholm Province) activities. "Dar Chełmski," in APAN, Papiery S. Kozickiego, sygn. 30, t. 7.

43. Evlogii, *Put' moei zhizni*, pp. 150–51. Evlogii stated, for example, that Count Zamoyski offered a cow to every family that converted to Catholicism. Similar accusations were repeated ad nauseam in *Okrainy Rossii*—see the essays from this journal collected under the title *Kholmskaia Rus' i poliaki* (St. Petersburg, 1907). The anonymous author of these articles is A. Budilovich, a close friend of Evlogii's, an Orthodox priest from the Kholm area and former teacher of assistant minister of internal affairs S. E. Kryzhanovskii. RGIA, f. 1327, op. 2, 1905, d. 18, l. 29.

44. Evlogii, *Put' moei zhizni*, p. 88. A short biography of Evlogii (his secular name was Vasilii Semenovich Grigorievskii) may be found in *Kholmskaia guberniia, Prilozhenie*, pp. 113–16. From December 1902 until June 1905, Evlogii's title was Episkop Liublinskii, Vikarii Kholmsko-Varshavskoi Eparkhii. *Kholmskaia guberniia* (Kholm, 1914), *Prilozhenie*, p. 114.

45. Evlogii, *Put' moei zhizni*, p. 124; "Uchrezhdenie samostoiatel'noi kholm-

skoi Eparkhii," *Kholmskaia guberniia*, p. 3; AGAD, GGW 7455. On Evlogii's election and the various ideas on measures to guarantee the election of a politically dependable Russian of Orthodox faith from the area, see RGIA, f. 1327, op. 2, 1905, d. 18; and AGAD, GGW 8860, 8965.

46. Evlogii, *Put' moei zhizni*, pp. 142, 149.

47. Jan Baudouin de Courtenay, *W sprawie porozumienia się ludów słowiańskich* (Warsaw, 1908), esp. pp. 27–30. Baudouin de Courtenay defends the individual's right to "national self-determination," to be of more than one nation or of no nation at all, regardless of origin. As he remarks, "A human being cannot be ethnographic material [*Człowiek nie może być materjałem etnograficznym*]" (p. 29).

48. Except V. Frantsev, who based his statistics on data gathered under the auspices of the Kholmskoe Sv.–Bogoroditskoe Bratstvo, a most Orthodox organization. Frantsev, *Karty russkogo*, p. xiv.

49. L. Dymsza, *Kholmskii vopros* (St. Petersburg, 1910), p. 31. Dymsza takes these figures from the *Obzor Sedletskoi Gubernii* for 1907 and 1909. It is possibly not a coincidence that this very A. Volzhin became the first governor of Kholm Province in 1913. Dymsza, the Polish Duma deputy from Siedlce Province, was a landowner and jurist. Part of Dymsza's personal archive is preserved in Moscow in GARF, f. 690. On Dymsza, see also the report from "Nachal'nik Sedletskogo gubernskogo zhandarmskogo upravleniia," November 13, 1907, in AGAD, PomGGW 727, k. 5. This report states that Dymsza and his wife regarded the Orthodox population of the area with great dislike and used extreme measures to polonize the area.

50. This lack of objective criteria distinguishing Russians and Poles was also manifest during deliberations regarding the election of a Duma delegate for the "Russian residents" of the Kholm area. At first the MVD strictly rejected the use of the religious factor *(priznak)* as incompatible with the post–April 17, 1905, religious freedom. In the end, in the Second and Third Dumas, however, the ministry was forced, faute de mieux, to adopt just this religious factor and elect the delegate, Evlogii, from the Orthodox congregations of the region. On the Duma elections from the Kholm area, see RGIA, f. 1327, op. 2, 1905, d. 18, and 1906, d. 65.

51. Dymsza, *Kholmskii vopros*, p. 37. Frantsev, *Karty russkogo*, p. xii. The failure to reach a compromise must be attributed to a variety of causes, most specifically the intractability of both sides. To quote one Polish source (and the sentiment was mutual among the Russians), "The Kholm question belongs to those issues in Polish politics that admit no compromise!" Tytus Komarnicki, *Obrona Chełmszczyzny w Dumie* (Warsaw, 1918), p. 31.

52. On the percentage of Orthodox population and Ukrainian *(malorusskii)* speakers in this area, see also Adam Zakrzewski (A. Z.), *Materialy k voprosu ob obrazovanii kholmskoi gubernii* (Warsaw, 1908), vol. 1, p. 63. Zakrzewski's views were closer to those of Jan Baudouin de Courtenay than to those of the majority of his compatriots. See, for example, his work *Zasada narodowości i przyszła Polska* (Warsaw, 1917), where he militates against Polish pretensions to the *kresy*, that is, the former western territory. Zakrzewski was also (and not entirely incidentally) a convinced Esperantist; see his *Historio de Esperanto, 1887–1912* (Warsaw, 1913).

53. Volume 2 of Zakrzewski, *Materialy*, is an update that takes into account the changes in the new government project, introduced to the Duma on April 24, 1909 (see pp. 30–33 for detailed statistics). The statistics in Dymsza, *Kholmskii vopros*, are especially useful because he gives statistics by *gmina* (commune), comparing seven different sources, both Russian and Polish. His statistics do not, however, include the area's Jewish population.

54. This sort of argument, emphasizing race *(plemennoi sostav)* over religion *(veroispovednyi printsip)* is used by Evlogii in the discussions of the Duma subcommittee on the Kholm project on November 9, 1911. RGIA, f. 821, op. 150, 1910, d. 210, ll. 25–26.

55. To be sure, the Catholic-Russian argument was not a completely new element in Russian nationalist discourse. The demand for depolonization *(raspoliachenie)* of the Catholic church in the Belorussian region rested on the same assumptions. See, for example, Vladimirov, *Istoriia raspoliacheniia*. However, as Vladimirov points out with considerable bitterness, when faced with strong Catholic opposition local authorities quickly abandoned *raspoliachenie*. That the authorities had previously frowned upon it is demonstrated by the case of one Planson, who was dismissed from government service because of his publication of a pamphlet on this subject. See "Ob uvolnenii ot sluzhby sovetnika smolenskogo gubernskogo pravleniia Plansona za napisanie vozzvanii k mirovym posrednikam o neobkhodimosti ustraneniia pol'skogo iazyka v katolicheskom bogosluzhenii," in RGIA, f. 1282, op. 2, 1868, d. 355. For a Polish view of this controversy, see Jan Przybyszewski, *Język rosyjski w katolickim rituale i w dodatkowem nabożeństwie* (Lvov, 1897). Przybyszewski goes so far as to call the use of Russian in Catholic services "a crime against God."

56. Frantsev, *Karty russkogo*, pp. xii, xiv.

57. Ibid., p. 20. The question read in Russian: "Na kakom iazyke govorit korennoe naselenie v nastoiashchee vremia?"

58. For a discussion of these statistics, see Stefan Dziewulski, *Statystyka projektu rządowego o wyodrębienie Chełmszczyzny w świetle krytyki* (Warsaw, 1910). For excruciatingly detailed statistics regarding the nationality and religion of the inhabitants of the future Kholm guberniia, see RGIA, f. 1278, op. 2, 1909, d. 883, ll. 316–71.

59. Evlogii remembers this visit in *Put' moei zhizni*, pp. 155–56. Here he recounts the oft-repeated anecdote that, when minister of internal affairs A. Bulygin failed to respond to the delegates' "Khristos voskrese!" (Christ has risen!), the mainly peasant delegation concluded that the rumors of the Tsar's and government's conversion to Catholicism were indeed true. Only when Nicholas II himself replied, "Voistinu voskres!" (Verily he did rise!), were the delegates reassured.

60. Some years earlier, on the text of Lublin governor Tkhorzhevskii's annual report for 1900, which proposed the creation of a separate Kholm Province, Nicholas II had written, "Ves'ma sochuvstvuiu etoi mysli" (I greatly sympathize with this idea), quoted in *Sprawa gubernii Chełmskiej*, p. 21.

61. Some of the petitions may be found in RGIA, f. 1288, op. 4, 1906, d. 73, ch. 1, ll. 41–70. Similar letters—but written by local Poles and Catholics and opposing the Kholm project—are collected in GARF, f. 5122, op. 1, 1907, dd. 39–43.

62. "Memoriia Soveta Ministrov," April 4, 1906, in RGIA, f. 1276, op. 2, 1906, d. 35, ll. 22–24; see also ll. 13–21 for the MVD *Predstavlenie*, "O vydelenii vostochnykh uezdov liublinskoi i sedletskoi gubernii iz Privislinskogo kraia" (March 6, 1906, no. 4645).

63. Ibid., ll. 42–74. The conference met from November 23 to December 14, 1906, and discussed such measures as the borders of the new province and the abolition of the Gregorian calendar there. Unlike later bodies within the Duma and the MVD, this conference did not count Archbishop Evlogii's name among its members (l. 42).

64. "Osobyi Zhurnal Soveta Ministrov" (January 3, 1907), in ibid., ll. 89A–92. See also the MVD's predstavlenie dated January 7, 1907, no. 409, in ibid., ll. 105–51. Despite the discrepancy in dates, it would appear that the Council of Ministers had

used this project (or a very similar text) in its discussions.

65. "Osobyi Zhurnal Soveta Ministrov" (January 13, 1909), in ibid., ll. 200–211.

66. RGIA, f. 1278, op. 2, 1909, d. 883, ll. 3–43; also in f. 1276, op. 2, 1906, d. 35, ll. 652–99. The Duma period of the Kholm question has received considerable attention in recent historiography. See Steinberg, "The Kholm Question"; Klaus Kindler, *Die Cholmer Frage, 1905–1918* (Frankfurt-am-Main, 1990); Avrekh, *Stolypin i tret'ia Duma*, pp. 108–50; Chmielewski, *Polish Question*, pp. 111–37, and "Separation of Chełm from Poland," *Polish Review* 15, no. 1 (winter 1970), pp. 67–86; M. Wierzchowski, "Sprawa Chełmszczyzny w rosyjskiej Dumie Państwowej," *Przegląd historyczny* 57, no. 1 (1966), pp. 97–125; Zygmunt Łukawski, "Koło Polskie w rosyjskiej Dumie Państwowej wobec kwestii chełmskiej," *Zeszyty naukowe Uniwersytetu Jagiellońskiego: Prace historyczne*, zeszyt 17 (Cracow, 1966), pp. 159–82; and Wieczorkiewicz, "Polityka rosyjska," pp. 479–682.

67. Dymsza claimed that officials in the area were guilty of harassment (and worse) of the Polish and Catholic population in the Kholm region. See, for these complaints, GARF, f. 690, op. 1, d. 56, and RGIA, f. 1276, op. 7, 1911, d. 617.

68. *GDSO* 3, s. 5, ch. 1, zased. 30 (November 25, 1911), col. 2608–20 (2619). I have translated the phrase *russkaia gosudarstvennost'* (a hazy term at best) as "the Russian state idea." The long quotation is from ibid., col. 2620.

69. For Polish and liberal opinions on the Kholm project see, for example, the following speeches: by Dymsza, in ibid., cols. 2620–50; by Uvarov (a progressive Russian), in ibid., zased. 31 (November 26, 1911), cols. 2692–711; by Harusewicz, in ibid., zased. 31 (November 26, 1911), cols. 2711–29; and by Rodichev (a Kadet), in ibid., zased. 36 (December 2, 1911), cols. 3159–71. For some of their arguments, see the speeches by Evlogii, in ibid., zased. 30, cols. 2650–66, and zased. 31, cols. 2675–92; by Markov 2, in ibid., zased. 46 (January 16, 1912), cols. 319–31; and by Alekseev, in ibid., zased. 50 (January 20, 1912), cols. 632–43.

70. It should be noted that the Duma subcommittee on the Kholm project was divided in its conclusions regarding the advisability of creating the Kholm Province. The majority report is found in "Formula perekhoda k ocherednym delam, predlagaemaia komissieiu po napravleniiu zakonodatel'nykh predpolozhenii k zakonoproektu Ministra Vnutrennikh Del o vydelenii iz sostava Tsarstva Pol'skogo vostochnykh chastei Liublinskoi i Sedletskoi gubernii s obrazovaniem iz nikh osoboi Kholmskoi gubernii," in *GDSO* 3, s. 5, *Prilozhenie*, no. 49 (13 pp.). The dissenting view (over twice as long as the majority report) appeared as the "Osoboe mnenie men'shinstva komissii," in ibid., no. 50 (30 pp.). The dissenters included Koło members Dymsza, Harusewicz, and Parczewski as well as the progressivist N. Rumiantsev, the Kadet A. Nikol'skii, and S. Maksudov, member of the Moslem group.

71. See "Zamechaniia chlena Gosudarstvennogo Soveta N. A. Zinov'eva," in RGIA, f. 1278, op. 2, 1909, d. 883, ll. 1147–54, and "Zapiska chlena Gosudarstvennogo Soveta I. A. Shebeko," in ibid., d. 883, ll. 1155–63.

72. As might be expected, the Polish members of the State Council bitterly attacked the project. See, for example, the following speeches: by Shebeko, in *GSSO*, s. 7 (1911–1912), zased. 75 (June 13, 1912), cols. 4922–40; by Khrzanovskii, in ibid., zased. 76, cols. 4987–96; and by Potocki, in ibid., zased. 76, cols. 5041–48. Ibid., zased. 77, col. 5202.

73. S. E. Kryzhanovskii's letter was dated April 4, 1910, and can be found in RGIA, f. 1276, op. 2, 1906, d. 35, ll. 267–69. "Ob obrazovanii mezhduvedomstvennoi komissii dlia ob"edineniia pravitel'stvennykh po kholmskomu kraiu meropriiatii," RGIA, f. 1276, op. 2, 1906, d. 35, ll. 285–87.

74. For the dealings of the commission, protocols, and discussions, see RGIA, f. 821, op. 10, 1912, dd. 233, 234, and 1913, dd. 241, 243.

75. For the nationalist view, see the many articles on Kholm in *Okrainy Rossii*, 1909–1912. Once again the dissenting voice on the right was Meshcherskii's. See "Boltovnia po kholmskomu voprosu," *Grazhdanin*, no. 4 (January 22, 1912). For the Polish side of the issue, see "Chełmszczyzna," *Myśl niepodległa*, no. 92 (March, 1909), pp. 341–46, and "W sprawie Chełmskiej," *Kraj*, no. 18 (May 7/20, 1909), p. 4.

The liberal Ukrainian view may be found in M. Hrushevs'kyi, "Za ukrainskuiu kost'," in *Osvobozhdenie i ukrainskii vopros* (St. Petersburg, 1907), pp. 278–91, originally published in *Rada*, nos. 2, 3, 4 (1907); O. Bilousenko, *Kholmska sprava* (Kiev, 1909); O. Bilousenko, "Ukrainskie momenty v kholmskom voprose," *Ukrainskaia zhizn'*, no. 3 (March 1912), pp. 10–23. An interesting exchange between two liberals—one sympathetic to the Poles, the other to the Ukrainians—is found in A. Pogodin, "Kholmskii vopros i ukrainskoe dvizhenie," *Moskovskii ezhenedel'nik* 3, no. 16 (April 13, 1908), pp. 43–50, and B. Kistiakovskii, "Kholmshchina i ukraintsy," in *Moskovskii Ezhenedel'nik* 3, no. 19 (May 13, 1908), pp. 32–46, and no. 20, pp. 17–28.

76. *Okrainy Rossii*, no. 17 (April 28, 1912), p. 252. The article is reacting to the Duma approval of the bill. See also Avrekh, *Stolypin i tret'ia Duma*, p. 147. Still, the governor of Siedlce Province (soon to be the first governor of Kholm) complained in his 1910 annual report that the Duma debates on the Kholm project were being artificially prolonged *(iskusstvenno-zatiazhnoi kharakter, pridannyi obsuzhdeniiu Kholmskogo voprosa v Gosudarstvennoi Dume)* and bewailed the negative effects of the ensuing delay on the morale of local "Russians." RGIA, *Chital'nyi Zal*, op. 1, d. 84A, 1910, p. 7.

77. RGIA, f. 821, op. 10, 1914, d. 250, ll. 67–69; RGIA, f. 1276, op. 10, 1914, d. 32, ll. 9v, 17–20; RGIA, f. 821, op. 10, 1913, d. 243, ll. 79–96.

78. The commission cited the negative attitude of the Roman curia as the main reason against introducing the Julian calendar to the Kholm guberniia. However, the hope was expressed that soon the curia would agree to such a change. RGIA, f. 1276, op. 10, 1914, d. 32, ll. 12v–13v. On economic measures, including building roads, increasing peasant credit, and encouraging Russian colonization in the area, see ibid., ll. 20v–28. On Ukrainophile elements, see ibid., l. 15v. At the Siedlce men's gymnasium in 1909 a Ukrainophile circle called Kholmshchina had been uncovered. RGIA, *Chital'nyi Zal*, op. 1, d. 84 (Siedlce, 1909), p. 6.

79. "Otkrytie Kholmskoi gubernii," *Kholmskaia guberniia, Prilozhenie*, pp. 75–100. See also "O prisposoblenii goroda Kholma k nadobnostiam gubernskogo goroda," in RGIA, f. 821, op. 10, 1912, d. 235.

80. On Kholm governor Volzhin's anti-Polish russifying measures, see RGIA, f. 821, op. 10, 1913, d. 249. The further measures are detailed in Chikhachev, *K obrazovaniiu kholmskoi gubernii*, pp. 163–73. For the signs, see RGIA, f. 821, op. 10, 1913, d. 249.

81. The decree *(postanovlenie)* bore the date August 27, 1913, and was printed as a "Special Supplement" *(Osoboe Pribavlenie)* to *Kholmskie Gubernskie Vedomosti*, no. 1 (September 14, 1913). Point 7 forbade the singing of "revolutionary hymns," point 8 the exhibition of national flags other than the Russian, and point 16 agitation against the Russian language.

82. On the Kholm area under the Polish Republic, see Bolesław Zimmer, *Miasto Chełm: Zarys historyczny* (Warsaw/Cracow, 1974), pp. 157–71. On the nationality issue in interwar Poland in general, see Stephan Horak, *Poland and Her National Minorities, 1919–1939* (New York, 1961), and the works of Jerzy Tomaszewski.

Conclusion

1. See, for example, Leopold Haimson, "The Problem of Social Stability in Urban Russia, 1905–1917," *Slavic Review* 23, no. 4 (December 1964), pp. 619–42, and 24, no. 1 (March 1965), pp. 1–22. A recent dissenting view is expressed in Lieven, *Nicholas II.*

2. On the Russian state and the Great Reforms, see Lincoln, *The Great Reforms.* A recent important collective work is Ben Eklof, John Bushnell, and Larissa Zakharova, eds., *Russia's Great Reforms, 1855–1881* (Bloomington, Ind., 1994).

3. The adjective *rossiiskii* refers to "Russian" in the state or geographic sense, while *russkii* (the much more usual and "warmer" term) is applied to Russian culture, language, and ethnicity. The dichotomy is precisely that of the two respective English terms "Hungarian" and "Magyar" (in Hungarian *magyar* covers both).

4. See, for example, Lieven, *Russia's Rulers under the Old Regime.*

5. In recent years, this topic has begun to receive the attention it deserves. See, for example, Yuri Slezkine, *Arctic Mirrors: Russia and the Small Peoples of the North* (Ithaca, N.Y., 1994); and Stephen Kotkin and David Wolff, eds., *Rediscovering Russia in Asia: Siberia and the Russian Far East* (Armonk, N.Y., 1995).

6. By the twentieth century, Ottoman possessions in the Balkan area were reduced almost to nothing. In the Austrian case, it must be remembered that until the 1866 defeat by Prussian armies at Sadova, the Habsburg Emperor Franz Joseph refused to grant even Hungarian demands. The Compromise of 1867 paved the way for explicit "magyarization" policies in Slovak and Romanian regions.

Selected Bibliography

Archival Sources

POLAND

Archiwum Akt Nowych (AAN), Warsaw.
    Akta Leona Wasilewskiego (sygn. 390).
    Akta Stanisława Dzierzbickiego (sygn. 93/II).

Archiwum Głównie Akt Dawnych (AGAD), Warsaw.
    General-gubernator Varshavskii (GGW).
    Pomoshchik general-gubernatora (PomGGW).
    Prokuror varshavskoi sudebnoi palaty (PVSP).

Archiwum Państwowie Miasta Głównego Warszawy (APW), Warsaw.
    T. 24.   Warszawski Wydział Ochrony Porządku i Bezpieczeństwa Publicznego 1897–1917.
    T. 27, cz. 1.   Zarząd Oberpolicmajstra Warszawskiego 1823–1918.
    T. 136.   Varshavskaia Gubernskaia komissiia po delam o Vyborakh v Gosudarstvennuiu Dumu (1905–1912).
    T. 151, cz. 1.   Kantseliariia Varshavskogo Gubernatora, stol 4 (1867–1915).

Archiwum Polskiej Akademii Nauk (APAN), Warsaw.
    Materiały A. Lednickiego (sygn. III–123).
    Papiery S. Kozickiego (sygn. 30).

Biblioteka Katolickiego Uniwersytetu w Lublinie (BKUL), Lublin.
    Papiery Jana Steckiego.

Wojewódzkie Archiwum Państwowie w Lublinie (WAPL), Lublin.
    Zespół Kanc. Gubernatora Lubelskiego (KGL) 1866–1917, sygn. 116.

RUSSIA

Gosudarstvennyi Arkhiv Rossiiskoi Federatsii (GARF), formerly Tsentral'nyi gosudarstvennyi arkhiv Oktiabr'skoi Revoliutsii (TsGAOR), Moscow.
    Fond 102:Departament politsii MVD.
    Fond 555:Guchkov Aleksandr.
    Fond 579:Miliukov Pavel.
    Fond 690:Dymsha Liubomir.
    Fond 1729:Sviatopolk-Mirskii Kniaz' Petr.
    Fond 5122:Pol'skie politicheskie organizatsii na territorii Rossii.

Rossiiskii gosudarstvennyi istoricheskii arkhiv (RGIA), formerly Tsentral'nyi gosudarstvennyi istoricheskii arkhiv (TsGIA), St. Petersburg.
    Fond 796:Kantseliariia Ober-Prokurora Sinoda.

Fond 821:MVD, Departament dukhovnykh del inostrannykh ispovedanii.
Fond 1022:Petrokovy Aleksandr i Petr Vasil'evich.
Fond 1149:Gosudarstvennyi Sovet. Departament zakonov.
Fond 1263:Komitet ministrov.
Fond 1270:Komitet po delam Tsarstva Pol'skogo.
Fond 1276:Sovet Ministrov.
Fond 1278:Gosudarstvennaia Duma.
Fond 1284:MVD. Departament obshchikh del.
Fond 1287:MVD. Khoziaistvennyi departament.
Fond 1288:MVD. Glavnoe upravlenie po delam mestnogo khoziaistva.
Fond 1327:Osoboe deloproizvodstvo po vyboram v Gosudarstvennuiu
     Dumu i Gosudarstvennyi Sovet.
Fond 1574:Pobedonostsev Konstantin Petrovich.
Fond 1622:Vitte Sergei Iul'evich.
Fond 1626:Goremykin Ivan Logginovich.

Periodical Sources

*Adres-kalendar': Obshchaia rospis' nachal'stvuiushchikh i prochikh dolzhn. lits po vsem up-
     ravleniiam v Rossiiskoi Imperii.* St. Petersburg, 1895–1915.
Ezhegodnik gazety "Rech'". St. Petersburg, 1912–1916.
Ezhegodnik Rossii. St. Petersburg, 1903–1916.
Grazhdanin. St. Petersburg, 1897–1913.
Kraj. St. Petersburg, 1894–1909.
Myśl niepodległa. Warsaw, 1906–1914.
Novyi voskhod. St. Petersburg, 1910–1913.
Okrainy Rossii. St. Petersburg, 1906–1912.
Polnoe sobranie zakonov Rossiiskoi Imperii (PSZ). Series 2 and 3. St. Petersburg,
     1864–1915.
Przegląd narodowy. Warsaw, 1908–1914.
Russkaia mysl'. St. Petersburg, 1894–1914.
Russkii vestnik. Moscow, 1894–1906.
Russkoe bogatstvo. St. Petersburg, 1903–1914.
Sbornik kluba russkikh natsionalistov. Kiev, 1909–1913.
Sobranie uzakonenii i rasporiazhenii pravitel'stva. St. Petersburg, 1894–1916.
Spisok grazhdanskim chinam pervykh trekh klassov. St. Petersburg, 1871–1915.
Ukrainskaia zhizn'. St. Petersburg, 1912–1914.
Vestnik Evropy. St. Petersburg, 1894–1915.

Works Cited

Aksakov, Ivan. *Pol'skii vopros i zapadno-russkoe delo: Sochineniia,* vol. 3. St. Petersburg,
     1900.
Alkar. *See* Kraushar, Aleksandr.
Alston, Patrick L. *Education and the State in Tsarist Russia.* Stanford, 1969.
Alter, Peter. *Nationalismus.* Frankfurt, 1985.
Amburger, Erik. *Geschichte der Behördenorganisation Rußlands von Peter dem Grossen
     bis 1917.* Leiden, 1966.
Anan'ich, Boris V., ed. *Krizis samoderzhaviia v Rossii, 1895–1917.* Leningrad, 1984.
Anderson, Benedict. *Imagined Communities: Reflections on the Origin and Spread of Na-
     tionalism.* London, 1983.

Andriewsky, Olga. "The Politics of National Identity: The Ukrainian Question in Russia, 1904–1912." Ph.D. diss., Harvard University, 1991.

Antonovich, P. *Chto perezhila kholmskaia Rus': Populiarno-istoricheskii ocherk.* Kholm, 1912.

Aronson, Irvin M. "The Attitudes of Russian Officials in the 1880s toward Jewish Assimilation and Emigration." *Slavic Review* 34, no. 1 (1975), pp. 1–18.

———. "Nationalism and Jewish Emancipation in Russia: The 1880s." *Nationalities Papers* 5, no. 2 (1977), pp. 167–82.

———. "The Prospects for the Emancipation of Russian Jewry during the 1880s." *Slavonic and East European Review* 55, no. 3 (1977), pp. 348–69.

———. "Russian Bureaucratic Attitudes towards Jews, 1881–1894." Ph.D. diss., Northwestern University, 1973.

———. *Troubled Waters: The Origins of the 1881 Anti-Jewish Pogroms in Russia.* Pittsburgh, 1990.

Arsen'ev, K., et al. *Intelligentsiia v Rossii: Sbornik statei.* St. Petersburg, 1910.

Artsybashev, M. M. *Griadushchaia gibel' Rossii.* St. Petersburg, 1908.

Ascher, Abraham. *The Revolution of 1905.* 2 vols. Stanford, 1988–1992.

Askenazy, Szymon. "Gubernia Chełmska." *Biblioteka Warszawska,* no. 1 (January 1909), pp. 213–30.

———. *Uniwersytet Warszawski.* Warsaw, 1905.

———, ed. *Sprawa gubernii chełmskiej.* Cracow, 1907.

Avineri, Shlomo. *The Making of Modern Zionism.* New York, 1981.

Avrekh, Aron Ia. *P. A. Stolypin i sud'by reform v Rossii.* Moscow, 1991.

———. *Stolypin i tret'ia Duma.* Moscow, 1968.

———. *Tsarizm i IV Duma, 1912–1914 gg.* Moscow, 1981.

———. *Tsarizm i tret'eiiun'skaia sistema.* Moscow, 1966.

———. "Vopros o zapadnom zemstve i bankrotstvo Stolypina." *Istoricheskie zapiski* 70 (1961), pp. 61–112.

A. Z. *See* Zakrzewski, Adam.

Balashev, I. *O politike Rossii v posledine veka i predistoiashchie ee zadachi.* St. Petersburg, 1914.

Balicki, Zygmunt. *Egoizm narodowy wobec etyki.* Lvov, 1902.

Balkanov, N. P., and V. E. Gertsenberg, eds. *Svod zakonov Rossiiskoi Imperii: Izdanie neofitsial'noe.* St. Petersburg, 1912.

Baron, Salo. *The Russian Jew under Tsars and Soviets.* New York, 1964.

Bartenev, Petr, ed. *Deviatnadtsatyi vek: Istoricheskii sbornik.* Moscow, 1872.

Bartoszewicz, Joachim. *Na Rusi: Polski stań posiadania.* Kiev, 1912.

Batiushkov, P. N. *Kholmskaia Rus': Istoricheskie sud'by russkogo Zabuzh'ia.* St. Petersburg, 1887.

———. *Podoliia: Istoricheskoe opisanie.* St. Petersburg, 1891.

———. *Volyn': Istoricheskie sud'by iugo-zapadnogo kraia.* St. Petersburg, 1888.

Baudouin de Courtenay, Jan. *Kwestia alfabetu litewskiego w państwie rosyjskim i jej rozwiązanie.* Cracow, 1904.

———. *W sprawie "antysemityzmu postępowego."* Cracow, 1911.

———. *W sprawie porozumienia się ludów słowiańskich.* Warsaw, 1908.

Bauer, H., A. Kappeler, and B. Roth, eds. *Die Nationalitäten des russischen Reiches in der Volkszählung von 1897.* 2 vols. Stuttgart, 1991.

Bauer, Otto. *Die Nationalitätenfrage und die Sozialdemokratie.* Vienna, 1975.

Beauvois, Daniel. *La Bataille de la terre en Ukraine, 1863–1914: Les Polonais et les conflits socio-ethniques.* Lille, 1993.

———. *Le Noble, le serf, et le revizor: La Noblesse polonaise entre le tsarisme et les masses ukrainiennes.* Paris, 1985.

————. *Polacy na Ukrainie, 1831–1863: Szlachta polska na Wołyniu, Podolu, i Kijowszczyźnie*. Paris, 1987.

————, ed. *Les Confins de l'ancienne Pologne: Ukraine, Lithuanie, Biélorussie, XVIe–XXe siècles*. Lille, 1988.

Belmont, Leo, and Jerzy Huzarski. *Zwycięstwo Romana Dmowskiego*. Warsaw, n.d. (ca. 1913).

Bendix, Reinhard. *Nation Building and Citizenship*. New York, 1964.

Berendts, E. N. *O proshlom i nastoiashchem russkoi administratsii: Zapiska sostavlennaia v dekabre 1903 goda*. St. Petersburg, 1913.

Berg, F., ed. *Materialy kommisii po ustroistvu byta evreev*. St. Petersburg, 1874.

Berg, N. *Zapiski o pol'skikh zagovorakh i vosstaniiakh*. Moscow, 1873.

Berger, David, ed. *The Legacy of Jewish Migration: 1881 and Its Impact*. New York, 1983.

Berk, Stephen M. *Year of Crisis, Year of Hope: Russian Jewry and the Pogroms of 1881–1882*. Westport, Conn., 1985.

Berlin, Isaiah. *Against the Current: Essays in the History of Ideas*. London, 1979.

Bikerman, I. M. *Cherta evreiskoi osedlosti*. St. Petersburg, 1911.

Bilousenko, O. *Kholmska sprava*. Kiev, 1909.

Blank, R. M. *Rol' evreiskogo naseleniia v ekonomicheskoi zhizni Rossii*. St. Petersburg, 1908.

Blejwas, Stanislaus A. *Realism in Polish Politics*. New Haven, Conn., 1984.

————. "Warsaw Positivism, 1864–1890: Organic Work as an Expression of National Survival in Nineteenth-Century Poland." Ph.D. diss., Columbia University, 1973.

Bliokh, I. S. *Budushchaia voina*. St. Petersburg, 1898.

————. *Sravnenie material'nogo byta i nravstvennogo sostoianiia v cherte osedlosti evreev i vne eia*. St. Petersburg, 1891.

Blobaum, Robert E. *Rewolucja: Russian Poland, 1904–1907*. Ithaca, N.Y., 1995.

Bloch, Jan. *See* Bliokh, I. S.

Bloom, Solomon. *The World of Nations: A Study of the National Implications of the Work of Karl Marx*. New York, 1967.

Bogdanovich, A. *Tri poslednikh samoderzhavtsa*. Moscow, 1990.

Bohon, John W. "Reactionary Politics in Russia, 1905–1909." Ph.D. diss., University of North Carolina, 1967.

Boiovich, M. M., ed. *Chleny Gosudarstvennoi Dumy: Tret'i sozyv, 1907–1912*. Moscow, 1910.

————. *Chleny Gosudarstvennoi Dumy (portrety i biografi)*. Moscow, 1906.

Bojarski, Józef. *Czasy Nerona w XIX w., czyli ostatnie chwile unii*. Lvov, 1878.

Borochov (Borokhov), Ber. *Klassovye momenty natsional'nogo kharaktera*. Odessa, 1906.

Borodkin, M. *Natsional'nost' v nauke (Molodomu pokoleniiu)*. St. Petersburg, 1912.

Borokhov. *See* Borochov, Ber.

Borschak, E. "Ukraine in the Russian Empire in the Nineteenth and Twentieth Centuries (1800–1917)." In *Ukraine: A Concise Encyclopaedia*, vol. 1, p. 667–89. Toronto, 1963.

Breuilly, John. *Nationalism and the State*. Chicago, 1982.

Bronsztajn, Szyja. *Ludność żydowska w Polsce w okresie międzywojennym: Studium statystyczne*. Wrocław, 1963.

Brooks, Jeffrey. *When Russia Learned to Read: Literacy and Popular Literature, 1861–1917*. Princeton, 1985.

Brutskus, B. D. *Statistika evreiskogo naseleniia*. St. Petersburg, 1909.

Brykalska, Maria. *Aleksander Wielopolski: Biografia.* 2 vols. Warsaw, 1987.

Budilovich, A. *Kholmskaia guberniia.* Kholm, 1914.

———. *Kholmskaia Rus' i poliaki.* St. Petersburg, 1907.

Bukowiecki, Stanisław [Drogoslav, pseud.]. *Rosya w Polsce.* Warsaw, 1914.

Burmistrova, T. Iu., and V. S. Gushakova. *Natsional'nyi vopros v programmakh i taktike politicheskikh partii v Rossii, 1905–1917 gg.* Moscow, 1976.

Butmi, G. *Vragi roda chelovecheskogo.* 4th ed. St. Petersburg, 1907.

———. *Zolotaia valiuta.* 3d ed. St. Petersburg, n.d.

Byrnes, Robert F. *Pobedonostsev: His Life and Thought.* Bloomington, Ind., 1968.

Cadzow, John F. "The Lithuanian Question in the Third State Duma." Ph.D. diss., Kent State University, 1972.

Cała, Alina. *Asymilacja Żydów w Królestwie Polskim, 1864–1897.* Warsaw, 1989.

Carnoy, Martin. *The State and Political Theory.* Princeton, 1984.

Chikhachev, Dmitrii N. *K obrazovaniiu kholmskoi gubernii: Doklad gosudarstvennoi Dume.* St. Petersburg, 1912.

———. *K voprosu o budushchem ustroistve Pol'shi.* Petrograd, 1917.

Chlebowczyk, Józef. *On Small and Young Nations of Europe: Nation-Forming Processes in Ethnic Borderlands in East-Central Europe.* Wrocław, 1980.

———. *O prawie do bytu małych i młodych narodów: Kwestia narodowa i procesy narodotwórcze we wschodniej Europie środkowej w dobie kapitalizmu (od schyłku XVIII do początków XX w.)* Warsaw, 1983.

———. *Procesy narodotwórcze we wschodniej Europie środkowej w dobie kapitalizmu.* Warsaw, 1975.

Chmielewski, Edward V. *The Polish Question in the Russian State Duma.* Knoxville, Tenn., 1970.

———. "Separation of Chełm from Poland." *Polish Review* 15, no. 1 (winter 1970), pp. 67–86.

———. "Stolypin and the Russian Ministerial Crisis of 1909." *California Slavic Studies* 4 (1967), pp. 1–38.

———. "Stolypin's Last Crisis." *California Slavic Studies* 3 (1964), pp. 95–126.

Chukovskii, Kornei. *The Poet and the Hangman (Nekrasov and Muravyov).* Ann Arbor, 1977.

Clowes, Edith W., Samuel D. Kassow, and James L. West, eds. *Between Tsar and People: Educated Society and the Quest for Public Identity in Late Imperial Russia.* Princeton, 1991.

Cohn, Norman. *Warrant for Genocide: The Myth of Jewish World-Conspiracy and the Protocols of the Elders of Zion.* Chico, Calif., 1981.

Connor, Walker. "A Nation Is a Nation, Is a State, Is an Ethnic Group, Is a . . . " *Ethnic and Racial Studies* 1, no. 4 (1974), pp. 377–400.

———. *The National Question in Marxist-Leninist Theory and Strategy.* Princeton, 1984.

Conroy, Mary S. *Peter Arkad'evich Stolypin: Practical Politics in Late Tsarist Russia.* Boulder, Colo., 1976.

———. "Stolypin's Attitude toward Local Self-Government." *Slavonic and East European Review* 46 (July 1968), pp. 446–61.

Corrsin, Stephen. "Political and Social Change in Warsaw from the January 1863 Insurrection to the First World War: Polish Politics and the Jewish Question." Ph.D. diss., University of Michigan, 1981.

———. *Warsaw before the First World War: Poles and Jews in the Third City of the Russian Empire, 1880–1914.* Boulder, Colo., 1989.

Crisp, Olga, and Linda Edmondson, eds. *Civil Rights in Imperial Russia*. Oxford, 1989.

Curtiss, John S. *Church and State in Russia: The Last Years of the Empire, 1900–1917*. New York, 1940.

Czarkowski, L. (S. Sękta). *Ostrzeżenie: W kwestii litewskiej słów kilka*. Wilno, 1907.

Czterdzieści lat prześladowania Unii na Podlasiu. Cracow, 1909.

Czyński, Edward. *Etnograficzno-statystyczny zarys liczebności i rozsiedlenia ludności polskiej*. Warsaw, 1909.

Dawidowicz, Lucy. *The Golden Tradition: Jewish Life and Thought in Eastern Europe*. New York, 1967.

Demchenka, Ia. *Evreiskoe ravnopravie ili russkoe poraboshchenie? Issledovanie tainykh evreiskikh planov i programm, napravlennykh k oslableniiu i razrusheniiu korennogo naseleniia i poraboshcheniiu ego evreistvu*. 2d ed. Kiev, 1907.

Dmowski, Roman. *Germaniia, Rossiia, i pol'skii vopros*. St. Petersburg, 1909.

————. *Myśli nowoczesnego Polaka*. Lvov, 1904.

————. *Niemcy, Rosya, i Kwestya Polska*. Lvov, 1908.

————. *Polityka polska i odbudowanie państwa*. Warsaw, 1926.

————. *Separatyzm Żydów i jego źródła*. Warsaw, 1909.

————. *Upadek myśli konserwatywnej w Polsce*. Warsaw, 1914.

Dobaczewska, Wanda. *Wilno i Wileńszczyzna w latach, 1863–1914: Dzieje ruchów społecznych i politycznych*. Wilno, 1938.

Dobianskii, F. K. *O litovskikh tatarakh*. Vil'na, 1906.

Dokumenty w sprawie gubernii chełmskiej. Cracow, 1908.

Doroshenko, Volodymyr. *Ukrainstvo v Rossii: Noviishi chasy*. Vienna, 1916.

Dovnar-Zapol'skii, M. V. *Narodnoe khoziaistvo Belorussii, 1861–1914 gg*. Minsk, 1926.

Drabkina, Elizaveta. *Natsional'nyi i kolonial'nyi voprosy v tsarskoi Rossii*. Moscow, 1930.

Dragomanov, Mikhail P. *Liberalizm i zemstvo v Rossii*. Geneva, 1889.

————. *Politicheskie sochineniia*. Edited by I. M. Grevs and B. A. Kistiakovskii. Moscow, 1908.

Drogoslav. *See* Bukowiecki, Stanisław.

Dubnov, Semen M. *Evrei v Rossii v tsarstvovanie Nikolaia II, 1894–1914*. Petrograd, 1922.

Dubnov, Semen M., and G. Ia. Krasnyi-Admoni, eds. *Materialy dlia istorii antievreiskikh pogromov v Rossii*. Petrograd, 1919–1923.

Dylągowa, Hanna. *Unia brzeska i unici w Królestwie Polskim*. Warsaw, 1989.

Dymsza (Dymsha), Lubomir. *Kholmskii vopros*. St. Petersburg, 1910.

Dziewulski, Stefan. "Statystyka ludności guberni lubelskiej i siedleckiej wobec projektu utworzenia gubernii chełmskiej." *Ekonomista* (Warsaw, 1909), pp. 157–93.

————. *Statystyka projektu rządowego o wyodrębienie Chełmszczyzny w świetle krytyki*. Warsaw, 1910.

Dziewulski, Stefan, and Henryk Radziszewski. *Warszawa*. 2 vols. Warsaw, 1913–1915.

Dzwonowski, Włodzimierz, ed. *Raport Neidgarta o rewizji senatorskiej w Królestwie Polskim*. Warsaw, 1916.

Edelman, Robert. *Gentry Politics on the Eve of the Russian Revolution: The Nationalist Party, 1907–1917*. New Brunswick, N.J., 1980.

————. *Proletarian Peasants: The Revolution of 1905 in Russia's Southwest*. Ithaca, N.Y., 1987.

Efremov, Serhii. *Evreis'ka sprava na Ukraini*. Kiev, 1909.

Eisenbach, Artur. *The Emancipation of the Jews in Poland, 1780–1870.* Oxford, 1991.

———. *Kwestia równouprawnienia Żydów w Królestwie Polskim.* Warsaw, 1972.

———. *Z dziejów ludności żydowskiej w Polsce w XVIII i XIX wieku: Studia i szkice.* Warsaw, 1983.

Eklof, Ben, John Bushnell, and Larissa Zakharova, eds. *Russia's Great Reforms, 1855–1881.* Bloomington, Ind., 1994.

Elenev, Fedor. *Pol'skaia tsivilizatsiia i eia vliianie na zapadnuiu Rus'.* St. Petersburg, 1863.

Emmons, Terence, and Wayne S. Vucinich, eds. *The Zemstvo in Russia: An Experiment in Local Self-Government.* Cambridge, U.K., 1982.

Eroshkin, Nikolai P. *Istoriia gosudarstvennykh uchrezhdenii dorevoliutsionnoi Rossii.* 2d ed. Moscow, 1968.

Esipov, V. *Avtonomiia Pol'shi, s tochki zreniia finansovykh, ekonomicheskikh i drugikh interesov Rossii.* Warsaw, 1907.

———. *Ocherk zhizni i byta Privislinskogo kraia.* Warsaw, 1909.

———. *Privislinskii krai.* Warsaw, 1907.

———. *Varshava i Lodz', ikh proshloe i nastoiashchee.* Warsaw, 1907.

———. *"Varshavskii dnevnik" za 50 let.* Warsaw, 1914.

Evlogii (Mitropolit). *Put' moei zhizni: Vospominaniia Mitropolita Evlogiia, izlozhennye po ego rasskazam T. Manukinoi.* Paris, 1947.

Evrei i voina. St. Petersburg, 1912.

Evrei v Privislinskom krae: Kharakteristika ikh deiatel'nosti sredi khristianskogo naseleniia etogo kraia. St. Petersburg, 1892.

Feldman, Wilhelm. *Dzieje polskiej myśli politycznej, 1863–1914.* 2d ed. Warsaw, 1933.

———. *Geschichte der politischen Ideen in Polen seit dessen Teilungen, 1795–1915.* Munich, 1917; reprint, Osnabrück, 1964.

Filevich, I. *Vopros o vozsoedinenii zapadno-russkikh uniatov v ego noveishei postanovke.* Warsaw, 1891.

Filipowicz, Tytus. *Polska i autonomia.* Warsaw, 1908.

Flynn, James T. "Uvarov and the 'Western Provinces': A Study of Russia's Polish Problem." *Slavonic and East European Review* 64, no. 2 (1986), pp. 212–36.

Folejewski, Józef. *O samorządzie ziemskim na Litwie i Białej Rusi.* Vil'na, 1911.

Frankel, Jonathan. *Prophecy and Politics: Socialism, Nationalism, and the Russian Jews, 1862–1917.* Cambridge, U.K., 1981.

Frankel, Jonathan, and S. J. Zipperstein, eds. *Assimilation and Community: The Jews in Nineteenth-Century Europe.* Cambridge, U.K., 1992.

Frantsev, Vladimir A. *Karty russkogo i pravoslavnogo naseleniia Kholmskoi Rusi.* Warsaw, 1909.

Frumkin, Jacob, et al., eds. *Russian Jewry, 1860–1917.* New York, 1966.

Fuks, Marian. *Prasa żydowska w Warszawie, 1823–1939.* Warsaw, 1979.

Gawroński, Franciszek Rawita. *Kwestia ruska wobec Austryi i Rosyi.* Cracow, 1913.

———. *Oderwanie Chełmszczyzny i Rusini.* Lvov, 1909.

Gelber, N. M. "Zur Geschichte der jüdischen Frage in Polen: Die polnische Judenreform unter Kaiser Alexander II und Marquis Wielopolski." *Zeitschrift für osteuropäische Geschichte* 4 (1913–1914), pp. 483–513.

Gellner, Ernest. "Ethnicity and Faith in Eastern Europe." *Daedalus* 119, no. 1 (winter 1990), pp. 279–80.

———. *Nations and Nationalism.* Ithaca, N.Y., 1983.

Gerth, H. H., and C. Wright Mills, eds. *From Max Weber: Essays in Sociology.* New York, 1958.

Gessen, Iulii I. *Evrei v Rossii: Ocherki obshchestvennoi, pravovoi i ekonomicheskoi zhizni russkikh evreev*. St. Petersburg, 1906.

Gleason, Abbot. *Young Russia*. Chicago, 1980.

Glinka, Luigi. *Diocesi ucraino-cattolica di Cholm (Liquidazione ed incorporazione alla Chiesa russo-ortodossa)*. Rome, 1975.

Gloger, Zygmunt, et al., eds. *Królestwo Polskie*. Warsaw, 1905.

Golczewski, Frank. *Polnisch-Jüdische Beziehungen, 1881–1922: Eine Studie zur Geschichte des Antisemitismus in Osteuropa*. Wiesbaden, 1981.

———, ed. *Geschichte der Ukraine*. Göttingen, 1993.

Goroda Rossii v 1910 g. St. Petersburg, 1914.

Gostowski, A. *Nasz przysły samorząd: Myśli, uwagi, projekty*. Warsaw, 1907.

Gosudarstvennaia Duma: Stenograficheskie otchety (GDSO). 37 vols. St. Petersburg, 1906–1917.

Gosudarstvennyi Sovet: Stenograficheskie otchety (GSSO). 25 vols. St. Petersburg, 1906–1917.

Grabowski, Ignacy. *Niewdzięczni gości: W sprawie żydowskiej*. Warsaw, 1912.

———. *Polacy, Żydzi, Rosjanie*. Warsaw, 1915.

Grabowski, Roman. "Likwidacja Kościoła Grekokatolickiego w Królestwie Polskim, 1864–1875." *Studenckie zeszyty naukowe Uniwersytetu Jagiellońskiego* 5 (Cracow, 1985), pp. 69–101.

Gradovskii, A. D. *Istoriia mestnogo upravleniia v Rossii*. St. Petersburg, 1868.

Greenberg, Louis. *The Jews in Russia*. 2 vols. New Haven, Conn., 1951.

Greenfeld, Liah. *Nationalism: Five Roads to Modernity*. Cambridge, Mass., 1992.

Groniowski, Krzysztof. *Uwłaszczenie chłopów w Polsce*. Warsaw, 1976.

Groniowski, Krzysztof, and Jerzy Skowronek. *Historia Polski, 1795–1914*. 3d ed. Warsaw, 1987.

Grushevskii, M. *See* Hrushevs'kyi, M.

Gurko, Vladimir I. *Features and Figures of the Past: Government and Opinion in the Reign of Nicholas II*. Stanford, 1939.

——— [V. R., pseud.]. *Ocherki Privislian'ia*. Moscow, 1897.

Guroff, Gregory, and Fred Carstensen, eds. *Entrepreneurship in Imperial Russia and the Soviet Union*. Princeton, 1983.

Hagen, Manfred. *Die Entfaltung politischer Öffentlichkeit in Rußland, 1906–1914*. Wiesbaden, 1982.

———. "Russification via 'Democratization'? Civil Service in the Baltic after 1906." *Journal of Baltic Studies* 9, no. 1 (spring 1978), pp. 56–65.

Hagen, William W. *Germans, Poles, and Jews: The Nationality Conflict in the Prussian East, 1771–1914*. Chicago, 1980.

Haimson, Leopold. "The Problem of Social Stability in Urban Russia, 1905–1917." *Slavic Review* 23, no. 4 (December 1964), pp. 619–42; 24, no. 1 (March 1965), pp. 1–22.

Halecki, Oskar. *From Florence to Brest, 1439–1596*. Hamden, Conn., 1968.

Hamm, Michael F. *Kiev: A Portrait, 1800–1917*. Princeton, 1993.

———, ed. *The City in Late Imperial Russia*. Bloomington, Ind., 1986.

———. *The City in Russian History*. Lexington, Ky., 1976.

Harcave, Sidney, ed. and trans. *The Memoirs of Count Witte*. Armonk, N.Y., 1990.

Haustein, Ulrich. *Sozialismus und nationale Frage in Polen*. Cologne, 1969.

Hellman, Manfred. *Grundzüge der Geschichte Litauens*. Darmstadt, 1966.

Herbaczewski, Józef A. *Głos bolu: Sprawa odrodzenia narodowego Litwy w związku ze sprawa wyzwolenia narodowego Polski*. Cracow, 1912.

Herzog, Elizabeth, and Mark Zborowski. *Life Is with People: The Jewish Little-Town of Eastern Europe.* New York, 1962.

Heuman, Susan Eva. "Bogdan Kistiakovskii and the Problem of Human Rights in the Russian Empire, 1899–1917." Ph.D. diss., Columbia University, 1977.

Horak, Stephan. *Poland and Her National Minorities, 1919–1939.* New York, 1961.

Hosking, Geoffrey. *The Russian Constitutional Experiment: Government and Duma, 1907–1914.* Cambridge, U.K., 1973.

Hroch, Miroslav. *Social Preconditions of National Revival in Europe: A Comparative Analysis of the Social Composition of Patriotic Groups among the Smaller European Nations.* Translated by Ben Fowkes. Cambridge, U.K., 1985.

Hrushevs'kyi, M. *K pol'sko-ukrainskim otnosheniiam Galitsii.* Kiev, 1905.

———. *Ocherk istorii ukrainskogo naroda.* 2d ed. St. Petersburg, 1906.

———. *Osvobozhdenie i ukrainskii vopros.* St. Petersburg, 1907.

———. *Za ukrains'kyi maslak / V spravy Kholmshchyny.* Kiev, 1907.

Iaroshevich, A. *Ocherki ekonomicheskoi zhizni iugo-zapadnogo kraia.* 3 vols. Kiev, 1908–1911.

Ilovaiskii, A. *Kratkie ocherki russkoi istorii: Kurs starshogo vozrasta.* Moscow, 1912.

Issledovaniia v Tsarstve Pol'skom (po vysochaishemu poveleniiu). 4 vols. St. Petersburg, n.d. (ca. 1865).

Istomin, Vladimir. "O russkom zemlevladenii v guberniiakh Privislinskogo kraia." *Moskovskie Vedomosti,* nos. 274–77 (November 11–15, 1906).

———. *Polozhenie "uniatskogo voprosa" v predelakh russkogo Zakona nakanune Ukaza 17 aprelia 1905 goda.* Moscow, 1907.

———. *Sovremennoe polozhenie russkogo voprosa v Privislinskom krae.* Moscow, 1906.

Istoricheskaia zapiska o kholmskoi Rusi i gorode Kholme, o sud'bakh Unii v kholmskom krae i sovremennom polozhenii v nem uniatskogo voprosa. St. Petersburg, 1902.

Ivancevich, Anthony Mario. "The Ukrainian National Movement and Russification." Ph.D. diss., Northwestern University, 1976.

Ivanovich, V. *Rossiiskie partii, soiuzy, i ligi.* St. Petersburg, 1906.

Iwaniec, Eugeniusz. *Z dziejów staroobrzędowców na ziemiach polskich, XVII–XX ww.* Warsaw, 1977.

Izgoev, A. *P. A. Stolypin: Ocherk zhizni i deiatel'nosti.* Moscow, 1912.

Jameson, Frederic. *The Prison-House of Language: A Critical Account of Structuralism and Russian Formalism.* Princeton, 1972.

Janowski, Aleksander. *Chełmszczyzna.* Warsaw/Lublin, 1918.

Janowsky, Oscar I. *The Jews and Minority Rights, 1898–1919.* New York, 1933.

Janus, Glenn Alfred. "The Polish Kolo, the Russian Duma, and the Question of Polish Autonomy." Ph.D. diss., Ohio State University, 1971.

Jaszczuk, Andrzej. *Spór pozytywistów z konserwatystami o przyszłość Polski, 1870–1903.* Warsaw, 1986.

Jeleński, Jan. *Nie bić żydów, ale im się nie dawać!* Warsaw, 1906.

Jobst, Kerstin S. "Die ukrainische Nationalbewegung bis 1917." In *Geschichte der Ukraine,* ed. F. Golczewski, pp. 156–71. Göttingen, 1993.

Jurgela, Constantine B. *The History of the Lithuanian Nation.* New York, 1948.

K voprosu o vydelenii Kholmskoi Rusi. St. Petersburg, 1906.

Kahan, Arcadius. "Notes on Jewish Entrepreneurship in Tsarist Russia." In *Entrepreneurship in Imperial Russia and the Soviet Union,* ed. G. Guroff and F. Carstensen, pp. 104–24. Princeton, 1983.

Kalabiński, Stanisław. *Antyanarodowa polityka Endecji w rewolucji, 1905–1907.* Warsaw, 1955.

————, ed. *Carat i klasy posiadające w walce z revolucja 1905–1907 w Królestwie Polskim: Materiały archiwalne.* Warsaw, 1956.

Kalabiński, Stanisław, and Feliks Tych. *Czwarte powstanie czy pierwsza rewolucja: Lata 1905–1907 na ziemiach polskich.* Warsaw, 1969.

Kappeler, Andreas. "Historische Voraussetzungen des Nationalitätenproblems im russischen Vielvölkerreich." *Geschichte und Gesellschaft* 8, no. 2 (1982), pp. 159–83.

————. *Rußland als Vielvölkerreich: Entstehung, Geschichte, Zerfall.* Munich, 1992.

————, ed. *The Formation of National Elites.* New York, 1992.

————. *Die Russen: Ihr Nationalbewußtsein in Geschichte und Gegenwart.* Cologne, 1990.

Kappeler, Andreas, et al., eds. *Die Deutschen im Russischen Reich.* Cologne, 1987.

Kareev, N. *Polonica: Sbornik statei po pol'skim delam, 1881–1905.* St. Petersburg, 1905.

Karetnikov, S. M. *Kholmskaia guberniia: Geografichesko-istoricheskii ocherk.* Lubny, 1913.

Kastelianskii, A. I., ed. *Formy natsional'nogo dvizheniia v sovremennykh gosudarstvakh: Avstro-Vengriia, Rossiia, Germaniia.* St. Petersburg, 1910.

Kelles-Krauz, Kazimierz. *Naród i historia: Wybór pism.* Warsaw, 1989.

Kholmskaia Rus' i poliaki. St. Petersburg, 1907.

Kholmskii vopros: Obzor russkoi periodicheskoi pechati. St. Petersburg, 1912.

Kieniewicz, Stefan. *Dramat trzezwych entuzjastów: O ludziach pracy organicznej.* Warsaw, 1964.

————. *The Emancipation of the Polish Peasantry.* Chicago, 1969.

————. *Historia Polski, 1795–1918.* Warsaw, 1970.

————. *Między ugodą i rewolucją (Andrzej Zamoyski w latach 1861–1862).* Warsaw, 1961.

————. *Powstanie styczniowe.* Warsaw, 1972.

————. *Warszawa w latach, 1795–1914.* Warsaw, 1976.

Kiepurska, Halina. *Warszawa w rewolucji, 1905–1907.* Warsaw, 1974.

Kiepurska, Halina, and Z. Pustula, eds. *Raporty Warszawskich Oberpolicmajstrów, 1892–1913.* Warsaw, 1971.

Kindler, Klaus. *Die Cholmer Frage, 1905–1918.* Frankfurt-am-Main, 1990.

Kirszrot, Jacob. *Prawa Żydów w Królestwie Polskim.* Warsaw, 1917.

Kistiakovskii, Bogdan [Ukrainets, pseud.]. "K voprosu o samostoiatel'noi ukrainskoi kul'ture: Pis'mo k redaktsii," *Russkaia mysl'* (May 1911), pp. 131–46.

Kizevetter, A. A. *Na rubezhe dvukh stoletii: Vospominaniia, 1881–1914.* Prague, 1929.

Kleinman, I. A. *Mezhdu molotom i nakoval'nei: Pol'sko-evreiskii krizis.* St. Petersburg, 1910.

Klier, John D. "The Concept of 'Jewish Emancipation' in a Russian Context." In *Civil Rights in Imperial Russia,* ed. Olga Crisp and Linda Edmondson, pp. 132–33. Oxford, 1989.

————. *Imperial Russia's Jewish Question, 1855–1881.* Cambridge, U.K., 1995.

————. "Russification and the Polish Revolt of 1863: Bad for the Jews?" *Polin* 1 (1986), pp. 91–106.

Klier, John D., and Shlomo Lambroza, eds. *Pogroms: Anti-Jewish Violence in Modern Russian History.* Cambridge, U.K., 1992.

Kmiecik, Zenon. *"Kraj" za czasów redaktorstwa Erazma Piltza.* Warsaw, 1969.

————. *Prasa warszawska, 1886–1904.* Wrocław, 1989.

————. *Prasa warszawska w latach, 1908–1918.* Warsaw, 1976.

Koialovich, M. O. *Istoriia russkogo samosoznaniia po istoricheskim pamiatnikam i nauchnym sochineniiam.* St. Petersburg, 1893.

————. *Istoriia vozsoedineniia zapadnorusskikh uniatov starykh vremen*. St. Petersburg, 1873.

————. *Litovskaia tserkovnaia Uniia*. 2 vols. St. Petersburg, 1859–1861.

Kokovtsov, Vladimir N. *Out of My Past: The Memoirs of Count Kokovtsov*. Edited by H. H. Fisher, translated by Laura Matveev. Stanford, 1935.

Kołodziejczyk, Ryszard. *Burżuazja polska w XIX i XX wieku: Szkice historyczne*. Warsaw, 1979.

————. *Jan Bloch, 1836–1902: Szkic do portretu "krola polskich kolei"*. Warsaw, 1983.

Komarnicki, Tytus. *Obrona Chełmszczyzny w Dumie*. Warsaw, 1918.

Konic, H. *Samorząd gminy w Królestwie Polskim w porównaniu z innemi krajami europejskimi*. Warsaw, 1906.

Korkunov, Nikolai M. *Russkoe gosudarstvennoe pravo*. 3d ed. 2 vols. St. Petersburg, 1899.

Kornilov, A. A. *Russkaia politika v Pol'she so vremeni razdelov do nachala XX veka*. Petrograd, 1915.

————. "Russkaia politika v Tsarstve Pol'skom do 1863 goda." *Russkaia mysl'*, no. 1 (1915), pp. 1–31; no. 3 (1915), pp. 1–36.

Kornilov, I. P. *Russkoe delo v Severo-zapadnom krae: Materialy dlia istorii vilenskogo uchebnogo okruga preimushchestvenno v murav'evskuiu epokhu*. St. Petersburg, 1908.

Korvin-Milevskii, Graf Ignatsii-Karl Oskarovich. *See* Korwin-Milewski, Ignacy.

Korwin-Milewski, Hipolit. *Les Eléments de la question lithuanienne*. Paris, 1918.

————. *Observations sur le conflit des langues polonaise et lithuanienne dans le diocèse de Wilna*. Paris, 1913.

————. *Siedemdziesiąt lat wspomnień, 1855–1925*. Poznań, 1930.

Korwin-Milewski (Korvin-Milevskii), Ignacy. *Golos pol'skogo dvorianina o vybore chlena gosudarstvennogo soveta v Vil'ne*. St. Petersburg, n.d. (ca. 1910).

————. *K chemu dolzhno stremit'sia litovskoe dvorianstvo*. St. Petersburg, n.d. (ca. 1912).

Korzec, Paweł. "Anti-Semitism in Poland as an Intellectual, Social, and Political Movement." In *Studies on Polish Jewry*, ed. Joshua Fishman, pp. 12–104. New York, 1974.

Koshevoi, V. P. "Mechty pol'skikh natsionalistov i deistvitel'nost'." *Ukrainskaia zhizn'* (November 1913).

Kostomarov, N. I. "Dve Russkie natsional'nosti: Pis'ma k redaktoru." *Osnova* (St. Petersburg) pt. 2 (March 1861), pp. 33–80.

Koszutski, Stanisław. *Nasz przemył wielki na początku XX wieku: Obraz statystyczno-ekonomiczny*. Warsaw, 1905.

————. *Nasze miasta i samorząd: Życie miast w Królestwie Polskim i reforma samorządowa*. Warsaw, 1915.

————. *Rozwój ekonomiczny Królestwa Polskiego w ostatnim trzydziestoleciu, 1870–1900*. Warsaw, 1905.

Kotkin, Stephen, and David Wolff, eds. *Rediscovering Russia in Asia: Siberia and the Russian Far East*. Armonk, N.Y., 1995.

Kovalevskii, P. I. *Aleksandr III: Tsar'-Natsionalist*. St. Petersburg, 1912.

————. *Istoriia Rossii s natsional'noi tochki zreniia*. St. Petersburg, 1912.

————. *Osnovy russkogo natsionalizma*. St. Petersburg, 1912.

Kraushar, Aleksandr [Alkar, pseud.]. *Czasy szkolne za Apuchtina: Kartka z pamiętnika, 1879–1897*. Warsaw, 1915.

Krawchenko, Bohdan. *Social Change and National Consciousness in Twentieth-Century Ukraine*. New York, 1985.

Kropotov, D. A. *Zhizn' gr. M. N. Murav'eva*. St. Petersburg, 1874.

Krynicki, K. *Rys geografii Królestwa Polskiego*. Warsaw, 1907.

Kryzhanovskii, Evfimii M. *Russkoe Zabuzh'e: Kholmshchina i Podliash'e*. With a foreword by I. Filevich. St. Petersburg, 1911.

———. *Sobranie sochinenii*. 3 vols. Kiev, 1890.

Kryzhanovskii, Sergei E. *Vospominaniia*. Berlin, n.d. (ca. 1938).

Krzemiński, S. *Dwadzieścia pięć lat Rosji w Polsce, 1863–1888*. Lvov, 1892.

Kuchinskii, Iosif. *Proekt vydeleniia Kholmshchiny na pochve russko-polskikh otnoshenii*. St. Petersburg, 1911.

Kula, Witold. *Historia gospodarcza Polski w dobie popowstaniowej, 1864–1918*. Warsaw, 1947.

Kul'turnye nuzhdy Kholmshchiny. St. Petersburg, 1912.

Kuropatkin, Aleksei N. *Rossiia dlia russkikh: Zadachi russkoi armii*. 3 vols. St. Petersburg, 1910.

Kutylowski, Bohdan. *Sprawa samorządu ziemskiego w prowincjach zachodnich*. St. Petersburg, 1909.

Kuz'min-Karavaev, V. D. *Proekt zemskogo upravleniia v 13-ti nezemskikh guberniiakh*. St. Petersburg, 1902.

———. *Upravlenie zemskim khoziaistvom v deviati zapadnykh guberniiakh*. St. Petersburg, 1904.

Kwestya litewska w prasie polskiej. Warsaw, 1905.

Lambroza, Shlomo. "The Pogrom Movement in Tsarist Russia, 1903–1906. " Ph.D. diss., Rutgers University, 1981.

Lange, Antoni. *O sprzeczności sprawy żydowskiej*. Warsaw, 1911.

———. *Sprawa żydowska jako zagadnienie ekonomiczne*. Warsaw, 1914.

Lavrinovich, Iu. *Kto ustroil pogromy v Rossii*. Berlin, 1908.

Lazarevskii, N. I., ed. *Zakonodatel'nye akty perekhodnogo vremeni, 1904–1905 gg*. St. Petersburg, 1907.

Lelewel, Joachim. *Geschichte Polens*. 2d ed. Leipzig, 1847.

Leliva, Graf. *See* Tyszkiewicz, Anton, Count.

Lenin, Vladimir I. "Kriticheskie zametki po natsional'nomu voprosu." In *Sobranie Sochinenii*, vol. 24, pp. 113–50. Moscow, 1961.

———. *Polnoe sobranie sochinenii*. Moscow, 1958–1969.

———. *The Right of Nations to Self-Determination: Selected Writings*. New York, 1951.

Leont'ev, K. N. *Natsional'naia politika, kak orudie vsemirnoi revoliutsii*. Moscow, 1889.

Leslie, Robert F. *Polish Politics and the Revolution of 1830*. London, 1956.

———. *Reform and Insurrection in Russian Poland, 1856–1865*. London, 1963.

———, ed. *The History of Poland Since 1863*. Cambridge, U.K., 1980.

Lew, Symcha. *Perokim yidishe geshikhte: Sotsiale un natsionale bavegungen bay yidn in poyln un rusland fun 1897 biz 1914*. Brooklyn, 1941.

Liber, George O. *Soviet Nationality Policy, Urban Growth, and Identity Change in the Ukrainian SSR, 1923–1934*. Cambridge, U.K., 1992.

Lichkov, A. "Iugo-zapadnyi krai po dannym perepisi 1897 g." *Kievskaia starina* 90 (September 1905), pp. 317–66.

Lieven, Dominic. *Nicholas II: Emperor of All the Russias*. London, 1993.

———. *Russia's Rulers under the Old Regime*. New Haven, 1989.

Likowski, Edward (Edmund). *Dzieje Kościoła Unickiego na Litwie i Rusi w XVIII i XIX wieku uważane głównie ze względu na przyczyny jego upadku*. 2d ed. Warsaw, 1906.

Lincoln, W. Bruce. *The Great Reforms: Autocracy, Bureaucracy, and the Politics of*

Change in Imperial Russia. DeKalb, Ill., 1990.

Lipiński, Waclaw. *Szlachta na Ukrainie: Udział jej w życiu narodu ukraińskiego na tle jego dziejów.* Cracow, 1909.

Liprandi, A. P. [A. Volynets, pseud.]. *Evreistvo i antisemitizm.* Khar'kov, 1914.

———. *Kak ostanovit' mirnoe zavoevanie nashikh okrain? Nemetskii vopros, sushchnost i znachenie ego v iugo-zapadnoi Rossii.* Kiev, 1890.

———. *Ravnopravie i evreiskii vopros.* Khar'kov, 1911.

Lisicki, Henryk. *Aleksander Wielopolski, 1803–1877.* 4 vols. Cracow, 1878–1879.

Liubanskii, F. L. *Opisanie imenii podol'skoi gubernii.* Vinnitsa, 1908.

Łossowski, Piotr. *Po tej i tamtej stronie Niemna: Stosunki polsko-litewskie, 1883–1939.* Warsaw, 1985.

Lotots'kyi, Oleksander. *Storinky minuloho.* 2 vols. Warsaw, 1933.

Löwe, Heinz-Dietrich. *Antisemitismus und reaktionäre Utopie.* Hamburg, 1978.

Luciani, Georges, ed. and trans. *Le Livre de la genèse du peuple ukrainien.* Paris, 1956.

Luckyj, George. *Young Ukraine: The Brotherhood of Saints Cyril and Methodius in Kiev, 1845–1847.* Ottawa, 1991.

Łukawski, Zygmunt. *Koło Polskie w rosyjskiej Dumie Państwowej, 1906–1909.* Wrocław, 1967.

———. "Koło Polskie w rosyjskiej Dumie Państwowej wobec kwestii chełmskiej." *Zeszyty naukowe Uniwersytetu Jagiellońskiego: Prace Historyczne,* zeszyt 17 (Cracow, 1966), pp. 159–82.

Lumer, Hyman, ed. *Lenin on the Jewish Question.* New York, 1974.

Luxemburg, Rosa. *Die inustrielle Entwicklung Polens.* Berlin, 1898.

Łużny, Ryszard, Franciszek Ziejka, and Andrzej Kępiński, eds. *Unia brzeska: Geneza, dzieje, i konsekwencje w kulturze narodów słowiańskich.* Cracow, 1994.

Maevskii, Vladimir. *Borets za blago Rossii: K stoletiiu so dnia rozhdeniia.* Madrid, 1962.

Magocsi, Paul R. *National Cultures and University Chairs.* Toronto, 1980.

Maliszewski, Edward. *Polacy i polskość na Litwie i Rusi.* Warsaw, 1914.

Marchlewski, Julian. *Antysemityzm i robotnicy.* Cracow, 1913.

Marek, P. S. *Ocherki po istorii prosveshcheniia evreev v Rossii: "Dva vospitaniia."* Moscow, 1909.

Markiewicz, Henryk. *Pozytywizm.* Warsaw, 1978.

McKenzie, Kermit E. "Zemstvo Organization and Role Within the Administrative Structure." In *The Zemstvo in Russia: An Experiment in Local Self-Government,* ed. Terence Emmons and Wayne S. Vucinich, pp. 31–78. Cambridge, U.K., 1982.

McReynolds, Louise. *The News under Russia's Old Regime: The Development of a Mass-Circulation Press.* Princeton, 1991.

Meier, F. *Nesostoiatel'nost' zakona o cherte osedlosti evreev.* Vil'na, 1910.

Melnik, Josef, ed. *Russen über Rußland: Ein Sammelwerk.* Frankfurt-am-Main, 1906.

Mendelsohn, Ezra. *Class Struggle in the Pale.* Cambridge, U.K., 1970.

———. "Jewish Assimilation in Lvov: The Case of Wilhelm Feldman." *Slavic Review* 28, no. 4 (December 1969), pp. 577–90.

———. *Zionism in Poland: The Formative Years, 1915–1926.* New Haven, Conn., 1981.

Meshcherskii, V. P. *Moi vospominaniia.* 3 vols. St. Petersburg, 1897–1912.

Miliukov, Paul. *Aleksander Lednicki jako rzecznik polsko-rosyjskiego porozumienia.* Warsaw, 1939.

———. *Political Memoirs, 1905–1917.* Edited by Arthur P. Mendel. Ann Arbor, 1967.

Milosz, Czeslaw. *Native Realm: A Search for Self-Definition.* Garden City, N.Y., 1968.

Minczeles, Henri. *Vilna, Wilno, Vilnius: La Jérusalem de Lituanie*. Paris, 1993.

Miron, Dan. *The Traveller Disguised: A Study in the Rise of Modern Yiddish Fiction in the Nineteenth Century*. New York, 1973.

Mommsen, Hans. *Die Sozialdemokratie und die Nationalitätenfrage im habsburgischen Vielvölkerstaat*. Vienna, 1963.

Mosolov, A. N. *Vilenskie ocherki, 1863–1865 gg. (Murav'evskoe vremia)*. St. Petersburg, 1898.

Mosse, W. E. "Imperial Favourite: V. P. Meshchersky and the *Grazhdanin*." *Slavonic and East European Review* 59, no. 4 (October 1981), pp. 529–47.

Moszczyński, Jerzy. *Fiziologia szowinizmu polskiego na tle rosyjsko-polskich stosunków*. Cracow, 1897.

Motyl, Alexander J. *Will the Non-Russians Rebel? State, Ethnicity, and Stability in the USSR*. Ithaca, N.Y., 1987.

Murav'ev, M. N. *Pamiati grafa M. N. Murav'eva usmiritelia pol'skogo miatezha 1863 g. i vozstanovitelia russkoi narodnosti i pravoslavnoi tserkvi v Severo-zapadnom krae Rossii*. Vil'na, 1898.

Mysh, M. I. *Rukovodstvo k russkim zakonam o evreiakh*. 4th ed. St. Petersburg, 1914.

Naimark, Norman. *The History of the "Proletariat": The Emergence of Marxism in the Kingdom of Poland, 1870–1887*. Boulder, Colo., 1979.

Nathans, Benjamin. "Beyond the Pale: The Jewish Encounter with Russia, 1840–1900." Ph.D. diss., University of California, Berkeley, 1995.

Natsionalisty v 3-ei Gosudarstvennoi Dume. St. Petersburg, 1912.

Neutatz, Dietmar. *Die "deutsche Frage" im Schwarzmeergebiet und in Wolhynien: Politik, Wirtschaft, Mentalitäten, und Alltag im Spannungsfeld von Nationalismus und Modernisierung, 1856–1914*. Stuttgart, 1993.

Niemojewski, Andrzej. *Doba obecna w Królestwie Polskim*. Cracow, 1905.

Nietyksza, Maria. *Rozwój miast i aglomeracji miejsko-przemysłowych w Królestwie Polskim, 1865–1914*. Warsaw, 1986.

Ob otmene stesnenii malorusskogo pechatnogo slova. St. Petersburg, 1910.

Ochmański, Jerzy. *Historia Litwy*. Wrocław, 1967.

Ochs, Michael Jerry. "St. Petersburg and the Jews of Russian Poland, 1862–1905." Ph.D. diss., Harvard University, 1986.

Offmański, Mieczysław [Orion, pseud.]. *Charakterystyka rządów Aleksandra III w Ziemiach Polskich, 1881–1894*. Lvov, 1895.

Ogranichitel'nye uzakoneniia i osobye zakonopolozheniia izdannye po soobrazheniiam natsional'nogo ili veroispovednogo svoistva libo obuslovlivaemym razlichiem polov. St. Petersburg, 1906–1907.

Ol'denburg, Sergei S. *Tsarstvovanie Imperatora Nikolaia II*. Munich, 1949; reprint, Washington, 1981.

Ol'shamovskii, Boleslav G. *Prava po zemlevladeniiu v zapadnom krae*. St. Petersburg, 1899.

Opalski, Magdalena, and Israel Bartal. *Poles and Jews: A Failed Brotherhood*. Hanover, N.H., 1992.

Orbach, Alexander. *New Voices of Russian Jewry: A Study of the Russian-Jewish Press of Odessa in the Era of the Great Reforms, 1860–1917*. Leiden, 1980.

Orion. *See* Offmański, Mieczysław.

Orlov, F. *Russkoe delo na Visle*. St. Petersburg, 1898.

Orshanskii, I. G. *Russkoe zakonodatel'stvo o evreiakh*. St. Petersburg, 1877.

Pamiętnik kijowski. 3 vols. London, 1959.

Pasternak, Ievhen. *Narys istorii Kholmshchyny i Pidliashshia: Novishi chasy*. Winnipeg, 1968.

Peled, Yoav. *Class and Ethnicity in the Pale: The Political Economy of Jewish Workers' Nationalism in Late Imperial Russia.* London, 1989.

"Perepiska N. A. Romanova i P. A. Stolypina." *Krasnyi Arkhiv* (1924), pp. 102–28.

Pervaia vseobshchaia perepis' naseleniia Rossiiskoi Imperii. 89 vols. St. Petersburg, 1899–1904.

Pervaia vseobshchaia perepis' naseleniia Rossiiskoi Imperii: Obshchii svod. 2 vols. St. Petersburg, 1905.

Petrov, P. N. *Istoriia rodov russkogo dvorianstva.* St. Petersburg, 1885.

Petrovich, Michael B. *The Emergence of Russian Panslavism, 1856–1870.* New York, 1958.

Petr Varta. *See* Piltz, Erazm.

Pietrzak-Pawlowska, Irena, ed. *Wielkomiejski rozwój Warszawy do 1918 r.* Warsaw, 1973.

Piłsudski, Józef. *Rok 1863.* Warsaw, 1989.

Piltz, Erazm. *La Politique russe en Pologne.* Lausanne, 1909.

———— [Petr Varta, pseud.]. *Povorotnyi moment v russko-pol'skikh otnosheniiakh: Tri stat'i Petra Varty.* St. Petersburg, 1897.

———— [Piotr Warta, pseud.]. *Z chwili obecnej.* St. Petersburg, 1907.

———— [Scriptor, pseud.]. *Nasze stronnictwa skrajne.* Cracow, 1903.

———— [Tensam, pseud.]. *W chwili ciężkej i trudnej.* Warsaw, 1912.

Piotr Warta. *See* Piltz, Erazm.

Pipes, Richard. *The Formation of the Soviet Union.* Cambridge, Mass., 1964.

————. "Peter Struve and Ukrainian Nationalism." *Harvard Ukrainian Studies* 3–4 (1979–1980), pp. 675–83.

————. *Struve: Liberal on the Left, 1870–1905.* Cambridge, Mass., 1970.

————. *Struve: Liberal on the Right, 1905–1944.* Cambridge, Mass., 1980.

Płochocki, L. *See* Wasilewski, Leon.

Po vekham: Sbornik statei ob intelligentsii i 'natsional'nom litse'. Moscow, 1909.

Poboóg-Malinowski, W. *Najnowsza historia polityczna Polski (Okres 1864–1914).* Gdańsk, 1991.

————. *Narodowa Demokracja, 1887–1918: Fakty i dokumenty.* Warsaw, 1933.

Podhorodecki, L. *Dzieje Kijowa.* Warsaw, 1982.

Podligailov, P. N. *Natsional'nye zadachi Rossii i mery k ikh osuchchestvleniiu.* St. Petersburg, 1888.

Podvig Murav'eva: Nastol'naia kniga praviteliam i pravitel'stvam. St. Petersburg, 1898.

"Poezdka po nekotorym mestnostiam Tsarstva Pol'skogo v oktiabre 1863 goda." In *Deviatnadtsatyi vek: Istoricheskii sbornik,* ed. Petr Bartenev, pp. 282–311. Moscow, 1872.

Pogodin, Aleksandr L. *Glavnye techeniia pol'skoi politicheskoi mysli, 1863–1907 gg.* St. Petersburg, 1907.

Pogromy v Rossii (po ofitsial'nym dannym). Berlin, n.d. (ca. 1907).

Poliaki i Evrei—Sbornik Statei: Materialy o pol'sko-evreiskom spore po povodu zakonoproekta o gorodskom samoupravlenii v Pol'she. Odessa, n.d. (ca. 1912).

Polozhenie ob upravlenii zemskim khoziaistvom v guberniiakh Vilenskoi, Vitebskoi, Volynskoi, Grodnenskoi, Kievskoi, Kovenskoi, Minskoi, Mogilevskoi, i Podol'skoi. St. Petersburg, 1903.

Pol'skii vopros v gazete "Rus'." St. Petersburg, 1905.

Porter, Brian A. "Who Is a Pole and Where Is Poland? Territory and Nation in the Rhetoric of Polish National Democracy." *Slavic Review* 51, no. 4 (winter 1992), pp. 639–53.

Potresov, A., L. Martov, and P. Maslov, eds. *Obshchestvennoe dvizhenie v Rossii v nachale XX-go veka*. 4 vols. St. Petersburg, 1909–1914.

Poznański, K. *Reforma szkolna w Królestwie Polskim w 1862 r.* Wrocław, 1968.

Pritsak, Omeljan. "The Pogroms of 1881." *Harvard Ukrainian Studies* 9 (1987), pp. 8–43.

Prymak, Thomas M. *Mykhailo Hrushevsky: The Politics of National Culture.* Toronto, 1987.

Przybyszewski, Jan. *Język rosyjski w katolickim rituale i w dodatkowem nabożeństwie.* Lvov, 1897.

Puzinas, Jonas. *Vorgeschichtsforschung und Nationalbewegung in Litauen.* Kaunas, 1935.

Radliński, Anatol. *Rosyjskie majoraty w Królestwie Polskim.* Warsaw, 1918.

Radziszewski, Henryk. *Warszawa: Gospodarstwo Miejskie.* Warsaw, 1915.

Raisin, Jacob. *The Haskalah Movement in Russia.* Philadelphia, 1913.

Rappaport, Herman, ed. *Reakcja Stołypinowska w Królestwie Polskim, 1907–1910.* Warsaw, 1974.

Ratch, V. *Svedeniia o pol'skom miatezhe 1863 goda v Severo-zapadnoi Rossii.* Vil'na, 1867.

Ratner, M. "Natsional'noe litso i natsional'nyi vopros." In *"Vekhi" kak znamenie vremeni: Sbornik statei.* Moscow, 1910.

Rawson, Don C. *Russian Rightists and the Revolution of 1905.* Cambridge, U.K., 1995.

Reinke, Nikolai. *Ocherk zakonodatel'stva Tsarstva Pol'skogo, 1807–1881 gg.* St. Petersburg, 1902.

Reymont, Władysław. *Z ziemi chełmskiej: Wyrażenia i notatki.* Warsaw, 1911.

Riasanovsky, Nicholas V. "Asia through Russian Eyes." In *Russia and Asia: Essays on the Influence of Russia on the Asian Peoples,* ed. Wayne S. Vucinich, pp. 3–29. Stanford, 1972.

———. *Nicholas I and Official Nationality in Russia, 1825–1855.* Berkeley, 1967.

———. *A Parting of Ways: Government and the Educated Public in Russia 1801–1855.* Oxford, 1976.

Robbins, Richard G. *The Tsar's Viceroys: Russian Provincial Governors in the Last Years of the Empire.* Ithaca, N.Y., 1987.

Rogger, Hans. *Jewish Policies and Right-Wing Politics in Imperial Russia.* Berkeley, 1986.

———. "Nationalism and the State: A Russian Dilemma." *Comparative Studies in Society and History* 4, no. 3 (April 1962), pp. 253–64.

———. *Russia in the Age of Modernization and Revolution, 1881–1917.* London, 1983.

Rogger, Hans, and Eugen Weber, eds. *The European Right: A Historical Profile.* Berkeley, 1965.

Römeris, Mykolas (Michał Romer). *Litwa: Studium o odrodzeniu narodu litewskiego.* Lwów, 1908.

———. *Stosunki etnograficzno-kulturalne na Litwie.* Cracow, 1906.

Roseveare, I. M. "From Reform to Rebellion: A. Wielopolski and the Polish Question, 1861–1863." *Canadian Slavic Studies* 3 (1969), pp. 263–85.

Rossiia i eia zapadnye okrainy: Otvet na "Ocherednye voprosy v Tsarstve Pol'skom." Kiev, 1903.

Rothschild, Josef. *Ethnopolitics.* New York, 1981.

Rychliński, St. "Liberalizm gospodarczy w Królestwie Polskiem po 1863 roku." *Ekonomista* 2 (1930), pp. 70–97.

Sabaliunas, Leonas. *Lithuanian Social Democracy in Perspective, 1893–1914.* Durham, N.C., 1990.

Sadovskii, V. V. "Ukrainskii vopros v tret'ei Dume." *Ukrainskaia zhizn'* no. 5 (May 1912), pp. 17–27.

Said, Edward. *Orientalism.* New York, 1979.

Sakhnovskii, V. G. *O Russkoi narodnosti: Natsional'nyi lik Rossii.* Moscow, 1914–1915.

Savchenko, Fedir. *The Suppression of the Ukrainian Activities in 1876 / Zaborona Ukrainstva 1876 r.* Munich, 1970.

Sbornik materialov ob ekonomicheskom polozhenii evreev v Rossii. 2 vols. St. Petersburg, 1904.

Sbornik pravitel'stvennykh rasporiazhenii po vodvoreniiu russkikh zemlevladel'tsev v Severo-zapadnom krae. 2d ed. Vil'na, 1886.

Sbornik uzakonenii i rasporiazhenii po zemlevladeniiu v Zapadnykh guberniiakh. Kiev, 1885.

Scriptor. See Piltz, Erazm.

Sedecki, W. *See* Unszlicht, Julian.

Senn, Alfred E. *The Emergence of Modern Lithuania.* New York, 1959.

Seton-Watson, Hugh. *Nations and States: An Enquiry into the Origins of Nations and the Politics of Nationalism.* London, 1977.

Shatzky, Jacob. *Geshikhte fun yidn in varshe.* 3 vols. New York, 1947–1953.

———. "Yidn in dem poylishn oyfshtand fun 1863." *YIVO historishe shriftn* 1 (Warsaw, 1929), pp. 423–68.

Shchebalskii, P. K. *Nikolai Alekseevich Miliutin i reformy v Tsarstve Pol'skom.* Moscow, 1882.

Shchegolev, S. N. *Ukrainskoe dvizhenie kak sovremennyi etap iuzhnorusskogo separatizma.* Kiev, 1912.

Sheremetev, S. D., ed. *Iz bumag Grafa M. N. Murav'eva.* St. Petersburg, 1898.

Shmakov, Aleksei S. *Evreiskii vopros na stsene vsemirnoi istorii.* Moscow, 1912.

———. *Svoboda i evrei.* Moscow, 1906.

Shul'gin, V. *Vybornoe zemstvo v iugo-zapadnom krae.* Kiev, 1909.

Sidorov, A. A. *Russkie i russkaia zhizn' v Varshave (1815–1895): Istoricheskii ocherk.* Warsaw, 1899–1900.

Sidorskii, Iosif. "Efim Mikhailovich Kryzhanovskii v 1865–1888 gg." *Russkaia starina* 66 (March 1890), pp. 717–26.

Simonenko, G. *Tsarstvo Pol'skoe sravnitel'no s Poznan'iu i Galitsiei: Publichnaia lektsiia.* Warsaw, 1878.

Skałkowski, Adam M. *Aleksander Wielopolski w świetle archiwów rodzinnych, 1803–1877.* 3 vols. Poznań, 1947.

Skvortsov, I. *Russkaia shkola v Privislin'e s 1879 po 1897 gg.* Warsaw, 1897.

Slavinskii, M. "Natsional'naia struktura Rossii i Velikorossy." In *Formy natsional'nogo dvizheniia v sovremennykh gosudarstvakh: Avstro-Vengriia, Rossiia, Germaniia,* ed. A. I. Kastelianskii, pp. 277–303. St. Petersburg, 1910.

———. "Russkaia intelligentsiia i natsional'nyi vopros." In *Intelligentsiia v Rossii: Sbornik statei,* ed. K. Arsen'ev et al. St. Petersburg, 1910.

Slezkine, Yuri. *Arctic Mirrors: Russia and the Small Peoples of the North.* Ithaca, N.Y., 1994.

Sliozberg, Genrik B. *Dorevoliutsionnyi stroi Rossii.* Paris, 1933.

———. *Obsledovanie polozheniia evreev.* St. Petersburg, 1907.

Słoniowa, Anna. *Sokrates Starynkiewicz.* Warsaw, 1981.

Smirnov, A. F. *Vosstanie 1863 goda v Litve i Belorussii.* Moscow, 1963.

Snyder, Louis L. *The Meaning of Nationalism.* New Brunswick, N.J., 1954.

Sonevitskii, I. *Kholmshchina: Ocherk proshlogo.* St. Petersburg, 1912.

Sosis, Israel. *Di geshikhte fun di yidishe gezelshaftlekhe shtremungen in rusland in 19 y"h.* Minsk, 1929.

Spasovich, V. *Sochineniia.* 10 vols. St. Petersburg, 1889–1902.

Spasovich, V., and E. Piltz, eds. *Ocherednye voprosy v Tsarstve Pol'skom*. St. Petersburg, 1902.

Spravka o predpolozhennykh meropriiatiiakh v otnoshenii Kholmskoi gubernii. St. Petersburg, 1912.

Sprawa gubernii Chełmskiej. Cracow, 1907.

Stalin, Iosif. *Marksizm i natsional'nyi vopros*. Moscow, 1939.

Stanislawski, Michael. *For Whom Do I Toil? Judah Leib Gordon and the Crisis of Russian Jewry*. Oxford, 1988.

Stankiewicz, Zbigniew. *Dzieje wielkości i upadku Aleksandra Wielopolskiego*. Wrocław, 1967.

Starczewski, Eugeniusz. *K volynskim vyboram*. Lutsk, 1906.

———. *Nasze sprawy*. Kiev, 1916.

———. *Sprawa polska*. 2d ed. Warsaw, 1913.

———. *Życie polskie na Ukrainie*. Kiev, 1907.

Starr, S. Frederick. *Decentralization and Self-Government in Russia, 1830–1870*. Princeton, 1972.

Staszyński, Edmund. *Polityka oświatowa caratu w Królestwie Polskim od powstania styczniowego do I. wojny światowej*. Warsaw, 1968.

Stegner, Tadeusz. *Liberałowie Królestwa Polskiego, 1904–1915*. Gdańsk, 1990.

———. "Władze carskie w Królestwie Polskim wobec Polskich opozycyjnych ugrupowań politycznych." *Dzieje Najnowsze* 15, no. 1 (1983), pp. 323–31.

Steinberg, Arthur K. "The Kholm Question in the Russian Duma Period, 1906–1912: Opinion and Action." Ph.D. diss., Kent State University, 1972.

Stempowski, S. *Pamiętniki, 1870–1914*. Wrocław, 1953.

Stojko, Wolodymyr. "The Attitude of the Russian Provisional Government towards the Non-Russian Peoples of the Empire." Ph.D. diss., New York University, 1969.

Stolypin, Petr A. *Gosudarstvennaia deiatel'nost' predsedatelia Soveta ministrov Statssekretaria Petra Arkad'evicha Stolypina*. 3 vols. St. Petersburg, 1911.

———. *P. A. Stolypin, 1862–1911*. Paris, n.d. (ca. 1927).

———. *Rechi v gosudarstvennoi Dume, 1906–1911*. St. Petersburg, n.d.

Strakhovsky, L. I. "Constitutional Aspects of the Imperial Russian Government's Policy toward National Minorities." *Journal of Modern History* 13 (December 1941), pp. 467–92.

Stroganov, Viktor. *Russkii natsionalizm, ego sushchnost', istoriia i zadachi*. St. Petersburg, 1912.

Stronnictwo Polityki Realnej i jego myśli przewodnie. Warsaw, 1906.

Struve, Petr B. *Na raznye temy*. St. Petersburg, 1902.

———. *Patriotica*. St. Petersburg, 1911.

Studnicki, Władysław. *Zarys statystyczno-ekonomiczny ziem północno-wschodnich z XXXVII tablicami statystycznemi*. Vil'na, 1922.

Subbotin, A. P. *V cherte evreiskoi osedlosti*. 2 vols. St. Petersburg, 1888–1890.

Subtelny, Orest. *Ukraine: A History*. Toronto, 1988.

Suligowski, Adolf (Suligovskii, Adol'f). "Gorodskoe upravlenie v guberniiakh Tsarstva Pol'skogo." *Vestnik Evropy* 37, no. 6 (June 1902), pp. 675–98.

———. *Istoricheskaia zapiska ob upravlenii gorodami v Tsarstve Pol'skom*. Warsaw, 1906.

———. *Miasto analfabetów*. Cracow, 1905.

———. *O reformie sądowej w Królestwie Polskiem*. Warsaw, 1875.

———. *Pisma*. 4 vols. Warsaw, 1916.

———. *Projekt przyszłego samorządu miejskiego.* Warsaw, 1911.

———. *Projekty ustaw samorządu miejskiego w Królestwie Polskiem.* Warsaw, 1906.

———. *Zapiska o sisteme gorodskogo upravleniia v guberniiakh Tsarstva Pol'skogo.* St. Petersburg, 1905.

Świętochowski, Aleksander. *Wspomnienia.* Wrocław, 1966.

Szacki, J. *See* Shatzky, Jacob.

Szeftel, Marc. *The Russian Constitution of April 23, 1906: Political Institutions of the Duma Monarchy.* Brussels, 1976.

Szporluk, Roman. *Communism and Nationalism: Karl Marx versus Friedrich List.* Oxford, 1988.

Szwarc, Andrzej. "Inteligencja Królestwa Polskiego w oczach władz carskich." In *Inteligencja polska XIX i XX wieku: Studia ofiarowane Henrykowi Jabłońskiemu*, pp. 217–33. Warsaw, 1985.

———. *Od Wielopolskiego do Stronnictwa polityki realnej: Zwolennicy ugody z Rosja, ich poglądy i próby działalności politycznej (1864–1905).* Warsaw, 1990.

Tajne dokumenty rosyjskie o niezbędności wyłączenia Rusi Chełmskiej z Królestwa Polskiego. Lublin, 1906.

Tajne dokumenty rządu rosyjskiego w sprawach polskich. 2d ed. London, 1899.

Tanty, Mieczysław. *Panslawizm, carat, Polacy: Zjazd słowiański w Moskwie 1867 roku.* Warsaw, 1970.

Taube, M. F., Baron [M. Vashutin, pseud.]. *K vozrozhdeniiu slaviano-russkogo samosoznaniia: Sbornik.* Petrograd, 1911.

Tennenbaum, H. "Rynki rosyjskie." In *Z Rosją czy przeciw Rosji?* Warsaw, 1916.

Tensam. *See* Piltz, Erazm.

Terej, J. *Idee, mity, realia: Szkice do dziejów Narodowej Demokracji.* Warsaw, 1971.

Thaden, Edward C. *Russia's Western Borderlands, 1710–1870.* Princeton, 1984.

———, ed. *Russification in the Baltic Provinces and Finland, 1855–1914.* Princeton, 1981.

Theweleit, Klaus. *Männerphantasien.* 2 vols. Frankfurt-am-Main, 1977–1978.

Tikhonov, T. I. *Zemstvo v Rossii i na okrainakh.* St. Petersburg, 1907.

Timberlake, Charles, ed. *Essays on Russian Liberalism.* Columbia, Mo., 1972.

Tkach, V. *Ocherki Kholmshchiny i Podliash'ia.* Kholm, 1911.

Tobias, Henry J. *The Jewish Bund in Russia: From Its Origins to 1905.* Stanford, 1972.

Tomaszewski, Jerzy. *Ojczyzna nie tylko Polaków: Mniejszości narodowe w Polsce w latach 1918–1939.* Warsaw, 1985.

———. *Rzeczpospolita wielu narodów.* Warsaw, 1985.

Toruńczyk, Barbara, ed. *Narodowa Demokracja.* London, 1983.

Troinitskii, N. A., ed., *Obshchii svod po Imperii rezul'tatov razrabotki dannykh pervoi vseobshchoi perepisi naseleniia Rossiiskoi Imperii.* St. Petersburg, 1905.

Trotsky, Leon. *My Life.* New York, 1930.

Trutovskii, Vladimir E. *Sovremennoe zemstvo.* Petrograd, 1915.

Tsylov, N., ed. *Sbornik rasporiazhenii grafa Mikhaila Nikolaevicha Murav'eva po usmireniiu pol'skogo miutezha v Severo-zapadnykh guberniiakh, 1863–1864.* Vil'na, 1866.

Turuk, F. *Belorusskoe dvizhenie: Ocherk istorii natsional'nogo i revoliutsionnogo dvizheniia Belorussov.* Moscow, 1921.

Tutkevich, D. V. *Chto takoe evrei?* Kiev, 1906.

Tvardovskaia, V. A. *Ideologiia poreformennogo samoderzhaviia (M. N. Katkov i ego izdaniia).* Moscow, 1978.

Tyszkiewicz, Anton, Count [Graf Leliva, pseud.]. *Russko-pol'skie otnosheniia: Ocherk.* Leipzig, 1895.

Ukraine: A Concise Encyclopaedia. Toronto, 1963.

Ukrainets. *See* Kistiakovskii, Bogdan.

Ukrainskii vopros. 3d ed. Moscow, 1917.

Unszlicht, Julian [W. Sedecki, pseud.]. *Socjal-litwactwo w Polsce: Z teorii i praktyki "Socjaldemokracji Królestwa Polskiego i Litwy"*. Cracow, 1911.

Urban, Jan. *Wśród Unitów na Podlasiu: Pamiętniki wycieczek misyjnych*. Cracow, 1923.

Urussov, S. D. *Memoirs of a Russian Governor*. Translated and edited by Herman Rosenthal. London, 1908.

Vago, Bela, ed. *Jewish Assimilation in Modern Times*. Boulder, Colo., 1981.

Vakar, Nicholas P. *Belorussia: The Making of a Nation*. Cambridge, Mass., 1956.

Vashutin, M. *See* Taube, M. F., Baron.

Vekhi: Sbornik statei o russkoi intelligentsii. 5th ed. Moscow, 1910.

Velitsyn, A. A. *Nemtsy v Rossii: Ocherki istoricheskogo razvitiia i nastoiashchogo polozheniia nemetskikh kolonii na iuge i vostoke Rossii*. St. Petersburg, 1893.

Verner, Andrew M. *The Crisis of Russian Autocracy: Nicholas II and the 1905 Revolution*. Princeton, 1990.

Veselovskii, Boris B. *Istoriia zemstva*. 4 vols. St. Petersburg, 1911.

Veselovskii, Boris B., and Z. G. Frenkel', eds. *Iubileinyi zemskii sbornik, 1864–1914*. St. Petersburg, 1914.

Veyne, Paul. *Comment on écrit l'histoire*. Paris, 1978.

Vital, David. *The Origins of Zionism*. Oxford, 1975.

Vitte, S. Iu. *See* Witte, Sergei Iu.

Vladimirov, A. P. *Istoriia raspoliacheniia zapadno-russkogo kostela*. Moscow, 1896.

———. "O polozhenii Pravoslaviia v severo-zapadnom krae." *Russkoe obozrenie* (February 1893), pp. 620–52; (March 1893), pp. 186–211; (April 1893), pp. 671–702.

———. "O russkom zemlevladenii v severo-zapadnom krae." *Russkoe obozrenie* (July 1894), pp. 217–41; (August 1894), pp. 748–67; (September 1894), pp. 171–92.

Volkov, F. K., M. S. Hrushevs'kyi, et al., eds. *Ukrainskii narod v ego proshlom i nastoiashchem*. 2 vols. St. Petersburg, 1914–1916.

Volynets, A. *See* Liprandi, A. P.

Von Laue, Theodore. *Sergei Witte and the Industrialization of Russia*. New York, 1974.

Voskobiynyk, Michael Hryhory. "The Nationalities Question in Russia in 1905–1907: A Study in the Origin of Modern Nationalism, with Special Reference to the Ukrainians." Ph.D. diss., University of Pennsylvania, 1972.

V. R. *See* Gurko, Vladimir I.

Vsepoddaneishii otchet o proizvedennoi v 1910 g. po Vysochaisemu poveleniiu Senatorom Neidgartom revizii pravitel'stvennykh i obshchestvennykh ustanovlenii Privislinskogo kraia i varshavskogo voennogo okruga. St. Petersburg, n.d.

Vzgliady N. A. Miliutina na uchebnoe delo v Tsarstve Pol'skom. St. Petersburg, 1897.

Walicki, Andrzej. *The Enlightenment and the Birth of Modern Nationhood: Polish Political Thought from Noble Republicanism to Tadeusz Kościuszko*. Notre Dame, Ind., 1989.

———. *Philosophy and Romantic Nationalism*. Oxford, 1982.

Wandycz, Piotr. *The Lands of Partitioned Poland, 1795–1918*. Seattle, 1974.

Wapiński, R. *Narodowa Demokracja, 1893–1939*. Wrocław, 1980.

Wasilewski, Leon. *Administracja rosyjska w Królestwie Polskiem*. Vienna, 1915.

———. *Dzieje męczeńskie Podlasia i Chełmszczyzny*. Cracow, 1918.

———. *Litwa i jej ludy*. Warsaw, 1907.

———. *Moje wspomnienia ukraińskie*. Warsaw, 1932.

———. *Polityka narodowościowa Rosyi*. Cracow, 1916.

————. *Rosya "konstytucyjna" wobec Polaków*. Cracow, 1913.

————. *Sovremennaia Pol'sha i ee politicheskie stremleniia*. St. Petersburg, 1906.

————. *Ukraina i sprawa ukraińska*. Cracow–New York, 1911.

———— [L. Płochocki, pseud.]. *Chełmszczyzna i sprawa jej oderwanie*. Cracow, 1912.

Wasiutyński, Bohdan. *Ludność żydowska w Królestwie Polskim*. Warsaw, 1911.

Wcislo, Francis William. *Reforming Rural Russia: State, Local Society, and National Politics, 1855–1914*. Princeton, 1990.

Weeks, T. "Defending Our Own: Government and the Russian Minority in the Kingdom of Poland, 1905–1914." *Russian Review* 54 (October 1995), pp. 539–51.

————. "Defining Us and Them: Poles and Russians in the 'Western Provinces,' 1863–1914." *Slavic Review* 53, no. 1 (spring 1994), pp. 26–40.

————. "The 'End' of the Uniate Church in the Russian Empire: The *Vozsoedinenie* of 1875," *Jahrbücher für Geschichte Osteuropas* 44, no.1 (1996).

Weinerman, Eli. "Racism, Racial Prejudice, and Jews in Late Imperial Russia." *Ethnic and Racial Studies* 17, no. 3 (July 1994), pp. 442–95.

Weissman, Neil M. *Reform in Tsarist Russia: The State Bureaucracy and Local Government, 1900–1914*. New Brunswick, N.J., 1981.

Whelan, Heide. *Alexander III and the State Council: Bureaucracy and Counter-Reform in Late Imperial Russia*. New Brunswick, N.J., 1982.

Wieczorkiewicz, Paweł Piotr. "Biskup Eulogiusz i oderwanie Chełmszczyzny od Królestwa Polskiego." In *Historia XIX i XX wieku: Studia i szkice. Prace ofiarowane Henrykowi Jabłońskiemu w siedemdziesiątą rocznicę urodzin*. Wrocław, 1979.

————. "Polityka rosyjska wobec Królestwa Polskiego w latach, 1909–1914." Ph.D. diss., University of Warsaw, 1976.

Wielhorski, Władysław. *Warunki rozwoju świadomości narodowej Litwinów i powstania współczesnego państwa litewskiego, 1861–1920*. Lvov, 1935.

Wiercieński, Henryk. *Jeszcze z powodu wydzielenia Chełmszczyzny*. Cracow, 1913.

————. *W sprawie wydzielenia Chełmszczyzny*. Warsaw, 1910.

————. *Ziemia chełmska i Podlasie*. Warsaw, n.d.

Wierzchowski, Mirosław. "Sprawa Chełmszczyzny w rosyjskiej Dumie Państwowej." *Przegląd historyczny* 57, no. 1 (1966), pp. 97–125.

————. *Sprawy Polski w III i IV Dumie*. Warsaw, 1966.

Witte (Vitte), Sergei Iu. *Samoderzhavie i zemstvo: Konfidentsial'naia zapiska Ministra finansov Stats-Sekretaria S. Iu. Vitte (1899 g.)*, ed. and introduced by R. N. S. (pseudonym for Petr B. Struve). Stuttgart, 1901.

————. *Vospominaniia*. 3 vols. Moscow, 1960.

————. *Zapiska b. ministra finansov stats-sekretaria Gr. S. Iu. Vitte*. St. Petersburg, 1908.

Yaney, George. *The Systemization of Russian Government: Social Evolution in the Domestic Administration of Imperial Russia, 1711–1905*. Urbana, Ill., 1973.

Zaionchkovskii, Petr A. *Kirillo-Mefodievskoe obshchestvo*. Moscow, 1959.

————. *Krizis samoderzhaviia na rubezhe, 1870–1880-kh godov*. Moscow, 1964.

————. *Rossiiskoe samoderzhavie v kontse XIX stoletiia*. Moscow, 1970.

Zajączkowski, Ananiasz. *Karaims in Poland: History, Language, Folklore, Science*. Warsaw, 1961.

Zakrzewski, Adam [A. Z., pseud.]. *Historio de Esperanto, 1887–1912*. Warsaw, 1913.

————. *Materialy k voprosu ob obrazovanii Kholmskoi gubernii*. 2 vols. Warsaw, 1908–1911.

————. *Pol'sha: Statistichesko-etnograficheskii ocherk*. Kiev, 1916.

————. *Zasada narodowości i przyszła Polska.* Warsaw, 1917.

Załęski, Witold. *Królestwo Polskie pod względem statystycznym.* Warsaw, 1901.

————. *Z statystyki porównawczej Królestwa Polskiego: Ludność i rolnictwo.* Warsaw, 1908.

Zamyslovskii, G., ed. *Pol'skii vopros v Gosudarstvennoi Dume III sozyva 1 sessii.* Vil'na, 1909.

Zaslavskii, David I., and S. Ivanovich. *Kadety i evrei.* Petrograd, 1916.

Ze stosunków litewsko-polskich. Głosy Litwinów: Audeatur et altera pars. Warsaw, 1907.

Zechlin, Erich. *Die Bevölkerungs- und Grundbesitzverteilung im Zartum Polen.* Berlin, 1916.

Zenkovsky, Alexander V. *Stolypin: Russia's Last Great Reformer.* Translated by Margaret Patoski. Princeton, N.J., 1986.

Zhabotinskii, Vladimir. *Fel'etony.* St. Petersburg, 1913.

Zimmer, Boleslaw. *Miasto Chełm: Zarys historyczny.* Warsaw/Cracow, 1974.

Zinberg, Israel. *A History of Jewish Literature.* 12 vols. Translated and edited by Bernard Martin. Cincinnati, 1978.

Zipperstein, Steven J. *Elusive Prophet: Ahad Ha'am and the Origins of Zionism.* Berkeley, 1993.

Zyzniewski, Stanley John. "Miljutin and the Polish Question." *Harvard Slavic Studies* 4 (1957), pp. 237–48.

————. "Russian Policy in the Congress Kingdom of Poland, 1863–1881." Ph.D. diss., Harvard University, 1956.

Index

DATE DUE